ELVIS PRESLEY

ELVIS PRESLEY

A Southern Life

JOEL WILLIAMSON

WITH DONALD L. SHAW

FOREWORD BY TED OWNBY

OXFORD
UNIVERSITY PRESS

OXFORD

UNIVERSITY PRESS

Oxford University Press is a department of the
University of Oxford. It furthers the University's objective
of excellence in research, scholarship, and education
by publishing worldwide.

Oxford   New York
Auckland   Cape Town   Dar es Salaam   Hong Kong   Karachi
Kuala Lumpur   Madrid   Melbourne   Mexico City   Nairobi
New Delhi   Shanghai   Taipei   Toronto

With offices in
Argentina   Austria   Brazil   Chile   Czech Republic   France   Greece
Guatemala   Hungary   Italy   Japan   Poland   Portugal   Singapore
South Korea   Switzerland   Thailand   Turkey   Ukraine   Vietnam

Oxford is a registered trade mark of Oxford University Press
in the UK and certain other countries.

Published in the United States of America by
Oxford University Press
198 Madison Avenue, New York, NY 10016

Library of Congress Cataloging-in-Publication Data
Williamson, Joel.
Elvis Presley : a southern life / Joel Williamson
with Donald L. Shaw ; foreword by Ted Ownby.
pages   cm
Includes bibliographical references and index.
ISBN 978-0-19-986317-4 (alk. paper)
1. Presley, Elvis, 1935–1977.
2. Rock musicians—United States—Biography.
I. Shaw, Donald Lewis.   II. Title.
ML420.P96W59   2014
782.42166092—dc23   [B]
2014011520

1 3 5 7 9 8 6 4 2

Printed in the United States of America
on acid-free paper

For Anna, Alethea, William, and Joelle

CONTENTS

FOREWORD

TED OWNBY

People respond to Elvis Presley with some pretty powerful emotions. People love him for some things, laugh at him for others, feel almost desperately sad about his decline and wasted potential, and sometimes get angry at him or people close to him.

In the 1950s the main emotions seem to have been lust and also fear. From 1954 to 1958, Elvis Presley's music in sound, look, and movement so appealed to young women that by his early twenties he became the subject of extraordinary female sexual fascination. They (not Sam Phillips or Tom Parker or even Presley himself) made Elvis Presley a powerful cultural figure, and for four years his appearances in person and on television and, less importantly, his recordings made him the subject of unprecedented public lust as a figure of sexual desire for people who, by the standards of their day, were not supposed to express or even possess such sexual desires.

Elvis Presley responded to these fascinations by performing onstage for only four years, and then by taking advantage of numerous opportunities to make money through the movies and to pursue sexual experiences with lots of young women. He did virtually nothing creative from 1958 to 1968, the year of his comeback television special, and only rarely and perhaps accidentally made music of much consequence. His fans stayed with him, though he feared he was not gaining many new fans, and in the last decade of his life he performed to loving but aging crowds in Las Vegas and in second-tier settings in smaller cities. He and his managers, bodyguards, and other supporters made choices that kept him in an unappealing, aesthetically unimaginative state in which he made uninspiring movies and (with a few exceptions) uninspiring music that relied on the fact that he was already a sex symbol. He lived an unhappy adulthood, fearful of bad publicity, overweight, oversexed, and overprotected, and took far more pills than human beings should take. The pills killed him.

That is a quick and far from complete summary of Joel Williamson's biography of Elvis Presley. Any book on a well-studied individual is bound to say things most readers already know or address topics that will be familiar. Most books on Presley have at least mentioned his rising from Southern poverty and obscurity, confounding categories about musical genre, race, and class, disturbing television censors and the parents of young women with his music and movement, and displaying unique musical creativity and maybe losing it. Scholars have analyzed Presley and his relationships with music[1] and race[2] and religion[3] and celebrity[4] and cultural rebellion.[5] Williamson's book draws from all of those approaches, but above all it is a book about Presley and sexual desire—the desire young women had for Presley, his desires for them, how both affected his life as an artist, and how all of those became intertwined with efforts to keep desire alive into Presley's middle age and beyond his death. The book seriously studies things that now seem clichés or easy jokes—squealing young women chasing performers into their dressing rooms, the phrase "Elvis has left the building," wardrobe changes and handing out scarves, passing encounters with actresses, pageant winners, and other fans, and entourage members who attracted women by asking if they'd like to meet Elvis. The important female

1. Peter Guralnick, *Last Train to Memphis: The Rise of Elvis Presley* (Boston: Little, Brown, 1994); Peter Guralnick, *Careless Love: The Unmaking of Elvis Presley* (Boston: Little, Brown, 1999).
2. Michael Bertrand, *Race, Rock, and Elvis* (Urbana: University of Illinois Press, 2000).
3. Charles Reagan Wilson, *Judgment and Grace in Dixie: Southern Faiths from Faulkner to Elvis* (Athens: University of Georgia Press, 1995).
4. Erika Doss, *Elvis Culture: Fans, Faith, and Image* (Lawrence: University Press of Kansas, 1999).
5. Vernon Chadwick, ed., *In Search of Elvis: Music, Race, Art, Religion* (Boulder, CO: Westview Press, 1997); E. Warren Perry, Jr., ed., *Echoes of Elvis: The Cultural Legacy of Elvis Presley* (Washington, DC: Smithsonian Institution Scholarly Press, 2011); Pete Daniel, *Lost Revolutions: The South in the 1950s* (Chapel Hill: University of North Carolina Press, 2000).

figures in Presley's life, Gladys Presley, Priscilla Beaulieu Presley, Linda Thompson, Ginger Alden, and Lisa Marie Presley, all are crucial to the story. As Williamson argues, Presley loved being loved, and that craving did not always lead in creative or happy directions.

Historians of Elvis Presley see the mid-1950s as a time of impressive and creative musical experimentation as the young man and his friends made new music out of a fascinating mixture of other available, mostly Southern, forms of music. Williamson emphasizes that this period of Presley's life was dominated by young women who responded to his music. The music was in fact sometimes creative, but soon it hardly mattered, since in public appearances no one could hear it. What the author of *Crucible of Race* and *William Faulkner* and other important works brings to the topic is a lifetime of provocative scholarship on the relationships between race and sexuality in southern history.[6] He helps us understand the young Presley in the settings where he heard and started to make music—fair, church, honky-tonk, public park, the *Louisiana Hayride*, the New York television shows—in part to show the dynamics of who was there, what was expected, and what his rebellion rebelled against. The young women screaming at Presley get their own history here, and Williamson discusses them through the combined histories of Southern white women who had been valued above all for purity and self-control and plain-folk evangelicals whose religion encouraged plenty of expressive music but discouraged open display of sexual desire.[7]

6. Joel Williamson, *The Crucible of Race: Black/White Relations in the American South since Emancipation* (New York: Oxford University Press, 1984); Joel Williamson, *William Faulkner and Southern History* (New York: Oxford University Press, 1993).

7. On young women in the mid-twentieth-century South, see Susan K. Cahn, *Sexual Reckonings: Southern Girls in a Troubling Age* (Cambridge, MA: Harvard University Press, 2007); Pippa Holloway, *Sexuality, Politics, and Social Control in Virginia, 1920–1945* (Chapel Hill: University of North Carolina Press, 2006). On Elvis Presley's female fans, see Mary Elizabeth Lasseter, "'That's Alright, Mama, Any Way You Do': Elvis, Sexuality, and Changing Southern Womanhood" (MA thesis, University of Mississippi, 2002). On Elvis Presley and female partners, see Alanna Nash, *Baby, Let's Play House: Elvis and the Women Who Loved Him* (New York: HarperCollins, 2010).

In response both to the frenzy of young women fans and to his own performance style onstage, Presley, even more than most other popular musicians, had to defend himself against charges that he posed a threat to good morals. He found those charges amazing and troubling, but he took advantage of female sexual desire for him from 1954 to his death, had physical relationships with countless young women, and lived in fear that the nature of his lifestyle would undermine his public support. Presley wanted to walk a line between being the object of desire and being a decent, religious, and patriotic American, but he frequently failed. Williamson makes a great deal of Presley's fears that a book by some of the bodyguards he had fired would reveal him as lecherous and indulgent.

Williamson argues that the contours of Presley's life were set by 1958, when he was twenty-three years old. Presley got stuck as the star in a grand drama about desire, and he enjoyed its benefits too much to break away from its limitations. One turning point came in 1968, when Presley surprised many people with a television special that was far more creative in music, dance, and look than most expected from a standard Christmas musical television special. Making what many saw as a comeback, Presley tried some things that were new, accepted some clothing choices that led to the style that defined him in his final decade, and, as Williamson emphasizes, played some older music surrounded by female fans who were no longer girls but grown women. The show was a high point because it once again pointed to Presley as a creative figure and object of desire. After that, Presley played primarily to older, loving fans in live performances, and his final years were generally sad and painful for the performer, his family and friends, and his fans. In retrospect, most of Presley's shows in the 1970s represented a long swan song.

I came to this book as a reader for Oxford University Press, and I found that it made an impression on me for the ways it mixes good scholarship with extraordinary empathy for a troubled and often frustrating individual. As I first read the manuscript, I found myself hoping, no matter how irrationally, that Presley could turn things around, and Williamson ponders some of the possibilities he considered. And I found myself wanting to hear and see performances I had never encountered. I watched the Comeback Special and the Aloha Special and listened to the early recordings. The book left me in a bit of a daze, and in truth, although it is a long book, I wanted it, like a really good concert, to keep going. With its focus on a unique, sometimes bizarre story, and with some details it is still hard to fathom, Williamson's book is not a case study of the problems of capitalism or mass culture or patriarchy. Nor, certainly, is it a celebrity biography. It is, instead, a thoughtful story of a fascinating individual life, and it is less about drawing conclusions and more about telling stories, often stories full of complications and context and extraordinary details. By emphasizing the relationships between Elvis Presley and the people who seemed to have mattered to him most—his female fans—the book helps us connect Presley's music more broadly to the social changes of Presley's time and more specifically to the uniqueness of his own personal circumstances. The book may not help us love its subject more or cause us to love him less, but it helps us understand him a lot better by seeing him in relation to the people who wanted so much from him.

So, what's new about Williamson's book? Is it just another story of the accomplishments, failings, and demise of a creative and influential individual? Many of the works on Elvis Presley deal with his Southern roots, his rebelliousness, his fans, certainly his music, and his extraordinary rise and personal and artistic decline. This volume will no doubt affect different readers in different ways, but I suspect its most unique, most powerful feature is its suggestion that the roots of Presley's failures lay in the roots of his rise to popularity. The mixture of youth, sex, race, and religion that made Elvis Presley's body and music so exciting and transgressive to his female fans and left Presley stuck in an identity created in his early twenties also let loose the mixture of easy sex, self-importance, and desire to cling to youth that were central to his failings and demise. Elvis Presley, as Joel Williamson shows, was not just another hero with big flaws. More important, the reasons for Presley's success were what ultimately led to his decline.

University of Mississippi
June 2014

PREFACE

Mississippi and Memphis are fascinating places. I suppose I always knew this, but it came home to me forcefully in 1984, when I taught at Millsaps College in Jackson as Eudora Welty Visiting Professor and at Rhodes College in Memphis. My hidden agenda in coming out from North Carolina was to pursue research for a book on William Faulkner. As the year progressed, however, I became increasingly interested in Elvis Presley in a scholarly way. In February of that year I visited Graceland. It was not crowded, not rushed at all, and the experience of the visitor much less structured than it is today.

On July 28, 1954, ten weeks after the initial Supreme Court Brown decision integrating public schools, Elvis sang "That's All Right" in the Overton Shell in Memphis. It was a black man's song, and white women went wild at the sight of Elvis's body—this beautiful young white male body—in motion as he sang. During the months that followed, "Elvis mania" swelled while the white South floated in dread, waiting for the Court's promised next move. How would integration be enforced? By federal soldiers with fixed bayonets as in Reconstruction after the Civil War? By Yankee policemen, such as federal marshals or the FBI? What would our girls do?

I began to ponder the question: "Why Elvis?" Why this amazing phenomenon springing up so suddenly, so powerfully from the soil of Southern culture and influencing people all around the globe?

Teenage girls in America created "Elvis." Why were these girls there in the Elvis venue in 1954, 1955, 1956, and 1957? Why did they express themselves sexually in such a revolutionary way?

These young women belonged to a very special generation in American history. They were teenagers, born as the Great Depression ended and World War II began. During the war, their early childhoods were often marked by absent fathers and, essentially, "single mothers." Some sixteen million men were away in the armed services and more than 400,000 of these were killed in combat. Millions more men were engaged in war work, often at a distance from home. A girl who turned sixteen in 1955 would have been born in 1939. She would have been two years old when America entered the war and six when it was over. Until late 1945 and early 1946, many of these girls lived with and among married but "single mothers" who, of necessity, did the work of two parents. It was a familial experience, unmatched in magnitude and duration in America since the Civil War.

During the war, all the girls in Elvis's audiences had lived in a world of man-made death and destruction. After the war, they lived in families that were virtually obsessive in their desire to produce children and acquire houses, cars, and clothes—to create all the good things of life.

The veterans who came home after World War II did not want to re-live the war in memory. They did not often talk about the slaughter they had witnessed overseas. Good men in that age were not supposed to flinch or cry, but rather absorb their physical and emotional hits and go resolutely on. And so they did, these men who were children during the heady prosperity of the 1920s, survived the Great Depression of the 1930s, and fought a desperate, obviously necessary and clearly moral war to the bitter end and won. They dedicated the remainder of their lives to fathering children and working diligently to ensure the perpetual comfort of their families. Ideally, their wives would stay home and care for these children.

After World War II, as very young girls, the females in Elvis's audiences had seen their mothers' bellies swell huge with pregnancy as often as nature allowed—once, twice, three times and more—while an increasing number of their younger brothers and sisters clutched at her sagging skirts. They helped their mothers mind their younger siblings, and they also helped neighboring mothers mind their children, all the tots and toddlers of the boomer generation. Babysitting—surrogate motherhood—became a new word to fit a novel and pervasive American institution as teenage girls were enlisted to help care for the sudden and massive flood of infants, toddlers, and tiny children that filled to overflowing the homes of the nation. In the lives of their own mothers and other mothers all around them, they saw their own future rise inexorably before them. They were slated to marry hard-working young men, bear child after child, and stay at home. Why did Elvis attract them?

The two key words, I realized, are "Southern culture." Elvis is the creature of that little postage stamp of earth in northeastern Mississippi that also gave birth to William Faulkner and Tennessee Williams. William Faulkner was born in New Albany, less than thirty miles northwest of the tiny shotgun house in which Elvis was born; Tennessee Williams was born in the Episcopal rectory in Columbus, about sixty miles south of Tupelo. Why did America's greatest writer in the twentieth century, America's greatest playwright in the twentieth century, and America's greatest entertainer in the twentieth century emerge from this same place? The answer, I think, lies in the history of the South and the particular history of the region.

A hundred years before Elvis was born, this land was populated and controlled by Native Americans, the Chickasaws. By the 1830s nearly all of the Indians were moved west to Oklahoma, and the land was quickly filled with African Americans and European Americans, with slaves and slaveholders, and with the plain folk of the Old South. Slavery dictated relations between men and women, and further it promoted a class structure that was hierarchical. Elvis was highly conscious of his place in that social hierarchy. Everyone born and reared in these Southern communities is conscious of his or her place. It is not so much a matter of simple class divisions as it is a matter of "who your people are." What does your family name mean, and how do you yourself fit into your family and clan and community? Elvis was well down in the hierarchy, and he never attempted to climb higher on the social ladder, regardless of his considerable wealth and global fame.

Perhaps Elvis knew enough to know that elite Memphis would not have accepted him anyway. Money can help one make it in Memphis, but not within a generation. Even so, poor boys and girls who do make it often do aspire to the columned mansion with surrounding grounds that they associate with gentility. Elvis bought that symbol when he acquired Graceland.

Graceland was created as a show piece, verily a signal to the world of wealth, social eminence, and elite culture. Elvis's sense of aesthetics alone was a gulf separating Elvis and his people from the elite of Memphis whose wealth was comparable to his own. When he moved in, one of the first things he did to change the landscape was to add a mobile home. When Elvis died, there were three mobile homes, two of them conspicuously large. In the later years a nurse who would monitor Elvis's drug addiction would work out of one of those trailers. Elvis was not at all a social rebel, no leveler of classes. But race and gender were other matters.

Looking at Elvis in 1984 and considering the matter of race, I very soon picked up on the Sam Phillips story—this Memphis white man who was recording black musicians and who allegedly said something to the effect that if he could just find a white singer with the Negro sound—the Negro feel—he could get rich. Phillips is a highly significant figure in the evolution of Southern culture. Had he been in politics or journalism, scholars would have called him a "Southern white liberal" and put him in the camp with such movers and shakers as Frank Porter Graham, president of the progressive University of North Carolina and Ralph McGill of the Atlanta *Constitution*. Phillips did not wait for the Supreme Court decision in *Brown v. Board of Education* to begin deliberately undermining the racial establishment in the South. He was a "cross-over" person, a person of one race who relates closely to the other race. Among whites in the early to mid-twentieth century these persons were rare but not unique. Often they were church people, professional or lay. They were also writers, and very often musicians. Given the compelling character of African American religion and music, this is not surprising. In Elvis, Sam Phillips found his white man with the Negro feel. Soon white women did too, and then the rest of us.

Let's consider Elvis's first great audience—that is, his early audience in the flesh. Those Memphis audiences in 1954, 1955, and into

1956 were vastly white, female, and young. The very first audience was Southern, even "Deep South Southern." In photographs the girls appear to be fourteen years old or in that neighborhood. The person who was female, white, Southern, and fourteen in 1954 was born about 1940 as the country was plunging deeper into World War II. Perhaps her father was away, among the millions of men in the American military. The need for soldiers was so great that men who had been in Parchman Prison with Elvis's father, Vernon, were released to join the service. Her father might not have been in the military but he might have taken a job in war work away from home, as did Vernon. In any event, all Americans suffered some of the physical and psychological pain of wartime. Priscilla Presley, for example, lost her father, a Navy pilot, in a crash that occurred just as the war came to a close.

Soon after that war ended, the Cold War with the Communists began, bringing with it omnipresent fears of the atomic bomb. At school, say, in the fourth grade, this girl might have participated in an air raid drill, crawling under her desk when the alarm sounded. Another killing war broke out in Korea when she was ten and wound down to an uneasy ceasefire when she was thirteen. This girl's family doggedly pursued the good life under the real danger of nuclear war and amidst fears of Communist subversion.

A threat of a very different order arose in May 1954, when the Supreme Court decided that her junior high school would be deseg-regated. Desegregation was a vital and potentially violent issue in the South and especially so in the Deep South, the black belt South, the Bible-belt South, the South where Elvis would find his first great live audiences. That is where Elvis found this girl who, with her friends, responded to him so enthusiastically he did not know what was happening. For the girls, it was escape from cultural restraint, however temporarily it might turn out to be for some. It was more than the music.

In the Southern white mind, race and sex are inextricably mixed, and it is not difficult to accept the idea that the primary purpose of segregation was to keep black males away from white females. Ideally, white women were expected to be pious, pure, domestic, and submissive, while the men provide and protect. Purity, of course, meant purity of body, but it also meant purity of mind and thought. No lusting by women allowed; no sex outside of marriage; no overt admiration and appetite for the male body; no overt expression of awareness of themselves as sexual creatures.

Then Elvis—with his mix of black and white rhythms, with his seeming indifference to race, with his exciting moving body—came along. During the months that followed his performance at Overton Shell in Memphis, "Elvis mania" swelled. In the audiences, the girls shrieked, danced, and stomped in expressions of their sexuality. Not every teenage girl in the lower Mississippi Valley became an Elvis girl, but enough did, and the movement spread through the black belt South, first in places where the numbers of black people relative to white people ran highest and where the tension over integration was greatest—from east Arkansas and Texas across to north Florida and up into eastern Virginia. Wherever Elvis played, the girls responded in the same demonstrative style as his first audiences.

"His audience was his true love," Priscilla Presley wrote in her book, *Elvis and Me*, her 1985 remembrance of her ex-husband. The engine that drove Elvis Presley for the rest of his life has never been stated more clearly. These teenage girls, not Elvis's managers, created "The First Elvis," without whom the Elvis that the world came to know and often celebrate during his life and after his death would not have existed. From 1954 to 1957, when Elvis performed live on stage, it was as if he and the teenage girls in his audience existed in a huge and protective bubble, alone, ecstatic, and away from the stultifying world.

Elvis became—and remains—a worldwide phenomenon. Graceland is one of the most visited homes in America, a quintessential piece of Southern culture where the spirit of a shy young man still seems to wander the house and its grounds. Elvis's dream included a son who would look like him and be with him in Graceland. But no daughter could look more like her father than his daughter, Lisa Marie. The feminine in the masculine and the masculine in the feminine are living contradictions, phenomena like no other in Western Civilization where dualism is virtually a religion. No duality may be more sacred than sexual duality.

No other phenomenon asserts more beautifully, more perfectly the oneness of us all. Elvis had a treasured masculine side...and a sensitive feminine side too. Perhaps we all do.

The gender world in which Margaret Mitchell of *Gone with the Wind* came to maturity was precisely the world into which the Elvis girls were born. The culture in which she suffered as a woman and finally flourished as a writer in the late 1930s was the culture that poured into the bodies of the Elvis girls virtually as they first stirred to life. In *Gone with the Wind*, it was Scarlett, not Melanie, who took charge of her life. Just two decades after publication of the novel, it seemed like the audiences for Elvis were filled with women who reflected Scarlett, cautiously bold, tentatively independent and, for a few hours at least, openly sexual. In *Gone with the Wind,* Scarlett raised a pistol and fired a bullet through the head of an intruding bummer who invaded her plantation home at Tara. As she did so, she glanced up at Melanie dragging a sword for their defense to the top of the stairs. Why, Scarlett exclaimed, she's just like me! As it turned out, it was not just Southern women who responded to Elvis's unique blend of musical cultures. It was American women, and in time women everywhere, and men, too.

ACKNOWLEDGMENTS

I would like to thank Donald Shaw, Kenan professor emeritus of journalism at the University of North Carolina, Chapel Hill. Professor Shaw met with me biweekly for the last several years and recruited special assistants to follow the manuscript through many changes, rewrites, and revisions. There have been many helpers. I mention in particular Melanie Hudak, Dr. Tom Terry, and my friend, Chapel Hill writer Joanna Catherine Scott. I appreciate my long association with the late Frank Ryan of the University Department of History. Of course I am grateful to Oxford editor Susan Ferber. Thank you also to my seminar students with whom I shared my research and insights, and who, in the back and forth discussion, inspired me with new ideas. Without all these brilliant and generous people, twenty-five years of labor would never have come to fruition in the publication of this book. Of course I owe a special debt of gratitude to my wife, Anna, and my children, Alethea, William, and Joelle. I feel I have been supported tenderly.

Joel Williamson
Chapel Hill, North Carolina
December 2013

ELVIS PRESLEY

INTRODUCTION

THE DEATH OF ELVIS

The call came to Memphis Fire Station No. 29 at 2:33 p.m. on Tuesday, August 16, 1977. The dispatcher indicated that someone at 3754 Elvis Presley Boulevard was having difficulty breathing. "Go to the front gate and go to the front of the mansion," the voice directed. Ambulance Unit No. 6 swung out of the station onto Elvis Presley Boulevard and headed south, siren wailing, advertising a speed that the ponderous machine had not yet achieved.

The two medics manning the ambulance recognized the address right away. The "mansion," as the dispatcher called it, was Elvis Presley's home, Graceland, three miles south of the fire station. They had been there often, to take care of fans fainting at the front gate and pedestrians injured by passing automobiles. Two years before, one of the medics, Charles Crosby, had come to assist Elvis's father, Vernon Presley, after he suffered a heart attack. He thought it might be Vernon again.

On this run Crosby was driving the ambulance. He was thirty-eight, stoutly built, dark-haired, and heavily mustached. His partner, Ulysses Jones, twenty-six, sat in the passenger seat. Members of the Memphis Fire Department, they had received eighty-eight hours of special training to become emergency medical technicians and had years of experience. On each call, they alternated between driving and riding in the back with the ill or injured. This time, Ulysses Jones would ride with the patient.

Crosby expertly threaded the boxy white, blue, and orange vehicle through the thin midafternoon traffic with lights flashing. Heat waves shimmered up from the asphalt in front of him. During the day, the mercury had risen into the mid-90s and hovered there. In a city not

3

yet fully air-conditioned, many working Memphians breathed the hot, damp air, mopped their brows, and thought fondly about getting home to an icy drink on their shady screened-in porches.

As the ambulance crested a low hill and swooped down the broad six-lane boulevard toward Graceland, the gates swung open and the crowd milling around the entrance parted. Making a wide sweeping turn to the left, the vehicle bounced heavily across the sidewalk and hurtled through the entranceway, striking one of the swinging metal gates a clanging blow. One of the several musical notes welded to the gate fell off. Crosby accelerated up the curving drive toward the mansion. He braked hard in front of the two-story, white-columned portico. Climbing down from the ambulance, Crosby and Jones were met by one of Elvis's bodyguards.

"He's upstairs," the man exclaimed, "and I think it's an OD."

Grabbing their equipment, the two medics rushed into the house and up the stairs. They pushed through Elvis's bedroom, noticing the deep-pile red rug and the huge unmade bed facing three television consoles, one for each of the three major networks. Passing through a wide doorway, they entered Elvis's enormous bathroom, what had been two rooms combined into a sitting room, dressing room, and bathroom. Ulysses Jones told a reporter later that day that he saw "as many as a dozen people huddled over the body of a man clothed in pajamas—a yellow top and blue bottoms."

At first sight Jones didn't recognize Elvis. The man was stretched out on his back on the thick red rug with his pajama top open and his bottoms pulled down below his knees. Rolls of fat girded his belly. He was very dark, almost black. Jones thought that he might have been a black man. "From his shoulders up, his skin was dark blue," he told a reporter for the *Memphis Press-Scimitar*. "Around his neck, which seemed fat and bloated, was a very large gold medallion. His sideburns were gray." A young man was pressing Elvis's chest rhythmically, while a middle-aged woman gave him mouth-to-mouth resuscitation. Jones knelt quickly to search for any sign of life in the prostrate form. He felt no pulse, and he saw no flicker of response when he flashed a penlight into his eyes. "Elvis was cold," he said, "unusually cold."

People in the room began frantically asking the medics what should be done. Suddenly, as if in response, one young man blurted out helpfully, "We think he OD'd." It was the second time the medics had heard that opinion. The man seemed to speak for the whole group. No one dissented, but Jones thought the statement caused "a kind of funny stir in the room." Elvis's employees were rigorously trained never to mention Elvis and drugs in the same breath. Elvis did not take "drugs" of any kind. If they ever had to say anything at all, they were to say that he was on "medication" prescribed by his physicians. One of the medics asked for the container that held the drugs taken by the victim. None was ever produced.

Jones and Crosby quickly concluded that emergency treatment in a hospital offered the only hope. It took five men to lift the body onto the stretcher. "He must have weighed 250 pounds," Crosby said.

With much difficulty, they negotiated the stretcher around the corners and down the stairs. Two men had to hold back Elvis's father, Vernon, as he cried and called out, "Son, I'm coming . . . I'll be there . . . I'll meet you there."

As they were about to leave, a Mercedes-Benz raced up the driveway and lurched to a stop. A stocky middle-aged man with a thatch of white hair dashed from the car and leaped into the back of the ambulance just as the doors closed. It was Elvis's doctor, George Nichopoulos.

Dr. "Nick" Nichopoulos

Four years later it would be established in court that during the seven and a half months preceding Elvis's death, from January 1, 1977, to August 16, 1977, Dr. Nichopoulos had written prescriptions for him for at least 8,805 pills, tablets, vials, and injectables. Going back to January 1975, the count was 19,012. The numbers defied belief, but they came from an experienced team of investigators who visited 153 pharmacies and spent 1,090 hours going through 6,570,175 prescriptions and then, with the aid of two secretaries, spent another 1,120 hours organizing the evidence. The drugs included uppers, downers, and powerful painkillers such as Dilaudid, Quaalude, Percodan, Demerol, and cocaine hydrochloride in quantities more appropriate for those terminally ill with cancer. In fact, at about 2:00 a.m. on the morning of his death, Dr. Nick was again ready to prescribe. He responded to a telephone call from Elvis by prescribing six doses of Dilaudid, an opiate that was Elvis's favorite drug. One of Elvis's bodyguards, Billy Stanley, drove over to Baptist Memorial Hospital, picked up the pills at the all-night pharmacy, and brought them to Graceland. The bodyguard said that he saw Elvis take the pills. The autopsy, however, showed no traces of Dilaudid in Elvis's body.

In the fall of 1981 the state tried Dr. Nichopoulos in criminal court for overprescribing drugs to Elvis and a number of other patients. Dr. Nick testified that if he had not given Elvis a large proportion of the drugs he demanded, other doctors would have. By supplying Elvis, he had at least some control over his patient's intake. His defense was weakened substantially by evidence that he had prescribed an excessive amount of drugs to at least ten other patients, including rock star Jerry Lee Lewis and his own teenage daughter, Chrissy.

On the other hand, it was clearly established that Elvis could, would, and did get any drug he wanted from show business doctors in Las Vegas and Los Angeles. One of his suppliers was a Las Vegas physician called "Flash" by Elvis's staff, since he would appear on a moment's notice, syringe in hand, ready to inject Elvis with whatever drug he wanted. The guys said that "Flash liked to attend Elvis's parties to mix with the overflow of attractive young women present and perhaps find a companion for the evening." At home in Memphis, Elvis would get packages containing drugs mailed from the West. Sometimes he sent his private plane, the four-engine *Lisa Marie*, to Las Vegas or Los Angeles to secure drugs from doctors in those cities and ferry them back to Memphis. Sometimes he flew out himself.

Dr. Nick, like Elvis's other physicians, had been seduced by the frothy glitter of show business, and with his tanned and striking appearance he fit right in. His style diverged from the practice of medicine that was increasingly a matter of business and less a matter of personal service. He was born and reared in Anniston, Alabama, where his father was a highly respected restaurant owner and businessman. George Nichopoulos, however, had not at first been a high achiever. He had not progressed smoothly through college and medical school. He had first entered the University of Alabama on a football scholarship, but dropped out before the school year ended, and he served in the army for two years. He was a student at Birmingham Southern University for a year and then moved on to the University of the South at Sewanee, where he earned his Bachelor of Science degree in 1951. He worked in a research lab at Vanderbilt University before his admission to the medical school in 1952. He failed biochemistry and physiology, was put on probation, and tried to make up for his failures during summer school, but failed again. In the fall, he was not readmitted. He moved to Memphis and for three years worked in the University of Tennessee's medical school. In 1956, he was readmitted to Vanderbilt Medical School, graduating in 1959. After finishing his training, in 1962 he entered practice in Memphis with several doctors who called themselves the Medical Group.

Other doctors looked askance at George Nichopoulos's personal and sartorial style. Too much informality, they thought. He allowed his patients, friends, and acquaintances to call him "Dr. Nick." He seemed unduly proud of the stylishly arranged thatch of white hair that crowned his head, and he was not averse to revealing his chest hair. He often wore his shirts open at the throat, showing off a very large, tasteless gold medallion suspended by a necklace and resting against his bare chest. The medallion was a special gift from Elvis Presley and marked him as a member of the star's inner circle, some of whom were macho young men who proudly called themselves "the Memphis Mafia." Dr. Nick usually sported a highly visible array of expensive rings, bracelets, and wristwatches, some of which were gifts from Elvis. Without his white smock and dangling stethoscope, one would have difficulty recognizing him as a doctor, even in a medical office or hospital. How could he command sufficient authority among his patients? his medical colleagues wondered. How could he justify his fees?

Dr. Nichopoulos was making his rounds at Doctors Hospital far out on the east side of Memphis when the call came that Elvis was in trouble. Dropping everything, he rushed to Graceland in the green Mercedes-Benz Elvis had given him. He was taken by surprise by the call. He had done everything he could think of to preserve Elvis's life in the face of his drug addiction, and he thought he was succeeding. He was looking forward to flying off in the *Lisa Marie* with Elvis to Portland, Maine, for a ten-day tour. For years the doctor had often toured with Elvis, carrying all the necessary drugs with him. Elvis would sometimes introduce him to his adoring audiences, publicly expressing his fond appreciation for his physician as thousands of people looked on and Dr. Nichopoulos stood in the spotlight graciously accepting their applause. Now and again, when Elvis was mad at Dr. Nick, he would punish him by not letting him come along on a tour.

The day before Elvis died, Dr. Nick had loaded up his bag at the Prescription House, a pharmacy just across the street from his office. Later, investigators found that for this ten-day trip, Dr. Nick had picked up 682 pills and tablets, including Dilaudids, Percodans, Amytals, Quaaludes, Dexadrines, and Bephetamines, along with 20 cc's of liquid Dilaudid.

Elvis paid the doctor $800 a day for his services on tours, which lasted from about ten to twenty days. He also paid the doctors with whom Nichopoulos practiced $1,000 a day to cover for him while he was gone. Between 1970 and 1977, Elvis paid Dr. Nick more than $76,000 for his services on the road and $147,000 to the medical group.

The material benefits that Dr. Nichopoulos enjoyed from his association with Elvis did not stop at gifts and fees. In 1975 he had persuaded Elvis to loan him $200,000 to build a house in a newly developing and affluent neighborhood well east of town. With a tennis court, a swimming pool, and an enclosed racquetball court, the banks found the home too costly even for its well-to-do neighborhood and refused to lend Dr. Nick the money he needed. Elvis did so, and before he passed away $55,000 more. They did draw up a paper shortly before Elvis's death that would pool the loans and obligate Nichopoulos to repay the amount over a period of twenty-five years at 7 percent interest, but Elvis never got around to signing the document.

Only days after the funeral, Vernon summoned Nichopoulos to Graceland and with insulting haste compelled him to sign a document in which he mortgaged his home to Elvis's estate for the total amount he owed. He also increased the interest rate to 8 percent and warned

Nichopoulos that if he was late on even one month's payment, fore-
closure would summarily follow. Vernon had never trusted Dr. Nick.
Court records indicate that as of June 27, 1979, Nichopoulos had not
missed a single payment and still owed the estate $245,807.33.

———

As the ambulance raced down the driveway and up the boulevard on the
afternoon of the death, Dr. Nichopoulos could not accept the reality
that lay before him. Working desperately on the body, the doctor kept
shouting to the dead man.

Later that day, Jones described the scene in the ambulance. "All the
way to the hospital," he said, "the doctor had this look of sheer disbe-
lief that this could happen to Elvis." He recalled that Dr. Nichopoulos
kept shouting, "Breathe, Elvis . . . come on, breathe for me."

BAPTIST MEMORIAL HOSPITAL

The ambulance left Graceland at 2:48, sixteen minutes after it arrived.
At 2:56, it pulled up at the emergency room at Baptist Memorial Hospital. The hospital maintained a superbly well trained crew of eighteen
doctors, nurses, and medical specialists to deal with life-or-death situations. Dubbed the Harvey Team, it could gather at a given point in the
building within minutes after the alert was sounded. Already assembled
and waiting when this patient arrived, the team rushed him into Emergency Room B and went to work. They had not been officially told
that it was Elvis. "Why are we working on this guy?" asked one young
medic, seeing that he was already dead. "Because he's Elvis Presley,"
answered one of her older teammates.

Ulysses Jones watched while the Harvey Team worked with professional steadiness. After some twenty minutes, they gave up. Dr. Nick
turned to Joe Esposito, Elvis's road manager. "There is nothing we can
do," he said. "We tried." Jones saw Nichopoulos's eyes begin to water
as he shepherded people out of the room. "Then he left too," Jones said,
"shutting the door behind him." Jones and Crosby drove Dr. Nick back
to Graceland in the ambulance.

The corpse was wheeled to the hospital morgue, where a resourceful, if graceless, newspaper photographer was lying on a gurney under a white sheet, pretending he was a cadaver, waiting for an opportunity to snap a photograph of Elvis's body. Such a photo would be worth thousands of dollars to the tabloids. The would-be photographer was quickly discovered and roughly expelled, and a guard was set until the autopsy began.

Sergeant John Peel of the Memphis Police Department arrived at Baptist Hospital about 3:45 p.m. and began to take notes for the official police report. He wrote that by 4:10 the body was already in the morgue. He had learned that the victim "appeared to have been sitting on commode & lunged forward." He "had gone to the bathroom to read." He noted that "Dr. Nick" had left the "hospital en route to get autopsy papers at Graceland." His last entry indicated that Dr. Nichopoulos "wouldn't give cause of death."

At Graceland, Nichopoulos secured Vernon Presley's signature to a document authorizing an autopsy of his son's body by the staff of Baptist Hospital, to be paid for by the Presley estate. Thus, Vernon might share—or not share—the resulting report with anyone he chose. If the object was to keep the cause of Elvis's death a secret, it was an excellent move both for the Presley family and for Dr. Nichopoulos. If Elvis died by his own hand from popping too many pills, only trusted people needed to know the truth, and the carefully constructed public image of Elvis would be secure. Also, if Dr. Nichopoulos had prescribed too many pills for Elvis, that fact might be kept from authorities who might otherwise take away his medical license or even bring him up on criminal charges.

The Cover-up

Baptist Hospital administrators realized that in dealing with the death of Elvis Presley they were involved in a public relations matter that might damage the hospital's sterling reputation. Over the years they had carefully concealed the nature and seriousness of his often embarrassing illnesses, including those resulting from drug abuse. Dr. Nichopoulos had

always checked Elvis into Baptist Hospital because he knew they were discreet. That was surely one reason why he ordered Charles Crosby to drive the ambulance some seven miles to Baptist Hospital rather than to the nearest emergency room, at Methodist South Hospital, only blocks away from Graceland.

The autopsy was conducted by a specially selected and highly skilled team of nine pathologists headed by the hospital's chief of pathology, Dr. E. Eric Muirhead. Dr. Jerry Francisco, the medical examiner for Shelby County, closely observed the proceedings. It would be his responsibility to declare to the world the official cause of Elvis Presley's death.

Early on, a meticulous dissection of the body revealed what Elvis did not die from. It was not heart failure, stroke, cancer, or lung disease—the usual killers. It also confirmed what his doctors already knew: Elvis was chronically ill with diabetes, glaucoma, and constipation. As they proceeded, the doctors saw evidence that his body had been wracked over a span of years by a large and constant stream of drugs. They had also studied his hospital records, which included two admissions for drug detoxification and methadone treatments. Over time, Elvis had, in effect, been poisoned. The bloated body, the puffy eyelids, and the constipation reflected the slow death. They prepared multiple specimens from the corpse's fluids and organs to be identified anonymously and sent to several well-respected laboratories across America for analysis. Chances seemed high that Elvis had, in fact, overdosed.

Dan Warlick, Dr. Francisco's aide, had driven to Graceland after Elvis's death was confirmed to investigate the scene. Several hours later, he summarized what he had found. Sadly, ignominiously, the crisis had come Tuesday morning while Elvis was sitting on the black leather padded seat on his black ceramic commode reading a book. There had been a trauma of some sort. Probably, Elvis stood up, dropped the book aside, took a halting short step or two, then sank to his knees and pitched forward. Perhaps he crawled a foot or two more before he collapsed, came to rest in the fetal position face down on the deep pile rug, and regurgitated slightly. Warlick told Dr. Francisco that the site had been cleaned up before he arrived, but even so, he had found two syringes and an empty medicine bag in Elvis's quarters. He thought that drugs were involved in the death.

Dr. Francisco seemed uninterested in Warlick's findings. He smoked a cigarette while Warlick talked. In front of them, the hospital pathologists continued to dissect Elvis's body, piece by piece, on a porcelain table. Francisco cut Warlick off before he had finished his report, but invited him to stay and witness the autopsy. The Shelby County medical examiner, perhaps, had already decided what the official cause of death would be.

Francisco and the hospital authorities knew that the world was waiting for their announcement about what killed Elvis Presley. News people were swarming around inside and outside of the hospital. Maurice Elliott, the hospital's vice president, knew that he had to give the journalists something to report. After Elvis's body had been wheeled away to the morgue, he told them that Elvis had been pronounced dead at 3:30 p.m., apparently of heart failure. He also scheduled a press conference with the pathologists for 8:00 p.m. As that hour approached, the pathologists were still working on the body and realized that they could not say with scientific certainty what had killed this man. They knew that he did not die of the usual causes, and they knew that addiction to drugs was the probable cause, but they could say nothing with confidence until they got the results back from the laboratories, if then. That would be a matter of weeks. The press and the world were not likely to wait patiently for their verdict.

At eight o'clock the hospital conference room was crowded with journalists when a team of doctors entered and took places behind tables in the front of the room. Dr. Francisco made himself the spokesman for the physicians. He sat down in front of a bank of microphones, flanked by Dr. Nichopoulos, Dr. Muirhead, and five other physicians. All of the hospital doctors still wore their white smocks, while Dr. Nick sported an open-necked black silk shirt, diamond rings, and gold jewelry.

Dr. Muirhead thought that Francisco would say that they would need to study the lab results before they could complete the autopsy and offer their judgment. Instead, Francisco opened with the flat statement that "the results of the autopsy are that the cause of death is cardiac arrhythmia due to undetermined heartbeat." Muirhead could not believe his ears. Francisco had not only presumed to speak for the hospital's team of pathologists, he had announced a conclusion that they had not reached. He said that Elvis had simply died of heart failure.

Francisco continued his indictment of Elvis's heart. "There are several cardiovascular diseases that are known to be present," he said. "One is a mild degree of hypertension that had been under treatment for some time, and that there was hardening of the arteries, the coronary arteries of the heart, known as coronary atherosclerosis." During the autopsy, the doctors had decided that these conditions were indeed present but not involved in Elvis's death. Francisco talked pointedly about the existence of these two conditions as if they were important, but he was also careful to indicate that they were not serious. He wasn't lying, but he really hadn't said anything of substance either.

If Francisco wanted the world to leap to the conclusion that Elvis died of a heart attack without his actually saying so, it was a brilliant presentation. The message was that Elvis's physicians had been monitoring his heart closely for a substantial period of time and there had been no indication that heart failure would kill him. The press and soon the world understood that a prestigious team of pathologists had said that Elvis died of heart failure, suddenly and without warning. It was a crisis that could not have been avoided. No one was at fault in Elvis's demise.

Francisco properly cautioned that the final and official determination of the cause of death would take days or weeks. Indeed, he warned, the cause "may never be discovered." Nevertheless, he proceeded to announce that he was absolutely certain of one thing: it was not drugs. Elvis was taking medication for high blood pressure and his colon problem, he said, but "there is no evidence of any chronic abuse of drugs, whatsoever." Again, Dr. Francisco was marvelously ingenious in his use of language. If he referred only to street drugs, he was correct. If he meant to include prescription drugs, he was lying.

Dr. Muirhead was sorely embarrassed for himself, his staff of pathologists, and his hospital. He later said that he wished he had spoken up, but did not because he did not know what the laboratory reports would show. Even later, he was silenced by the fact that the autopsy report belonged to Elvis's estate, not to the state, and hence was not public knowledge.

During the press conference, Dr. Francisco did not invite Dr. Muirhead or any of the other pathologists to speak after he finished, but rather turned the microphone directly over to Dr. Nichopoulos. Dr. Nick seemed "positively jubilant" over the medical examiner's pronouncement that drugs were in no way involved and, in effect, no one was responsible for Elvis's death. He told the journalists that he had been Elvis's private physician for a decade and he knew positively that he had not been taking hard drugs. "If he was taking cocaine," he declared, "I would have known about it." He had given Elvis a complete physical only five days before, he said. "He was getting over an eye infection and a sore throat, but overall he was a healthy man." Elvis's death was simply a bolt out of the blue, a tragedy that no one could have prevented.

What Killed Elvis

Several weeks later, Baptist Hospital pathologists received the laboratory reports. They revealed a number of prescription drugs present at toxic or near-toxic levels in the specimens tested, in particular codeine, which was present at many times the therapeutic level. The pathologists concluded that Elvis died from a reaction to drugs. Virtually unanimously, medical experts involved in Memphis and elsewhere agreed that it was the combination of many drugs, "polypharmacy" as they called it, that killed Elvis.

On October 18, Dr. Muirhead presented the meticulously prepared report to Vernon Presley at Graceland. Vernon did not make the information public, and Dr. Muirhead did not feel that he could ethically do so. However, journalists and other interested parties soon managed to learn the contents of the report, at first in part and eventually in full.

Foremost among the journalists was Beth J. Tamke, a hard-driving young reporter for the *Commercial Appeal*. On October 22, 1977, she published a complete description of the findings of one of the labs that analyzed the specimens taken from Elvis's body, proving that Francisco was wrong. She had researched the literature thoroughly and learned, as she wrote, that Placidyl, which the labs had found and Francisco had declared was not present, was "lethal when combined with codeine," as it had been. The "polypharmacy" diagnosis was correct. Beth Tamke was so aggressive and so effective in getting out the true drug story behind Elvis's death that her editor took her off the case and assigned her trivial pieces. "I wrote stories about Legionnaire's disease, about cricks in the neck, about water on the knee," she told the Memphis writer James P. Cole. Ironically, she also was assigned to write obituaries.

Under fire from several directions, Dr. Francisco ignored the lab results and the opinions of other pathologists. He gave heart disease as the probable cause on the official death certificate and ruled that Elvis died a "natural" death rather than an "accidental" death, which an OD would have been labeled. Over the decades that followed, he held to that position steadfastly and with a seemingly happy defiance.

Jerry Francisco was a self-assured and strong-minded man. He loved his work, and he was sure that he did it well. Every year his office certified the deaths of about three thousand people in Shelby County, about a third of which required some investigation. In accomplishing his formidable task expeditiously, Dr. Francisco seemed to be guided when possible by the ancient and usually wise dictum "Let the dead bury the dead." To that, he added a Francisco addendum, "And let life go on."

On one revealing occasion, both he and Dr. Muirhead testified in a civil case involving a claim against an insurance company brought by the relatives of a man who had died, predictably, of a heart condition long known to his doctors. Dr. Muirhead testified that the man died of natural causes, his failing heart, which meant that his family could not claim the insurance money. Dr. Francisco persuaded the jury that he died from accidental causes because the man happened to hit his head on an object as he fell to the floor just before he died. The insurance company paid the claim. When Muirhead criticized Francisco, he replied, "Eric, you just don't know how to play the game."

Dr. Nick on Trial

One result of Elvis's death was that Dr. Nichopoulos's practice of medicine came under close scrutiny. In January 1980, a panel of five doctors commissioned by the Tennessee Board of Medical Examiners to judge his treatment of Elvis and a number of other patients began a hearing in the chambers of the Memphis City Council. The doctors concluded that Dr. Nick was, as one member of the panel worded it, "not a bad doctor." He was simply too sympathetic to his patients and too quick to write prescriptions for people who just dropped in at his office. They suspended his license for three months and put him on probation for three years.

In the fall of 1981, local authorities, under the direction of the state attorney general, charged Nichopoulos with violating a law against doctors overprescribing drugs. The previous year a panel of five doctors had let Dr. Nick go with a slap on the wrist and an indulgent smile; now, the state's prosecutors were determined to put him behind bars for years. Nichopoulos hired James Neal to defend him, reputedly for $150,000. Neal had won national fame as the legal counsel for the Senate committee that brought Richard Nixon down from the White House following the Watergate cover-up.

Neal's defense of Dr. Nick was brilliant. He portrayed the doctor as the Good Samaritan who put the welfare of his sorely afflicted patients far above his own. In Elvis's case, Dr. Nick had shown great compassion, faithfully treating an exceedingly difficult patient over many years. Neal also cleverly managed to use the "polypharmacy" argument to exonerate his client from sole and punishable blame in the death of Elvis. He questioned one expert witness for the prosecution after another, going down the list of drugs found in Elvis's body one by one. Tell me, Doctor, he would say, which drug killed him? Was it codeine? "No." Was it Dilaudid? "No." The witness would have to answer "no" to each question because it was the combination of drugs that did Elvis in and no single one. The jury had no difficulty deciding that there was indeed reasonable doubt that Dr. Nick had done anything at all illegal in Elvis's case or in any of the other cases. Rather, the good doctor cared very much, personally as well as professionally, about his patients. They returned a verdict of "not guilty."

———

An amazing array of wild theories sprang up to explain Elvis's untimely death. Within a few days of his passing, Dr. Nick, seemingly desperate, told Vernon that Elvis was actually dying from bone cancer. Thus, it was merciful that he died as quickly as he did and escaped the agony that would have come. Another story asserted that someone came into his bathroom and delivered a karate chop to the neck that did him in. Elvis was an ardent karate fan, and the young men in his coterie had become expert in the art. One alienated friend might easily have gained entry into the bathroom and given him the lethal chop. Vernon, at least at first, was absolutely convinced that someone had killed his son. He commissioned Dick Grob, the chief of security at Graceland, to find the culprit.

Still another idea floated about claiming that Elvis was not dead. He had paid a man who was terminally ill to undergo plastic surgery to look exactly like him and then commit suicide. The money was to go to the man's family. Elvis, thus relieved of the burden of his celebrity, now lived happily in some unknown land under an assumed name.

Very knowledgeable people differ widely on exactly what killed Elvis. One highly creative yet plausible theory is that his excessive straining on the toilet somehow cut off the circulation of blood to his heart; hence the sudden pain that led him to stand up and fall forward. It was a heart attack after all, even though his affinity for "downers" had brought about the phenomenally high level of constipation that triggered the attack.

Another creative but plausible scenario held that during that last night he mistakenly took the codeine pills supplied by his dentist, rather than the Dilaudid prescribed by his doctor, since the pills were virtually indistinguishable. No Dilaudid was found in his body during the autopsy, while codeine was at a lethal level for an ordinary person. It was well known that Elvis was highly allergic to codeine; hence the pain just before he died.

Yet another plausible theory is that Elvis carelessly downed the codeine pills his dentist had given him, and those, combined with a host of other drugs he ordinarily took, produced a lethal reaction. Dr. Nichopoulos himself had established a routine "protocol" in which three separate packets of drugs were to be given to Elvis when he needed to go to sleep. Elvis definitely took all three of these that morning, downing the last at about 8:30 a.m. Quite possibly, the depressants he took trying to induce sleep reduced his breathing to the critical level. He had frequently suffered such episodes before and come terribly close to dying—saved only by the vigilance of his caretakers. That morning, no one was watching. For some reason—perhaps involving a reaction to the codeine and attempts to move his bowels—he experienced pain and fright while sitting on the toilet. Alarmed, he stood up, dropped the book he was reading, stumbled forward, and fell face down in the fetal position. He struggled weakly and drooled on the rug. Unable to breathe, he died.

The young man who met the medics when they first arrived at the front door of Graceland had already made the correct diagnosis of an overdose even before the experts saw the body.

DAVID BRINKLEY ON *THE NIGHTLY NEWS*, AUGUST 16, 1977

"Elvis Presley died today," David Brinkley declared at the beginning of the six o'clock NBC *Nightly News* on August 16. "He was forty-two. Apparently it was a heart attack," he continued in his dry, staccato, and compelling style. "He was found in his home in Memphis not breathing. His road manager tried to revive him. He failed. A hospital tried to revive him. It failed. His doctor pronounced him dead at three o'clock this afternoon, the end at an early age of one of the two most spectacular careers in the history of entertainment, the other being Frank Sinatra."

Brinkley said Presley was very near the peak of his career when he was drafted into the army and "actually trained as a tank man" rather than serving as a performer entertaining for the troops. "He sold records in the multiples of millions, made millions, bought a string of Cadillacs, one after another, gave away a string of Cadillacs to people he liked. And along the way he was married to Priscilla Anne Beaulieu. The very symbol of sex for all the millions of . . . uh . . . hundreds of thousands of teenagers, he was married only once and then relatively late. The couple had one child, a daughter. The marriage did not last very long. It ended in divorce.

"He was a part of American popular history," Brinkley continued. "In the 1950s, the great swing era of Benny Goodman, Artie Shaw, and Tommy Dorsey was about dead. Big band pop music had turned into what was called Bop or Bee Bop, remote, obscure, and bloodless, nobody liked it, nobody could dance to it. And then here came Elvis with a hot, stomping, steaming, sexy kind of music that turned on young people as pop music never had before. Others came along, including the Beatles, but they were all indebted to him and most of them said so."

Coolly and calmly, David Brinkley gave Elvis the obituary that the country wanted to hear. He was a fine young man of the lower social orders who had risen to fame and fortune by his talent to become one of America's top entertainers. A true patriot, Elvis had served in the army; he became rich; he was generous; and he was a father. Now Elvis was dead; he was forty-two.

The Woman at the Gate—"A Heart of Gold"

There were millions of Americans—especially women—who loved Elvis. Their feelings could hardly be expressed in words. Many of them journeyed to Graceland to mourn his death.

NBC sent a television reporter, Jackson Bain, to capture the scene and interview some of the people present. On Wednesday, the film clip appeared on the early morning *Today Show*, hosted by Jane Pauley. She began by explaining that Elvis came to Memphis for "a better life." His "parents were hard-working people," and Elvis became a "truck driver like his father." She announced that his father, Vernon, was opening up Graceland for two hours that afternoon for a public viewing of the body.

At sunrise, Bain had positioned himself at the twin black metal gates at the foot of the driveway that led up the low hill to the front entrance of the house at Graceland and interviewed some of the people present. At one point he approached an attractive, long-haired, blonde in her midthirties. She and her family had begun to drive from California to Memphis to visit the Graceland site before they heard of Elvis's death.

One can imagine the family getting into their car in the predawn hours in California, traveling for a couple of days over the Rocky Mountains and across the Great Plains, then hearing the news of Elvis's death on the car radio. They pressed on to Memphis through the night and arrived at the gates at first light.

"Why have you come here?" Bain asked the woman. "Why do you feel close to Elvis Presley?"

"We were on our way from California to see him when we heard the news that it had happened," she replied in the shocked, sad tone of someone recounting events immediately after the sudden death of a loved one.

"But why are you here?" Bain persisted. "What makes you feel close to the man?"

"I just love him," she answered. "I love his generosity, his talent, everything about him. He has a heart of gold." For at least two generations, millions of Americans have agreed.

PART I

THE BUBBLE

PART I

THE BUBBLE

CHAPTER ONE

THE DREAM

THE SHELL

The girls first discovered Elvis in July 1954 in the Overton Shell, an open-air theater with a covered stage in Overton Park in Memphis. All sorts of entertainment happened at the Shell. In the days before air-conditioning, affluent Memphians might go there on a warm summer evening to enjoy a performance of *The Merry Widow*, the light opera that Jeanette MacDonald delightfully introduced to America on film in 1934.

On this evening, Friday, July 30, the show was country and western. The bill was put together by Bob Neal, a popular Memphis radio personality and promoter whose early morning program reached listeners on farms and in villages far out into the hinterland while they were milking cows and cracking eggs on the edges of hot frying pans. The headliner for this evening was Slim Whitman, whose latest hit record was entitled "Indian Love Call." Sam Phillips, the owner of Sun Records, had persuaded Neal to add Elvis to the program. During the previous four weeks, he had managed with amazing success the creation, the broadcast by radio, and the local distribution of Elvis's first record. On one side Elvis had done a black blues song—"That's All Right, Mama"—and on the other a country number—"Blue Moon of Kentucky." He was now slated to do on stage what he had done on the record.

Elvis was exceedingly anxious that the audience at the Shell might not appreciate his performance. In those days, country singers, such as those who achieved stardom on *The Grand Ole Opry*, broadcast from Nashville, Tennessee, on Saturday nights, did not do black songs.

Furthermore, he had done both songs in a style that no one had ever heard before. These folks in the Shell had bought tickets to hear familiar and uncomplicated country and western music. What Elvis and his guitarist, Scotty Moore, and his bass fiddle player, Bill Black, were doing was not country. It was not hillbilly, not pop, not gospel, and not blues. It was neither black nor white, neither sacred nor—quite—profane. Yet it was somehow influenced by all these things.

When Sam arrived at the Shell, he found an agitated Elvis waiting for him on the steps at the rear of the stage. Four decades later, he described the scene to Elvis's biographer Peter Guralnick.

"Man, I'm so glad to see you, Mr. Phillips . . . I—I—I—I just didn't know what I was going to do," Elvis stammered.

Sam reassured Elvis. He was absolutely certain that the world would soon recognize their achievement, if not here, then elsewhere.

When their turn came, Elvis and his two fellow band members stepped nervously onto the stage and faced an audience of some two thousand people. Stiffly, he adjusted the microphone, stepped back, and jumped into "That's All Right, Mama," the A-side of their record. It was a blues song recorded several years earlier by a black singer, Arthur "Big Boy" Crudup. Elvis raised up on the balls of his feet, leaned forward into the microphone, and curled his upper lip into the sneer that would become known around the world.

"That's all right, mama," he sang, moving his whole body with the music, "any—wa-ay you do."

Sliding into the thick, thumping sound, Elvis stepped back from the mike, savaging the strings of his guitar and shaking all over while Scotty and Bill each took a turn doing the instrumental. They heard and saw the audience responding loudly and physically to their rendition of "That's All Right." Almost automatically, they swung into the only other number they had polished for their repertoire, the B-side of their record, "Blue Moon of Kentucky." Bill Monroe, the soon-to-be King of Bluegrass, had done it before in a high keening tenor, dripping with nostalgia for a rural and romantic past. Elvis, using his God-given rich and versatile voice, perfected by practice, gave it a different turn. Just as "That's All Right" was not black anymore, "Blue Moon" was no longer hillbilly; it was joyous, country-come-to-town and damn glad to be there.

The crowd in front of the stage broke loose. On stage, the performers themselves did not know what to make of the ruckus. "I was scared stiff," Elvis later confessed. "Everyone was hollering and I didn't know what they were hollering at."

Scotty Moore described the scene. "During the instrumental parts," he said, "Elvis would back off from the mike and be playing and shaking, and the crowd would go wild, but he thought they were actually making fun of him." Two years later, Elvis recalled that when he came offstage he asked his manager, "What did I do?" His manager told him it was the way he was "wiggling" his legs that caused all the excitement. Elvis took the hint.

"I went back out for an encore," he said, "and I did a little more, and the more I did, the wilder they went."

It was the girls who went wild, and Elvis gave them more of what they obviously wanted—the movement of his body. This was the beginning of a phenomenon that determined his early career, an amazingly intimate relationship between Elvis onstage and the women in his audiences. While the record had to do with race on one side and the loss of a rural past on the other, the stage performance had everything to do with sex and traditional gender roles.

As it evolved over the next two years in the South, this performance by young white women in the Elvis venue was unprecedented in character and unmatched in magnitude. Huge crowds of women were determined to express themselves as sexual creatures in a highly visible public arena. In 1956 and 1957, they exported their revolution to young women in the North and West.

FINDING THE AUDIENCE

After the triumph at the Shell, Sam Phillips immediately booked Elvis for an appearance on *The Grand Ole Opry* in Nashville. This time, Elvis skipped the black blues song "That's All Right," but even his rendition of "Blue Moon of Kentucky" drew only polite applause. Undaunted, Sam promptly put Elvis and his band on the *Louisiana Hayride* in Shreveport, Louisiana. The *Hayride* was less prestigious than *The Grand Ole Opry*, but its radio reach was wide, and it was famous for giving beginners a good start.

On October 16, during the first of their two performances on the *Hayride* on Saturday evening, Elvis, Scotty, and Bill got much the same response as at *The Grand Ole Opry*. At the second show later that evening, however, they had a younger audience that exploded, shouting and screaming enthusiastically. They were on course again.

When they were invited to return for second and third weeks, the composition of the audience in the 3,800-seat auditorium shifted in a remarkable fashion. "The young ladies started showing up," recalled Frank Page, the avuncular, baritone-voiced announcer for the *Hayride*. As Page remembered, "Elvis wiggled his leg a bit, snarled a bit, and let his hair hang down." The young women responded. Page said that "the audience changed as the demeanor of the act changed." The act changed as the audience changed, too. Elvis would become notorious among fellow entertainers for that obsession, doing what the girls wanted him to do, envied and often hated for his success in achieving that goal.

Recognizing Elvis's entertainment value, the *Hayride* immediately booked him for a full year. He was to appear every Saturday night, do two shows of a dozen minutes each, and be paid $18. Meanwhile, Sam had brought Elvis, Scotty, and Bill—soon to be known as "the Blue Moon Boys"—back into the studio to produce a second highly successful record: "Good Rockin' Tonight" backed by "I Don't Care If the Sun Don't Shine."

In the fall of 1954, Bob Neal took on the job of managing public performances by the Blue Moon Boys. He had no difficulty at all booking them into high school auditoriums and public meeting halls within driving distance of Memphis. What had been scattered appearances soon became well-organized tours in which the boys performed almost every night for a week or two, often driving at breakneck speeds to get from one engagement to the next. One ten-day tour, for example, began on Wednesday, January 12, 1955, at the municipal auditorium in Clarksdale, Mississippi, some seventy-five miles south of Memphis, moved west across the Mississippi River on the thirteenth to play in the Catholic Club Auditorium in Helena, Arkansas, then Marianna, Arkansas, on the fourteenth and the *Hayride* in Shreveport on the fifteenth. The tour then recrossed the river to play through northeastern Mississippi and northwestern Alabama at Booneville, Corinth, and Sheffield. It ended at the National Guard Armory in Sikeston, Missouri, on January 21.

The *Hayride* was widely broadcast on Shreveport's 50,000-watt radio station KWKH. Every Saturday night it reached up to twenty-eight states, and on the third Saturday of every month, 198 CBS stations carried the program. The *Hayride* opened the way for Elvis's live performances over a broad territory in the South and West. Soon he was playing all over Texas, from East Texas towns such as Gladewater, Texarkana, and Houston to West Texas towns such as Midland and Odessa.

Elvis was popular enough in Midland, where the more affluent people in the oil industry in the Permian Basin made their homes, but he was even more popular in Odessa, where the workers, vastly Southern and vastly white, lived. In Odessa, he headlined a show on January 4, and on February 2 he was part of a tour package that drew an audience of four thousand. For Elvis, this was a huge crowd. He earned $150 for that performance, an amount that would have seemed astronomically high to him only a few months before.

February 6, 1955—six months into his career—was the day that marked a revolutionary change in the life of Elvis Presley. On that day, Bob Neal introduced him to the legendary promoter Colonel Tom Parker, the man who had managed the country singer Eddy Arnold to national success as a touring performer and an RCA recording star. Arnold finally rebelled against Parker's drive for total control over his life as well as his work and fired him. Parker eventually entered into a partnership with another only slightly lesser star, Hank Snow, a diminutive Canadian with a guitar and a peculiarly nasal voice whose song "I'm Movin' On" ranked No. 1 for twenty-one weeks on the country and western chart in 1950.

The meeting between the Colonel, Elvis, Neal, and Sam Phillips occurred in a restaurant booth located in the Holiday Inn just across the street from Memphis's Ellis Auditorium, where Elvis was performing. Phillips took a strong and immediate dislike of the always commanding Colonel. The Colonel yielded not an inch to Sam, and Sam soon left. Nevertheless, what came out of the meeting was a valuable new beginning for Elvis. Within two weeks, the Colonel began to book him for tours with stars from *The Grand Ole Opry*. On February 14, Parker included Elvis in a short tour with the Hank Snow Jamboree. The tour opened with two shows at North Junior High School in Roswell, New Mexico, moved through Texas, and ended on Friday, February 18, in Monroe, Louisiana, just in time for Elvis to appear on the *Hayride* in Shreveport the next night.

Elvis, Scotty, and Bill were now running at a hectic pace. In February, they did twenty-two shows in twenty-three days, stretching from the American Legion Hall in Carlsbad, New Mexico, in the West to the high school auditorium in Ripley, Mississippi, in the east and from the Golden Cadillac Club in New Orleans up to Robinson Auditorium in Little Rock, Arkansas.

ON THE ROAD

Life on the road was exhilarating for Elvis, Scotty, and Bill, but it was also exhausting. With no planes and no trains, they would perform in the evening and drive night and day to get to the next engagement, Bill's big bass fiddle strapped to the top of the car like some huge dead beast brought down by a hunter's gunfire. Happily for the Blue Moon Boys, they had the loan of Scotty's wife's car—virtually permanently, it turned out, after three hundred thousand miles on the road. But Bobbie Moore missed tooling around Memphis in her brand-new 1954 four-door Chevrolet Bel Air with a white top, blue body, and white sidewall tires. It was not easy for her to commute to her job as a clerk in the huge regional Sears, Roebuck office in Memphis while the boys were on the road. Bobbie was the one who kept up monthly payments on the car and paid numerous repair bills. Ironically, Elvis later gave hundreds of cars and pickup trucks to friends, acquaintances, and even strangers, but he never gave one to Bobbie.

When Bobbie's car wore out, Elvis bought himself a 1951 Lincoln. He painted ELVIS PRESLEY—SUN RECORDS on the door. They wrecked that one. Next, Elvis bought a 1954 Cadillac. This car burned while he was driving from Home, Alabama, to Texarkana, Texas, with a girl he had invited to join him for the trip. He barely managed to empty the trunk of the car before everything was consumed by fire. The guys were following behind in another car, and the troupe nearly missed getting to their next show on time. He bought a new 1955 pink and white Cadillac and had his name painted on the door.

Linked to the *Hayride* and through Colonel Parker to *The Grand Ole Opry*, Elvis often toured with country and western performers who were well established and drew large and adoring crowds. One of these acts was a brother-sister team, Jim Ed and Maxine Brown, whose record "Looking Back to See (If You Were Looking Back at Me)" had just hit No. 1 on the country music charts nationally. Elvis attempted, without success, to woo Maxine.

In late February, Colonel Parker added Elvis to another Grand Ole Opry tour with a star-studded ensemble that featured "Mother Maybelle and the Carter Sisters" and comic Whitey Ford, "the Duke of Paducah." The Carters were RCA recording stars and the most talented and beloved female gospel group in America. "The Duke," from Paducah, Kentucky, was country's most adored comedian. "I'm going back to the wagon, folks," he would shout out at the end of his semi-soliloquy in mock exasperation at having been in town. "These shoes are killing me."

Whitey's tagline was loaded with meaning for audiences who lived in the country or, having been born and reared in the country, had moved to town. World War II, especially, had brought a lot of country folks to town either permanently or for the duration, who experienced the shock of urban living. Whitey's line drew upon their deep and disturbing feelings about the strictures of town life versus the natural freedom of life in the country. The "back to the wagon" phrase drew upon a practice these people knew well. Into the 1930s and even the 1940s, some country people would hitch their mules and horses to wagons on occasional Saturday mornings and drive to town to hang out, chew tobacco, talk, or drink and play pool in "cafes" on the side streets, or even conduct a little business, while a self-ordained minister would preach the gospel on a corner of the square, and the women and children shopped and socialized.

Whitey Ford, the Carter family, and other entertainers spoke powerfully to millions of plain white Southerners in a language that outsiders could sometimes admire but never fully understand. On tour, the Grand Ole Opry Show often drew audiences of several thousand. They had come to see and hear country and gospel singers, and early on there was a degree of shock at Elvis's unique style. But adults did not walk out, and the teenage girls were increasingly numerous and increasingly explosive, a fact the press noted.

———

Elvis's music was different, just as Sam had wanted, and the huge popularity of two more new recordings ("Milk Cow Blues Boogie," which came out in January 1955, and "Baby, Let's Play House," which appeared in April) clearly marked his success as a singer. But neither Sam nor anyone else had expected such a wildly emotional reaction on the part of the young women in Elvis's audiences at the mere site of his body in motion.

"I hadn't thought of him in terms of a physical specimen," Sam declared looking back. "I wasn't thinking, 'Is he going to look good onstage, is he going to be a great performer?'"

Sam was so intensely focused on the sound of the music that he missed the sight. But then, Sam was a man and very conscious of his masculinity. "I was just looking for something nobody could categorize," he said.

The girls loved what Elvis did. Many other people either tolerated it condescendingly or hated it bitterly. Elvis himself could not understand why anyone would be upset by his onstage movements. "I jump around because it's the way I feel," he explained. "I can't even sing with a beat at all if I stand still." Movement came naturally with his music, he said, and both were innocent.

The girls were innocent too, Elvis insisted, denying charges that they indulged in lascivious behavior during his performances. They were not bad girls, Scotty Moore agreed. They were not camp followers or groupies, he asserted. They were "all nice girls, well scrubbed, well dressed."

Even so, Scotty admitted, there was sex on the road, and a lot of it. Elvis was like a "young stud at a rodeo," he said, and "they could have named him Man o' War." Elvis was highly active sexually, but Scotty somehow felt the need to deny strenuously rumors that Elvis was bisexual or homosexual. "He'd have been the first one to lay someone out if a man made an advance on him, I can tell you that," he declared. "If he was prejudiced about anything, that was it." Rumors about Elvis's sexual orientation arose, he thought, because Elvis wore eye makeup. He started using mascara for performances, Scotty said. Afterward, "he just wore it all the time." Then Scotty leaped to another thought. "Let's face it," he said, "the man was damned near too pretty to be a man." Elvis looked like a girl and acted like a sexual superman; the girls looked innocent and acted like Jezebels. Good girls behaving like nymphomaniacs caused consternation among both friends and foes.

Sonny West, who eventually became one of Elvis's bodyguards, captured the phenomenon perfectly. Sonny was a young enlisted man in the air force stationed in the Southwest. He was large, dark, and handsome with, it seems, a ready appetite for young women. He met a local girl and went with her to an Elvis performance at the rodeo grounds. As Sonny described her in the so-called bodyguard book—*Elvis: What Happened?*—she "was a quiet, corn-fed Southwestern girl whose demeanor and looks suggested that when someone invented virginity and apple pie, they must have had her in mind." He recalled that "the dainty face and the Sunday-best dress she was wearing told him immediately to resist cursing in her presence and scrap any thoughts of ever scoring."

A half hour later, this young woman was, in Sonny's limited understanding, "behaving totally out of character." She acted "like a sex-starved little nymphet," he declared. "Believe me," Sonny insisted, "this gal changed right before my eyes." Sonny's perception was that Elvis had caused the girl to become something that she was not. Like some wizard, he had waved a magic wand and created a miracle in defiance of nature. Sonny continued: "If someone had grabbed that lady right there and then and dragged her off to bed, it would have happened there and then. Every time he moved, it seemed like a couple of hundred gals were getting it off."

Sonny never did, as he delicately worded his ambition, "score with the lady." Indeed, he said, "after the show my gal just went back to what she was like before. It was as if all that carrying on was for Elvis and nobody else." It never occurred to Sonny that his date's "carrying on" was not for Elvis, but for herself. He saw her as a nice girl, and he could only make sense of her behavior by describing it as "totally out of character."

Sonny's limited universe, restricted by a sort of testosterone-driven tunnel vision, was not rare among American males in the 1950s. Women were to be passive, not active, in sexual and all other relations, submissive and undemanding. In the broad round of life, women were not to be the creators and controllers of their sexual pleasures. Men certainly did not exist to be used sexually by women as they pleased. Men worthy of the name could not imagine a male stripper for a female audience— a male Gypsy Rose Lee or Tempest Storm. Men who sold their bodies for sex were gigolos, Italians in tight pants, or effete Europeans, and something less than real men. Most men—like most women—could not imagine themselves as "sex objects." What women saw as their role in life during the week was confirmed in church on Sunday. Their lot was God-given—as Paul had tried to teach those amazingly slow learners, the Corinthians—"For man did not come from woman, but woman from man; neither was man created for woman, but woman for man," he preached.

In the eyes of young people in the South, there were two groups: good girls and bad girls. Good girls were not to be pressed aggressively into sex. Bad girls (theoretically) hardly had to be pressed at all. The trick was to "sex" the girl in question: Was she a good girl . . . or a bad girl? Sonny West thought he could tell.

Offstage, Elvis offered himself as a male replica of Sonny's prim and proper date, a "good girl." He was a convincing angel, a perfectly mannered, seemingly pure and even virginal Southern boy. Onstage he was a devil, pumped up with carnal knowledge and a predatory attitude, a satyr ready to ravish whichever young maiden might venture near. Both Elvises seemed real, yet they were incompatible. For some years, the teddy bear denied all knowledge of the tiger.

On February 16, 1955, the singer and disc jockey Roy Orbison first saw Elvis come onstage in the high school field house in Odessa, Texas. "First thing he came out and spat out a piece of gum," Roy recalled. Elvis spit on the floor and was not genteel in his remarks to the audience. "His diction was real coarse, like a truck driver's," Roy said. "I can't overemphasize how shocking he looked and seemed that night." Swiveling his hips, bumping and grinding suggestively, curling his upper lip and snarling, he was raw and outrageous. Yet he had a voice, a talent, an unmatchable feel for the music that vibrated through his audiences. "Just a real raw cat singing like a bird," Roy said. "His energy was incredible, his instinct was just amazing."

Roy stretched for an analogy and came to David Lynch's film *Blue Velvet.* "Actually it affected me exactly the same way as when I first saw that David Lynch film," he said. "I just didn't know what to make of it. There was just no reference point in the culture to compare it." It was outrageous and irresistible.

Roy's analogy was marvelously insightful, given the movie's plot, specifically the attempt by an exceedingly unlovely and violent homosexual man to seduce a handsome and virginal young man. The Elvis that Roy saw onstage was not a nice man. Rather, he was "raw," spitting out his gum, talking in a "real coarse" manner, curling his lip and snarling. He was ready and eager to take each girl in the audience sexually, by force if need be, "then and there," to use Sonny West's phrase. In the bubble with Elvis, the girl would seemingly have sex emotionally, but she would only dance—in plain sight in the auditorium of the high school she attended, or in a public arena in the community in which she lived. There was indeed no conventional reference point to which the performance of the girls could be compared, as they amazingly rebelled against Southern social conventions.

Just as the girls were "prim and proper" before and after the performance, so too, it seemed, was Elvis. He didn't curse, smoke, or drink. He loved his mother and gospel music. He was unfailingly mannerly and exceedingly deferential to his elders. "Yes, ma'am," he would respond, and "Yes, sir."

Elvis deferred offstage, but onstage he had no qualms at all when it came to competing with older performers as well as his contemporaries for attention. Talented and ruthless, he wanted to win totally and exclusively the love and adoration of every audience he met. He had an uncanny ability for finding his audience, feeling out its desires, and playing to them. Tillman Franks, a veteran showman who organized tours for *Louisiana Hayride* performers, described Elvis in action: "He would study a crowd. He would look at them, see that he's gotten through to them, and then give them a little bit more. He had electricity between him and the audience. Elvis masterminded the situation. He was a genius at it." Elvis himself gloried in his talent, and he used it aggressively. He also adjusted quickly to the fact that his audiences too gloried in his talent, and he used that adoration aggressively. Moreover, he adjusted quickly to the fact that his audiences had become distinctly female and very young. He did not intend that result and rued that young men often resented him, but he did nothing to pander to male audiences.

FORBIDDEN FRUIT

In May 1955, the Elvis comet flamed across the Southern sky for all America to see. Elvis was included in a Hank Snow All-Star Jamboree tour that began in New Orleans, traveled for seven days through Alabama and Florida, then moved northward into North Carolina and Virginia for six more days. The show was purely country and gospel—except for Elvis. Star performers Hank Snow, Slim Whitman, Faron Young, and Mother Maybelle and the Carter Sisters drew the crowds, but the bill also included youngsters such as Elvis and Jimmie Rodgers Snow, Hank Snow's twenty-year-old son. The newcomers came on first, then, after an intermission, the stars. Already no young performer dared follow Elvis, so he ended the opening set. After the first night, the manager put him at the end of the whole show. Nobody, not even Hank Snow, wanted to follow Elvis. After Elvis and the girls had met, no sensible professional dared enter the steaming hot and churning waters.

During this tour, Jimmie Rodgers Snow was Elvis's roommate. Jimmie had first met Elvis in February in Lubbock, Texas, where the Colonel had booked him to share the stage with "the hillbilly cat." He was shocked by Elvis's attire, "a chartreuse jacket and black pants with a white stripe down the side." Bad enough offstage, in Jimmie's eyes, Elvis was worse onstage. Elvis's gyrations were outrageous, and yet "the kids were just going wild."

Talking to Elvis, Jimmie quickly got over his shock. Elvis expressed great admiration for Jimmie's father and sang favorite passages from Hank Snow's more obscure numbers. Jimmie was amazed at his knowledge and persuaded by his sincerity. Soon, he not only liked Elvis, he wanted to be Elvis.

On the tour, Jimmie focused on Elvis like the eye of a movie camera. In Mobile, he watched the girls chase Elvis across a football field. In the tour cities, he would catch shots of Elvis cruising about in his new pink and white Cadillac with girls all around. As Elvis's roommate, he was an especially intimate witness.

"He would run the women," Jimmie said. "He'd run two or three of them in one night." Jimmie was not sure whether he was having sex with each one. Elvis did not say and Jimmie did not ask. He gave Elvis plenty of freedom for his activities. "If I thought he was going to run some women in the room with him, I didn't stay," he said. Thoughtfully, he concluded, "I just think he wanted them around. It was a sense of insecurity, I guess, because I don't think he was a user. He just loved women, and I think they knew that."

Florida was the Colonel's very special domain. He had lived there during much of his adult life, and he prepared the ground thoroughly for Elvis's arrival. His public relations person for the Florida portion of the tour was Mae Axton, journalist, country songwriter, and English teacher at Paxon High School in Jacksonville. Mae was born in Texas and reared in Oklahoma, the daughter of a U.S. congressman. Writing an article for a magazine had led her to an interest in country music and a number of publicity projects in Florida for Colonel Parker and Hank Snow. She interviewed Elvis on radio before the May 7 performance in Daytona Beach. He called her "Miz Axton" so many times that she pressed him to use her first name. Elvis persisted in addressing her as "ma'am."

Mae was superb at her work, but nobody could have prepared Florida for Elvis. An Orlando reporter, a woman who preferred the annual spring performances of the Metropolitan Opera in Atlanta, was amazed by the rawness of the whole show but especially by the physicality of the "hillbilly fan" who whistled shrilly through his teeth, barked like a dog, and stomped the floor over the performances of such singers as Faron Young and Martha Carson. "But what really stole the show," she wrote, "was this 20-year-old sensation, Elvis Presley, a real sex box as far as the teenage girls are concerned." The girls "squealed themselves silly over this fellow in orange coat and sideburns." Afterward, the "girlies" surrounded him asking for his autograph. "He would give each a long, slow look with drooped eyelids and comply. They ate it up."

The crescendo event came at the Gator Bowl in Jacksonville on May 13 with a crowd of fourteen thousand. Elvis's act was the last, and as he left the stage he made a serious mistake. "Girls," he said flirtatiously, "I'll see you all backstage." Then came the stampede. Elvis made it to the locker room with a screaming herd of teenage girls in hot pursuit. By the time help arrived, he was perched on top of one of the stalls in the toilet. Mae Axton and other staff members rushed in to save him. He looked "sheepish and scared," she said, "like 'wat'd I do?'" His coat was torn and his shirt was shredded. The girls had already reached up to take his ankle boots, his socks, and his belt. He was down to his pants, and the girls were stretching up and pulling at those when more defenders arrived. Mae saw one small girl with what looked like a hump on her back. When Faron Young kicked at her in a valiant attempt to keep Elvis's pants on his body, Elvis's boots fell out of her clothes and the hump disappeared. The girls were determined, it seemed, to strip Elvis bare.

In the parking lot, Elvis's new Cadillac fared no better. It was covered with lipstick, scratches made with fingernail files, and writings with various instruments as girls attempted to leave their names, love notes, and phone numbers. Parts of his car were even ripped off and taken away. The Cadillac was a wreck. Adults were horrified. The girls were out of control. Another view, a more accurate one, was that the girls were in control, at least in the time and place where Elvis was in performance.

Mae saw one of her former high school students, then a student nurse, in the crowd. The young woman didn't even know who Elvis was, had not heard of him before the show. But she was "just *ahhh*," Mae said. "All of them were."

"Hey, honey, what is it about this kid?" she asked.

"Awww, Miz Axton," the girl replied, "he's just a great big beautiful hunk of forbidden fruit."

"ELVIS" MEANS MONEY

In Jacksonville, Colonel Parker caught the vision of a prosperous future unfolding before him. Mae said that was when the Colonel "got dollar marks in his eyes." Parker himself told an associate that this was "the real eye opener." Soon he would become the man in total charge of Elvis's career. Elvis would become his only client.

The Florida tour and the "panty raid" on Elvis by the girls in Jacksonville in May 1955 marked the great divide between Elvis as a purely Southern performer, with a Southern recording company, a Southern audience, and a Southern manager, and his explosion onto the national scene. His rapid rise compelled attention from major recording companies in the music industry. By then, he had made two more records with Sun Studios, and Sam Phillips was finding that he could not keep up with the demand. The Colonel was well connected through Eddy Arnold and Hank Snow with RCA. It happened that RCA's country and western promotion manager, Chick Crumpacker, was in Richmond on May 16 when the "All Star Jamboree" came to town. He saw Elvis perform at the Mosque Theater. A graduate of the Northwestern School of Music and a sophisticated musician, Chick was astounded. Later, he could not even remember what Elvis sang—perhaps "Ba-by, ba-by, ba-uh-by, let's play house"—but he remembered the style and the response of the audience. Elvis belched into the mike, then took out his chewing gum and threw it into the crowd. This was wild enough, but what really got the audience, Chick recalled, "was his energy and the way he sang the songs."

The next morning, while Chick was having breakfast with the Colonel and Hank Snow in the restaurant of the Thomas Jefferson Hotel, Elvis walked in. Again, Chick was amazed. "He was so unassuming," he said. Elvis looked around nervously and then joined them. It was the split between devil and angel that everyone saw who knew Elvis. Chick thought Elvis was very smart. He flattered people, and they liked him. Chick certainly did. During the meeting, the Colonel acted as if Elvis were already "his boy." This was just ten months after Elvis had first appeared in the Shell in Overton Park.

All through the summer and fall of 1955, with Bob Neal as their manager, Elvis and the Blue Moon Boys continued to play the Southern circuits, mostly in the Lower South. Their well-traveled beats were in Texas, Arkansas, Louisiana, and Mississippi. The character of the venues was very much what they had been: the St. Francis County Fair and Livestock Show in Forrest City, Arkansas; the Boys Club Gymnasium in Paris, Texas; the high school auditorium in Midland, Texas; and the Slavonian Lodge Auditorium in Biloxi, Mississippi. In October, after another sweep into North Carolina and Virginia, they worked through the Deep South yet again. By now the rituals were set, the girls and Elvis each doing their parts.

In August, they had added drummer D. J. Fontana to the group. D. J. had been the house drummer for the *Hayride*. He had first played with the Blue Moon Boys from behind a curtain. Country fans attending *Hayride* shows did not approve of drums in a band. Now D. J. came out from behind the curtain. He was an exceedingly valuable addition to the group, in part because of a special talent he had developed while playing for strippers in Shreveport nightclubs. He now adapted his skill for punctuating the bumps and grinds of female strippers to Elvis's movements.

Also in August, the band came out with their fifth and final record with Sam and Sun Studios. "Mystery Train" was a bluesy number that had to do with the singer putting his lover on a departing train. "It was the greatest thing I ever did on Elvis," Sam later judged. "It was pure rhythm. At the end, Elvis was laughing, because he didn't think it was a take, but I'm sorry, it was a fucking masterpiece!"

Meanwhile, Colonel Parker was working his wiles to become Elvis's manager. He was especially wooing Elvis's parents, Vernon and Gladys. Elvis was only twenty years old; his parents were still his legal guardians and were obligated to sign any contract. Vernon was quickly persuaded. Gladys was skeptical and held back. The violence wreaked on her son during the Jacksonville riot had shaken her, and she did not trust the Colonel. Parker backed off, but shrewdly brought out his big guns. He had *Grand Ole Opry* stars Whitey Ford and Hank Snow talk to Gladys and Vernon on numerous occasions by phone and in person. Only with Parker, they insisted repeatedly, would Elvis realize the great success that his talent deserved. On August 15, 1955, Parker got their signatures on an agreement that labeled him "special adviser" to Elvis and Bob Neal for a year. The devil was in the detail. Effectively, it tied Elvis tightly to the Colonel. He won exclusive rights to manage a hundred of Elvis's appearances during the next year. Elvis and his three musicians all together would be paid $200 for each performance, a very modest sum.

Colonel Parker also gained the crucially important right to renegotiate all of Elvis's contracts. Three months later, on November 21, 1955, he concluded intensive and not-very-open negotiations that generated a package of three new contracts that revolutionized Elvis's career and lasted a lifetime. Sam Phillips was out. He got $35,000 in cash and release from the $5,000 that he owed Elvis in royalties. Elvis moved from Sun Records to RCA and thus gained instant exposure nationally and, within a year, internationally. His sheet music would be published by one of the most influential music publishing houses in the country, Hill and Range. And, at last, the Colonel would become Elvis's exclusive manager when Bob Neal's contact ran out in March 1956.

THE BUBBLE

By the fall of 1955, Elvis and the Blue Moon Boys were often the only act on the bill. Elvis was the show and the crowds were getting larger. Overwhelmingly, they were dominated by young women. Sometimes there were thousands of teenage girls, and they knew just how to behave on an Elvis occasion. What had been a curious performance before now became an incredible spectacle. It was as if each girl and Elvis had created a magic space, a huge bubble in which they existed alone together, isolated, ecstatic, and exclusive of the dreary world. Increasingly, the girls sent up such a roar that Elvis's voice and the music could not even be heard. His performances became totally visual, and the girls responded to his every move as he sang—audibly, visibly, physically, and without inhibition. Their performance became the dominant performance. The girls might as well have been on the bill. It was a collaboration.

Scotty Moore was there every time, and he described the phenomenon perfectly. At the first note of the first song the din from the girls rose to a fever pitch, and it stayed there at a steady roar. "The only way I could describe the sound is that it was like, you know, if you dive into a swimming pool—that rush of noise that you get," Scotty said. "It would be so loud that all you could hear in your ears was that sound." The band could hear neither Elvis's voice nor their own instruments. They played by watching Elvis's movements.

Elvis, of course, could not even hear himself. Scotty was amazed at Elvis's control in the midst of it all. "I never saw him break meter," he said. Once the song started, the musicians all watched Elvis. They would use eye movements to communicate while watching Elvis's arms and legs to see where he was in the song. Scotty later joked that it was the only time in his life as a musician that he had been "directed by an ass."

During 1955, Elvis performed live on stage at least 234 times, but in only two cities outside the South: Indianapolis, Indiana, and Cleveland, Ohio. The 1955 performances were not only Southern, they were black belt Southern, areas where the proportion of blacks to whites ran high. Virtually all of Elvis's performances in 1955—and all of those in 1954—occurred in states where slavery had been a central cultural institution less than a century before, where lynching by hanging and burning and race rioting had been rampant only fifty years before—the alleged result of the rape, or attempt to rape, or the desire to rape white women by black men, and, most immediately, where tension over the integration of the races in the public schools was then rising to white-hot intensity. In January and February 1956, with Colonel Parker in charge, "Elvis mania" exploded out of the South.

On May 17, 1954, the United States Supreme Court ruled in the case of *Brown v. The Board of Education of Topeka, Kansas*, that the public schools in America were to be desegregated. Ten weeks later, Elvis performed in the Overton Shell. The Court said that it would rule on how the decision was to be enforced in its May term a year later. In that year, all during the time of Elvis's meteoric rise in the black belt South, the white South waited in dread. Its girls and boys were to be forced into close association with huge numbers of black boys and girls—especially they feared the closeness of black boys to white girls. In May 1955, the Court said that the decision would be enforced by federal district courts on a case-by-case basis. The white South breathed a collective sigh of relief. Southern white judges would rule on suits for desegregation in Southern communities. Being Southerners, they would presumably rule against such suits.

Soon, however, the South was again thrown into turmoil. Southern-born federal judges in the South ruled for desegregation, some because they thought it was right, all because they recognized that it was and would inevitably become the law of the land. Those teenage white girls who were so vigorously demonstrating their sexuality before Elvis in school auditoriums were about to be virtually thrown into the arms of young black males, supposedly notorious for their lack of inhibition in such matters. The hopefully innate virtue and purity of young white women was about to be severely tested in the very places where Elvis often performed. Not everyone was sure they would pass the test.

ELVIS OUTSIDE THE SOUTH AND EVERYWHERE

In 1956, only New England and the Great Northwest were spared the Elvis onslaught. In 1957, only New England remained inviolate. Wherever Elvis went outside the South, girls in his audiences behaved exactly like their Southern sisters. The "Elvis mania," as critics liked to call it, was totally exportable.

At first, Elvis did not always play to full houses outside the South. For example, in May 1956, in St. Paul, Minnesota, only 3,000 fans attended an afternoon performance in an auditorium that could hold 17,000. Nevertheless, these 3,000 raised such a ruckus that local police had to surround Elvis to get him out, but not before the girls managed to get close enough to rip his coat in half. The next day in La Crosse, Wisconsin, the 7:00 p.m. show was sold out to an audience of 4,000. But the 9:30 show drew only 1,200. It was almost as if the best defense Midwestern parents could manage was to curfew their daughters out of a late-night Elvis show.

The next year, 1957, Elvis shows everywhere were almost all sellouts, and the crowds were huge. In March, the Chicago show drew 13,000; in September, his audience numbered 15,000 in Seattle and Portland, and in Vancouver, British Columbia, it swelled to 26,500. In Vancouver, for about fifty minutes of a planned one-hour show, the Royal Canadian Mounted Police managed to hold the crowd back from the stage erected on the playing field of the Empire Stadium. Finally, the Colonel, fearing for the safety of "his boy," pulled Elvis—a resistant Elvis—off the stage and fled. George Klein, one of Elvis's Memphis friends, was traveling with the tour on this occasion. As George ran for safety, he looked back to see the entire wooden stage rise up in the air and turn over. Music stands, sheet music, and instruments flew in every direction as fans grabbed whatever they could get. The music critic for the *Vancouver Province,* Dr. Ida Halpern, denounced the whole thing as "subsidized sex." It was, she said, "an artificial and unhealthy exploitation of the enthusiasm of youth's mind and body."

Elvis ranged north and west, but he also maintained his bastion in the South, especially the Deep South. In October 1956, he performed in the Cotton Bowl in Dallas for some 26,500 wildly enthusiastic teenagers. They all seemed to have cameras with flashbulbs. "We went around the park on the back of that Cadillac," D. J. Fontana recalled, "and all you could see was just thousands of bulbs going off. I thought, 'What's this guy done?' " Never before in Dallas had so many people paid to see a single performer. Onstage, the musicians again never even heard their own instruments nor a word that Elvis sang. The uproar, the "hysteria," lasted through the whole show and continued as Elvis and the band leaped into the Cadillac and sped away.

"Whatever was going on here didn't seem to have much to do with music anymore," concluded Michael Gray and Roger Osborne in their 1966 book, *The Elvis Atlas*. It did not, of course. It had everything to do with sex—female sex. The girls had made it that way.

"I Hope I Never Wake Up"

Observers were nonplused by the performance of these young women. Not the least of those puzzled was Elvis himself. "It never ceases to amaze me," he said and shook his head. He struggled to understand the astonishing phenomenon of which he was a part. "I watch my audiences and I listen to them and I know we're all getting something out of our system but none of us knows what it is," he said. He insisted, however, that whatever it was, "it ain't nasty."

Elvis's assertion that neither he nor the girls knew what "it" was challenges belief. How could he not know? Even Sonny West saw at first sight that it was all about sex. Was Elvis really terribly naive or brilliantly disingenuous? He was always clever in projecting his "good boy" image offstage and in public, and perhaps he was dissembling. More likely, this new life was just too good to give up, and he was determined to brush past any threat to its continuance.

Always, Elvis's primary response to criticism was to make common cause with the girls in his audiences. He was adamant in his defense of the young women. It was the one point where his compulsively deferential manner to anyone with any power seemed on the verge of shattering. What the girls did was okay, he insisted, even if it involved injury to his body. "I've been scratched and bitten," he said. "I accept it with a broad mind because actually they don't intend to hurt you. They just want pieces of you for souvenirs."

The romance between Elvis and the girls—or more accurately between Elvis and each girl—created millions of separate fantasies. The time and place where they met was their special and private space. Elvis described the feeling for himself and the girls just right. It is like a "dream," he said, and "I hope I never wake up."

CHAPTER TWO

KILLERS OF THE DREAM

Even wise and excellent students of the Elvis phenomenon have written about it as a "mania," as if these girls had fallen into some sort of insanity. The girls were "hysterical," a psychotic illness allegedly peculiar to women. As the number of young women at Elvis occasions swelled into the thousands and then tens of thousands, many people were profoundly disturbed, even deeply frightened by what they saw. They felt that things were getting more and more out of control.

If the girls were "out of control," it was only in the sense that the rebels who staged the Boston Tea Party during the American Revolution, or stormed the Bastille in 1789, or sat-in, rode-in, and marched-in during the civil rights movement in the early 1960s were out of control. In certain times and places, the girls were in control. That was precisely the problem. They turned Elvis occasions into what they wanted them to be.

The girls decided it was much more satisfying to see Elvis than to hear him. By the hundreds and the thousands, they wanted to hear their own voices, to move their own bodies, to express themselves as sexual creatures on those occasions. Some were even ready to do violence to the police and other girls to get, as Elvis said, a piece of him. No shrinking violets or swooning maidens, they were more like warrior women, Amazons, whose bodies had power.

Adult Americans were horrified. They saw Elvis as the culprit and they saw what he did, but they had great difficulty articulating exactly what it was that he did to perpetrate the crime. His public performances were points where the social corruption came to a head and burst forth most powerfully. In 1956 and 1957, as he moved from city to city in the North and West as well as in the South, it fell to journalists everywhere to describe and interpret Elvis's actions onstage. They tortured metaphors and struggled mightily for language to do their job.

THE PRESS

One ploy was to describe Elvis as a person who was, in effect, physically ill. The *Buffalo Courier-Express* likened him to a man with chronic and painful indigestion. The *Columbus* (Ohio) *Citizen* thought his "continual flexing of the hands, gyrating of the knees, and facial expressions" suggested acute appendicitis. Others said he was "spastic," "epileptic," or afflicted by "St. Vitus Dance." Another tactic was to depict him as an animal—predatory like a panther or silly like a goose. The *Tacoma* (Washington) *News-Tribune* stretched to make a very unkind analogy, declaring that Elvis "strutted like a duck, his hands dangling loosely in front of him." The *Miami Herald* declared flatly that "the boy is a show business freak," while its companion the *Daily News* dismissed him as simply "stupid."

It is striking—and revealing—that the one image Elvis's critics most often used in their attempts to describe their revulsion at his performance was that of the female stripper. In Los Angeles, after witnessing an Elvis show, a reporter for *Variety* declared that a "stripper who tried anything like it would find herself a guest of the county," meaning that she would be thrown into the county jail. Journalists in Waco and Amarillo emphasized his "bumps and grinds," while in Omaha the *World-Herald* asserted that his "gyrations" were "simply no more than a male cooch dance complete with bumps and grinds." St. Paul declared him "nothing more than a male burlesque dancer," while Topeka asserted that he "would put a burlesque queen to shame." The *Savannah Morning News* was kinder but held to the analogy. "Women have discovered burlesque," the reporter said, "and they love it.

Paul Wilder, writing in the *Tampa Morning Telegraph*, wrapped up the Elvis stripper image in a couple of sentences. Elvis was "America's only male hoochy-kootch dancer," he declared after attending a show. "He wrestled microphones, slunk panther-like across the stage with a masculine version of Marilyn Monroe's wiggle in every jerking step, and blasted his feminine heart-wilting voice into every cranny of the huge armory."

Elvis was not simply a stripper out to entertain an audience and earn a living; he was a stripper who used nefarious means to pursue an evil and specific end—the destruction of female purity. His performances were not merely sensual, they were deliberately lewd. He was sullen, sulky, and sinister. "His performance was the most disgusting exhibition this reporter has ever seen," Marjorie Howe wrote in the *Sioux City Journal*. "He has a sulky look and his infrequent smile is almost surly." Critics thought that Elvis was unhappy with society for no good reason, and it was outrageous that he took every opportunity to show the world his contempt for its ways. His whole body, it seemed, mocked the stunning inadequacy of the mainstream world. An Oakland writer resented his "staggering, sulking walk," which seemed to say that he just couldn't take the stupidity of his elders anymore.

Elvis was bad, but the girls were worse. When Elvis appeared on-stage, the girls screamed mindlessly. "You couldn't hear Elvis in the front row," Betty Schiebel wrote in the *San Antonio Light*. "Uproar exploded each time he looked as though he might open his mouth," she continued. "A flood of white teeth from Elvis, a loose-hipped slur of dance steps, a Brando-like gaze from his soulful blue eyes, and the floor vibrated from 6,000 stamping feet, whistles shattered the air." Onstage, Elvis moved his body vigorously, and outrageously. "He comes across like the midnight express. He kicks, slinks, shimmies and gyrates.

Writers struggled to find words to describe the girls' performances. They "exploded" in La Crosse, Wisconsin, "screamed" in Hawaii, and in New Orleans set up a "din of squealing." In Amarillo, "the air raid siren screams" rose as Elvis "worked himself into an orgiastic rhythm, losing himself to the savage beat." In Shreveport the girls yelled "like Zulus every time he moved a muscle." In Long Beach they "whistled, screamed, wept, stomped their feet, jumped up on their seats, ran up and down the aisles and shrieked over and over again, 'Ohhh Elvis, Elvis!'"

————

A reporter in Seattle said it sounded "like 12,000 girls having their heads shaved at once." This image is both problematical and fascinating. As World War II came to an end, the newsreels often showed French and Italian women who had consorted with German soldiers having their heads shaved and then being put on public display, marking them as tramps and traitors. Readers of the Bible might be reminded of St. Paul's dictate to the Corinthians. "If a woman does not cover her head, she should have her hair cut off," Paul preached, because "it is just as though her head were shaved" (1 Corinthians 11:5–6). For Paul, the woman covered her head as a sign of respect for the man; shaving the heads of twelve thousand girls in Seattle suggests censuring them for rejecting the authority of men. Indeed, by their behavior at an Elvis concert female fans could be seen as betraying future husbands, and defying fathers, lovers, boyfriends, self-appointed censors, and most pointedly policemen, whose sole purpose was to preserve law and order in society.

SOMETHING HAD TO BE DONE

As Elvis rose, the counterrevolution gathered strength. Something had to be done. He was corrupting the moral fiber of the young women in America. The opposition won a victory when the girls of Notre Dame High School in St. Louis were persuaded to recant their sins. Publicly and ceremoniously, they burned an Elvis effigy and their Elvis icons— photographs, records, and teddy bears—in a "bonfire of the vanities." St. Louis was one of the cities in America where the Elvis girls broke out in amazing numbers. On October 21, 22, and 23, 1955, he played three shows in the Missouri Theater. On January 1, 1956, only two months later, he filled the Civic Auditorium with girls. On Thursday, March 29, 1957, the 10,800 seats in the Auditorium were sold out to Elvis enthusiasts.

Even the FBI took notice of the Elvis phenomenon and swung into action. It eventually gathered more than a thousand pages in its "Elvis File," the FBI file most often requested by the public. One FBI informant in La Crosse, Wisconsin, declared that an Elvis performance in May 1956 was "the filthiest and most harmful production that ever came to La Crosse for exhibition to teenagers." It was "sexual gratification on stage" and "a strip-tease with clothes on." He thought that Elvis "may possibly be a drug addict and sexual pervert." J. Edgar Hoover, the director of the FBI, knew all about "sexual perverts," and his agency was already well aware of Elvis's subversive potential. Hoover saw Communists everywhere and knew that they often worked their insidious ways through "fellow travelers" and unwitting human tools. Elvis was a good candidate to become a Communist dupe and needed watching. Ironically, authorities in Communist Russia did not like Elvis either and wanted to exclude him from the country, along with other evidence of decadence in the capitalist West.

TELEVISION AND FILM—BURSTING THE BUBBLE

The revolution of the Elvis girls was not crushed by the police. It was not squelched by irate parents rising up and refusing to allow their daughters to attend an Elvis concert, late night or otherwise. Ironically, it was killed by Tom Parker's ambition to win Elvis an audience of millions rather than thousands and thus gain a huge increase in revenue. Parker changed the venue of Elvis's performance first from stage to television and then from television to film. As the venue changed, the audience changed radically both in numbers and composition. As it grew to millions, the girls no longer dominated.

In 1955, Elvis appeared live onstage more than 230 times. During the first half of 1956, counting 28 performances in the Frontier Hotel in Las Vegas, he came onstage 122 times. In the last half of 1956, including his television appearances, he came onstage only 22 times. For all of 1957, the number was 20. In 1958, before he went into the army in March, he didn't perform onstage at all.

In 1956, television became Elvis's medium. In the first ten months of that year, he was on national television ten times, watched by an audience of well over two hundred million. In 1957, he did only one television show, appearing on *The Ed Sullivan Show* in January, and then no more. He was going into movies. His first movie came out in the fall of 1956. In 1957, he did three more films.

Television destroyed the assembly of girls, the actual palpable meeting place where they could openly express their deepest feelings and experience by their numbers and share rituals giving them a heady sense of power and liberation. Television, in effect, burned their churches and dispersed the faithful.

Film continued and deepened the process. The movie house brought them together again, but in more limited numbers and venues, a confined and darkened space to view images closely prescribed and controlled, prefabricated, and literally canned by men. There was no piece of the living Elvis here, no performance shaped creatively to the expression of their own deep feelings and immediate desires. Beginning with television and ending with film, the girls lost control.

Even so, the passions that women felt for Elvis did not die. His early fans were as ardent as ever, probably even more ardent at a deeper level, more reflective as each communed with Elvis in the privacy of her own bedroom. Paradoxically, as Elvis became more remote and mechanical, ecstasies became deeper, more individual and personal. Girls and women bought and played Elvis records and lived whatever fantasies they wanted to live. They bought the photographs and read the magazine stories. They saw the movies over and over. Now and again, they made the pilgrimage to the gates of Graceland, perhaps to see Elvis flash by in his car or simply to gaze up at the blacked-out windows of his bedroom on the second floor of the mansion. The passion that women felt for the idea of Elvis did not go underground; it was not hidden, or secretive. It was simply diffused.

TELEVISION

Elvis's first foray into television came on January 28, 1956, with his appearance on CBS's *Stage Show*. The hosts, big band leaders Jimmy and Tommy Dorsey, had been giants in music in the 1940s, but they and their show were losing audience in the 1950s while NBC's mellow-voiced Perry Como was crooning his way into the hearts of affluent Americans hungry for order, peace, and complacency. Both shows appeared at the same time every week. Como enjoyed 34.7 percent of the national TV audience, while the Dorseys at 18.4 percent had only about half as much. Notwithstanding the Dorseys' low market share, Elvis performed for thirteen million Americans that first evening. After he returned for five more performances, ending on March 24, Como was down to 30.1 percent and *Stage Show* was up to 20.9 percent. Eighteen months into his career, Elvis had the power to take huge chunks of the national audience away from one of America's most popular singers.

In July 1956, Elvis discarded his flashy clothes and donned formal attire, a tuxedo, for his appearance on *The Steve Allen Show*. Allen's attempt to make fun of Elvis by having him dress so and sing "you ain't nothing but a hound dog" to a real live "hound dog" on national television accrued to Elvis's benefit, as he bore the ordeal with dignity. Allen became the shallow, vapid teenager, relishing humor where there really was none. Elvis became, ironically, the gracious adult. A *Newsweek* writer pronounced Allen's ethics "questionable."

The most popular variety TV program in America in the mid-1950s was *The Ed Sullivan Show*. Sullivan was deeply conservative and hated the provocative sexual displays that brought Elvis such wildly demonstrative female audiences. But he hated more the prospect of a loss in his ratings. Finally, and reluctantly, he booked Elvis for Sunday night, September 9, 1956. Sullivan himself did not preside over the engagement. The show was filmed in Los Angeles, and Sullivan, amazingly, sent in the Hollywood actor Charles Laughton, an Englishman, to host. That evening, the Sullivan show—without Sullivan—drew an astounding rating of 82.6 percent and an audience of some fifty million people, the largest ever for a variety show in America.

One month later, Sullivan himself reluctantly consented to host Elvis's second appearance on his show. This was the famous occasion on which he did not allow the camera to reveal Elvis below the waist. This minor measure of censorship advertised the lower half of Elvis's body in a degree unmatched for the lower half of any body, male or female, in the twentieth century. Far from taking offense, Elvis seemed to see the humor in this. His audience seemed to agree with him.

Meanwhile, in the spring of 1956 Elvis's new record "Heartbreak Hotel"—written by Mae Boren Axton, who had done such good work advertising his tour in Florida the previous year—had hit the top of all three charts: country and western, rhythm and blues, and popular music. This was a triple score across categories that was unprecedented and another indicator that cultural fragmentation in America was diminishing. In July, his record "Hound Dog," backed by "Don't Be Cruel," sold one million copies in eighteen days.

On November 21, Elvis made his film debut in 550 movie theaters across America. *Love Me Tender* was a low-budget film for which he got only $100,000, but it repaid its total cost at the box office in only three days. Elvis was moving into the third medium of his entertainment career—movies.

KILLING OFF THE FIRST ELVIS

Elvis was rapidly rising, but there was a drag on his ascent. Ironically, it was the very image that he had labored so hard to construct after the revelation in the Overton Shell in July 1954. The image that Elvis had cultivated so successfully with teenage white girls was absolutely offensive to many Americans. Elvis fans were devoted, but they represented a relatively narrow band in the total population. Across the gender line, white boys might like Elvis's music and admire his rebellious style to some degree, but they might also see him as a rival for female attention. The great mass of adult Americans, if they deigned to notice Elvis at all, hated him and feared his influence. Thus, to increase his audience, he needed to virtually destroy his hard-won public persona and create another with broad appeal. Brilliantly managed by Colonel Parker, Elvis did precisely that.

As compelling public displays by mass gatherings of orgiastic young women diminished in frequency in 1956, the image of Elvis as a menace to the morals of America began to fade. The powerful and spontaneous relationship that he and the girls had created was broken, as the girls lost the power to tell Elvis in person and onstage what they wanted him to do and how to do it. The Colonel took charge and cultivated an image of Elvis as a safe and sane young man. His performances came to be very carefully constructed and projected onto television and movie screens.

As Elvis's appearances on television fell from the menu after January 1957 and he moved only to film, control of the Elvis image by the

Colonel and his associates became nearly total. They strove to adjust the image to take advantage of the broad new market, which was older, increasingly male as well as female, and international as well as national. Overall, they proved highly adept at fine-tuning their message—completing four movies over the two years before Elvis entered the army. Ironically, Elvis in the can became vastly more visible and valuable than Elvis in real life and onstage.

THE NEW ELVIS

Elvis gave up live audiences numbering thousands, but he gained television and movie audiences numbering millions, with commensurate increases in income. He gloried in his new celebrity, and he loved the money—or, more deeply, the things that money could buy. He was a person of gargantuan appetites for food, cars, clothes, houses, friends (mostly young males), and girls (one after another). The girls did not forget Elvis, Elvis did not forget the girls, and others came to know and became fans of the young Mississippi man who blended the black and white music of the Deep South.

Elvis was rolling in money, and he rolled easily into projecting the new image of himself. Even early in 1956, there were signs that he was no longer entirely at ease performing as the girls wanted him to perform.

In mid-February, after his third appearance on the Dorsey television show, Elvis was touring in North Carolina with a show put together by the Colonel. As usual, the music was country and gospel, not everyone in the troupe liked Elvis's music, and many hated the way he took audiences away from them. One of these was Ira Louvin, who with his brother, Charlie, sang duets beautifully in seemingly impossibly high keys. Ira was short-tempered and irascible, and he despised Elvis. Elvis, on the other hand, loved the music the Louvin brothers made; they were his mother's favorite singers. He would stand in the wings and relish their performances. On February 14, 1956, in Wilson, North Carolina, the Colonel had ordered the troupe to do a third show without pay because the local promoter had oversold the two shows scheduled, largely because so many girls wanted to see Elvis. Ira flew into a rage. In an interview years later, Charlie Louvin painted a scene in which Ira "went on and on about who did this Presley kid think he was, that no-talent sonofabitch, trying to take over their music—and fuck the Colonel anyway."

The Colonel finally agreed to pay the performers for the third show, but a couple of days later, just before Elvis and his band were to fly off from Winston-Salem to New York for his fourth TV appearance on the Dorseys' *Stage Show*, Ira turned his guns on Elvis himself. As often happened while on tour, Elvis and others were backstage gathered around a piano singing gospel songs.

"Boy, this is my favorite music," Elvis exclaimed.

Ira put himself in Elvis's face, bristling. "Why, you white nigger, if that's your favorite music, why don't you do that out yonder?" he demanded furiously. "Why do you do that nigger trash out there?"

"When I'm out there, I do what they want to hear," Elvis responded. "When I'm back here, I can do what I want to do." Ira did not accept his explanation.

"Ira tried to strangle him," Charlie said.

Elvis was never one to back down from physical combat. On the contrary, past performances would lead one to expect Elvis to bash his fist into the mouth of anyone who called him a "white nigger." It seems likely that his encounter with Ira Louvin shook him to his roots. Ira demanded to know what he was doing as a man—a white man—and as an artist. In effect, Ira offered to fight him man-to-man. Elvis didn't know quite what to do—fight, fly, or faint. "What would a real man do?" was the question. A week later, after doing a show in Jacksonville, Florida, Elvis collapsed in the parking lot. The doctor diagnosed exhaustion and put him into the hospital for the night. The next morning, Elvis bragged about how the nurses would not leave him alone. Strangely, he also claimed privately that he had not passed out; he was just trying to get the attention of Anita Carter, a beauty and one of the highly respected singing Carter sisters.

———

Elvis changed willingly and eagerly. Driven by his obsession with pleasing whatever audience was before him, he revolutionized his stage manner and projected an image strikingly different from the one he had labored so hard to build with the girls. His biographer Peter Guralnick called it a "radical metamorphosis," and he thought that it happened within a few days before Elvis's television appearance with Milton Berle in San Diego on April 3, 1956. Berle was one of the creators of early American television, bringing to it a genius for manic slapstick humor. On this occasion, Berle was doing his show from the flight deck of the U.S. Navy's aircraft carrier *Hancock*. The audience could hardly have been more unlike those of Elvis's early career. It was significantly male—made up of young sailors, their officers, and invited guests. No venue could have been more masculine than a giant and powerful ship of war, an arena dedicated to defending America from Communist aggression. Berle dressed up comically as an Elvis look-alike and played out a skit with Elvis in which he was Elvis's twin brother who had "taught him everything he knows." Dressed like an exaggerated Elvis, Berle managed to parody brilliantly—as only he could—the image of Elvis that the girls loved.

Elvis looked on in amazement. He became a fond and indulgent adult. Berle was the fool. No more bumps and grinds into the microphone by Elvis, no more spitting saliva-laden gum onto the deck or into an audience of girls, no more stripteases. His clothes were dark, neat, and unflashy. His hair was less greased. His very body—legs apart, feet firmly planted on the flight deck, arms in easy, comfortable motion—bespoke balance and unhaste. Elvis was at ease with the world, no rebel, no threat. Indeed, he was at one with this new and very broad audience. "It may not be as clear to the little girls," Peter Guralnick explained, "but there is no aggression in the act."

In June, Elvis did another show with Berle in Los Angeles. The rating for the first show in San Diego was 30 percent. The second improved upon that number.

In September 1956, with his initial appearance on *The Ed Sullivan Show*, Elvis reached his first really vast audience—fifty million people. During his visit to New York in October for his second appearance, he offered himself to America as a sane, sensible, and very appealing young man whose true character had previously been unrecognized.

The *New York Times* was delighted to discover the real Elvis as he moved about the city before the show. It happily reported that "the idol of rock 'n' roll juveniles also surprised an afternoon press interview by demonstrating to adult reporters that he is a polite, personable, quick-witted and charming young man." Elvis was a "young man," not a "boy," and the girls were simply young, that is, "juveniles." "Adult reporters"—not young reporters—were highly approving of the "young man," the *Times* said. The gap between Elvis and the older generations was rapidly closing as if it had never existed.

During his run on the Sullivan show that evening, Elvis was a living model of great success folded into unshakable modesty. Pressed to tone down his by-then well-known and eagerly anticipated sex-laden signals, he did so with a youthful good humor that endeared him to his audience. There was no need for Sullivan to limit the focus of the cameras to the top half of his body. No one among the millions of viewers in his or her right mind could believe that this young man was a menace to society. His bad-boy behavior was nothing more than theater, good acting, and good-humored teasing. Milton Berle had parodied the earlier Elvis; now Elvis parodied himself, and delightfully so.

Again, he ended his appearance with a public relations bull's-eye. His closing line for the evening eviscerated the bad-boy Elvis image. "May God bless you as he has blessed me," he said to his audience with a deferential bow and a sweeping gesture.

Elvis quickly perfected his appealing persona for his interviewers. He was performing offstage now, and he manifested his marvelous talent for "reading" his audience and giving them exactly what they wanted. He was proud and humble. He knew that he was great, but his modesty was unshakable. "Teenagers are my life and triumph," he asserted earnestly and honestly. "I'd be nowhere without them," but their parents need not fear, he insisted. He wished he could sit down and talk with those who regarded him as a bad influence on their children. He was sure he could persuade them otherwise because he knew he had done nothing wrong. "I've examined my conscience and asked myself if I led anybody astray even indirectly, and I'm at peace with my conscience." The Bible told him, he declared to the world, that one reaps what he sows. His own salvation was at stake, and he would not risk that. "If I did think I was bad for people, I would go back to driving a truck," he declared, "and I really mean this."

Later that afternoon, Elvis allowed himself to be inoculated for polio with the newly perfected Salk vaccine. He took the needle in a very public proceeding during which he applauded a medicine that helped "so many kids and adults too." The press again warmly applauded Elvis for his service to the American people.

Back in Memphis, Elvis appeared and spoke at the yearly "Road-E-O" safe-driving contest for teenagers in which he urged youngsters to follow the rules of the road. It was another brilliantly targeted, well-publicized event. If there had ever been a generational war going on, Elvis had switched sides.

On January 6, 1957, Elvis concluded his third performance on *The Ed Sullivan Show* by reverently singing a mainline religious song, "Peace in the Valley." No rock, no roll, not even a Pentecostal shout. Sullivan himself was now at peace with Elvis and ended by giving him his priceless stamp of approval. He held up his hand in his usual casually commanding and masterful way to halt uproarious applause. "I wanted to say to Elvis Presley and the country," he declared, "that this is a real decent, fine boy." Ed closed by asking for "a tremendous hand for a very nice person." Elvis was mentally awake, morally straight, sanitized, certified, and approved for nationwide consumption.

Then, having conquered television, Elvis all but disappeared from it for more than a decade. The single exception was an appearance on the Frank Sinatra show in 1960 immediately after his release from the army. He gave up live performances too, except for three in 1961 when he did two shows at Ellis Auditorium in Memphis for "Elvis Presley Day" and another at Pearl Harbor in Honolulu to support turning the sunken battleship *Arizona* into a national monument. To hear Elvis, fans had to buy a record. To see a moving, talking, singing image of him after 1957 and before 1968, they had to go to the movies. For eleven years out of twenty-three years of his career, Elvis was available only on records and in films.

CREATING THE "GOOD ELVIS"

In the beginning, it was by no means certain that Elvis's films would be merely vehicles for his musical talent. The possibility of re-creating Elvis as a film star with acting talent of some magnitude and making a profit seemed real. The formula for moving a highly successful performer from his or her original venue to success in the movies was already well established, most notably by singer Bing Crosby, dancer Fred Astaire, ice skater Sonja Henie, and even swimmer Johnny Weissmuller (Tarzan). Frank Sinatra had done even better. In 1953 he had established himself as a serious, unsinging, and convincing dramatic actor in the movie *From Here to Eternity*.

Elvis's chances for crossing over were heightened significantly by the death of the young actor James Dean in an auto accident in September 1956. The original "rebel without a cause," Dean had made his reputation in the film *East of Eden*. His death left a huge vacuum in the hearts of young Americans. The first Elvis, the Elvis the girls had created, was an obvious candidate to replace him.

In April 1956, just after his appearance on the USS *Hancock* with Milton Berle, Elvis did a screen test at Paramount Studios in which he "lip-sang" "Blue Suede Shoes" and then acted out a part in a scene from a prospective film, *The Rainmaker*. Burt Lancaster was cast in the movie as the Rainmaker. For his screen test, Elvis read the part of the Rainmaker's younger brother. Afterward, he complained that the character wasn't suitable for him. He told producer Hal Wallis that he would like to play a part "more like myself, so I wouldn't have to do any excess acting." Wallis was amused. The Rainmaker's brother was young and naive.

To professionals, Elvis's screen test indicated a high potential for singing in the movies and a low potential for acting. As it happened, however, his first film did not showcase his musical talent. An ambivalent screen test led to an amateurish performance in *Love Me Tender*, a story set in the Civil War South. At the end of the tale, the youthful character played by Elvis died melodramatically, making way for his sexy widow, played by Debra Paget, to marry his strikingly mature older brother, played by star Richard Egan, to whom she had been engaged before he went off to the Confederate Army only to be mistakenly reported as killed in battle, ostensibly leaving her free, ridiculously, to take Elvis as her boy-husband.

Obviously, this was not *Gone with the Wind*. Elvis seemed to be the only actor who took more than a workmanlike interest in his or her performance in this vaguely incestuous play. He was exceedingly earnest, highly energetic, and totally unbelievable. Elvis's character, on the way to his eventual demise, slid improbably into song four times. The most memorable song, "Love Me Tender," became the name of the film almost as an afterthought, replacing the flat but descriptive original title, *The Reno Brothers*.

Seldom thereafter did Hollywood attempt to promote Elvis as a serious dramatic talent. In his heart of hearts, Elvis wanted nothing more than to become a great actor on the order of James Dean or Marlon Brando, but he hobbled himself by adamantly refusing to take any acting lessons, insisting that he simply wanted to be himself onscreen. Hollywood honored his wish. They asked no "excess acting" of him and made excellent profits from cheap movies.

In his second movie, *Loving You* (1957), Elvis sang seven songs, and a costar added three more. In *Jailhouse Rock* (1957), he burst into song six times. In *King Creole* (1957), he sang eleven songs in a film that lasted 116 minutes. Many critics say this was his best film ever.

In the first three films that he did after *Love Me Tender*, all released the same year, Elvis was clearly the star, and all the storylines said that here we are giving you the real Elvis doing the real story of his life. In *Loving You*, he is a young truck driver named Deke Rivers who has a God-given gift for singing. Unscrupulous managers use his voice and his overwhelming sex appeal to advance his fantastically successful career and reap the profits. Naive and innocent, Deke becomes confused by the attentions of a bad woman on one side and the love of a good girl on the other. He runs away. Older and somehow wiser from his suffering, he returns to perform on a major national television show where everyone sees that he is really a noble young man. Furthermore, he gets the girl.

In *Jailhouse Rock*, Elvis is a young man justly convicted of manslaughter for accidentally killing a man in a barroom brawl. However, like Deke Rivers in *Loving You*, he finds redemption through a natural gift for song, a gift discovered in prison by his wise, musically talented, and significantly older cellmate.

In *King Creole*, Elvis is a young man rebelling against his father. Working in a New Orleans nightclub called King Creole, he gets involved with gangsters and a bad girl, drops out of high school, is tempted to join a street gang, gets knifed in a fight, comes to his senses, reconciles with his family, and falls in love with a good girl. Having seen the light, he develops his singing skills and is thereby saved.

In each of the films, Elvis plays the part of a young man who made some really serious mistakes. In each, he is redeemed primarily by his God-given musical talent and innate goodness, but also with the aid of wise and sympathetic adults. The real message seems to be that if young Elvis Presley had indeed transgressed as charged, he had suffered severely as he should have, repented, and confessed his sins. Now he would be good. Adult persons had aided him in his redemption and could fairly and graciously readmit him to the communion. Now his good work, including manifestations of his gift for song, reflected their good work. He and they were one.

THE NEW ELVIS IN PERSON

The tide of public regard for Elvis had turned visibly favorable in January 1957, when arch conservative and arch anti-Communist crusader Ed Sullivan said to Elvis in essence, "Go, and sin no more." The image of the good Elvis swelled in March when RCA released Elvis's first gospel album, *Peace in the Valley*, which concluded with "Take My Hand, Precious Lord." It established Elvis's credentials as a deeply spiritual and Christian person. Elvis won gold and platinum awards from RCA for selling huge numbers of their records. Eventually, some two billion of his records were distributed around the world. But he won only two Grammy Awards for his records, both for gospel albums. Elvis's image as a good person rose yet again when all of America learned in April 1957 that he had moved his beloved mother into a mansion on a hill in Memphis. Marvelously, even providentially, the mansion was already named Graceland.

Meanwhile, Elvis was also busy proving himself a virtuous citizen of the highest order by conspicuously supporting charities with gifts of money and by personal appearances to support noble causes. Regularly, he made sizable, calculated, and well-publicized contributions to local charities, especially the Cynthia Milk Fund for poor children. In December 1956, he was at Ellis Auditorium for the annual all–African American *Goodwill Review*, organized to raise money for the needy, particularly needy African American children. He watched the show from backstage. He was not allowed by the Colonel to perform there or anywhere else without a contract and careful preparation. But he did come onstage for an introduction and in response to a request that he do "a little something" for the African American audience, he gave them a "little wiggle." The young women in the crowd "went crazy."

Nat O. Williams, a leading African American journalist in Memphis, was amazed and somewhat disturbed that these middle-class black girls went wild over the mere sight of Elvis but had uttered no screams for the highly talented black guitarist and singer B. B. King, who had just performed. He wrote that "a thousand black, brown, and beige teenage girls in the audience blended their alto and soprano voices in one wild crescendo of sound that rent the rafters and took off like scalded cats in the direction of Elvis." Williams suspected that such behavior reflected "a basic integration in attitude and aspiration which had been festering in the minds of most of your folks' women folk all along." Black girls loved Elvis just like white girls loved Elvis. The race line seemed to evaporate.

COLONEL PARKER

Colonel Parker assiduously orchestrated everything for maximum positive publicity and income. Elvis was not only a great talent worthy of the high cost of his hire; he was also a model citizen and an adorable person, worthy of respect not only from female teens but also from young men and adults, rich and poor, blacks and whites.

Parker radically changed Elvis's venues; Elvis radically changed his image. The Colonel was only following the money; Elvis was giving his changing audience what he felt they wanted with uncanny accuracy. It came to be that Elvis's new image and its broad acceptance in the nation worked powerfully to improve the projection of a united America confronting the Communist menace, a projection that was very much needed in a Cold War that had recently heated up to a near disaster in Korea and would soon become an absolute disaster in Vietnam. Elvis brought blacks and whites together as if there were no race line in America. He also significantly melted the lines that might divide generations and genders, and religions and classes in the nation.

The Army

In 1958, Tom Parker pulled off the last act in the image shift of the century. He persuaded a very—even bitterly—reluctant Elvis to submit to being drafted into the United States Army for two years as if he were an ordinary unprivileged American boy. He also managed to get Elvis to publicly and repeatedly express his willingness—even eagerness—to embrace his patriotic duty, even though Elvis, privately and personally, was not at all elated by the prospect of military service and at times resented the imposition. He had a horror of being forgotten, of sinking back into relative anonymity.

Colonel Parker's gamble paid off handsomely. Elvis's fans remained loyal. During his service and for a few years into the 1960s, they bought his records and went to his movies as never before. The result was that his gross income rose to millions of dollars a year. But most of all, his image went from black to white and then to absolutely golden. For adult and conservative Americans in the mid-1950s, Elvis had been evil incarnate—literally a walking, talking, singing, and dancing devil in the flesh. He returned from valiant service at his post on the front line of freedom in Europe in March 1960, strikingly crisp, clean, and neat in his army uniform with his sergeant's stripes on his arm. Elvis Presley was a brave defender of the American way, the nation's poster boy in the Cold War against Communism. The onstage Elvis of the first two years of his career was left, essentially, to living memory, and the girls went on with their lives.

PART II

WHY ELVIS?

CHAPTER THREE

VERNON AND GLADYS

THE PHOTOGRAPH

One photograph of the small Presley family captures the essence of their lives then and thereafter. Elvis, about three years old, is posed with Gladys and Vernon. Elvis is standing, and his parents are sitting on either side of him.

The exact date of the picture is unknown. Decades later it showed up in the photograph collection of the Official Elvis Presley Fan Club in Leicester, England. Interviews with pediatricians, pediatric nurses, mothers, fathers, grandmothers, and grandfathers have estimated Elvis's age.

The blank, clean, slightly gray background is probably the concrete wall of the brand-new Lee County jail in Tupelo. Vernon is a prisoner, having been arrested on November 16, 1937, for forging a check. The county jail had recently been built by the Works Progress Administration (WPA), a New Deal project to employ the unemployed. Previously, county prisoners had been lodged in the run-down town jail. Only the white prisoners were moved to the new jail.

In the photograph, mother, child, and father are close, body to body as if huddled against a coming moment of separation. Gladys's left arm reaches behind and across Elvis's back to Vernon. Her open hand rests lightly on Vernon's left shoulder, as if to hold him in gently, to affirm her presence with him. It is a hand that seeks to comfort, but its loose openness signals her powerlessness.

Vernon had been charged with forging a check on Orville Bean, the dairy farmer who was his landlord and employer. He had been arrested and arraigned during the fall term of criminal court. He pled not guilty, but he would not get a speedy trial. His plea came too late for him to be tried in the fall term of court. His case would have to wait for the spring term, which began six months later on Monday, May 23, 1938. Before the court convened that spring, the local papers were full of suggestions that the docket was overfull and that justice in Lee County must be meted out more rapidly than before.

Only days before Vernon's case would have been tried, he changed his plea to guilty. Justice swiftly followed. On Wednesday, May 25, Judge Thomas H. Johnston sentenced Vernon to three years in the state penitentiary. He got no credit for the six months he had spent in the county jail. After sentencing came the anxious wait before the prison guards trucked him off to Parchman Farm.

On Saturday, May 28, Circuit Court Clerk Joe J. Kilgo wrote out the papers committing Vernon and eleven other convicts to Parchman. The twelve men waited in the county jail for the dreaded arrival of "Long Chain Charley," a sergeant on the guard force at Parchman who circulated through the state collecting convicts for transport to prison. He always brought a long chain to which he shackled his prisoners to prevent their escape.

Six months in the county jail waiting for a trial had been bad enough, but there was always at least some hope for relief. Orville Bean might decide not to press charges against Vernon. Relatives and friends might somehow intervene. If it came to a trial, a good lawyer might rise to defend him and the jury might find him innocent. Having changed his plea to guilty, Vernon faced the certainty of serving at hard labor in a notoriously tough prison for three long years, years in which he could not come home every night to his wife and child in their little two-room wooden house in East Tupelo nor earn money to support them.

Sensing the pathos in the photograph does not require knowledge of its history. The bodies of the man and woman are tense with anxiety and dread. The child is anxious and confused. Vernon has put his hat on his head as if making ready to leave. He faces the camera, but his eyes cut to his left as if watching fearfully for someone or something to appear that he already hears. Gladys also stares to the left, her body stiff.

The little boy's gaze is less focused, as if he were told to look at the camera but senses something he needs to see off to the left too. He wears bib overalls over a dark, long-sleeved shirt, charmingly trimmed with white cuffs and a white collar. Gladys is a talented seamstress. She wears a flower-print dress. Her dress, like Elvis's shirt, is attractively set off by a collar of a different color. Elvis, like his father, wears a hat. His hat seems almost man-sized, cocked at a rakish angle on his round little head. His full cherubic lips are twisted down to the right as if he realizes that he should say something and set his jaw in some certain way to assert an attitude, but he doesn't know what to say or how.

This is the earliest photograph of Elvis. The photographer was most likely a friend or a relative who had driven Gladys and Elvis a couple of miles over from their home in East Tupelo. It was a defining moment in the lives of Elvis, Gladys, and Vernon Presley, individually and collectively. The very fact of the visit, the camera, and the one photograph that has been preserved indicates that they understood that they were at a critical juncture in their lives. The petty and foolish crime that Vernon committed in the fall of 1937, when he was twenty-one, Gladys twenty-five, and Elvis less than three, deeply marked their lives.

The Crime

Vernon was barely seventeen in June 1933, when he married twenty-one-year-old Gladys. He gave his age to the registrar in the Pontotoc County courthouse as twenty-one. Gladys gave her age as nineteen, a minor fiction that she maintained and even improved upon in later years. Elvis only learned his mother's true age after she died. Pontotoc was the next county west of Lee County. Vernon and Gladys were driven over by a couple, Marshall and Vona Mae Brown, who were close friends and who served as witnesses to what was, at first, a secret wedding. Marshall Brown lent Vernon the $3 for them to get married. Vernon was afraid to tell his father, Jessie Presley, that he was married and continued to live at home. Gladys continued to live with her family until Vernon finally gained the courage to announce the news. Then Gladys joined him in his father's house.

Jessie, like Vernon, worked for Orville Bean on the dairy farm, but he was not an ordinary laborer, nor an ordinary man. Born in 1896, Jessie D. McClowell Presley had grown up on tenant farms several miles east of Tupelo. His mother, Rosella Presley, was fiercely independent. She never married, had ten children by at least two men, and never identified the fathers of any of her children. She headed up her own household and reared her family on a sequence of small farms that she worked for a share of the crops.

Rosella's father, Dunnan Presley Jr., had deserted her, her mother, and her sister, Rosalinda, one Sunday morning while they were at church. They came home, and he was gone. He had decided to return to his previous wife and child. He had not bothered divorcing that wife before marrying Rosella's mother. Indeed, he never divorced any of his four wives. One historian asserted that during the Civil War he enlisted in the Confederate Army twice and deserted twice. Each time he enlisted, he collected a substantial bounty. He signed up for the cavalry, where they gave him a large amount of money to buy a horse. He simply evaporated with the money. It was also said that many years later Dunnan attempted to collect a pension for having served—with honor—in the Confederate Army.

Jessie's father—Elvis's great-grandfather—was probably John Steele, whom the census of 1900 shows to be Rosella's neighbor. A tenant farmer with a separate and, presumably, legal family, John was said to be part Cherokee. If documents in the courthouse reliably prescribed who had sex with whom to produce a child, Elvis's name would have probably been Elvis Aron Steele. Instead, the Presley name comes down from that peripatetic polygamist and two-time deserter from the Confederate Army, Dunnan Presley Jr.

Jessie Presley—Elvis's grandfather, also known as "J. D." or "Dee"— was bright, assertive, and strikingly handsome. At age seventeen he married a farm girl, Minnie Mae Hood, who was eight years his senior. Families in the Hood clan often owned their own farms, and Minnie Mae herself was not poor or totally dependent. Lee County Chancery Court records indicate that on September 28, 1948, she leased one hundred acres of farmland for a share of principal crops—a quarter of the cotton, a quarter of the hay, and a third of the corn. She also bought a one-acre lot in a Tupelo-area subdivision. She signified her agreement to that transaction by making an X (her mark) on the document, so she was possibly illiterate.

Court records also show that Jessie was not poor, though some of his money might have come from his marriage to Minnie Mae. In 1923, he bought a house and lot, not in the less expensive, country-come-to-town appendage called East Tupelo where the Presley family first settled, but rather on Jackson Street in Tupelo itself. A year later, he traded his equity in that house for $400 in cash and a new 1924 Chevrolet touring car. One can easily imagine a dapper Jessie tooling over to East Tupelo showing off his new car to kinfolk and friends, top down, Minnie Mae by his side, and eight-year-old Vernon in the back. Jessie was a hell-raiser, a drinker, a womanizer, and a fighter, and he sometimes spent Saturday nights in jail, but he always had a job and money in his pocket.

The same could not be said of the grown-up Vernon Presley, Jessie's youngest son. Although Vernon was strikingly handsome like his father, he was terribly insecure. He dressed like a dandy and strutted about like a peacock, but until Elvis became wealthy, his finances were exceedingly precarious. Repeatedly, other people had to pull Vernon out of holes that he had dug.

A year after his marriage, probably in April 1934, Gladys became pregnant. That fall, Jessie, Vernon, and his older brother, Vester, built the little house in East Tupelo with two rooms and a front porch where Elvis would be born. It was located next door to Jessie's substantial four-room house on Old Saltillo Road. Within the family, Jessie's house was called "the big house." Vester was always a good brother to Vernon, and Jessie clearly favored Vester over Vernon.

Orville Bean provided the land and the cash, $180, to buy the materials to build the house. There is no record in the Lee County courthouse that Vernon ever bought or began to buy the house and lot. Surely this was another very common case in which a farm owner allowed a farm laborer to build a house on his land to live in while he worked for the employer. Most likely, Vernon, teenage husband and father-to-be, paid his rent with labor on Bean's farm.

Vernon and Gladys moved into their new home in December 1934. At 4:00 a.m. on the icy cold morning of January 8, 1935, Elvis's twin brother, Jessie Garon, was born. Jessie was stillborn. That afternoon, thirteen-year-old Catherine Hall, who lived next door, saw him lying in a tiny casket by the window. The baby was perfectly formed. Catherine thought he was merely asleep and not dead. She was horrified. Someone had made a terrible mistake. They were about to bury a live baby! One of Vernon's sisters soon assured her that Jessie Garon was dead and that he would be buried nearby in the cemetery across the road from the Baptist church in Priceville, a community at the top of the long hill above the house. He would be buried near all the Presleys there, she said, so he would not be lonely.

Thirty minutes after Jessie Garon's birth, Elvis Aron appeared. Gladys had a very difficult labor, and she and Elvis subsequently spent some days in the county hospital. The expenses of Elvis's birth and Gladys's medical care ($15 for the birth) were paid by the county welfare department. Vernon could not pay for his son's birth, but he did give him his own beautifully euphonic middle name, Elvis. For his middle name, Aron, he gave him an adaptation of the first name of his best friend, Aaron Kennedy. Elvis later added an *a* to spell his name as Aaron.

"Elvis" was a very unusual name, but it was not original with the Presleys. When Elvis's father, Vernon Elvis Presley, was born in 1916 there was a little boy named Elvis Tucker living nearby. In the census of 1920, Jessie and Minnie Mae were listed as farmers living a dozen or so miles east of Tupelo in Itawamba County. Spencer and Bell Tucker tenanted a farm close by and were probably relatives of Minnie Mae. They had named their oldest son, who was five years old in 1920, Elvis.

Vernon was not a habitual criminal, but he often thought he deserved more than he got and sometimes simply took things that did not belong to him. Mostly he resisted steady labor, a mode of behavior that he had hit upon to rebel against his hard-working and domineering father. For years, he had been a great disappointment to Jessie, who responded to his son's inadequacies with strict discipline. At one point, he sent fifteen-year-old Vernon off to live and work with relatives, hoping for a change, but to no avail. After his marriage, Vernon worked at a succession of jobs and succeeded at none. Then he tried forgery.

In 1937, he had raised a pig to some unknown degree of maturity. Needing money, he sold the animal to Orville Bean for $4. Why he did not sell it to a more generous buyer is not clear. Bean probably already owned a part of the pig, the result of having provided housing or feed or both for the animal. Such sharing arrangements between farm owners and workers were ordinary in the always poor, low-wage Southern economy.

Whatever the provenance of the pig, Vernon felt that he had been cheated out of his just return. He had probably been drinking with Travis Smith, who was Gladys's younger brother, and another young man named Lether Gable when the three of them decided to alter the amount of Bean's check. Travis later told his son Billy that they had added a zero to the $4.00 to make it $40.00 and changed the writing to read "forty" instead of "four." Vernon did the necessary penmanship because Travis could not read or write. With no children and unmarried, Travis and Lether took their share of the loot and lit out for Texas, expecting to get rich. They very soon returned, each with only a new shirt, new trousers, and a huge wide-brimmed Texas hat to show for their venture. The police arrested them virtually as soon as they stepped down from the train in Tupelo.

The ink had hardly dried on the forged check before the sheriff grabbed Vernon and locked him up in the Lee County jail. On November 16, the three young men were arraigned in criminal court, pled not guilty, and were held over for trial in the May 1938 term. Thus, self-pity and stupidity left Vernon confined in the county jail for six months.

Vernon's father did not lift a finger to help his son. Instead, Jessie used the circumstances to rebuke Vernon more publicly, pointedly, and viciously than ever before. Jessie had the resources to bail Vernon out of jail pending trial and bring him home to his wife and child. But he did not. Instead, he cosigned the $500 bond that freed Travis Smith, Gladys's brother, until the court convened in May 1938. Other persons provided bail for Lether Gable, including at least one of his relatives.

The message was clear. Family and clan counted for everyone except Vernon. Both Travis and Lether were freed on bail on January 4, 1938, four days before Elvis's third birthday. Of the three conspirators, only Vernon was left in jail, where he could contemplate the error of his ways and ponder the depth of his father's rejection.

For two months before and four months after his third birthday, Elvis only saw his father as a prisoner in the county jail in Tupelo. His very first vivid memories of his father—his first memories of family life, of the three of them together—would be from those emotionally wrenching visits. Many of his early memories would be of traveling the long mile over the causeway across the flat bottom land on either side of Mud Creek from East Tupelo to Tupelo in some generous person's car, entering the jail, encountering the guard with a badge and a gun, his father's eager and needy embrace, the awkward and anxious conversation, and then, finally, alone again with his mother in the little house in East Tupelo.

Criminal court convened for the spring term on Monday, May 23, and on Wednesday, May 25, Vernon, Travis, and Lether again stood before Judge Johnston. They had changed their pleas to guilty. Gladys would have been there, seated in the audience, and she would have had Elvis by her side. They would have watched anxiously as Vernon stood to receive his sentence. The judge faced a crowded calendar, and he wasted no time in sentencing each man to three years in the state penitentiary, Parchman, in the Mississippi Delta more than a hundred miles west of Tupelo.

LOWER-CLASS CRIME IN THE GREAT DEPRESSION

In retrospect, three years in the state penitentiary seems a harsh penalty for a failed attempt to settle a minor difference over the value of a pig. But there was more going on in America just then than pig stealing. It was the Great Depression and times were hard. People were stealing to eat, making bootleg whiskey to survive, and joining in labor strikes. Some, like Bonnie Parker and Clyde Barrow, took to robbing banks across the South, in the process killing guards and police officers. Lee County had its own experience with bank robbery in 1932 when "Machine Gun" Kelly walked into the Citizens' State Bank in Tupelo in broad daylight, emptied its coffers, and made a clean getaway with some $17,000. Kelly was soon taken quietly by the FBI at the home of his very respectable parents in Memphis.

Vernon's difficulty with his employer was personal, but it was exacerbated by the malaise of the Great Depression. If workers living on a landlord's land in a house that the landlord owned felt they could violate the landlord's property with such impunity, the economic and social order of society would disintegrate into chaos. All things considered, Bean had treated Vernon and his little family generously. Vernon, in return, cheated him. Further, he did not even have the decency to flee after the crime; rather, he pled not guilty, as if Bean, not he, had done something wrong. It was okay, he seemed to say by his actions, to appropriate the property of the well-to-do when you felt that they had given you less than you deserved.

If Bean wanted Vernon punished, it was understandable. Also, the severity with which District Attorney Floyd W. Cunningham and Judge Johnston came down on Vernon and his cohort was a function of the times. Vernon's case occurred in the midst of a severe labor crisis in Tupelo. The city was exceedingly proud of its eager embrace of industrialization and modernity in previous decades, including a Carnation Milk Company processing plant. On the south side of town, there was a large locally owned textile mill employing several hundred workers. The workers and their families lived in small but comfortable wooden houses around the mill, a "mill village" built and owned by the company. The company flourished during the 1920s, but in the 1930s profits narrowed and wages shrank, and hardship in the village rose. By 1937, organizers for the United Textile Workers had moved into Tupelo. In mid-April 1938, one organizer, Jimmie Cox, was seized by a gang of eight men, thrown into a car, and driven out into the country. He was then tied to a tree, his pants removed, and whipped severely with belts. Threatened with being dragged behind a car with a rope around his neck, Cox promised to leave the area. The men left. Cox walked on to the nearest town, Pontotoc, and telephoned for help. Sarah Potter was in Tupelo as a representative of the International Ladies' Garment Workers Union. She reported the event to the sheriff's office and the press. Two days later, the sheriff's office announced that it would act on the matter only if Cox filed a proper affidavit. No one was ever tried for the crime.

All over America, labor unrest was rampant in 1937 and 1938. Auto workers, steel workers, and textile workers rose in militancy, and factory owners and civil authorities showed a readiness for violent response. Throughout the South, governors in textile states ordered out the National Guard to protect the mills. Guardsmen built circular "machine-gun nests" of sandbags around the mills in World War I fashion and manned them with soldiers wearing tin pan helmets and carrying machine guns. It was as if they were about to fight a class war in which masses of workers would swarm out of their hiding places in the villages and attempt to seize possession of the factory buildings. National survival, it seemed to many Americans, was at stake.

In Tupelo, striking workers were forcibly evicted from their mill houses by local toughs specially deputized for the task. One of these men was Lee Turner. He was sixty-two years old and notorious for sudden fits of anger and acts of violence. Turner's brief authority seems to have gone to his head. Soon after the evictions were completed, one day on the streets of Tupelo he flew into a rage at an unoffending young man passing through town and shot him to death. With Turner's "second shot," the *Tupelo Daily News* said, the young man "fell forward on his face." The paper identified him as a war veteran, deplored the crime, and urged stiff justice for his killer. Turner was tried two days after Vernon was sentenced, quickly found guilty, and sentenced to serve the remainder of his "natural life" in Parchman. That weekend this irascible and violent old man, like Vernon, sat in his cell on the first floor of the county jail waiting for "Long Chain Charley" to come for him. At Parchman, there were many other men like Turner, violent men, killers with short tempers, waiting for Vernon to join them.

PARCHMAN FARM

On Wednesday, June 1, Vernon, prisoner number 12231, was registered at the prison hospital in Parchman. He was twenty-one years old, five feet ten and one-half inches tall, and weighed 147 pounds. He described himself as a farmer. He could read and write and professed five years of schooling. Asked to identify his "primary family," he chose to name neither his wife nor his mother but rather, pathetically, his father alone, "J. D. Presley."

The prison record describes Vernon as having an oval face, arched eyebrows, a concave nose, a small mouth, good teeth, and a medium complexion. His body was unscarred. Indeed, the prison registrar recorded no identifying marks at all on Vernon's body, which made him a rarity in that way among inmates.

In contrast, Vernon's brother-in-law Travis Smith bore marks of a hard life, physically and mentally. In his early twenties, he could neither read nor write and had no schooling. Travis's face was "narrow" and his complexion was "sallow." His teeth were "bad" and his build was "small." He stood five feet seven and one-half inches tall and weighed 129 pounds. He bore a tattoo, "NBB," on his right forearm. A tattoo in that time and place advertised a willingness to fight, to take pain and also to give it. "Don't tread on me," it said, sometimes literally with an image of a coiled snake. Travis also had a number of scars, including a cut scar on his left thigh. For Travis's occupation, the registrar wrote "none." Lether Gable gave his occupation as truck driver. Like Travis, he was slight of build and scarred, including a cut scar on his upper lip. Vernon was about to enter an institution that by design was full of Mississippi's most ruthless and violent men, men who were practiced in and relished violence. They loved to beat, shoot, knife, rape, and sometimes kill.

Parchman Farm was essentially a twenty-thousand-acre plantation spread over a six-by-eight-mile rectangle that used hundreds of convict laborers to produce a cash crop, cotton, for the benefit of the state. Idleness among prisoners was no problem there. The mode of operation was one that Mississippi knew well, having perfected the practice during slavery; it was a plantation using forced labor to produce cotton and most of the goods necessary to sustain itself. The goal at Parchman, achieved year after year, was to show a profit by growing, reaping, and selling a huge cotton crop. Parchman did not pay its laborers, and there was never a labor shortage. Even in its very first year, 1905, the prison fed $185,000 into the state treasury.

Parchman, awful as it was for its inmates, was conceived and instituted as a reform measure. It replaced the convict lease system in which prisoners, both white and black, were rented out to private entrepreneurs, often treated with great cruelty, and sometimes worked to death. In the 1880s, William Faulkner's great-grandfather built his railroad from Ripley to Pontotoc using convicts rented from the state at the rate of $50 a year. When some people complained that he starved and beat those men, he replied that they were fed as well as any people on poor relief and were not abused physically.

In view of the fact that the great majority of convicts in Mississippi were black, it is ironic that the reform in the state's prison system was the work of the state's formative racist, Governor James K. Vardaman. In terms of humane treatment, it was the white prisoners he was concerned about, but he was also mindful of the money to be made by the state's using convict labor, white as well as black, and the patronage opportunities he would gain in staffing a prison. Vardaman led the state in purchasing the Parchman plantation. The new penitentiary would house white convicts, but it was also designed to contain the very worst members of the majority black population in the state.

Vardaman, like many other leading whites in the black belt South at the turn of the century, felt that blacks in America freed from the stringent controls of slavery were retrogressing to their natural state of savagery. In freedom, the veneer of civilization was falling away, as evinced by the vast increase in the number of attacks on white women by "black beast rapists." Over several generations, black people would simply die away, destroyed by their own inadequacies. Meanwhile, they must be rigorously contained. Such was the contemporary white view. "You cannot create something when there is nothing to build on," Governor Vardaman declared. "But they can be well trained, and that is the best that can be done with the genuine Negro." Parchman Farm was created to make the most out of the worst black men in Mississippi.

Originally about 90 percent of the inmates were black, but the number of whites rose rapidly between 1917 and 1925, from 149 to 280, more than 20 percent of the total. Almost a third of whites in 1925 were "bootleggers," having violated state liquor laws. By the time Vernon arrived in 1938, during the Great Depression, whites made up about 30 percent of prisoners.

In Vernon's time, there were a dozen field camps spread across the forty-eight square miles of absolutely flat Delta landscape that was Parchman. Camps 4 and 5 held white prisoners. Prison records indicate that Vernon was in Camp 5, along with Travis, Lether Gable, and about 150 other convicts. Each camp was isolated and largely self-supporting, growing and preparing its own food, doing its laundry outside in large wash pots, repairing its tools, and caring for its livestock. Each camp was under the absolute authority of one man, the sergeant, who lived in a house on the grounds with his family and earned $50 a month. He was assisted by white "drivers" who literally drove the men before them in the fields. If the task was to chop the grass away from the stalk of the cotton plant using a hoe, each man would have a row to hoe. If there were 150 men, they would work 150 rows simultaneously, forming a "long line" moving across the field. The driver would ride behind on his horse, carrying a "bull whip," strips of leather fixed to a handle, used to reprimand laggards. Occasionally, a convict with a bad attitude would be stripped, held on the ground between the rows, and lashed until welts rose and blood oozed.

The real guards at Parchman, the men who were liable to kill a man attempting to escape, were also convicts, designated as "trusties." Trusties wore uniforms marked by vertical, rather than horizontal, stripes. Some of these were armed with guns and served as "shooters." The trusties enforced discipline and prevented escapes. They were chosen for the job precisely because they were the most violent and vicious white men in the prison. They had already demonstrated to the state they were capable of mayhem and murder.

There would be several shooters for every hundred men. When the men were working in a field, the shooters would draw a "gun line" around the area. Any man crossing the line without permission from the shooters automatically became a target, at short range for a shotgun, at long range for a Winchester rifle. Any shooter who brought a man down, either dead or alive, would be rewarded, perhaps even with a full pardon from the governor.

The shooters also guarded the men at night. They were housed at one end of the long, one-story barracks, separated from other prisoners by the dining hall. At the other end of the building, ordinary prisoners like Vernon and Travis slept in bunks set at regular intervals in two long lines, heads to the walls with an aisle in between. Shooters did not fraternize with other inmates. At night, they patrolled the grounds around the building, deliberately making menacing noises so that the inmates always knew they were there, watching and ready.

VERNON IN PARCHMAN

This was the tight, violent, fear-filled cage that Vernon walked into on June 1, 1938. He could expect to be in that cage—with a token allowance for extra work, called "Sunday work"—into the spring of 1941. Before Parchman, Vernon had been able to indulge his penchant for low performance and suffer only the disapproval of his father or Orville Bean. Now he would work hard or else suffer lashes on his heretofore smooth and unmarked back. Apparently, he did not learn this lesson quickly enough. "The story went around that Vernon got bullwhipped," his nephew Billy Smith, Travis's son, said later, "and that's why he never went shirtless after that."

The workday for Vernon and everyone else at Parchman began at 4:30 a.m. when the steam whistle sounded at the power station in Front Camp. The shooters turned on the lights and moved noisily through the barracks, rousing the men. After a breakfast of biscuits and syrup, they marched to the fields to begin their tasks at first light. Each day brought its quota of work for each man, so many rows to plant or hoe, so much wood to cut, two hundred pounds of cotton to pick at harvest time. Laggards would be whipped while others were made to watch. The sergeant might decide to improve discipline by publicly and ceremoniously whipping a lazy, rebellious, or simply unfortunate inmate. The man would be stripped and held spread-eagle on the ground while the others were made to watch. The sergeant or one of his minions would lay on lashes with a three-foot by six-inch leather strap known as "Black Annie." The severity of the whipping was arbitrary. "There is no telling what punishment will be used in this prison," one convict said. "It all depends on how mad the sergeant is, as to whether you get fifteen or fifty lashes." The whole camp might be disciplined by being forced to sleep outside the barracks at night regardless of the weather. Sometimes, when the sergeant was especially mad, they had to spend the night outside next to the open cesspools.

Crimes against property brought most men to Parchman, but there they joined Mississippi's most violent criminals, who were well practiced in violence with guns, knives, clubs, and fists. A new convict who was a slow learner would be in trouble immediately, not only from the drivers and shooters but also from other convicts.

On one occasion a young newcomer casually sat down on the bunk of another prisoner. The man flew into a rage and stabbed him to death.

In Camp 5 Vernon was caged with men lifted out of their communities all over Mississippi precisely because of their proclivity to use force to take whatever they wanted—including sex. Travis Smith, with his own scars and tattoo, might evince a defiance and pride that would not endear him to prison authorities, but his appearance would say to other prisoners that he was not an easy target of abuse. In a fight his opponent might suffer more pain.

In such an order, smooth-skinned and unscarred Vernon Presley would not stand very high. Strikingly handsome and twenty-two years old, he would be a target. Travis would defend him, but ultimately his protection would have to come from the authorities, and Vernon would need it. His good looks, the very quality that caused women to follow him with their eyes and caused Gladys to adore him when he was only sixteen years old and to marry him when he was barely seventeen, was a liability in Camp 5. Moreover, he was vain about his looks, a penchant he was not likely to shed with his incarceration. Other prisoners would see Vernon as unmanly, but their words for him would be much less kind than that.

Vernon must have been terrified as he lay in his bunk at night, hearing the scurrying sounds and seeing the dim shapes of men moving around him. If half of the men in Camp 5 engaged in homosexual relations, the usual proportion in prison, he must have heard whispered conversations and sometimes curses, slaps, grunts, and the sounds of men forcing themselves upon other men. He must have despaired as he thought about the next three years of his life.

Later, when Vernon had become Elvis's "business manager" at Graceland, he was harsh and callous to his employees. Elvis would reply to the complainers, "You just don't know what Daddy's been through." Elvis knew very well what his father had been through, but he never told. It was only after Elvis died that the tabloids exposed the fact that Vernon had been a convict in Parchman.

ELVIS AND GLADYS AT PARCHMAN

The first and third Sundays of every month were visiting days at Parchman. Sunday, June 5, 1938, would have been a visiting day, but it seems unlikely that Gladys and Elvis would have come to Parchman so soon after Vernon's arrival. They came on Sunday, June 19, or Sunday, July 3, or both. Certainly, Vernon and Gladys were writing back and forth. A penny postcard that Vernon wrote to Gladys on Friday, July 8, suggests that Gladys had already found friends and relatives upon whom she could rely to drive her and Elvis to Parchman for those visits. On the postcard, Vernon urged Gladys to come on the third Sunday in July, the seventeenth.

> *friday*
> Dear gladys
> I will right you a few
> lines to let you no I am
> alright hope you all
> the same I was glad
> to here that the baby
> was better I hope
> he is alright now
> you all come this
> 3 sunday if you can

and tell Mr. powel
to come to I want
to tell him something
well i will
close answer
    soon
with love
from Vernon

Among those who drove Gladys and Elvis to Parchman for those visits on the first and third Sundays was F. L. Bobo, the man who owned the hardware store in Tupelo. Vernon's uncle Noah Presley, Rosella's oldest son, was another. He opened a grocery store in East Tupelo in the 1920s, and in 1936, when the village was incorporated as a town, he became its first mayor. Under his leadership, the little town got water, sewer, and power lines. It was, in fact, the first town in America to receive power from the New Deal's Tennessee Valley Authority.

Gladys, according to custom and in the phrase of the time, would offer to pay the friend or relative for "the gas and oil" if she could afford it or promise to pay later if she could not. Gladys would sit in the front seat with the driver. Elvis would stand or sit in the back, listening to his mother talking to the man, always filling the silence with her voice, working to knit up the raveled fabric of family life, making everything whole by stringing out words and weaving the strands together. She is grateful for the ride, she says, and worried to death.

Elvis would look out at the rolling land, cotton plants raising dark green leaves to the sun, the new white concrete highway unfolding ahead, riding from east to west through the Sunday morning quiet of the main streets of the little towns along the way. If they took the fastest way and the best roads, they followed what is now Highway 278. They went through Pontotoc, where Vernon and Gladys had married five years earlier, then on to Oxford, where forty-year-old William Faulkner lived in his rickety and almost barren antebellum mansion on the south side of town.

Approaching Oxford's courthouse square from the south side, Elvis would see the Confederate soldier carved in stone atop the impossibly high pedestal gazing steadily southward down the town's main street. They would turn right and drive counterclockwise around the square, which Faulkner's fictional Benjy Compson had circled every Sunday afternoon. Almost surely, they never visited the University of Mississippi just blocks away.

They would drive west out of Oxford, cross the Tallahatchie River on a bridge near Batesville, and roll out onto the marvelously flat and seemingly endless expanse of the Delta. Turning south at Marks, they passed through the hamlets of Tutwiler, Rome, and Minot and came at last to Parchman, having traveled some 115 miles in a few hours.

There would be cars ahead of them, parked on the right shoulder of the road outside the prison gate, people inside waiting for visiting hours to begin. They would take their place at the end of the line, shut off the engine, and wait. Elvis, looking out the windows on the right side of the car, would see no walls, no bars, only a high wire fence, a gathering of buildings at Front Camp, and the towering smokestack of the powerhouse.

At the given hour, the prison gates would swing open. Drivers down the line would start their engines and begin to roll forward. One by one, they would swing right and stream through the stone pillars and iron gates of the entranceway. They would not be stopped by the guards there. Elvis, his mother, and the driver would ride by the huge Victorian house in which the superintendent lived and drive out across the flat land to Camp 5.

CAMP 5

At Camp 5, visitors would be screened for contraband and then allowed to pass into the area. On cold or rainy days, they would visit in the dining area of the barracks. On good days, they could visit in the yard, walking around or sitting on benches at long tables used for outside meals. The camp did not look like a prison and lacked bars, walls, and even fences.

On the first visit, Vernon would have been in prison garb, horizontal black and white stripes, loose top and baggy bottom. The meeting must have been emotional, and Elvis probably carried the whole scene of their first meeting in Parchman the rest of his life, the memory not only of Parchman prison and his father in stripes, but also of his sense of his father's fear that the Presleys would embrace. The driver would shake hands with Vernon. Travis, Gladys's brother, would be there too. Then they would sit and talk, in the Southern way, about the more comfortable subjects, putting the best face on things, knowing by tone and body language that there were harsh things underneath that should not be pushed into words. After a time, Vernon and Gladys would rise and move away from Travis and Elvis. They needed to talk privately, to be together. Eventually, they probably had sex, a practice allowed and even encouraged by the authorities. Vernon's survival virtually required Gladys's attention. Gladys made Vernon a man—especially inside Parchman.

Parchman was one of the few prisons in America where male prisoners were allowed "conjugal visiting." It began when the administration allowed whole truckloads of black prostitutes to visit the black camps on certain Saturdays and Sundays. In time, the prisoners in each camp, using leftover materials, constructed houses with separate rooms to provide a modicum of privacy for couples. These structures were painted red and called "Red Houses." Later, white prisoners also erected Red Houses. White female visitors were more carefully screened than black, and as the institution matured, white prisoners were allowed to take only their legal wives to the Red Houses. By the time Vernon got to Parchman, conjugal visiting was fine-tuned to protect the sensitivities of all parties. A numbered key to each numbered room in the Red House was placed on a key board discreetly located.

Prison officials said sexual visitation cut down on homosexual activity and the fights that grew out of that activity. It kept families together and preserved outside ties. Inmates, they thought, were generally more contented. Also, it was a privilege that could be taken away to punish the unruly.

While his parents were gone, Elvis might have sat at the picnic-like table with the man who had driven them over, and maybe his uncle Travis. Everyone always said that Travis was like Gladys, outgoing and friendly, but also that he suffered no insult lightly.

Finally came the drive home, four hours or so, the windows of the car rolled down to catch the slightly cooling air, the sun setting bright orange behind them. As night came on, Elvis would crawl into the front seat and curl into his mother's lap, his head resting against her breast, feeling her heart beat, hearing her talk to the man again.

He would drift off to sleep. Then he would wake slowly. The car was motionless, making the clanking noises of connected metal cooling. Strong arms were lifting him up carefully, holding him against a broad chest, and then lowering him to the bed. He felt his weight melt onto the mattress, his clothes being pulled gently off, his mother crawling into bed beside him, holding him close.

Friends and neighbors remember this time well. Soon after Vernon went to jail, Gladys and Elvis would sit on the front porch of their little two-room house. Elvis could not do enough for his mother.

"Mama, would you like a glass of water?" he would ask. He would sit at her feet and rest his arm on her knee. He would stroke her face, smooth her eyebrows, and pat her head. "There, there, my little baby," he would say. Elvis was there, and he was only three years old.

Elvis felt deeply his mother's anguish—and his own. People recalled him sometimes "bawling so hard he couldn't catch his breath."

THE ASSEMBLY OF GOD

On Sundays when they did not go to Parchman, Gladys and Elvis went to the Assembly of God Tabernacle at the bottom of the hill below their house in East Tupelo. One neighbor recalled that they "went every time the door was open." They went Sunday mornings, Sunday evenings, and during the week when there were prayer meetings or revivals. Gladys's uncle Gains Mansell, the minister, had built the little church with his own hands and led the congregation of some two to three score souls who worshipped there. Gladys might well feel that she had a special place, a refuge, in a church built and led by one of her own people. Both Smiths and Presleys belonged to the Assembly of God.

Throughout his life, Elvis's fundamental religious beliefs were the beliefs he had acquired through the Assembly of God. He thought that the true believer could achieve an exceedingly intimate and mystical re-lationship with God. True believers were few and far between, but God gave them miraculous powers that other people did not have. They could heal the sick, prophesy, and perform miracles. Elvis knew that he was a true believer.

The Assembly of God was organized as a denomination in 1914. It grew out of the Pentecostal and Holiness movements that surged through the South in the previous decade's spiritual rebellions against the materialism of modernity. Consciously devaluing worldly posses-sions, the Assembly of God focused on the blessings of the Holy Spirit and on a very personal closeness to God in this life and the next.

Pentecostals believed that they each had a "crisis" experience, a moment when they faced the sinful lives they had lived and the Holy Spirit miracu-lously came down upon them and changed their lives forever. They could name the exact date and circumstances of their conversion, the time and place that they came to know God intimately. Pentecostals asserted that the saved person possessed special powers. By prayer and a "laying on of hands," they could heal the sick. They might "speak in tongues," that is, stand with their body quivering, raise their open hands to heaven, and speak words in a holy language. The Holiness movement came mostly out of the Methodist Episcopal Church, South, formed by Southern Meth-odists who had seceded from the national church in 1844 over slavery. More specifically, the Holiness impulse grew out of Wesleyan Methodism, a purist tradition within Methodism. Holiness people felt that the conver-sion experience produced a person who would not only possess the Holy Spirit but would also by the grace of God undergo "sanctification," a purification. The sanctified person manifested the Holy Spirit by abstain-ing from smoking, chewing tobacco, drinking alcohol, dancing, mixed swimming, wearing jewelry, and a long list of other things that varied somewhat from one congregation to another. Women were to dress mod-estly, not wear makeup, and not cut their hair short. More positively, Ho-liness people believed that the converted experienced marvelous things of a mystical nature, such as visions, prophecies, and awarenesses.

Flowing with and into the Pentecostal and Holiness movements was the conviction that the believers were restoring the primitive Christian

church. In effect, the restoration of the primitive church bypassed materialism and modernity in all of its forms. It carried one directly back
to a powerful intimacy with Jesus and through Jesus to a communion
with the Holy Spirit and the possession of holy powers. The Pentecostal, Holiness, and Restorationist movements all took strong hold in the
rural South in the early decades of the twentieth century, particularly
among those who were losing out in the race for material wealth in
the modern world. As displaced rural folk—often having moved down
from farm owners to farm tenants to farm workers—they migrated into
towns and cities, as they did to Tupelo and Memphis. They brought
their beliefs and their churches with them. Also, rural migrants who had
been Baptists, Methodists, and Presbyterians in the country often did
not feel comfortable in the mainline uptown churches dominated by an
affluent, educated, and worldly-minded elite. Many deserted the church
into which they had been born and joined the new denominations—the
Assembly of God Church, the Church of God, the Pentecostal Holiness
Church, and the Fire-Baptized Holiness Church. They did so as whole
families and clans. Many others, like the Presleys later in Memphis,
became virtually unchurched in the move from country to city.

The Assembly of God church in East Tupelo housed a small congregation in a tiny building, but both the people and the place were
charged with the spirit of God. They saw themselves as an island of faith
in a sinful world. They would carry on until Jesus Christ came to earth
again, a family of the faithful, banded together in church and out. They
addressed one another as "Brother" or "Sister." Jesus, the Son of God,
was near, and the spirit of God was always with them, but especially
when they came together to pray, preach, and sing. "He walks with me,
and he talks with me," they would sing, "and he tells me I am his own."

Singing was vital to the religious experience. Frank Smith, "Brother
Frank," a minister who followed Gains Mansell to lead the Assembly of
God church in East Tupelo, played the guitar and sang. The congregation joined in with faces lifted, voices strong with conviction, and hands
double-clapping. "Where could I go but to the Lord," they would sing
joyfully, standing and dancing to the music. The piano would play and
the singing would go on, the same song over and over, the same words

rendered with increasing fervor each time. "Where could I go . . ." The piano sounded like a pedal-driven player piano; each note rang out clearly, distinctly, mechanically, predictably, faithfully.

During the sermon, members of the congregation raised their faces and arms toward heaven and audibly affirmed the minister's message. "Praise the Lord!" they would call out. As the Spirit seized them, they cried, laughed, shouted, fainted, jerked, and spoke in tongues. There would be a woman who would raise one arm high, palm open, and wave her hand slowly, smoothly back and forth as if signaling her presence to a heaven already in sight. There would be a man who could only express his jubilation physically, running, jumping over the backs of benches, and shouting. Some people would fall to the floor and lie perfectly still as if slain by the Holy Spirit, and some would fall and roll back and forth crying and moaning. Finally the minister's speech would slow and soften, the piano would begin to play quietly, and the congregation, exhausted and ecstatic, would subside with a shuffling of feet and a scattering of low cries. "Yes, Lord." "Amen." "Yes, Lord." It was as if a torrential rain had passed over them, washing away the trash and filth of earthly life, leaving them cleansed and quiet.

These Christians felt the spirit of God with an intimacy and a power that mainline churches had found during the Great Awakenings of the eighteenth and nineteenth centuries, but had lost. The people in the uptown churches had become sedate, subdued, and cerebral in their worship. They looked down upon the people in such churches as the Assembly of God as ignorant and overly emotional and called them "Holy Rollers" in derision. Meanwhile, the Pentecostal and Holiness churches could barely contain the joyous and noisy fervor of their worshippers.

Members of the Assembly of God in East Tupelo recall Elvis at about age three toddling down the aisle toward the singers at the front of the church enthralled, his little mouth and voice attempting to imitate theirs. They would sing about "the wonder-working" power of the spirit or how on that "glad day" they would "fly away . . . to Glory." Later, Elvis repeatedly asserted that he liked gospel music best of all. "It more or less puts your mind to rest," he said. Then he reached down into that defining past of his childhood, and added: "At least it does mine, since I was two."

Elvis was two years old when he began to go to church with his mother alone. When he was three and four years old, every Sunday he went either to Parchman or to the little church at the bottom of the hill in East Tupelo. After he became successful, he ceased going to any church at all. He excused himself by saying that his presence would be disruptive. But he was famous among fellow entertainers for holding impromptu gospel singing sessions backstage between performances. Sometimes he would close his eyes as others sang and seem transported. Now and again onstage he would have his gospel group sing a hymn while he listened raptly, seemingly truly transported and unmindful of the audience. Only a few hours before he died, he was playing the piano and singing gospel songs at Graceland while his cousin, his cousin's wife, and his fiancée listened.

GETTING VERNON OUT OF PARCHMAN

Gladys did more than visit Vernon in Parchman and serve as his lifeline. She got him released.

Mississippi had no parole board, and prison officials gave no paroles. The governor might pardon convicts, which he occasionally did for political or personal reasons. In addition, there were various loosely defined processes by which a convict might secure a "suspended" sentence, which would be authorized by the governor and would allow the convict to leave prison before he had served his full time and remain out during good behavior. Bad behavior would send him back to Parchman.

A suspended sentence was rarely achieved. For Vernon to get his sentence suspended, the judge who sentenced him, the district attorney who prosecuted him, and his local sheriff would have to approve. Letters, petitions, and personal entreaties might encourage officials to leniency. A devoted, chaste, and faithful wife and little children needing his support would also help. Finally, a key person in the process was the sergeant who commanded his camp in prison. He had a veto, as it were, and Vernon himself had to please that man. He had to be responsive to authority and promise to be a responsible citizen, worker, husband, and father. He had to "walk the line," as Johnny Cash would later sing so convincingly that some people thought he had actually served time in prison and on parole, which he had not.

Between Gladys's work outside and Vernon's behavior inside, the authorities were persuaded to suspend Vernon's sentence for six months beginning on February 6, 1939. Billy Smith, Travis's son, understood that his aunt Gladys got up a petition and got Vernon out of Parchman as a hardship case. The record in Mississippi state archives shows that Governor Hugh White, who signed the order, was persuaded to do so by a petition of the citizens of Lee County and a letter from O. S. Bean, the party on whom the checks were forged. Surely it was Gladys who, by explaining her needs—including the means to support Elvis—and manifesting her virtues, convinced influential people to sign the petition and Orville Bean to write that letter.

During the week when Vernon was released from Parchman on a suspended sentence, Gladys took part in two social events in East Tupelo reported by the *Tupelo Daily News* on Saturday, February 10, 1939. Her event on Sunday, February 4, was warm and personal. The *News* reported that "Miss Dora Harris and Miss Gladys Presley visited friends at Wheeler," a village about twenty miles north of Tupelo.

On Tuesday, February 6, the *News* announced that Vernon Presley was released from Parchman with a suspended sentence. Two days later, on Thursday, Gladys was one of eight "ladies" who came together for a sewing circle. The *News* reported that event on Saturday: "A sewing circle composed of the following ladies, Misses Gladys Pressley [*sic*], Dora Harris, Dora Alred, Sarah Cloyd, and Mrs. Luna Buse and Mrs. Nora Clarks met at the home of Mrs. Elmo Holloway Thursday afternoon at [type missing in the newspaper] o'clock. Mrs. Nell Peck of Tupelo is instructing the group in sewing. Coke and tea was served as refreshments." The *News* misspelled the Presley name as Pressley once. Much more strikingly, it identified Gladys as "Miss," not "Mrs.," Presley twice. Where in the world was Vernon?

In truth, Gladys herself fulfilled the role of a husband in Southern white culture during the fifteen months that Vernon was in the county jail and Parchman. She was the "provider and protector" for the family. She had also marvelously fulfilled three of the four ideals prescribed for women. She was pious, pure, and domestic. But she was not at all submissive. She got her husband out of the Mississippi state prison.

After serving less than nine months of a three-year sentence, Vernon was back home. Travis Smith and Lether Gable were not out, nor would they be out until 1941, when they had served their full sentences. Authorities might have decided that they were not hardship cases, or that they were primarily responsible for the forgery and Vernon had been seduced by them.

SENTENCE SUSPENDED

By the time Vernon returned, Gladys and Elvis had left the little house in East Tupelo and moved in with her cousin Frank Richards, his wife, Leona, and their children on the south side of Tupelo. Gladys was working nearby at the Mid-South Laundry while Leona watched the children. The commercial laundry was another sign of modernity coming to the South and Tupelo. Many middle-class white people no longer boiled their clothes in black iron wash pots in their backyards or gave their business to African American washerwomen, who worked wash pots at their own homes. Instead, they "counted" out their wash on a "laundry list" at the beginning of the week, bundled it up, and sent it to the laundry, where large machines did the hard labor of cleaning; white men in delivery trucks brought it back before the weekend neatly folded and bundled.

Vernon needed to go to work soon after he got out of prison, not only to earn a living for his family but also to prove himself worthy of his freedom. In 1939, as the Great Depression dragged on, anyone would have had trouble finding a new job quickly. Vernon had a reputation as undependable and lazy before; now he was also a convicted criminal. Any employer would regard him with a suspicious eye. Even his friends began to shun him. Billy Smith, his nephew, said, "No, he's gone to jail. It's best not to socialize because people might think I'll get into trouble with him."

In the mid-1980s, there was a vague memory in the Tupelo community that Vernon first got a job helping build public outhouses. The memory is close to the truth. In fact, in early May, Vernon was enrolled as a WPA worker and assigned to the Sanitation Project in Lee County. He would work 140 hours each month for $30.10. By July, he was upgraded in skill to carpenter and cement finisher, and his pay was raised to $52 a month. In those terribly hard times, when the cost of food, housing, and clothing was minimal, this was high security indeed.

The Presleys needed all the security they could get, and Vernon needed to show the authorities that he deserved the suspension of his sentence. On August 6, his suspension would end. Before that time, authorities would have to make a judgment. Would Vernon be sent back to Parchman or not?

Some friends and relatives in East Tupelo discounted the seriousness of Vernon's crime, chalking it up to Orville Bean's mercenary and vindictive nature. Others did not, and across the creek in Tupelo proper the Lee County gentry was not likely to see his incarceration as a total miscarriage of justice. Certain members of the elite had endorsed his temporary release. Their judgment, reputations, and honor were at stake, and they would be aware of his performance. Most immediately, sheriff's deputies and town police would be watching. His release had been based on his continued good behavior. One misstep and the authorities would send him back to Camp 5, where the sergeant would surely resent Vernon's betrayal of his trust. His days of freedom were literally numbered and steadily dwindling. He did not have much time to prove himself worthy of an extension of the suspension of his sentence. It was almost a godsend that the WPA gave him a job in early May.

The little family was under tremendous pressure, and it showed. They did things in their sleep—like moving their mattress and bedclothes from the bedstead to the floor in the middle of the night and waking up the next morning surprised to find themselves thus lowered. For a time, Elvis walked in his sleep, moving about at night with his eyes wide open.

During this trying time, family and clan were vital to the survival of the Presleys, especially the Richards, with whom they lived. Apparently mother, father, and little boy all slept together in the same iron-work, wire-spring, tick-mattress bed. They had done so from the beginning in the little house on Old Saltillo Road. For people born to large families on tenant farms, there was nothing at all shocking about many bodies sleeping in a single bed. On cold winter nights, it was comforting to snuggle under layers of homemade quilts on a mattress filled with chicken or turkey feathers or freshly dried corn shucks surrounded by other family members. Smiths and Presleys had for generations considered themselves lucky to have any bed at all to sleep in and a roof over their heads.

Little Elvis was profoundly affected by his father's absence and made anxious by his return. Signs suggest, however, that Elvis was not resentful toward Vernon. The ordeal of his incarceration seemed to thicken the bonds tying the family together. The prime mover in that process was Gladys.

Gladys loved Vernon and did not forsake him. In the crisis that he created, she became the provider and protector as well as wife and mother. Her smile, her touch, her approval were vital to her husband, and her relation to him was important to the community. Her virtue provided an umbrella under which Vernon could find a measure of protection in a larger world that held him in low regard as a man. Such consideration as he got from the community was largely the gift of Gladys.

As spring passed into summer, the possibility of Vernon's return to Parchman must have loomed before the family. Their fate was in the hands of the local gentry. An extension came through only on the day before the deadline. On August 5, Governor White authorized ninety more days of freedom for Vernon for good behavior while out on former suspension. The new date was November 3. Vernon had passed the six-month test; now he faced another countdown of days. On November 3, 1939, two years after he was first arrested, on the very day that Vernon's three-month reprieve ended, he received an indefinite suspension of his sentence.

The relief for the Presleys must have been tremendous. If Vernon behaved himself, presumably he—and they—would never have to see Parchman again. Yet he had not served out his sentence, and any misbehavior, any trouble at all with the law, would leave him vulnerable to a summary proceeding and two more years of prison. His future lay most immediately in the hands of the city and county police, before whose eyes he moved daily. They knew him—by face, by name, and by character. They knew what he had done, and they certainly knew they had the power to treat him in an arbitrary manner if they wanted. Vernon's vulnerability must have weighed heavily upon Gladys, and the anxieties of both parents must have passed into the consciousness of their son, now almost five years old.

ON BECOMING A BOY

During his formative years, it is said, in order to become a man and a father himself, a boy needs a manly father as a model, and especially so in the early years of his life. Elvis's mother had to fill the space left by his father's absence in prison. Gladys, not Vernon, became the provider and protector. She became the model for that role in family life.

If Elvis read the realities accurately, he understood that his mother—not his father—had such power. Her power was the limited but certain power that a lower-class white woman might muster in the cultural order of the Deep South. A good woman—pious, pure, and faithful to family—was entitled to maintenance and protection by chivalrous men, manly men at the top who had power. The formula was very clear. She needed to make them aware of her virtuous character, to make her hardship felt by them, to be deferential in her demeanor, and to manifest to her benefactors her gratitude to them for everything they did for her and hers. The very stuffing of a Southern gentleman demanded that he do his duty to good people of the lower orders in his community, to "deserving" people and to women in particular. Deference from them compelled maintenance and protection from the elite. Thus, Mr. Bobo, the owner of the hardware store in Tupelo, spent entire Sundays, his day off, driving Gladys and Elvis to Parchman and back.

Elvis would understand early and clearly that he was born into the lower orders of society. He must have known that even in the Presley and Smith clans his father stood near or at the bottom. Vernon was not the man his father, Jessie, was, nor the public-spirited citizen his uncle Noah was. Among men at large, including criminals, Elvis's father had little if any respect. Most importantly, Elvis knew from his mother's example that in reaching up from the bottom one gained a modicum of respect and security only by making visible one's best self along with one's needs, by manifesting a distinctly deferential manner to people with power, and by clear and repeated statements of gratitude for any recognition or gifts received. "Thank you. Thank you very much," he would later say repeatedly to his audiences with a bow of the head and a bend of the body.

Elvis as a child understood very well the realities of life for himself at the very bottom of the social order among whites. He learned to deal effectively with the disabilities he suffered because of his class, not in the way of his father, but rather in the way of his mother. Gladys played the game and survived; Vernon dumbly defied the hierarchy and paid the especially severe penalties imposed on a faulty white man of the lower orders—including the humiliation of Parchman, the unmanning that went with serving time there. During a significant portion of the period when Elvis was learning how to be a boy, Gladys, not Vernon, became the adult model for Elvis. Through her, he learned to appreciate and himself practice the ways of white women of the lower orders in Southern culture. In dealing with the world, he became a master at the game.

CHAPTER FOUR

EAST TUPELO AND TUPELO

THE WAR

Vernon continued working with the Lee County Sanitation Project into
1941. At some point he took a job with the S and W Construction
Company in Sardis, Mississippi, seventy miles west of Tupelo. Possibly
the company had been engaged by the U.S. government during the
New Deal to help build a dam—"the largest earthen dam in America,"
locals would boast—across the Tallahatchie River nearby. For decades
Sardis Lake and its recreation area would be a favored resort for residents from miles around. On Saturday, January 24, 1942, Vernon quit
his job, citing ill health.

By then, America was at war, and at first Vernon seemed eager to
leave Lee County and take advantage of well-paying job opportunities abundantly available elsewhere. On August 1, 1942, he was living
with Gladys and Elvis in Ozark, Alabama, some three hundred miles
southeast of Tupelo, where he worked for the J. H. Jones Construction Company. On August 8, he began a job at the Ferguson-Oman
Gulf Ordnance plant in Aberdeen, Mississippi, only forty miles south
of Tupelo. On November 22, he went back to work for the S and W
Construction Company, this time in Como over in the Delta, where he
helped build a camp for prisoners of war. Como was named for the
Italian lake, and the camp was intended for captured Japanese soldiers,
but it came to hold Germans, initially some of those captured in the
North African campaign. Within two weeks of Vernon's arrival, however, construction on the camp was coming to an end. Vernon asked
his friend and fellow worker Bill Parham if he had received a notice of

termination. Bill had not. Vernon had. But because of the war, he knew exactly what to do. "Well," Vernon said to Bill, "guess I'll be going up to Memphis now to look for work." Within a week he had found it. On December 12, he began work with Dunn Construction Company at a military base near Millington, Tennessee, a dozen miles north of Memphis. He left that job after nine weeks.

In the year 1942, Vernon held five jobs. Despite the inconstancy of his labor, he was making money at a rate that must have amazed and delighted him. He had qualified as a carpenter with the WPA, and in all of these jobs he was a card-carrying member of the carpenters union. With time-and-a-half for overtime, he was making about $50 a week. In the WPA, he had made $52 a month. Manpower was in such great demand that Parchman was suspending the sentences of men who would agree to join the war effort.

Working away from home, Vernon lived in communities where he had no local reputation. He did not have to tell anyone that he had served time as a convicted criminal in Parchman. He was freed from the scrutiny of police officers in Tupelo and Lee County, distanced from the humiliation of having been jailed. He could offer himself to strangers, both women and men, as a man in an image that he desired, tall, handsome, and intelligent, and, for a time at least, be accepted in that image.

In 1943, Vernon continued his peripatetic ways. In mid-February, he quit his job in Millington and within the month was working at the Pepsi-Cola bottling plant back in Tupelo. Several weeks later, on April 29, when he left Pepsi, the clerk made a note on his last pay slip. "Gone to shipyard," it said. On May 16, Vernon started working at the Moss Point Shipyard on the Gulf Coast near Pascagoula, Mississippi. This time, Gladys and Elvis went with him, as well as his cousin Sales Presley and his wife, Annie, and their two little girls. The work was hard, but exceedingly well paid. Vernon got $1.20 an hour for a forty-hour workweek and $1.80 an hour for overtime. Workers and families lived in slapped-together quarters made of wood, canvas, and screen. It was not comfortable, especially as summer heat rose and insects came on, but Gladys and Elvis had the company of Annie and her kids. Elvis was eight years old. He took a liking to Annie's baby, Diane, and would carry her around riding astraddle his hip, his arm around her waist.

On Sunday, June 20, five weeks after they had arrived, Sales and Annie decided to go back to Tupelo. Vernon and Gladys decided to stay. Within hours, Vernon, Gladys, and Elvis threw their things into their car and headed north. About noon Sales, Annie, and the girls were at a roadside stand having lunch at an outside table. Annie looked up to see the Vernon Presley family in their car turning off the highway. Joining them, Gladys delivered the explanation. "We're not staying down there alone," she declared, "watching all those uptown folks eating shrimps and oysters."

Vernon took Gladys and Elvis with him to live in Ozark, Alabama, and Pascagoula, Mississippi, but otherwise they stayed home while he went off to do war work. At first, they lived with Frank and Leona Richards and then shared a duplex in East Tupelo with Vester Presley and his wife, Clettes, Gladys's sister. Their baby daughter, Patsy, was Elvis's "double first cousin," not a rare phenomenon in close-knit Southern communities in which brothers and sisters sometimes married brothers and sisters; she would later become Vernon's loyal and very able secretary at Graceland. When Vernon was doing war work elsewhere, he sometimes came home on weekends, but mostly it was Gladys and Elvis alone again.

On one occasion, Vernon was very much needed, and he was not there. While he was working in Como, Gladys was brought to the hospital in Tupelo on a stretcher. She was in great pain. Elvis was holding her hand and crying. Gladys, it turned out, was having a miscarriage. She was distressed about the cost. She had only $10 to live on until Vernon returned, she said, and could not pay the hospital bill. Nurse Leona Moore told her not to worry. The county paid in situations such as hers. Still distressed, Gladys asked what would become of Elvis. Again, Nurse Moore said not to worry; she would send for Vernon's uncle Noah Presley to come and get him.

After Elvis died, Vernon insisted that he tried real hard to find a place in Memphis where he could live with his family and do war work too. He said he would knock on a door, in Memphis, that was advertising a place to rent. The landlord would ask about his family. A wife was okay, it seems, but when he said that he had a little boy, he would be sent away, sometimes abruptly as if he had presumed too much. Vernon implied that Elvis, simply by his existence, caused this separation between himself and Gladys. It was not easy, but other people came to Memphis to work during the war and found housing for their spouses and their children. Moreover, he had brought Gladys and Elvis with him to Ozark and Moss Point where he found lucrative war work, but soon quit both jobs.

All of this—the money, the knowledge that he was in high demand as a worker, perhaps the interest of attractive women whose husbands were away in the war, the relative lack of competition from other young men, the sheer distance from the Lee County jail and Parchman Farm—gave Vernon in his midtwenties more than enough to inflate his ego. World War II, it seems, was liberating Africa, Europe, Asia, and Vernon Presley.

Returning from Pascagoula and settling his family in East Tupelo again during the summer of 1943, Vernon went to work for L. P. McCarty and Son, a wholesale grocery business in Tupelo. Although he described himself on his income tax statement for 1943 as a salesman for McCarty and Son, there was not much selling to do in his job. He actually drove a truck delivering goods ordered by grocery stores for a dozen or more miles around Tupelo. It was a great job for a man who liked moving about, driving a truck, and, most of all, avoiding a boss who watched his every move. He stuck with that job, with one or two interruptions, for the next five years. The problem was that the job did not pay well.

The difference in weekly earnings between Vernon's war work and his truck driving was glaringly evident in his 1943 tax statement. At the shipyard near Pascagoula, he had earned $353 in five weeks, or about $70 a week. In working for McCarty for almost six months, he was paid $540, or about $21 a week. For the whole year, he earned $1,233, about $24 a week. Vernon apparently spent a lot of days in the first half of 1943 not working at all. His pay at McCarty's was very low, but it was a job he clearly liked.

ELVIS IN SCHOOL

While the war raged on, Elvis attended elementary school. In September 1941, he entered the first grade at East Tupelo Consolidated School. The consolidated school was created in 1926 by bringing together a number of small schools in the area. Economies of scale paid off magnificently in central heating, electric lighting, indoor plumbing, a gym, a playing field, and a student body that rose to about seven hundred students in twelve grades taught by thirty-six teachers—a comfortable ratio of about twenty students for each teacher. Superbly led by educator Ross Lawhon and staffed by well-educated and highly dedicated teachers, the new school became known as the best-run school in the county. It provided country kids—many of them bused in—with a substantial measure of preparation for their entrance into the modern world. For example, the high school under Lawhon developed special programs in agriculture, home economics, and business. Soon it also produced winning football teams, award-winning bands, and a well-deserved pride in itself. In the mid-1930s, it added a lunchroom—yet another highly successful project of the WPA—which allowed more hours to be added to the students' school day.

Gladys, who had perhaps achieved a third-grade level of education, was totally supportive of Elvis's schooling. Neighbors noted that every morning for years she would walk him the few blocks to and from school. For both mother and son, the public school was a bastion of order, sympathy, and steady support in a household that was recurrently thrown into turmoil and anxiety by the husband and father.

Elvis also enjoyed his first great success as an entertainer during these early school years. In 1943, at age eight, he sang on local radio accompanied on guitar by a man who had become his living idol, country and western singer Mississippi Slim. Slim's real name was Carvel Lee Ausborn. He regularly performed on Tupelo's station WELO, often with a local band, the Lee County Ramblers.

All over the South in pretelevision days there were country and western musicians like Mississippi Slim performing regularly on local radio, often sponsored by the producer of some miracle elixir or an economically priced furniture company, just as surely as the noontime obituaries would be sponsored by a local funeral home and read between clips of the hymn "Rock of Ages, Cleft for Me." Around town, the performer would stand out with his bold attire. In a community where men wore either overalls or khakis or coats and ties according to their station in life, he would stride about in cowboy boots, a silver buckle on his belt, dangling tassels on his jacket, and a ten-gallon hat. Usually, just in case you might not know who he was, he also carried his guitar wherever he went. Often he had a side-kick, younger, shorter, thinner, less handsome, and less voluble than he.

In Anderson County, South Carolina, for example, the singing cowboy was called "Tex." He performed on WAIM along with his apprentice, "Georgia Boy." They were sponsored by Hadacol, a marvelously restorative drink sold by a highly successful entrepreneur who floated into town and began to bottle the product in a small red-brick building on South Main Street that had been a corner branch of the Great Atlantic and Pacific Tea Company, "the A&P," before the advent of self-service required large stores with grocery carts and checkout stands. The Hadacol man covered all the windows in his building, and the door was always closed as if visitors were not welcome. The contents of Hadacol were both secret and suspect, like Coca-Cola, which many contemporaries thought contained a touch of cocaine. Somehow, local authorities were never able to determine exactly what was in Hadacol or what might be wrong with it. Knowing persons thought that the major active ingredient, unadvertised, was alcohol of a high proof. In any event, many local ladies of undeniable sobriety testified to its great medicinal value. Meanwhile, the Hadacol king bought one of the largest and most famous houses on North Main Street and tooled around at least three counties in a huge automobile.

Elvis was enthralled by Mississippi Slim. Ernest Bowen, an announcer at WELO, said that Elvis got Slim's attention by "following him around like a pet dog." Elvis tried to attend every show Slim put on at WELO, often hitch-hiking over from East Tupelo. Reggie Bell, one of the Lee County Wranglers, would sometimes pick Elvis up in front of the C&A Cleaners in East Tupelo and bring him to the station, where he would sit quietly and watch the show. Reggie worked regularly as an automobile mechanic. Finally, on one glorious occasion, Slim played guitar while Elvis sang on WELO's Saturday afternoon amateur program. After the show, Slim declared that Elvis had done pretty well considering his age, but complained that "the kid can't keep time." Even so, subsequently he sometimes had Elvis sing on his show.

In September 1945, when he was ten, Elvis's gift as a singer led his elementary school to enter him in the talent contest held yearly in Tupelo as a part of the annual Mississippi-Alabama Mid-South State Fair and Dairy Show. His talent had been discovered by his fifth-grade teacher, Mrs. J. C. (Oleta) Grimes, the daughter of Orville Bean. She persuaded the principal of the East Tupelo Consolidated School to enter him into the contest as a candidate sponsored by the school. In the show, Elvis stood on a box behind the microphone and sang "Old Shep," one of his favorites. Winners were identified by popular applause from an audience of about two thousand people. Elvis won fifth place. He had found his prestige piece—his singing voice.

A Bad Year—1946

On August 18, 1945, three days after the Japanese surrendered in Tokyo Bay, Vernon put down $200 in cash toward buying a brand-new, solid ("tongue-in-groove wooden siding") four-room house on Berry Street at the foot of the hill just below the little house where Elvis was born. The purchase price was $2,000. The seller was Orville Bean, the man who more than any other had sent Vernon to prison and then did more, perhaps, than any other man to get him out by writing a letter to the governor. Now, Bean supplied the Presleys with their second house.

Vernon always spent whatever money he made and spent it quickly. Where he got $200 to make a down payment on this new home is unknown. Quite possibly, he got it from his mother, Minnie Mae. Probably Minnie Mae brought her own assets to her marriage to Jessie and likely managed to keep some of them after the marriage. Just as Jessie clearly preferred his son Vester, Minnie Mae clearly favored Vernon.

In 1945, the Presleys moved up in the world, but during 1946 they fell terribly—very close to the bottom. In July, they lost their new

house. Vernon and Gladys had not done the basic math on the mortgage and fell behind in their payments. The math was not difficult.
Vernon had committed himself to pay $30 a month on the loan when
about $24 would have been much more manageable. His weekly pay
was only $22, which came to roughly $95 a month. After taxes and
other expenses, the Presleys would have mighty little to live on. In those
times, the rule of thumb was that rent or mortgage payments should
not exceed a quarter of one's income. It was a good rule, and for the
great majority of people it worked well.

Bean took possession of the house again and sold it to Vernon's friend
Aaron Kennedy for $3,000. Aaron made a very substantial down payment
of $760. Why Vernon himself did not resell his house for the $1,000 over
what he had paid is a mystery. Certainly he was behind in his payments
and could be held responsible for paying them off even if Bean foreclosed
the mortgage. As it was, the mortgage was not legally foreclosed; there
is no record of such a proceeding in the records of the Probate Court in
the Lee County courthouse. Perhaps he was simply unwilling to enter a
contest with Bean, and his friend Aaron bailed him out of the difficulty.

The rapid escalation in the value of the Berry Street house signaled a
national phenomenon that determined where the Presley family would
live over the next several years. After the war, as veterans came home
and rejoined or started families, there was a severe housing shortage in
America. Vernon had actually beat the veterans to the market and got
an excellent house at a good price before the crunch came. But in 1946
the veterans were home again, and the competition for any place to live
became exceedingly keen. For the Presleys from 1946 into 1954, the
struggle was always hard, and too often it was desperate.

TUPELO PROPER

In July 1946, when Elvis was eleven, the family moved out of its sturdy
new four-room home in East Tupelo and settled in a shack on the edge
of the city dump in Tupelo proper. The run-down wooden structure
they occupied on Mulberry Alley lay on the eastern edge of town in a
mostly black neighborhood called "Shake-Rag." The name came from

the assumption that the people who lived there wore rags. On wash days, they hung out their clothes on a line to dry. If there was wind, the raggedy clothes shook, signaling the poverty of the residents. In the eyes of the community, a white man in either Tupelo or East Tupelo could not have sunk further down in housing his family.

When Elvis started the sixth grade at Milam Junior High School in Tupelo in September 1946, his exceedingly low status in the social hierarchy became painfully apparent. East Tupelo had its own public school, and Milam included all the children of the wealthiest, best-educated, and most prestigious families in town as well as the poorest. Everyone in the school—students, teachers, and principal—was exceedingly conscious of precisely where in the social pyramid he or she and everyone else stood. It all depended on who "your people" were. Elvis was at the bottom, if not somewhere below the bottom, because his father was Vernon Presley, an ex-convict who drove a delivery truck, and he lived in a run-down shack in Shake-Rag near the city dump and among blacks. Evelyn Helms, also a student at Milam, recalled how other students used to laugh at Elvis because his house had no front porch.

Elvis's lack of status at Milam is still clearly visible in the formal photograph taken of his sixth-grade homeroom class. The students are posed with their teacher on several steps leading up to the school. Elvis, relatively slender and small, is the only one of twenty-four students (twelve girls and twelve boys) wearing overalls. His feet were hidden, but he is the only one without shoes. In East Tupelo, a school boy of eleven in overalls and barefooted in warm weather would have been totally unremarkable. Elvis is also the only child in the photograph not clearly smiling or making a pleasing face for the camera. Elvis felt keenly the class prejudices of his schoolmates. During the 1946–47 and 1947–48 school years, from boyhood into puberty, he felt it virtually every day.

SUNDAYS

Saving grace for the Presleys would come on Sundays. Vernon's employer allowed him to use the company truck to carry his family the long flat mile across the causeway and bridge over to East Tupelo to attend the Assembly of God Tabernacle. The building was not grand, but it was their church, and Vernon was still a deacon.

The congregation had a new minister, nineteen-year-old Frank Smith from Meridian, Mississippi. Reverend Smith sang and played the guitar. The Presleys joined in the singing. They sang about getting along with "meager fare" in this life, but flying away to glory on some future happy morning. One song they surely sang declared that "this world is not my home, I have no mansion here" and then moved on to contemplate their future life in a superior mansion in the sky. The Presleys decidedly had no mansion here, but in that little church on the edge of a swamp that had been drained to make a mile-wide stretch of farmland, they had a home for their souls. A literal reading of the Bible gave them a universe, and their songs gave them a simple and practical philosophy to deal with a life that seemed unfair and precarious. In those years in the South, new songs flowed into a continuing stream of gospel music to generate worldviews that made the lives of believers comprehensible, manageable, and even joyous in the face of a rapidly changing and often threatening material world. A line from one of the favorites of those years declared that "I heard a wreck on the highway, but I didn't hear nobody pray." Lyrics compressed truth into a few words like poetry. Put to music, they were easily remembered, savored, and earnestly and endlessly repeated. The church was a place where family and faith joined to make life whole, to put their minds at ease.

Elvis's homeroom teacher in the sixth grade, his first year at Milam, was Mrs. Dewey M. Camp. While organizing a talent show among her students at the beginning of the school year, she discovered Elvis. "He was so good," she recalled forty years later, so good in fact that she took him around to perform in the other two sixth-grade classrooms. His audiences were impressed, and every day thereafter he brought his guitar to school and would play and sing at the mere hint of an invitation.

Elvis got an audience, but he did not get acceptance. "Then, as now, if you weren't in the clique you were out," recalled Evelyn Riley, another Milam student. "We did enjoy listening to him sing. But Elvis was not popular."

1010 NORTH GREEN

In 1947, the Presleys moved into a comfortable little house at 1010 North Green Street, several blocks north of downtown. It was a house that almost no white people in Tupelo would have taken. It sat squarely in the middle of what whites called "Darktown." Elvis at age twelve could look out a back window of his home and see the black public school a hundred yards or so across a narrow weed-and-vine-covered ravine. Several buildings south on Green Street, above and just at the crest of a long, low hill, was the intersection that marked the heart of the African American community in Tupelo. All around this center were black-owned stores, cafes, a pool hall, a barber shop, a beauty parlor, a funeral parlor, the African American Masonic Lodge, the Elks Club, the African Methodist Episcopal Church, other churches, the black high school, the black graveyard, and the Sterling Library for African-Americans.

When Elvis walked to town or school he would have walked the short distance south up to the crest of the hill, then down the long slope on Green. On his left he might pass a pool hall with black music pulsing out of a jukebox, voices talking and laughing, the click and clatter of sticks and billiard balls, the hooded lamps and clouds of tobacco smoke over green baize covered tables. Green Street ran down the low hill alongside the white cemetery for a very long block, then through the more affluent part of town. At Jefferson Street, Elvis could turn right and walk three blocks to Milam school or left a couple of blocks to downtown where he might see a movie at the upscale Lyric Theater, across the street from the stone Confederate soldier on the courthouse square. More likely he would walk on down to the Strand Theater on West Main Street, where the movies were less pretentious and tickets, at ten cents each, were cheaper.

In East Tupelo, Elvis had lived in a virtually all-white community. Overwhelmingly, the whites there were working class. On North Green, he lived in the middle of a black world, where he gained an intimacy with that culture that was rare among white people. Elvis's exposure was different even from that of his parents, since he came to know the black community in Tupelo in ways that only a twelve- and thirteen-year-old white boy could know it. On Saturday afternoons, he walked past the bustling black businesses. On Saturday nights, he sensed all around him the excitement—music, talking, dancing, drinking, wooing, and fighting. Then, on Sunday mornings, he witnessed the quiet, decorous, best-dressed gatherings of worshippers in the church yards near his home, followed by the rich thick sound of gospel singing welling up and out of the churches and filling the air.

After the Presleys moved to Memphis in 1948, Elvis needed no tutoring in what black culture was about. He did not have to go to Beale Street in Memphis to begin to learn about black people, black life, and black music—blues, gospel, and honky-tonk. Without a doubt, with his almost miraculous ear and passion for music, virtually any music, he drank in those sounds and sights on North Green Street. When he was twelve and thirteen, they became a part of him.

The Presleys Recover

After moving over to Tupelo in 1946, Gladys went back to work at the Mid-South Laundry. If Vernon could not provide adequately for the family, then she must make up the difference. If Elvis wore overalls to school, she would see that they were clean overalls, properly ironed.

Soon after the move to North Green Street, Vernon's mother, Minnie Mae, moved in with them. Her husband, Jessie, had simply taken off in 1946 and never came back. In 1947, he sued Minnie Mae for a divorce. In his usual bold and outrageous way, he claimed that she had deserted him. She refused to join him, he said. Consequently, he refused to send her any money. Minnie Mae told the court that Jessie had deserted her, but the court gave Jessie his divorce and did not require him to pay alimony. Jessie eventually settled in Louisville, Kentucky, became a night watchman in the Pepsi-Cola bottling plant, and married a school-teacher. Much later, when his grandson Elvis became famous, Jessie attempted to put out his own record and become a singing star himself. He thought it was only right that he become rich and famous too. Jessie knew no modesty.

In 1947, the Presleys became relatively prosperous again, as their income tax return for the year shows. Vernon apparently worked about half the year for McCarty, earning $887, and the other half for another grocery company, D. W. Food Products, earning $756. Gladys worked as a seamstress at Reed Brothers, a department store, earning $269. Together, Vernon and Gladys earned $1,913, almost $160 a month.

The Presleys were definitely no longer poor, and their consumption rate went up. By February 1947, they had acquired a 1936 Chevrolet, and they paid for its repair in that month and again in April. In November, they bought a linoleum rug, a heater, a new mattress and springs, and an amazingly large number of pillows—eight pairs. They paid $17.30 down on the $77.50 price of these items. They made monthly payments until September 24, 1951, when the payments ceased. In October 1959, a letter requesting payment of the $22.76 balance was honored by Elvis's Memphis accountant. In January 1948, the Presleys bought a Philco radio-phonograph and paid $9 for sixty quarts of buttermilk apparently delivered to their doorstep by the Carr-Myers Dairy. In February, they bought an oil stove. In the same month, Gladys took Elvis down to the town library and got him a library card.

CHAPTER FIVE

MEMPHIS

Elvis had hardly started the eighth grade at Milam in September 1948 before one Saturday night in early November his father and his mother loaded him and all their movable belongings into and on the top of their 1937 Plymouth and headed for Memphis.

Long after they left—almost fled—under cover of darkness, some people believed that the reason was that "the law" had its eye on Vernon again. He had been dealing liquor out of his delivery truck, they thought. Also, there was an impression that vagrant animals—livestock with cash value, like pigs—had disappeared in the wake of Vernon's passing vehicle as it moved through the countryside. Suspicious-minded police officers might pick Vernon up and send him back to Parchman just because they didn't like him, his looks, and his manner, deacon of the East Tupelo Assembly of God Tabernacle or not.

Vernon's attitude did not help. As he grew older, he seemed to sink deeper into his sense of himself as persecuted and seriously undervalued in the world. He deserved more than he got. Whatever seemingly bad things he had done were justified by circumstances that were beyond his control.

In any event, Vernon and Gladys left Tupelo, where at least in 1947 they had enjoyed a very good income, and they went to Memphis, where they had no jobs and no place to live. There was no clear pull for them in Memphis, which implies that they felt a push to leave Tupelo and Lee County. Local people later recalled that L. P. McCarty fired Vernon sometime before he left Tupelo for reasons that are not clear. That probability is supported by the fact that Vernon began to borrow significant sums of money in April and May 1948. The amounts escalated in August and October. In April, Vernon took out a $120 loan from Tower Loan Brokers to be paid back in twenty monthly installments of $6 each. In May, he borrowed $63 to be paid back in twelve monthly installments of $5.30 each. In August, he borrowed $200 to be paid back in twenty weekly installments of $10 each. On October 19, he again borrowed $200 to be paid back in twenty weekly installments of $10 each. On Saturday night, November 6, he, Gladys, and Elvis left for Memphis. Probably portions of the $200 loans were used to repay previous loans. Probably the last loan also supplied the meager funds for Vernon to relocate his family.

It is easy to imagine thirteen-year-old Elvis crowded into the back seat of the car in the dark hours of Saturday night and Sunday morning with bundles of clothing and bedding, the car loaded on top and in the trunk with every household effect they could carry, the dash lights dimly lighting the faces of his parents, the headlights reaching up the white concrete highway. "We were broke, man," Elvis would later say earnestly to his friends in describing those times, "and we left Tupelo overnight." Finally, Elvis might sleep curled up in the back seat and then wake up early Sunday morning parked on a broad street in downtown Memphis, hearing the rich tones of the tolling bells of the old and elegant downtown churches—Calvary Episcopal Church on Second Street and the Presbyterian Church nearby. The Catholic Church was farther up Third Street—really the "Main Street" in Memphis—and across the street from the large apartment complex that was Lauderdale Courts.

On Sunday morning, only a week before, he had heard the bells of the African American churches at the top of the hill on the north side of Tupelo where he lived.

ROAMING LOVERS

Vernon knew Memphis well enough, and he knew what to do. He rented a room in a rooming house for $11 a week for his family at 370 Washington Street very near downtown. Travis Smith and his wife and two little boys, Bobby and Billy, also came to Memphis around the same time and moved into the same rooming house. Vernon and Travis took to the streets looking for work. Family tradition says that they actually wore holes in the soles of their shoes and had to stuff them with newspapers before they finally found jobs at Precision Tool. The plant was some two miles south on Kansas Street, and getting to work and back in Vernon's aging car was a challenge.

On Monday, November 8, 1948, Elvis began the eighth grade at Humes High School several blocks northeast of the rooming house on Washington. Gladys soon got a job sewing at Fashion Curtains nearby on Poplar Avenue. In February 1949, Vernon found employment closer to home. He got a job moving buckets at the United Paint Company, an easy walk to the north at Concord and Winchester Avenue. His pay was 83 cents an hour. With overtime, he could make up to about $40 a week at United Paint. By mid-June, the family had moved into one room of a large, red-brick Victorian mansion at 572 Poplar Avenue, several blocks northeast of downtown.

The Presley quarters in the rooming house on Poplar were much worse than at 1010 North Green Street back in Tupelo and close to on par with Shake-Rag. Their room, number 7, on the first floor, had a sixteen-foot-high ceiling and was one of sixteen rented rooms in the house. They cooked their meals on a hot plate and shared a bath down the hall with several other families and roomers and a colony of cockroaches. The rent was only $9.50 a week. A white man could hardly have found cheaper or worse housing for his family in Memphis. From time to time, Minnie Mae came up from Mississippi to join this already crowded household, living in a single room; at other times, she stayed with her other children.

GETTING INTO LAUDERDALE COURTS

On Friday, June 17, 1949, Ms. Jane Richardson called on the Presleys in their room at 472 Poplar. Ms. Richardson worked for the Memphis Housing Authority, where the Presleys had applied for an apartment in public housing, a highly desirable commodity in postwar Memphis. She had come to interview the family, observe their surroundings, and make a recommendation. It was a life-shaping event for the Presleys. Fortunately, Ms. Richardson's notes from her visit have been preserved.

Minnie Mae was absent on this occasion. Vernon was also absent, presumably at work. Gladys and Elvis were there. He was then fourteen years old. Mother and son would be scrubbed clean, plainly and neatly dressed, waiting in a room also carefully cleaned and neatly arranged. Gladys, representing the Presley family, introduced her son and answered the lady's questions. Elvis sat quietly by, attentive to the proceedings between the two women.

Ms. Richardson had power. She could provide Gladys the kind of housing her family so sorely needed. Gladys's skill in dealing with authority to save her family was on trial again, much as it had been when she secured the suspension of Vernon's prison sentence.

Gladys played her cards superbly. Ms. Richardson was appalled to learn that mother, son, and father "cook, eat, and sleep in one room." They shared a single bath with other roomers and had "no privacy." Of course, they had no phone, and their car, probably the 1937 Plymouth, in which they had trekked to Memphis, was barely operational, which impacted Vernon's ability to get to his job and earn a living for the family.

Ms. Richardson came to understand that Vernon was a steady, willing, and even eager worker. He earned 83 cents an hour at the paint company, which translated to $33.20 a week before taxes and withholding. Moreover, Ms. Richardson learned that Vernon was a diligent breadwinner who put in so much overtime that he brought in $40.38 a week. Vernon thus earned a very respectable $2,100 a year, which put their income well over the minimum required for public housing, but also kept it safely under the $2,500 that would have made them too prosperous to qualify.

Gladys apparently did not tell Ms. Richardson that she had worked at Fashion Curtains and might do so again, or take another job that might put their income above the limit. Also, she did not tell her that Minnie Mae had been a part of their household and might be so again. Instead, Ms. Richardson learned that every month Vernon sent $10 to his mother, who lived in West Point, Mississippi, and was dependent on him. Soon, Memphis city directories would reveal that Minnie Mae was back in the Vernon Presley household. They described her as a "widow," a more comfortable category, it seems, than "divorcée." Thus, Vernon emerged as a man who labored long, hard, and faithfully not only to provide for his wife and son but also to help support his dependent mother. The family had fallen into dire circumstances, but not from any dereliction of duty on his part.

Ms. Richardson bought what Gladys sold. By the time she wrote her report, sympathy had turned to respect if not indeed admiration. She remarked particularly on Mrs. Presley's son. "Nice boy," she wrote of Elvis. "They seem very nice and deserving," she concluded. Ms. Richardson even went so far as to recommend housing the Presleys in Lauderdale Courts if it were possible, rather than another complex farther away from the center of town, because it was "near husband's work."

Had Vernon walked into the room at the end of the interview, Ms. Richardson would have been at first favorably impressed. He was a fine figure of a man. He was intelligent and could appear mannerly, particularly to women. Had they talked for a while and had she begun to question him she would have perceived that self-pitying, whining, dodging character that marked his life and marred the lives of his wife and son. Vernon was not a steady worker, and he did not want to be a steady worker. During eighteen months in 1942 and 1943 he was either fired or quit work nine times. He did not like being under the eye and thumb of a boss. In the language of the day, he was "shiftless." He developed illnesses, and he missed days of work. Vernon apparently simply preferred to stay at home and do whatever he wanted to do or do nothing at all. In 1949, he turned thirty-three years old and was doing nothing to improve his income to support his family. In the early 1940s, he had been employed as a carpenter and for a time had paid dues to the carpenters union. In 1955, Elvis told an interviewer that his father "didn't have no trade."

Back in business-minded and progressive Tupelo, friends and relatives were doing better materially than ever before. Indeed, all over the South people had not done so well since before the Civil War, and—relatively speaking—they were doing better than any other region in the nation. During the Great Depression, President Franklin D. Roosevelt had declared that the South was "the nation's number one economic problem." In the 1950s that was decidedly not the case. Yet the best that Vernon had been able to do for his family after nine months in Memphis was to put four people (including extended visits from Minnie Mae) in a room with a hot plate for a stove and a cockroach-infested bathroom down the hall they shared with several other rooms full of people.

Even as a boy, Elvis more than made up for Vernon as a model man. In getting the family into Lauderdale Courts, he did so just by sitting there clean and well dressed, quiet, polite, and attentive while his mother painted an appealing family portrait for Ms. Richardson, who could give her the one thing she most wanted in this world, a decent place to live with the two people in the world she most loved. Her husband and her son were and always would be the center of her life, but especially Elvis.

It worked. Gladys divined what Jane Richardson and her superiors wanted and needed to see and hear, and she gave it to them in a superb performance. The authorities decided that the Presleys were among the "deserving" poor—to use Ms. Richardson's most significant and highly charged word. On Tuesday, September 20, 1949, they moved into apartment number 328 at 185 Winchester Avenue in Lauderdale Courts. Elvis had his own bedroom, Vernon and Gladys theirs. The Presleys had a full kitchen, a private bath, and a separate living room. With 689 square feet of floor space, with plumbing, electricity, and heating all managed for them, it was a palace in Memphis for the Presleys. Moreover, they were paying 10 percent less rent than they had paid for the single room on Poplar Avenue.

Gladys and Elvis played their deferential roles as white people of the lower orders to the hilt. Ms. Richardson was absolutely convinced that the whole family was "nice and deserving." All Vernon needed to empower fully his innate capacity as an excellent provider was decent housing within walking distance of his job. To the latter end, Ms. Richardson recommended specifically that the Presleys be assigned to Lauderdale Courts, the most desired public housing in Memphis.

Lauderdale Courts was a world unto itself—almost. The qualifier is necessary because the property was managed by Southern-born federal authorities who ruled from outside and "by the book." They kept the buildings in very good repair and the grounds neat and attractive. They also made regular announced inspections inside each apartment. Elvis would always remember his mother—not his father—preparing for those inspections, scrubbing the floors on her hands and knees, cleaning the stove and the toilet, and putting things in order, after working so hard all day at the hospital down the street. It was, in part, the image game again, making an appealing face to show people with power over her life. This game, however, was well worth the trouble. In her whole life, Gladys never lived in one place longer than she lived in the Courts, and before that she had never lived so well. In the sense that she knew what the rules were, she had never lived so securely.

Lauderdale Courts contained about four hundred apartments. Some were in single-story buildings, but most were in three-story structures, all surrounded by lawns, trees, and connecting concrete walkways. The Presley apartment was in the building in the northwest corner of the complex. The building faced on Winchester Avenue to the north and sided on Third Street to the west, a major north-south thoroughfare in the city. In the Presleys' building each of three entranceways led to nine apartments, three on each of the three floors. Their apartment was near the center of the building on the first floor, to the right of the north-facing entranceway. Elvis's bedroom window looked out on Winchester, the walkways, and the grassy yard.

A jog to the left from the front door of Elvis's building was North Third Street. Several blocks south on Third was the elegant Peabody Hotel, and two blocks farther was Beale Street, the core of black life in Memphis and for more than a hundred miles all around. Elvis had easy access to the center of the city, to the very hub and heart of the whole Mid-South. Only New Orleans rivaled it to the south, Atlanta to the east, St. Louis to the north, and nothing at all to the west.

In that it was all white and relatively classless, living in Lauderdale Courts was for Elvis somewhat like going back to East Tupelo. But this federal initiative in public housing was totally new and revolutionary in Southern culture. The race issue was quickly and simply sidestepped by strictly segregating apartment complexes. In Memphis, Lauderdale Courts was carefully created as all white and working class. African

Americans eligible for public housing dwelled exclusively in Dixie Homes several blocks to the east.

In the white South in the twentieth century, an individual's place in the pyramidal social hierarchy was indicated by numerous markers, including church membership, residence, style of dress, use of language, body language, circle of friends, and a certain use of titles in talking to one another. Blacks ordinarily would be called by their first names, plain white men would be called by their family names, and upper-class white men would be addressed by their titles—Mister, Professor, Reverend, Judge, Doctor, Colonel, Major, or Captain. There were rewards for keeping one's place in the societal order and punishments for transgressions. In Tupelo, a man's employer, minister, the mayor, the sheriff, and his landlord knew all about him, and they knew all about his relatives, "his people." For example, Dr. Green, a prominent Tupelo physician, owned the house at 1010 North Green Street that the Presleys lived in before going to Memphis. Dr. Green had put them into the house, and he could put them out, just as he pleased.

More to the point for the Presleys, Orville Bean was the descendant of large landowners and slaveholders, and he and others like him might have lost extreme wealth with slavery, but they possessed the knowledge and the manners to rule. He had put Vernon into prison and then played a major role in getting him out. He had also put him and his family into two houses and took them out of both. In Lauderdale Courts, relations between landlord and tenant were formalized and depersonalized. Tenants had rights. They could petition and appeal. They also had certain responsibilities, the appearance of cleanliness and orderliness, and paying the rent—in the Presleys' case $35 a month. The duties were clearly defined, and beyond those obligations they lived their private lives very much as they pleased.

Lauderdale Courts, in effect, represented an extraordinary experiment in social engineering within Southern culture. It sought out and recognized worth among working-class whites, and it devoted substantial public resources to their elevation. It was totally fitting that this was a New Deal—an outside—idea. The Courts offered dignity, security, and upward mobility to people of the lower orders just as did other New Deal programs such as the WPA. The goal was obscured a bit during World War II when space in Lauderdale was often given to serving the war effort. After the war, however, scores of young people came out of the Courts to become, eventually, business people, teachers, nurses, and lawyers. Hundreds attended public schools and acquired skills that landed them solidly in the middle class. The usual progression was to go to school, get and keep a job, develop a trade, marry, rent a home, and then buy one of their own. Soon there would be children, but only two or three, not the half dozen or more that many of their grandparents had reared.

In creating Lauderdale Courts, federal authorities in Memphis took a horizontal slice out of the Southern social pyramid, set it down as a whole piece on the northeastern edge of downtown, and gave it a significant measure of immunity from the informal and arbitrary sanctions that enforced the usual hierarchy. Economically speaking, in the Courts all whites looked alike. They were not poor, they were not on welfare, they earned their livelihood and paid their rent by working. Within the Courts, there was absolutely no pyramid of wealth, nor was there a social pyramid. For people who had suffered the slings and arrows of outrageous Southern white classism, as had Gladys, Vernon, and Elvis, it was a haven. Or it should have been, if Vernon had just kept working steadily and paid the rent.

HUMES HIGH

During the same month that the Presleys moved into Lauderdale Courts, September 1949, Elvis entered the ninth grade at Humes High School. At Humes, as in the Courts, the social pyramid was also truncated. It was a public school in a working-class neighborhood. Memphis city directories from 1949 to 1953 list household after household around Humes headed by house painters, delivery men, and drugstore clerks. A walk through the neighborhood at the end of the twentieth century showed many of their houses still standing, modest one-story wooden structures with wide front porches, screen doors, and swings hanging from chains.

Very few Humes students came from affluent families, and some came from poor families or families whose economic security was impaired by the absence of a breadwinning father. The latter was the case with George Klein, who became a favorite with both teachers and fellow students at Humes and would become a close, lifelong friend of Elvis after Elvis became a star. According to the city directories, George lived alone with his mother, Bertha Klein, in a house on Manassas Street just across the street from Humes High. Mrs. Klein worked as a seamstress in the Mid-South's premier men's clothing store, Halle's, on Main Street.

At Humes High, a working-class boy or girl, even a poor boy or girl, could stand out as a student leader, a scholar, an athlete, or a musician. George Klein stood out as a gadfly. Small and slight, bright and energetic, he was into everything—sports writer, sports announcer, sports manager (armed on the field with towels and water buckets for the players), editor of the yearbook, and class president. He was everywhere, seemingly, at the same time. His peripatetic nature was recognized, tolerated, and even valued by fellow students. When he and Elvis graduated in the class of 1953, George was voted "the most likely to succeed."

All of the kids in the eighth grade or above who lived in Lauderdale Courts attended Humes High. The democratic synergy of the two institutions was impressive. The Courts offered decent living space for the working poor, while Humes offered a way up to the comforts of middle-class life. Public housing was for the fortunate few; public education was for everyone. Thanks to Gladys, Elvis had both.

In the early years of the twentieth century, the controlling elite in the Southern states created public school systems out of whole cloth as a part of the effort to integrate the mass of white people into the culture they ruled, even as they pushed black people further away. Every child was required by law to attend school, and for white kids, the law was enforced with surprising consistency. One result was that talented children of the lower classes often developed the prospect, ambition, and means to rise into the middle orders and sometimes higher. The elite adopted the most talented of those who arose from the masses—even though it often took three generations to do so. The great mass entered the working class and earned relatively comfortable livings.

Such was the case with three teenage boys who became Elvis's closest friends. All three attended Humes High and lived in the Courts, two in Elvis's building. Farley Guy's father, who had worked for a railroad, died in 1949, and his mother moved into Lauderdale Courts. He loved horses and spent most of his adult life managing the stable at Shelby Farms in Memphis. Farley lived in the apartment just above Elvis, and their friend Paul Dougher lived directly above Farley. Evan "Buzzy" Forbess lived in an apartment nearby. Everyone recognized that he was one of Elvis's best friends during his high school years. Buzzy, though slight of build, was a football star. He spent the rest of his life working for Memphis's Light, Gas, and Water Division and came to live in a comfortable home in a white working-class neighborhood on the north side of town.

LIVING IN THE COURTS

Elvis lived in the Presley apartment in Lauderdale Courts for more than three years, longer than anywhere else in his life other than Graceland. These were critical years for Elvis, years in which he moved through puberty to young manhood. Everything should have gone smoothly for the Presleys. Vernon's job at the paint company meshed well with living in the Courts. Not only was it just down the street, his earnings there should have supported the family well. The Housing Authority had worked out the numbers carefully. With his salary, a family of three could occupy the two-bedroom apartment for $35 a month and live securely and comfortably. Hundreds of other tenants in Lauderdale managed just fine over the years, but within a year the Presleys were falling behind in their rent and were in danger of eviction. In the crisis, Gladys went back to work, first at Fashion Curtains, and later—for about ten days—tending the large coffee urn at Britling Cafeteria a few blocks over on Main Street.

Also during the summer of 1950, Vernon got a great idea for increasing the family income: he bought a push lawn mower for Elvis. Elvis and his friends started mowing lawns in the neighborhood. Vernon later liked to tell the story of how Elvis came home after his first day in the business. He put 50 cents on the table, as if that were the total return. Then he laughed and pulled $7 out of his pocket. Vernon was delighted. This was income that would not be reported to the housing authorities—or to the IRS.

In the fall of 1950, Elvis got a steady job working from 5 to 10 p.m. as an usher at Loew's State Theater on Main Street. In those days, movies ran continuously in an always darkened theater. The movie programs included a weekly news film and usually a cartoon. In an upscale theater, teenage ushers dressed in smart uniforms and equipped with flashlights escorted newcomers to their seats. When Gladys learned that Elvis was falling asleep in class, she made him quit this job. That fall, Elvis also got another uniform in which he showed pride. He joined the ROTC (Reserve Officer Training Corps) at Humes High. Photographs in the yearbook for the 1950–51 school year show him fitting into the student body neatly and not conspicuously.

As soon as school was out in June 1951, Elvis went to work at Precision Tool, by that time practically a family workplace for the Smith and Presley men in Memphis. His uncles Travis and Johnny Smith worked there, as did a cousin or two. The Korean War was raging then, and the company was producing casings for artillery shells at a high rate. Workers were in great demand, and Elvis was soon doing his part for the war effort by operating a drill press making rocket shells. He earned $27 a week.

Also in June, Vernon received a $10-a-month raise at United Paint. That raise was a curse in disguise. The paint company duly reported the increase to the Housing Authority, which raised the rent on the Presley apartment. Vernon felt the pressure. In September, he ceased making payments on furniture he had bought in Tupelo in November 1947. Elvis was now sixteen and no longer required by law to attend school. Vernon wanted him to quit school, take a regular job, and bring home some money. Gladys would not hear of it.

Back in school during the fall of 1951 for his junior year, Elvis at sixteen seemed a more self-confident young man. He was growing sideburns, so thin still that he was using hair coloring to prove that the sideburns were truly there. He also let his hair grow long and tortured it in several ways with applications that gave it a stuck-down look. He probably got his tonsorial ideas from the movies. In particular, he idolized the actor Tony Curtis, whose head was usually crowned with black, shiny, slicked-back hair. During the school day, everyone noticed that Elvis paid a lot of attention to his hair. His voice was changing, and his acne was on the rise.

Elvis also began to wear unusual clothes. As the school year progressed, other students raised eyebrows at his two-toned western-style shirts and stared unbelievingly at his black pants with pink stripes down the sides. The striped-pants concept might have come from his usher's uniform, though fellow students thought the effect made him look like a carhop in a drive-in restaurant or a bellboy at the Peabody Hotel. He had probably begun to acquire some of his clothes from Lansky Brothers, a store on Beale Street that catered to style-conscious young black men.

Elvis stood out in the student body for his style, but in no other way. His grades were a marvel of modesty. He belonged to a lot of clubs just as other kids did, but held no offices. That fall he did make an attempt to gain some masculine distinction. Elvis went out for football, but the coach said he would have to cut his hair to join the team. He declined, saying that he had to work anyway.

Actually, it appears Elvis did not work during the fall of 1951, but Gladys did. She took a job as a nurse's aide at St. Joseph's Hospital, just down the hill from her front door. It was the most gratifying work that she had ever done. Naturally outgoing and nurturing, she came to be respected, valued, and very much liked by patients and staff. Further, she earned $24 a week, more than she had ever made. In February 1952, however, she had to quit. The Housing Authority notified the Presleys that they were now making too much money to remain in their apartment under the present contract and threatened eviction. The Presleys apparently felt that they needed more spending money than the housing authorities allowed.

Vernon petitioned the Housing Authority for relief. He explained their excess income even as he pointed out that they did not have income enough. Again, he was the blameless victim of circumstances.

The trouble began some time before when he had not been able to work. There had been "illness in family," he wrote. It was Vernon who was ill. He had hurt his back. Hence, Gladys had gone to work of necessity, but now had quit. "Wife is working," he declared, "to help pay out of debt. Bills are pressing—and don't want to be sued." Vernon's illness, presumably, was unavoidable, and the family was struggling in good faith to make things right.

With seemingly infinite institutional patience, the Housing Authority gave the Presleys a new lease that would, presumably, fit their circumstances as described by Vernon. Rent would be reduced to $43 a month and maximum income would be set at $3,000 a year. By that time, if he were working full-time, Vernon's annual income might approach $2,400, or $200 a month. The new figure left a good margin for occasional earnings for Gladys. Also, Elvis might pick up a dollar or two here and there that would not be reported.

But Gladys and Elvis were not working, and in the early spring of 1952 the Presleys were broke again. About this time, Elvis's shop teacher saw that he lingered in the shop when the other students had gone to the cafeteria for lunch. He found that Elvis did not even have the price of the meal. The teacher gave Elvis lunch money then and continued to do so as needed. Vernon later confessed that some days he could not give his son more than a quarter for his lunch at school. It seems likely that some days he could not even give him a quarter.

The Presleys were again behind in their rent during that spring of 1952. They owed $43.74 in back rent and were being charged $1 a day penalty until the bill was paid. Once more, they faced eviction. Elvis went back to ushering at Loew's Theater. Five weeks into the job the manager caught him scuffling with another usher. The girl at the concession stand had been passing free candy to Elvis, the other young man had ratted on her, and Elvis wanted to hurt him.

There was probably much more to Elvis's aggressive action than first meets the eye. His mother had been forced to quit the job she loved at St. Joseph's, the family was broke and in danger of eviction, he was working as best he could while going to school, and it was all because Vernon could not manage to work steadily. In *Elvis and Gladys* Elaine

Dundy made much out of Elvis's attack on his fellow usher as "misdirected rage." The real target, she insisted, was Vernon.

Elvis was not able to confront his father directly. Nor could he confront his mother, who always sheltered his father. Instead, he assaulted a young man, ostensibly to defend the honor of a young woman passing out food and drink who might lose her job because of her kindness to him. Elaine Dundy argued persuasively that Elvis then and later showed himself "incapable of confronting his real enemies head on." It was, she said, his "fatal flaw."

Again and again Elvis's father had failed to take care of his wife and his son as any good man should. Vernon had a well-paying job at the paint company, and in Lauderdale Courts they should have been secure. But Vernon had developed that most mysterious, unaccountable, and debilitating of male ailments, the "bad back," which recurrently threw him out of work and the family into desperate financial straits. Gladys and Elvis had taken jobs attempting to make up the difference, but Gladys's very success in earning money at female labors—nursing, sewing, serving up coffee at Britling Cafeteria—brought threats of eviction from their home. Surely Vernon could have found another job that would not have strained his back, but he apparently made no effort to do so. There is no indication that he ever signed up with the state employment office to find suitable work, which Elvis himself did after he turned eighteen and even before he finished high school.

Although Vernon could hardly find lunch money for Elvis in the spring of 1952, he found money in June 1952 to buy a 1941 Lincoln Coupe and encouraged Elvis to think of it as "his." Elvis was thrilled. "My daddy was something wonderful to me," he told an interviewer in 1956, recalling the purchase. Fellow students at Humes saw Elvis driving the car—with cardboard substituting for one window—so much that they thought it did belong to him. Using the car, seventeen-year-old Elvis could commute to any paying job in or around Memphis, which he promptly did.

The Presley family finances here are puzzling, as always. In March 1953, they filed their federal tax form for 1952. It showed that Gladys earned $555.70 at St. Joseph's Hospital and Vernon earned $2,781.13

from United Paint. The two of them earned $3,336.83, or about $278 a month. Vernon alone averaged about $231 a month. It seems that even without Gladys working they should have been able to pay the $35, $43, or even $50 monthly rent for their apartment, enjoy a comfortable lifestyle, and also save enough to tide the family over during Vernon's illnesses. Yet he could not give his son more than 25 cents a day for his lunch at school. How could that be? Obviously, the Presleys were spenders, not savers. For them, paying the rent was clearly less important than buying or doing things. Their difficulties arose from a passion for consumption as well as inconsistency in earnings. They were simply unable to balance the family books. It was as if they could not count.

In the summer of 1952, after his junior year in high school, Elvis went to work in an upholstery shop and in one month made $109. After that, he went to work full-time, from 3 to 11 p.m., at MARL Metal Products, a furniture assembling company on Georgia Street near the river. No doubt the '41 Lincoln was very useful in getting Elvis the two miles to work and back every day. It was during that summer, Gladys later proudly remembered, that Elvis would take it upon himself to pay the bill at the grocery store, $25 to $30 a month. "We didn't ask him to do it," she added. "He'd just do it himself."

Elvis was eager to drop out of school and get permanent employment to help support the family. Vernon was totally supportive of Elvis's ambition. Gladys was adamantly opposed, and Vernon backed down.

In September 1952, Elvis went back to Humes to begin his senior year but kept his job at the metal shop. Again, he began to fall asleep in class. Mildred Scrivener, Elvis's homeroom and history teacher for the twelfth grade, saw him wake up when the end-of-class bell sounded one day. "Elvis, like a little boy, raised his head, got to his feet, and wandered out like a sleepwalker," she recalled. In applying for the job at the metal works, Elvis made himself exactly a year older than he was. In a penciled draft of their 1952 income tax form, the Presleys reported no income from Elvis.

"It got so hard on him," Gladys remembered, "he was so beat all the time, we made him quit." She went back to work at St. Joseph's Hospital. In November 1952, the Housing Authority projected the Presley family yearly income at $4,133, or about $344 a month, the highest yet. By common calculation, they should have been able easily to pay up to $86 a month in rent. Their projected income got them yet another eviction notice on November 17, 1952. They were to move out by February 28, 1953, more than three months later. Yet again, at least for the moment, the Presleys were too prosperous to enjoy the shelter of public housing. They would have to make room for some less fortunate family.

This time, they determined, seemingly with bitterness, to leave Lauderdale Courts. They left seven weeks before they were required to leave. After all, with a projected income of $80 a week, surely they could make it on their own. On January 7, 1953, the day before Elvis turned eighteen, they moved out of the Courts. Perhaps they stayed for a short time with kinfolk on Cypress Street in the lumber yards north of town. Soon, however, they were rooming at 698 Saffarans Avenue, just north of the Humes High campus.

By April, they were more permanently located at 462 Alabama Avenue, sharing a house with Rabbi Alfred Fruchter and his wife, Jeanette. Their landlord was a widow whose husband had been a kosher butcher. The rent was $50 a month. Elvis turned on electricity and gas for the Fruchters on the Sabbath when they as Orthodox Jews could not do so for themselves. The Fruchters and the landlady sometimes helped the Presleys with their finances. "They never had much," Mrs. Fruchter said, but every Saturday morning Vernon and Elvis would "polish that old Lincoln like it was a Cadillac."

GLADYS—TROUBLE IN MIND

The Presleys seemed comfortable in their new home on Alabama Avenue, but the years of strain, struggle, and anxiety had taken its toll on Gladys. Her decline had already become apparent in Lauderdale Courts. Farley Guy remembered her as "a sort of sickly woman." He recalled that "she walked around a lot dressing only in her housecoat and gown." Minnie Mae stayed with them often. "Mister Presley was always real quiet and smiling all the time. No matter what mood he may have been in at the time, he was always smiling." In April 1952, when Gladys turned forty, the family was behind in their rent, and she began to brood about her life and its losses. She had lost two babies, but she dwelled specially on the death of Elvis's twin.

Gladys began to worry about her looks. She was several years Vernon's senior, though later she usually would claim that she was the same age as her husband. Trying to look younger, she blackened her hair more deeply. She altered the color of her lipstick. She used eye shadow and a bit of mascara to emphasize her dark eyes. She began to take diet pills, hoping to lose weight. She and Vernon often went to the movies and stopped off for a beer on the way home. Now Gladys began to drink more than one or two beers on such occasions. In time, she did not need to be in a bar to drink them.

Coming home at night, Elvis would find his mother in moods that must have frightened him. She was either very happy, very excited, or she was sad and tearful, remembering him in his childhood. He would try to calm her down, petting her, calling her "baby," and using the especially intimate loving language they had developed in his childhood.

Increasingly it became apparent to Elvis that his father would never steadily support or take care of his mother financially or emotionally. That duty would fall to him, and he was ready and eager to begin. Nothing was more important to him. Buzzy Forbess remembered that Elvis, Farley Guy, and he would sit around and talk about what they wanted to do with their lives. Farley wanted to be a baseball player. Buzzy wanted to be a football player. And "Elvis always said he wanted a job where he could provide for his mother and father."

During the summer of 1952, the problem reached a crisis point. It was then that Elvis began to pay the grocery bills without telling either parent. He might have connected Gladys's extreme moods, her drinking, and other disturbing signs in her behavior to Vernon's inability to earn a steady income and save them from recurrent threats of eviction and other humiliating circumstances. Quietly paying the grocery bills was a way of helping his mother without embarrassing his father.

As an adult looking back, Elvis would say to his friends with emphasis, "We were poor, man!" Vernon's federal tax returns show that the Presleys earned enough money to live comfortably. They were definitely not poor. Friends and neighbors were sometimes amazed at the things that the Presleys had—a telephone, a record player, a radio, a car. Yet they were recurrently in dire financial straits.

It must have seemed to Elvis that his family had little or no power in the world, and neither did he. He was frustrated, angry, and rebellious. His rebellions assumed forms that were strikingly apparent. He began to cultivate differences that appeared bizarre to his schoolmates and were bound to excite animosities, especially from other boys. It was as if he were asking for a fight. He may have been a rebel with a compelling cause, but the cause was exceedingly unclear.

In the fall of 1952, when Elvis decided to return to school for his senior year instead of going to work full-time, his clothes, hair, and demeanor seemed to explode in a riot of difference. Nobody else in school looked like him. He would wear dress pants when other boys would wear ordinary pants. He would wear loafers when they wore shoes. He acquired a chest-hugging black bolero jacket and a pink and black sports coat. Sometimes, he wore his coat and tied a scarf around his neck like an ascot. He continued to wear trousers with colored stripes down the sides. He treated his hair as his crowning glory, letting it grow long, pouring on the stickum, and combing it often and carefully. One day, he showed up at school having given himself a permanent wave. All of this came from the movies, from Lansky's clothing store on Beale Street, and from Elvis's fertile imagination in matters of dress and appearance.

The goal was to look different, to stand out by assaulting the eye with objects that were out of place. The disjunction compelled attention and sent a message. Ultimately, it was a play for attention, for audience, a cry for recognition of looks, talent, and worth. First it demanded attention; then it invited rejection; then, hopefully, consideration and acceptance.

Elvis got attention, but not always the kind he would have liked. He stood out in a manner that some students, themselves adolescent and vulnerable, took as defiant and insulting. Elvis was weird, "queer," a target for would-be lynchers, and he brought it upon himself. Later in life, he recalled with great bitterness that in this stage of his life it was as if some people said, "Hey, look at that squirrel up there in the trees—let's *get* him!" He was never physically attacked, but the threats were real. His friends from the Courts, both girls and boys, defended him always.

SENIOR YEAR

At the very same time that Elvis was presenting an image of generalized and bold rebellion to the world, he was offering every sign of deference to the authorities in his life, and they responded accordingly. As always, he answered his elders with "yes, sir" and "yes, ma'am." His home-room teacher, Mildred Scrivener, was highly sympathetic to Elvis, and so too were other teachers. When he finished Humes High, the year-book picked Elvis and two others out of a class of a couple hundred to label as "teacher's pet." He obviously felt the need to advertise his distress in his provocative appearance and at the same time plead to sympathetic authorities for protection and relief, working hard for it with the tools that his mother had taught him to use.

Recognition came much too late at Humes High for Elvis's overall happiness there, but it came just in time to begin the revolution that would change his life. As it happened, Miss Scrivener was in charge of managing the school's annual "Minstrel Show," scheduled for Thursday evening, April 9, 1953. Such productions were typical in high schools all over the South. A school band provided the music. More than a dozen students in blackface, seated onstage in a long row of chairs, sang and swayed. "End men" on either side of the singers, also in blackface, shook tambourines, talked loudly back and forth, and made jokes, while "Mr. Interlocutor," a white-faced, elegantly suited white student seated in the middle of the group, acted as the master of ceremonies. Schools could easily buy packets from music publishers that laid everything out—music, words, costumes—for the players.

At Humes that year, the Minstrel Show was combined with a talent contest. After the "Grand Opening," little five-year-old Helen Pittman did her baton twirling act. Later in the program, the Arwood twin girls did their baton twirling act. A quartet sang, three girls played the xylophone, and individuals sang, danced, did acrobatics, and played various instruments. Joanna Massarano, for instance, did a solo on her accordion.

At appropriate times all through the show, the band played, the singers sang, and the tambourines rang. One of their songs, "Kentucky Babe," was a required number in any high school minstrel show. "Fly away, Kentucky babe," it went. "Fly away to rest. Fly a-wayyyy… a-wayyyy…a-wayyyy…" They would sing lustily, heads up, mouths open wide, young voices charming and delightful, but not quite in harmony.

Elvis signed himself up for Miss Scrivener's show. He was number sixteen on the bill of twenty-two acts. He came after a student sang "Old Man River" (no doubt in blackface) and the band and singers did "Beautiful Ohio," another staple of a minstrel show.

When Elvis's turn came, he strung his guitar around his neck and slouched out onto the stage. For a few moments, he affected the manner of a shy and surly youth, looking sideways at the audience of more than fifteen hundred students and teachers. Then he swung his body around and plunged into "Till I Waltz Again with You," a song recently made very popular by "the little girl with the big voice," Teresa Brewer. The audience was briefly aghast, then highly responsive, making a great clamor and ending with loud applause. It was said that one eighth-grade girl actually fainted.

Audience response determined the winner, and it was Miss Scrivener who made the call. "It's you, Elvis," she said. "Go on out there." Elvis went out for his encore and again received tumultuous applause. "They really liked me, Miss Scrivener," he exclaimed ecstatically to her as he came offstage again. "They really liked me."

Recalling the scene years later, Elvis saw the occasion as one in which his performance onstage radically changed the way his peers saw him. "I wasn't popular in school," he said. "I wasn't dating anybody [there]. I failed music—only thing I ever failed. And then they entered me in this talent show…It was amazing how popular I became after that." In fact, Elvis had dated girls in Lauderdale Courts, and he never failed a music class. In Elvis's mind "they," not "I," entered "me" in the talent show. It was as if some authority must give him a stage and an audience, and only then would he become someone really worth knowing.

Emotionally, Gladys and Vernon were the two most important people in Elvis's life. Yet it was three female teachers in the public schools in Tupelo and Memphis who first gave Elvis the opportunity to develop his powerful talent for entertaining and, in the process, a feeling of self-worth in the broad world.

JOBS

On Wednesday evening, June 3, Elvis graduated from Humes High. Two months earlier, on March 26, he had walked into the Tennessee Employment Security Office and put his occupational future in their hands. In filling out his part of the application form, he wrote that he was five feet eleven inches in height and weighed 150 pounds. For recreation, he liked "sing[ing], playing ball, working on car, going to movies." In answer to the question of how he had prepared himself for the workforce, he wrote that he would finish Humes High and had taken two years each of English, wood shop, ROTC, and science. In addition, he had belonged to the speech and biology clubs. The woman who interviewed him said that he "wants factory work at once—must help father work off financial obligations." He also indicated that he "owns an automobile."

Elvis took a battery of tests, which led the interviewer to conclude that he "was mechanically inclined, but should avoid fine work with fingers." Elvis himself had said that he would not want to be a machine operator, "but thought [he] might like industrial maint. [maintenance] + repair." The woman who interviewed Elvis read him well. "Rather flashily dressed—'playboy' type," she wrote, but immediately noted that his appearance was belied "by fact [that he] has worked hard past 3 summers." With all of the talk about mechanical skills, she nevertheless wrote that he "wants a job dealing with people."

On May 6 Elvis was in the employment office again, but no entry was made in his record. The office called on July 1 and referred him to the M. B. Parker Company, a machine shop, for a temporary job as an "assembler." He began work the same day at 90 cents an hour. His take-home pay was about $33 a week. Each week, he took a few dollars out for himself and gave the rest to his father, not his mother. Vernon took it.

Elvis's job with Parker ended on Wednesday, July 29, and the next Monday, August 3, he was back in the employment office again. He was not happy with work in a factory and "expressed [a] desire for a job where he could keep clean." The people in the office tried to oblige. On August 5, they put him in touch with Sears, Roebuck, but Elvis could not get an interview. The next day, he got two interviews, one to work as a "delivery boy" for $35 a week and another at Kroger's, a grocery chain, but neither hired him. Six weeks later, having garnered no other leads from the employment office, Elvis went back to Precision Tool. He had only worked one month out of three since finishing high school.

Elvis worked for Precision Tool for six and a half months, quitting on March 19, 1954. His tax return for 1953 showed that his taxable income from Parker was about $130 and from Precision $786. His total taxable income from July 1 to the end of the year was $916. A pay slip for March 1956 indicated that he was then getting $62 for a forty-hour workweek and that his pay after deductions would amount to about $40. As far as we know, Elvis, unlike his father, never missed a day of work once he had a job.

CHAPTER SIX

DIXIE LOCKE AND SAM PHILLIPS

DIXIE LOCKE

In the fall and winter of 1953–54 Elvis worked steadily. In the normal course of events, he would have a time of youthful bachelorhood in which there would be a number of girls, then one girl, and soon marriage and children. He passed through the first stage, and in January 1954, when he was nineteen years old, he found that one girl. Her name was Dixie Locke. He loved her, it seems, virtually on first sight. And she him.

Before Dixie, Elvis was not marvelously successful in his courtships. It was not for lack of trying. Even as a young boy back in Tupelo, he had been interested in girls, but his choices were less interested in him. Magdalene Morgan was a tall, handsome girl the same age as Elvis. At age ten, they were photographed together, charmingly standing side by side, she taller than he, in the church yard in East Tupelo. When he was thirteen years old, several weeks before the Presleys left for Memphis, Elvis took his parents' marriage license and wrote his name in the space with his father's and Magdalene's name in the space with his mother's. Interviewed decades later, Magdalene was amazed that he had done that. They were friends and they had held hands, she said, but she never thought of their relationship as a romance

Elvis's first love in the Courts was Betty McMahan. Betty lived on the third floor above him. When she first moved in she talked to him from the open window of her apartment while he stood in the yard below. She would not come down, she said, because she felt she didn't have anything decent to wear. Soon there was a knock on her door. It was Elvis; he had brought her a pair of blue jeans.

Betty began dating a boy from Arkansas, but already Elvis was courting fourteen-year-old Billie Wardlaw, who lived just across the hall from Betty. "Elvis was a great kisser," Billie later recalled, but he was very shy. Happily for Elvis, when they played the kissing game "spin the bottle," they did so in the dark. Also, when Elvis played his guitar and sang at teenage parties in the Courts, he insisted on having the lights turned out. Often he performed especially for the girls. His aunt Lillian thought that he preferred the company of girls much more than that of boys. "He was different with the girls," she remembered.

Elvis definitely needed female attention. He worked hard to get it, and when he got it he was very possessive. When he lost it, he suffered acutely. Billie Wardlaw experienced this cycle. She met a sailor at the USO Club on Third Street and began to date him while she was still seeing Elvis. He was very upset. One day he happened to see a young man's picture in her wallet and responded violently. "He grabbed it out of my purse and began stomping and grinding it into the ground with the heel of his shoe," she recalled. One night she finally announced to Elvis that she was ending their relationship, and "he started crying." She had never before seen "a man, or a boy, cry," she said.

Elvis's popularity in high school came a bit too late for him to find a new girlfriend there. He probably continued to date girls from the Courts, and certainly he began a long and close friendship with his cousin Gene Smith, with whom he double-dated. Gene also worked at Precision Tool. Using code words, Elvis and Gene had created a way of communicating with each other that other people had difficulty understanding. No doubt, the girls they were with found them more than a little strange as the four of them drove around in the old 1941 Lincoln to the movies, the drive-ins, and the parks with the boys gibbering away in their own language.

DIXIE

In January 1954, Elvis began attending the Assembly of God Church on McLemore Avenue, some two miles south of downtown. His cousin Gene came with him. Perhaps they went there to meet girls, but for

Elvis there was much more to it than that. He wanted to sing in a gospel quartet. For years, he had attended Saturday all-night gospel sings at Ellis Auditorium, two blocks from the Courts. Recently, those events had been organized by the Blackwood Brothers gospel quartet, which had moved its "home church" from Shenandoah, Iowa, to this much more suitable church in Memphis. Elvis could not hope, of course, to sing with the Blackwood Brothers, but there were also amateur quartets around, one of which had been spawned by the Blackwoods out of the church on McLemore. As he had learned to do, without demanding attention, he was putting himself in the eye of those who had the power to do something with his talent, to put him on a stage in front of an audience and let him sing.

At church, Elvis met Dixie Locke. Fifteen, bright, balanced, and beautiful, Dixie first saw Elvis soon after he began to attend church. Tall, clothed in pink and black with long, greasy, dark blond hair, he stood out in a crowd. "He was just so different," she recalled for Elvis's biographer Peter Guralnick some four decades later. "All the other guys were replicas of their dads." Elvis decidedly was not a replica of his dad.

One Sunday while seeming to talk casually with some of her friends at church, Dixie deliberately talked loudly enough for Elvis to hear that she was going skating with girlfriends at the Rainbow Rollerdrome on Saturday. When she got to the Rollerdrome that night, she saw him. He was wearing his bolero jacket over a ruffled shirt and pegged black pants with pink stripes down the legs. She introduced herself to him. "Yeah, I know," he said, hanging his head, then raising it and tossing his hair sidewise. Of course he knew who she was; that was why he was there after a week of sanding down artillery shells and measuring the thickness of shell casings at Precision Tool.

Elvis invited Dixie for a Coke. Then he began to talk. And talk. He talked until ten o'clock and still that was not enough. He invited her to K's Drive-In for hamburgers and milkshakes. She sat close to him in the old Lincoln and gave him a chaste kiss in the drive-in parking lot. They ate and talked, and talked some more, and finally he drove her home; she lived just off South Third Street. Elvis had found an audience of one—other than his mother—who accepted and liked him for who he was. As for Dixie, she knew that it was love. The next night they went to the movies.

Dixie's parents and three sisters were not so sure about this boy. The hair and the pink clothes gave them pause. One of Dixie's sisters had eloped at fourteen and was back home again. Her father grilled Elvis. Mr. Locke was a big man, six-two and strong. The boys who came calling on his daughters were generally intimidated by him. Elvis, as always, met authority with cast-down eyes and great deference. "Yes, sir. No, sir," he would say. Dixie's mother grilled her in the kitchen while her father talked to Elvis in the front room of the flat in which they lived on the south side of town. Dixie defended Elvis vigorously. Looks deceive, she said. She had met him at church. He was nice.

Elvis was exceedingly anxious about introducing Dixie to his parents. He thought the Lockes were of a higher social class. In reality, he was probably impressed by the fact that Mr. Locke worked hard to earn a steady support for his wife and four girls. The Lockes seemed to feel secure in a way he had never known.

Two weeks later, Dixie met the Presleys at their home on Alabama Avenue. Mrs. Presley sent Elvis and Vernon out of the room and then interrogated Dixie. Mr. Presley seemed to have nothing to say. He was out of work with a bad back. Mrs. Presley was no longer working at St. Joseph's Hospital. Elvis was the only one working and the sole support for his family. Even so, the Presleys had a television set, a telephone, and a piano, all possessions the Lockes did not have. A day or so later, Dixie asked Elvis what his mother thought of her. She learned that Gladys really liked her. What Vernon thought seemed not to matter.

After the first meeting, Gladys rushed to embrace Dixie with striking rapidity. They talked over the phone often and at length, Dixie using a neighbor's phone. Dixie began taking the bus up to Alabama Avenue after school while Elvis was still at work. They developed a woman-to-woman relationship centered on Elvis that did not include him. Gladys shared her recipes with Dixie and took her to a Stanley Products house party, where a local woman invited homemakers from all around the neighborhood to socialize, try out utensils, and buy household goods at low prices. Gladys and Dixie often went shopping together, maybe to get something personal—like clothing—for Elvis. They talked about him a lot.

Once, a girl from the Courts stopped by while Dixie was there. She seemed to have some special claim on Elvis and the Presleys. When the girl left the room to prepare a drink for the three of them, Gladys reprimanded Dixie. "I could just pinch you," she said. "Why did you sit there and let her take over? Don't you ever do that again. You know you're just as at home here as Elvis is. You get up and do something next time, just like you would if you were in your own home." Gladys was like a second mother to her, Dixie thought. Obviously, Gladys was training Dixie to become Elvis's wife.

Dixie soon saw that the Presley family was very different from other families. They seemed uneasy in the world, suspicious. "Mrs. Presley was a very humble person," she said. "It was almost like she felt inferior around people where she didn't feel like she quite fit in." Vernon was strange. "I never saw him be unkind. I never saw him drink or be unruly," she said. "I'm sure he was a very loving husband and devoted to his family." But "it was like he was an outsider, really, he wasn't part of Elvis and Mrs. Presley's group." Elvis and Gladys loved and respected each other, Dixie thought, but "I didn't think there was a lot of respect for him during that time."

Dixie compared Vernon unfavorably with her father. Vernon's "bad back" was excuse enough for him to stay home rather than go to work. Dixie's father also did heavy lifting in his job with the Railway Express Company, which transported packages, parcels, and freight rapidly. Dixie had seen her dad "go to work with a brace on his back for years." Her father was a real man, a provider and a protector, and Vernon was something less.

It was not that Vernon was bedridden or housebound by his affliction. Occasionally, he even drove down to pick Dixie up after school and bring her home to meet Elvis when he got home from work. But when Vernon did not feel like driving, Dixie had to take the bus. Vernon was not dependable. "It was almost like Elvis was the father," Dixie concluded, "and his dad was just the little boy.

CROWN ELECTRIC

On Friday, March 19, 1954, Elvis quit his job at Precision Tool after they made him get a haircut. He was so ashamed of his new look that he hid behind a clothesline full of clothes so that Dixie's mother could not take his picture. The loss of income must have thrown the Presley household into turmoil again. Two weeks later, on Tuesday, April 6, Elvis was back at the state employment office. He told them that he had worked at Precision Tool for six and one-half months and was in the process of doing a "reevaluation" of his place in the workforce. He did not bring up his previous preferences for working with people or keeping clean, nor even in machine maintenance. Now he thought that a "machinist appr. [apprentice] job would be fine." He "really wants to operate [a] 'big lathe,'" the interviewer noted, putting "big lathe" in quotes. Probably, Elvis equated "big lathe" with big money, and the quotes inserted by the interviewer indicated to the staff that they should not narrow their search for a fitting place for Elvis in the working world to operating a large lathe. Nor did they. This time they made a match for Elvis that included love as well as money, but not much money.

On April 20, 1954, the employment office sent Elvis to interview for a job with Crown Electric Company on Poplar Avenue just around the corner from where he lived. The company was owned and run by Jim and Gladys Tipler, a middle-aged couple. Before Elvis came for the interview, the woman who sent him called from the employment office to tell the Tiplers that he was a nice boy who simply looked different. The Tiplers hired him immediately after he said that all he wanted to do was to take care of his mother. Soon he was driving a Crown Electric panel truck delivering supplies to electricians who were working all around town. Women in public schools and women in public housing had saved Elvis before. Now women in the public employment service did the job.

Elvis's take-home pay was about $41 a week, substantially less than the $62 a week he had earned at Precision Tool. But, just as Vernon during World War II found driving a truck delivering goods to grocery stores much more congenial than working as a carpenter in wartime jobs, Elvis found driving a delivery truck for an electrical contractor much more congenial than working in a plant producing artillery shells. Earning money, after all, did not seem to be the most important thing in the world for either man. Elvis could keep relatively clean, do his hair how he pleased, deal with people, and drive a truck around Memphis and its environs all day with his guitar by his side. Sometimes Dixie joined him in the panel truck.

Every Friday Elvis continued turning over his pay to his father, taking out just enough to take Dixie to a double-feature movie at Suzore No. 2, have hamburgers and milkshakes at the drive-ins, and buy gasoline for the Lincoln. During the winter and spring, Elvis also took Dixie to gospel sings at Ellis Auditorium, to the annual Minstrel Show at Humes High in March, and to the talent contest there in April. Dixie came over to the Presleys' for Easter dinner on Sunday, April 18, and in early May they attended the Cotton Carnival and an Oral Roberts revival. It was a beautiful life. Possibly, Elvis was again at the employment office on June 4 and 29. With a take-home salary of $41 a week and rent at $50 a month, perhaps the Presleys were in money trouble again, and Elvis was thinking "big lathes" again. In any event, nothing happened.

Elvis and Dixie were always together when not at work or in school. Often they were alone, and at times they were with Elvis's kinfolk. Indeed, the Presleys seemed to have few friends who were not kinfolk. Elvis's closest male friend was still his cousin Gene Smith. When Elvis took Dixie over to Humes High during school hours for a visit, she met boys who had previously been his friends both there and in the Courts but learned that he no longer saw them.

It seemed to Dixie that increasingly she and Gladys were his whole life. He began to talk to Dixie in the baby-talk way he talked to his mother. He would put his face up close to her face and tell her how sweet she looked. He did so in front of Gladys, and Dixie was afraid it might offend her, but she continued in her affectionate ways. Everyone seemed to assume that they would marry, and everyone seemed fond of the idea. At one point they talked of running off to Hernando, Mississippi, just across the state line to get married. It could be done in Mississippi in a matter of hours, start to finish, provided that both parties were either black or white and over thirteen years old. They decided, however, to wait a while.

Dixie was not aware of the depth of Elvis's ambition for a career as a singer. She thought he was simply a boy who loved music and played the guitar for fun. She did notice, however, that his shyness did not at all preclude his performing informally before any audience if someone asked. Elvis, she saw, loved attention, any attention. She had seen it in Bible class when the new kid with the long hair and strange clothes engaged himself intensely in whatever subject was under discussion. Increasingly, she realized how Elvis would work hard not merely for attention but to be the center of attention, however briefly, whatever the audience. It was one role in which he felt comfortable. Dixie saw that he could perform easily for a roomful of people. She thought he could perform as easily for thousands.

Dixie also learned that Elvis adored gospel music. They faithfully attended the monthly all-night sings that the Blackwood Brothers organized. She knew that he aspired to sing with an amateur gospel quartet, but it came as a total surprise that he also aspired to sing country and western. She went with him one night to the Bel Air, a country and western nightclub, where the management gave him a trial run. He was clearly a failure. Elvis seemed to be a natural-born truck driver, the audience implied by its response.

On July 3, Dixie and her family left for a two-week vacation to visit relatives in Florida. When she returned she found that the young man she expected to marry had become a celebrity in Memphis. The catalyst for the change was a brilliant young record producer named Sam Phillips.

Sam Phillips

Sam Phillips, born in 1924, was reared on a two-hundred-acre farm near Florence in northwestern Alabama, where he drank thirstily from the broad stream of black culture that flowed all around him. As a boy, he would stand outside an African Methodist Episcopal church just down the road from his own church and listen while the congregation sang and music poured out of the open doors.

More intimately, there was an older black man, Uncle Silas Payne, who worked for his father. Silas would tell him stories about mythical sausage and butter-cake trees in Africa and about the Molasses River. It was as if both man and boy had taken their script from Joel Chandler Harris's Uncle Remus tales. Uncle Silas was Uncle Remus, comfortably settled on the floor of the open doorway of his cabin on the mountain, smoking his pipe, telling stories to Mars Tom. At Uncle Silas's feet young Sam learned about the richness and wisdom of black life and made it his mission to convey it to white people. Uncle Silas also played the guitar and the harmonica and told Sam about Beale Street in Memphis.

Sam loved music, but his experience as a musician ended when he left high school and gave up playing the tuba in the school band. His genius, he soon discovered, was in reproducing music by electronic means. In 1945, Sam came to Memphis with a wife, a son, and four years of experience in radio in northern Alabama and, briefly, Nashville, Tennessee. He went to work for station WREC, where his older brother Jud sang with the Jolly Boys Quartet. Soon, he became the engineer for the nighttime nationwide broadcast over CBS of the big bands that played in the rooftop Skyway Room of the Peabody Hotel. Increasingly, he grew frustrated with the formulaic, stiff, stilted manner of the big bands. He was irritated by the sight of the always carefully made-up beautiful girl singer attired in an evening gown sitting on the stage, hands folded demurely in her lap, and the rows of identically dressed musicians all mechanically turning the pages of their music at the right moment in spite of the fact that they had played the same song in the same way a thousand times and could have written it out from memory. It was all too boringly predictable. "I was shooting for that damn row that hadn't been plowed," he told Elvis's biographer Peter Guralnick four decades later, using the imagery of his rural origins.

In January 1950, Sam established his storefront Memphis Recording Service at 706 Union Avenue, a few blocks east of the WREC studios in the Peabody Hotel. His company would do anything, record anything—weddings, bar mitzvahs, recitals, anniversaries—to survive, but Sam put it there, he said, to give some of the "great Negro artists" a chance to be heard. He said he wanted "genuine, untutored Negro" music. He wanted "Negroes with field mud on their boots and patches in their overalls . . . battered instruments and unfettered techniques."

Sam survived, but barely. He was working eighteen hours a day. In the studio, he was recording "cotton patch blues" as well as rhythm and blues. Sometimes he sent his recordings to a "race" label—such as Chess in Chicago or RPM located in the Watts area of Los Angeles—which would market the record through its well-established networks. One of his best records, appearing in late 1951, was B. B. King's "Three O'Clock Blues." Another, "Rocket 88" by Ike Turner and his saxophonist and sometimes singer Jackie Brenston, held first place on the nationwide rhythm and blues chart for seventeen weeks. Seminal in the R&B movement, it became a classic. All in the same day, Sam might wire a baseball stadium for sound, go to the studio to record primal blues man Howlin' Wolf (Chester Burnett), then go on to the Peabody for the late-night Skyway broadcast.

Respected by his fellow workers for his skills as an electronics engineer, Sam nevertheless had to pay for his unorthodox interest in black people. At the radio station in the Peabody someone might say to him, "Well, you smell okay. I guess you haven't been hanging around those niggers today." White Southerners who manifested too much respect for black people earned epithets such as "nigger lover" and paid a price in the white world for their lack of conformity. Only a fool would tamper with established race relations.

Sam was working day and night, seven days a week, with a wife and two sons to support. Twice he suffered nervous breakdowns and retreated to the Gartley-Ramsey Hospital, a private—and discreet—resort for emotionally exhausted persons. Located on Jackson Avenue in a huge two-story Victorian house with a wide, wrap-around porch, the hospital was just around the corner from Humes High on Manassas.

William Faulkner, whose bouts with alcohol recurrently forced him into such retreats, would have been in the Gartley-Ramsey about the same time as Sam Phillips. Perhaps Sam and the silent and brooding Faulkner, both men who struggled with racial and class orthodoxies in their native South, sat in rocking chairs on the broad front porch of the Gartley-Ramsey, watching Elvis Presley, the shambling teenager, making his less-than-eager way down Jackson from his home in the Courts to Humes High.

In June 1951, when Sam's boss remarked critically on his absences, suggesting that his other business endeavors impinged on his work at the radio station, he quit his job at WREC. Then he was on his own—but not quite.

MARION KEISKER

Marion Keisker was an amazing woman. Born in 1917, she was heard on WREC in 1929 on a weekly children's show, *Wynken, Blynken, and Nod.* In 1938, she graduated in both English and Medieval French from Southwestern (now Rhodes) College, Memphis's highly prestigious private school. She married, gave birth to a son, continued her career in radio, and later divorced. In 1946, she began to host the *Meet Kitty Kelly* talk show on WREC five days a week. While she was becoming a well-known and very popular radio personality, she was also writing, producing, and directing as many as a dozen shows in addition to her own, including the nightly *Treasury Bandstand* broadcast from the WREC studio in the Peabody Hotel basement.

"He was a beautiful young man," Marion said of Sam in describing to Peter Guralnick how it all began in 1950. "Beautiful beyond belief, but still that country touch, that country rawness. He was slim and had those incredible eyes . . . with touches of real elegance, beautifully groomed, terrible about his hair." Marion sounded like a woman in love, and she acted the same.

She was with Sam when he discovered the empty building in just the right location, a few blocks east of the Peabody, just off Union and a few blocks north of Beale Street. "One day we were riding along," she recalled years later, "and he saw that spot on Union, and he said, 'That's the spot I want!'" Continuing her story, Marion switched to the first person plural. "With many difficulties, we got the place, and we raised the money, and between us we did everything," she said. "We laid all the tile, and we painted the acoustic boards, I put in the bathroom, Sam put in the control room—what little equipment he had always had to be the best." Soon the business opened as the Memphis Recording Service.

Why was Marion there? "I knew nothing about the music, and I didn't care a bit," she said. Also, she was not into the business of social revolution. "My association, my contribution, my participation was based totally on my personal relationship with Sam in a way that is totally unbelievable to me now. All I wanted to do was to make it possible for him to fulfill his vision—all I wanted to do was to do what would make him happy."

Divorced and raising a nine-year-old son, she nevertheless quit her job at WREC and went to work with Sam. She was receptionist, secretary, typist, bookkeeper, everything up front. Sam, when he was there, either worked in the studio in back or took his current visitor to what was called "the conference room," actually the third booth on the window side in Mrs. Taylor's cafe next door.

SUN RECORDS

In early 1952, encouraged by the success of recordings he had produced for other companies, Sam established his own label, Sun Records. By the summer of 1953, he had scored a big hit with blues man Rufus Thomas's "Bear Cat." Two others soon followed: "Feelin' Good" by Little Junior Parker and "Just Walkin' in the Rain" by the Prisonaires. Both rose into the charts that fall. The Prisonaires were, literally, black prisoners brought over from the state penitentiary in Nashville. Both the warden and the governor, Frank Clement, supported the rehabilitation of criminals, and this was a very visible and audible move in that direction. It was probably the first time ever that uniformed and armed prison guards had attended a recording session in a studio.

African American artists soon learned that Sam Phillips was the man in Memphis who understood their music, who was fair, and who might record and sell their work. They were drawn to the little storefront studio on Union Avenue, and he recorded many of them, including Howlin' Wolf, B. B. ("Blues Boy") King, and Ike Turner, the first husband of Tina Turner.

Ike Turner, like blues pioneer Muddy Waters, came out of that amazingly rich wellspring of creativity in the Mississippi Delta, Clarksdale. In the 1910s, it was the childhood home of Tennessee Williams. In the early 1920s, Clarksdale was also the playground for sexually challenged and desperately searching William Faulkner and his older bachelor buddy, the Oxford lawyer Phil Stone. It was a place where they could drink and gamble, often at the elite but famously profligate Moon Lake Club north of town. Recurrently, Memphis reformers drove bootleggers, gamblers, madams, and prostitutes out of the city, and many took refuge in and around Clarksdale, where they continued their operations unabated. Faulkner soaked it all up, and it poured forth magnificently in his fiction.

Faulkner had a beautifully supportive female friend in Clarksdale, a uniquely marvelously independent young woman named Eula Dorothy Wilcox. "Dot" owned a "beauty parlor," a vital institution in every Southern community that totally excluded men and gave women a place to regularly express their thoughts and feelings. Born in Oklahoma, Dot was orphaned at twelve and put herself through beautician's school. She opened her own shop in Clarksdale, bought a house, and erected a high, solid wooden fence around it. Just as some black businessmen ran all-black businesses, drew their money from black people, and thus gained some insulation from white people, Dot had an all-woman business that drew its money from women and gave her some insulation from that male-dominated world. William Faulkner, Tennessee Williams, and Elvis Presley were all born within seventy-five miles of one another in northeastern Mississippi. Sam Phillips was born just across the state line in northwestern Alabama. This was the very heartland of slavery in America in the generation before the Civil War and the heartland of repressive racism for generations after. Slavery, and after slavery race, permeated the culture and tortured Southerners both black and white. It was precisely the complex, unrelenting, and deeply painful frustrations generated by Southern culture that informed the art of Faulkner and Williams—and Presley—and gave it great power. In the black belt South, the suffering was extraordinarily keen and compelled expression, the kind of expression that could only come with art—with writing, with music, and with performance. It was precisely because the culture wracked its people with such emotional violence over generations that its artists in the twentieth century achieved such power in interpreting humanity in America. The strikingly close geographical congruence of the origins of these highly creative people is no coincidence.

Sam Phillips shared that culture. He too felt keenly the disjunction between what was and what ought, humanely, to be. He was an artist who dedicated his life to the ideal that people should be able to express freely what they felt, to be what they felt themselves truly to be. His medium was technical—sound electronically rendered—but it was art too, just like fiction, song, or performance. Sam began with blacks and moved on to whites. What he did with whites was informed by what he had done with blacks.

THE VERY FIRST ELVIS RECORD

It was Marion Keisker who was there up front at her desk in the Sun studio one Saturday morning in the summer of 1953 when young Elvis Presley, then age eighteen, walked in. He was white and working class. He was probably unemployed, having worked only one month during that whole summer. It was another steaming hot day in Memphis, and the Venetian blinds were already slanting against the south-side sun beyond the plate glass windows on either side of the front door. In her midthirties, cool and crisp in her starched cotton dress, fair of skin, red-blond hair fixed in a permanent wave, Marion, like her radio talk show persona Kitty Kelly, could meet anyone with poise, with real but measured interest, including this rather strange-looking boy with the long sideburns.

For Elvis it was an exciting, upbeat day. In Marion's memory, however, she associated that first meeting with Elvis with tears—her tears.

Sam had spoken harshly to her. Sometimes, in her memory, Sam is in the studio arguing with a partner over money; sometimes he's in the restaurant next door. Both were common occurrences.

Marion recalled vividly the image of the teenager poking his head in shyly through the doorway. She noted the hair—long, dirty-blond, and greasy. He approached her desk, diffidently, almost sliding forward. She asked if she could help him. Then her exact memory faded again. Perhaps he said, actually mumbled, that he wanted to make a record "to surprise my mother." Or, perhaps he said, "I just wanted to hear what I sounded like." She gave him the price: $3.98, the cost of eight trips to the movies for his date and himself at Suzore No. 2 on Main Street. Not cheap, but it was something he had thought about carefully and wanted very much to do. While they waited for Sam to call Elvis into the studio, they talked.

"If you know anyone that needs a singer," he said. The tip of his hidden agenda became barely visible. He was looking for a job as a singer. He had recently won the talent contest at Humes High; he knew he had talent. He did not want to work in a machine shop, at Sears and Roebuck or Kroger, or take a job as a delivery boy, all possibilities generated for him by the Tennessee Employment Security Office that summer. He was announcing his availability as a singer. Not knowing what else to do, he pushed his shyness in front of Marion, a woman who seemed receptive to him. He was not begging, but asking, hoping.

"What kind of singer are you?" Marion asked.

"I sing all kinds," Elvis replied.

"Who do you sound like?" asked Marion, patient, encouraging.

"I don't sound like nobody," Elvis said.

Marion tried yet again, "What do you sing . . . hillbilly?" she suggested.

"I sing hillbilly," he said.

"Well, who do you sound like in hillbilly?"

"I don't sound like nobody," he said again.

Later, in the studio, Sam watched through the glass window of the control booth while Elvis performed. Elvis did not, indeed, sound like anyone else. He sang and picked at the battered, beat-up guitar that he never played very well and often carried about with him as if to draw attention. First came "My Happiness," a 1948 hit. It was a sweet, melting, sentimental ballad that he had sung scores of times for his friends. On the flip side, he did "That's When Your Heartaches Begin," a weepy song made a favorite among whites by a black group called the Ink Spots. Elvis ran out of song before he ran out of recording time and simply terminated the session. "That's the end," he announced.

Elvis looked at Sam in the control booth. Sam nodded and said he was an "interesting" singer.

"We might give you a call sometime," he said. Sam asked Marion to write down Elvis's name, and she noted beside it: "Good ballad singer. Hold."

Out front at her desk, Marion typed out the titles of his songs and his name for the labels. Elvis lingered, talking with Marion. But Mr. Phillips did not come out. After a while, Elvis took his shiny black, brittle acetate disc and left.

All fall Elvis would drop by the studio—or Mrs. Taylor's cafe next door—and talk to Marion. He could talk to women. Mr. Phillips would be in and out, but very busy. Sun Records was alive and moving, but finances were precarious, and Sam was under tremendous pressure. In January, Elvis cut another record for himself. This time he did two country songs, "Casual Love Affair" and "I'll Never Stand in Your Way." Sam saw possibility, but still he was noncommittal. It was all right, though. By then, there was the church on McLemore, offering him heady proximity to the Blackwood Brothers . . . and to Dixie Locke.

THE STARLITE WRANGLERS

Sam Phillips was determined to give talented African Americans an outlet for expressing their art, and he was no less committed to talented whites of the lower social orders. It was almost as if he were waging a war on privilege, on people at the top who allowed little or no chance to those who were born without advantages. "I don't remember when," he told Peter Guralnick, "I thought to myself: suppose that I would have been born a little bit more down on the economic ladder. I think

I felt from the beginning the total inequality of man's inhumanity to his brother." Sam rejected Southern social orthodoxy. He was fiercely individual, and he was, in his own unideological, self-determined, and driven way, a rebel against the established order.

Sam began with African Americans, and in 1953 he was achieving some success. By the spring of 1954, however, he was also well into a search for talent among working-class men on the white side of the line. One group he recorded was the Starlite Wranglers, led by Scotty Moore. Scotty's daytime job was "blocking" (cleaning and reshaping) men's hats in his brother's dry-cleaning shop on McLean Street just north of the zoo in Overton Park and, incidentally, within a hundred yards or so of where Tennessee Williams's grandparents lived and a backyard nearby where amateur actors had presented his first performed play in 1935. Scotty's other job, the one he truly loved, was playing his guitar with the Wranglers, a country and western band that performed in honky-tonks in and around Memphis. Also in the band was Scotty's best friend, Bill Black, who played bass fiddle. Bill was a "tire builder" at the Firestone plant on the north side of town. Other Wranglers also worked at Firestone. Both they and their audiences were very much "country come to town," virtually from the cotton patch to the production line.

Scotty himself was reared on a farm near Humboldt, Tennessee, seventy-five miles northeast of Memphis. His full name was Winfield Scott Moore, named after his father, who was named after the general who took Mexico City in 1847 during the Mexican War. It was a war dear to the hearts of the slaveholders in the Old Southwest. Victory meant that their land, the American South, extended through West Texas, New Mexico, Arizona, and California all the way to the Pacific Ocean. After the war, the South was filled with little Winfields or Winfield Scotts and dotted with little towns named for the war's battle sites—Monterey, Buena Vista, and Saltillo. At sixteen, Scotty falsified his age to join the navy and was sent to Korea, the global struggle that would so deeply mark him, Elvis, and other young people of their generation.

By 1953, twenty-two-year-old Scotty was in Memphis working in his brother's laundry. He was already the father of two children, but his wife had left him and took the children back to her hometown, Bremerton, Washington. His guitar, not his wife, was the love of his life. He had just acquired a Gibson ES-295 semiacoustic jazz guitar. It was "feminine," he said. "I could make out with the Gibson." Even so, in June, he married again. He had met Bobbie Moore at Shadow Lawn, one of the raucous night spots around Memphis where he played on weekends.

Scotty recruited the musicians who made up the Starlite Wranglers, put them in matching cowboy hats and shirts, and even constructed a six-foot star out of Christmas lights to background their performances. He secured bookings in and around Memphis and got them a regular radio spot on station KWEM across the river in West Memphis. Also in West Memphis, a month after his marriage to Bobbie, he got an aspiring young country singer pregnant. His daughter was six years old before he knew she existed.

Scotty well understood that real success in bookings required radio play, and radio play required a record. Like many others, he thought that Sam Phillips was the man who held the keys to the kingdom. In the spring of 1954, the Wranglers made their record. It sold only several hundred copies, but it brought Scotty and Sam together. Scotty got into the habit of dropping by the studio almost every afternoon after work. He and Sam often consulted over coffee in "the conference room," trying to figure out where music ought to go. Both men were always on the lookout for talent.

Sam wanted to make a record like no one had ever made before. He wanted to show the world what raw, untutored, unfettered talent could do. He could not say exactly what the sound would be, he told Scotty, but he would know it when he heard it.

Is This the Right Place?

On Saturday, June 26, 1954, Sam saw his chance. The same man who had sent him a hit with the Prisonaires had mailed a recording of a song: "Without You." It was an amateurish production; Sam said it sounded like a fusion between a sentimental Irish tenor and the Ink

Spots. Yet it was intriguing, and it brought to mind the voice of the strange-looking kid who was still hanging around the shop talking to Marion.

Sam asked Marion to call Elvis and invite him to come down to the studio. She telephoned him at home on Alabama Avenue, several blocks away. "Can you be here at the studio by three?" she asked. Elvis later loved to tell the story. "I was there by the time she hung up the phone," he would say and laugh.

Sam and Elvis tried hard with the new song, but just never got a feel for it. Sam did not then send Elvis away. On the contrary, he kept him there all afternoon. They tried virtually every song, or fragment of song, that Elvis could remember. As Elvis's spirit sank, Sam caught his eye, nodded, and spoke reassuringly. "You're doing just fine," he said. "Now just relax. Let me hear something that really means something to you now."

As Sam later recalled, what he wanted was communication, music that would communicate the richness of life among Southern blacks and unprivileged whites. Big bands were not the only musicians worth hearing. The wall against innovation might be breached with young people. Sam knew that they listened to black music on their radios, even if they didn't buy the records. There was a restlessness that bred tolerance among young people, he thought, almost a need to break out and experiment with something new, whatever it might be, black or white.

Sam was impatient for success, but he had tremendous control. He probed and pondered. He knew that Elvis had something. It was precisely the kind of raw untrained talent that he had sought and found among black artists. But he was not asking Elvis to sing "black." He was asking him to sing what he felt.

Elvis had not clicked on the first try. Someone less perceptive and less determined than Sam might have passed this young man by as another investment that had not paid off. Instead, he enlisted Scotty Moore to work with Elvis. He did so during another "coffee conference" with Scotty and Marion at Mrs. Taylor's cafe on Saturday afternoon, July 3. Encouraged by Sam, Scotty invited Elvis over to his house on July 4.

Bobbie Moore remembered Elvis coming up the walk to her front door. He was a study in color: pink pants, as she recalled, with a black stripe running down the side of each leg, white lacy shirt, and white buck shoes. He was carrying his guitar.

"Is this the right place?" he asked.

Bobbie invited Elvis in and brought Scotty up from a back room where he was practicing his guitar. She offered Elvis a Coke. Then Scotty sent Bobbie down the street to ask Bill Black to join them.

During the first month of their marriage, Scotty and Bobbie had lived in a room in his boarding house. Then for almost a year they lived with kinfolk. In June 1954, just a month before, they had moved onto the same street with Bill and only three doors away. Scotty wanted to be close to Bill in North Memphis, where he lived to be near his day job at the Firestone plant. To make more room for his family, Bill kept his big bass fiddle in Scotty's living room.

Bill arrived, and Elvis ran through every song he could think of. Scotty was astounded at the number and range of songs that Elvis knew—"every damn song in the world," he said, from Eddy Arnold to Billy Eckstine.

Down the street, Bobbie visited with Evelyn Black for an hour or two. When she returned, they were still at it. She recalled Elvis singing a lot of "Because" songs—"I Love You Because (You Understand Me)," "Because of You," "Just Because You Think You're So Pretty." Evelyn was thinking that he was only a pimply-face kid with greasy, duck tailed hair.

After Elvis left, Scotty asked Bill what he thought.

"Well, he didn't impress me too damned much," Bill said.

Scotty thought that Elvis had a good voice and good timing, but nothing new jumped out from the material. He called Sam. Elvis did know a lot of rhythm and blues songs, he said. They agreed that it was worth bringing Elvis into the studio for another audition. Sam did not think they would need any of the other Starlite Wranglers as backup musicians, just Scotty and Bill.

Early the next morning, Bobbie left for her job in the billing department at Sears, Roebuck. Scotty left for the dry-cleaning shop, as always carrying his guitar for lunchtime practice.

Wynette Pugh, age twelve, was probably in and out of the steamy laundry that day, as she was all during that summer. Her mother worked in the laundry office. They had come to Memphis from Itawamba County in northeastern Mississippi, near Tupelo. Her father died before she was born. He had been a locally famous musician, and she grew up in a house full of musical instruments and an aura of music. Wynette loved to hear Scotty play his guitar. Later, she would stick around to listen as Scotty and Elvis practiced in an upstairs room in the laundry, balancing her fascination with the music against her apprehension of having to walk home in the dark alongside the zoo in Overton Park with its growling lions, silently slithering snakes, and shrieking monkeys. As a teenager, Wynette moved to Birmingham, where she began a long, difficult, and determined rise as a country singer. With success, she changed her name from Wynette Pugh to Tammy Wynette, and married George Jones, one of the great country singers of his time. George turned out to be severely unbalanced and very alcoholic, and Tammy's great song turned out to be "Stand by Your Man." Sorely taxed, Tammy finally gave up on her man, divorced George, and gained the fame she deserved.

SAM'S FIRST ELVIS RECORD

Monday evening, July 5, Sam was again in the control booth. The three musicians were in the sound room. Again Sam trolled patiently, one song after another. Nothing worked. Elvis, Scotty, and Bill were exhausted. They had worked all day at their regular jobs while the temperature in Memphis climbed from the mid-70s at dawn to 100 degrees in the early afternoon and the humidity hovered at 92 percent. The dreary prospect of having to go to work the next morning rose before them. About midnight, they were lying about in various stages of collapse. Sam was in his control room adjusting his equipment. Suddenly Elvis jumped up and started flailing away at his guitar and singing a blues song, "That's All Right, Mama." Bill, never reverent toward his instrument, was sitting on his bass fiddle. He leaped up and joined in, then Scotty. Sam knew the song right away. It had been first recorded in

1946 (as just "That's All Right") by the black singer Arthur "Big Boy" Crudup.

Lights do sometimes flash on the road to Damascus. The light flashed for Sam, and he saw Elvis as if for the first time, a white boy picking up on a black man's song. "That's All Right" was a song that Elvis simply by his color and youth had no right doing. Because Elvis was not born and reared black, his rendering could never be black. Yet Elvis was a young white man to whom this black man's song meant something, something he could feel in his own life, feel around him, and express in his singing. Elvis's performance was an appropriation from another culture, a piece plucked out of its original setting and plunked down in his world. Of necessity, it was new, a mutation, in itself a creation.

It was a song with a message. It was about a universal and vital issue—how men and women relate to one another. When Elvis said, "That's all right, mama," he was singing about his world. Vernon and Gladys, Minnie Mae and Jessie Presley, Elvis and Dixie. It was about all those men and women, mamas and papas that he had known, white folks, not black folks, plain white folks. The lyrics suggested the possibility of a more comfortable relationship between the sexes than obtained among adult whites in the patriarchal South in the 1950s. "That's all right, mama, any way you do." It was wisdom out of the mouths of babes, out of a new and rising generation free for a moment at least from the crippling baggage of maturity.

Poking his head through the doorway of the engineer's room, Sam asked, "What are y'all doing?"

"Just foolin' around," Scotty replied.

"Well, it didn't sound too bad," Sam said. "Try it again."

After several tries during which Sam moved Elvis closer to or away from the microphone, they turned on the tape recorder and ran through the whole song. Sam played it back.

"Man, that's good," he declared. "It's different."

They needed a song for the back side of the record, but it was almost 2:00 a.m. before they finished the A-side. Well satisfied with what they had done, they decided to quit for the night. Tuesday morning everyone went back to his day job. That evening they came together again in the studio to try for a B-side, thinking that it should in some way match the A-side. Nothing worked. They came together on Wednesday evening and ranged through every song they could think of, black and white, pop and country. Again, nothing worked. Sam decided to put the record on the air with just one side and see what happened.

On Thursday evening about 9:40, Sam's good friend Dewey Phillips, a disc jockey at station WHBQ, played "That's All Right, Mama" on his show, *Red, Hot, and Blue*. Dewey, who kept up a boisterous, often nonsensical, and always rebellious patter between records, was exceedingly popular with young white people. One of his ploys was to call people he didn't like "pissants" on the air, a practice so close to using foul language that it jeopardized the station's FCC license. Dewey played black music as well as white, a practice that distressed many white parents. Often young whites would listen to him secretly. One white teenager, for example, practiced football with his high school team every afternoon, then helped out at his father's filling station before he went home. After dinner, he went into his bedroom, put his radio under the covers of his bed so that his parents couldn't hear it, tuned it in to Dewey, and crawled in beside it, pulling the covers over his head.

The response to Elvis's record was immediate and massive. The phones began to ring on the first play. Dewey played the record seven times in a row, and still the phones kept ringing. Dewey's fans could not get enough. Some of the callers were black. Dewey actually favored black music over white on his show, and listeners generally thought that this new singer was black. Dewey fixed that quickly. He brought Elvis in for an interview right away and elicited the fact that he had gone to Humes High School, an all-white institution. Memphians then knew instantly that the singer was white, and the sound was thus even more remarkable. Simultaneously, they knew more. Humes was not only white, it was also working class.

The next day, orders began to pour into Sun Records and soon rose to five thousand. And still they had no back side for the record. Friday, Saturday, and Sunday they came together in the little studio. Again they ran through the spectrum, song after song. They were still thinking that it should somehow match the blues song on the front side.

It was Bill Black who found the back side, probably on Sunday. During a lull in the proceedings, Scotty recalled, Bill "jumped up and grabbed his bass and started slapping it, at a fast tempo, singing 'Blue Moon of Kentucky' in a high falsetto voice." Elvis joined in, then Scotty on his guitar. Again Sam knew it when he heard it. Poking his head through the doorway of the control booth, he shouted, "Hey, that's the one!"

Given the A-side of the record, so obviously inspired by black blues, Bill had no right to think of this one for the flip side. It was not blues or rhythm and blues. On the other hand, in terms of his all-white, grass-roots country heritage, Bill had every right to think of it. It was about as white as one could get.

"Blue Moon of Kentucky" had become a hit in 1947, a year after Crudup did "That's All Right." It was recorded by Bill Monroe and his band. The lyrics bespeak the usual lament over the loss of a lover. The novel element is that the lover asks the blue moon to "shine on the one that's gone and proved untrue." He laments but accepts his loss, and wishes her well, blessed by that marvelous moon. Monroe had sung the song in a high keening voice and played it in waltz time. Listeners of *The Grand Ole Opry* knew Monroe's rendition well, and they loved this hillbilly lament.

"Blue Moon of Kentucky" as rendered by Bill Monroe and the Blue Grass Boys was back-looking. The keening sound that carried the message might be read as a yearning for family and community and the soft healing light of the moon on the hills of home. It was definitely not a celebration of moving on with life in the big city and such things as the great Firestone plant in north Memphis where Bill Black and other Starlite Wranglers made tires, or Precision Tool where Smiths and Presleys made artillery shells.

Sam, Elvis, Bill, and Scotty began to work on the song. By now, they were well attuned to one another. After one of the takes, Sam announced his judgment from the control room. His voice can still be heard on the tape.

"Hell, that's different," he said. "That's a pop song now, nearly about."

Elvis, Bill, and Scotty totally turned the mood of "Blue Moon of Kentucky" around. They made a record that was upbeat and bubbling over with exuberance. Instructions on sheet music printed in 1978 advised a "Bright 'jump' tempo." The past on the farm was just fine, but also we are okay in the city today, it seemed to say, working in the shop or factory or driving a truck.

The record was indeed different, and Sam as engineer added to the difference of the sound in the final product. He had invented a double taping process that gave more body to the music he recorded. Scotty Moore said that "Sam treated Elvis as another instrument and he kept his voice closer to the mike than was the norm at the time." The norm was to put "the singer's voice way out front." Revolutionary innovation in the electronic arts—so much a part of Elvis's rise in records, radio, television, and film—was there in his first great, popular, and commercial success. "Sleepy Eyed" John Lepley, a very popular country DJ on WHHM, described "Blue Moon of Kentucky" and "That's All Right, Mama" as highlights of Elvis's attraction.

Sam made copies of the completed record and passed them out to Memphis disc jockeys. Dewey Phillips still loved the A-side; others liked the B-side, "Blue Moon of Kentucky." Soon the B-side was more popular in Memphis than the A-side. On this and the next record they would make, the artists were identified as "Elvis, Scotty, and Bill." On the third they became "Elvis and the Blue Moon Boys."

On July 27, Edwin Howard, an entertainment reporter for the *Memphis Press-Scimitar*, interviewed Elvis, his first ever with the press. Fortunately, Marion Keisker, who brought him to the newspaper office for the interview during his lunch-hour break, did most of the talking. Elvis seemed happy enough in simply responding "yes, sir" and "no, sir" to the reporter's questions. "The odd thing" about the new record, Marion said, "is that both sides seem to be equally popular on pop, folk and race record programs." And then she captured the Elvis phenomenon succinctly and perfectly in a single sentence, not only for the moment but for decades to come. "This boy has something that seems to appeal to everybody," she said.

Forty-three years later, Scotty Moore looked back on what they had done. On one side, he said, "Elvis took a blues song and sang it white."

On the other, "he took a country song and gave it a bluesy spin." It should not have worked, Scotty thought, this blending of black and white, but "in the laid-back, anything goes atmosphere of Sam's studio, it seemed perfect." What was new was not the songs, nor even, so much, the music. It was the people who made—and heard—the music. "Blue Moon of Kentucky" had the same sort of feel as "That's All Right." "After that," he said, "we sort of had our direction."

CHAPTER SEVEN

A GIRL IN THE BED

The Loss of Dixie

When Dixie returned after two weeks of vacation, she was surprised to find that her young man had become a local celebrity. She was very proud of him and, for a time, shared in the excitement. She sat with Evelyn Black and Bobbie Moore, "the girls," while the boys practiced at Scotty's house. She went with Elvis downtown to the studios of WHBQ in the Hotel Chisca to visit his new friend Dewey Phillips, the frenetic, racy-talking disc jockey. Ironically, she felt at ease with Dewey, but when she met Sam Phillips at Sun Studios she did not feel warmly welcomed.

Sam was intensely focused elsewhere, and perhaps he wanted no distractions. He was working feverishly to get an audience for Elvis. He succeeded in getting Bob Neal to add him to the country and western show Bob was organizing for July 30 at the Shell in Overton Park. Name recognition for such a newcomer as Elvis was not easily achieved. His name itself was a problem. Few people in the world had ever even heard of anyone named "Elvis." One newspaper advertisement for the show gave his name as "Ellis" Presley. Another left him off the bill altogether. His high school yearbooks once had the same difficulties with "Elvis."

On the way to the performance, Elvis drove his 1941 Lincoln coupe from his house on Alabama Avenue to the south side of town to pick up Dixie. In the car she sat close, nestled supportively beside him, not quite sixteen, long dark hair, round of limb, fair and smooth of skin. Elvis drove north, then turned east on Poplar Avenue toward the park. He was exceedingly anxious and drummed the fingers of one hand nervously on the dashboard as he drove. Dixie herself was fearful that the audience might not appreciate his unique style. This was, after all, a country and western show. It featured Slim Whitman, whose latest record, "Indian Love Call," was all the rage, and Billy Walker ("the Tall Texan"), who had just made it with "Thank You for Calling."

Elvis went backstage, and Dixie took her seat among some two thousand people arrayed in tiered rows facing the stage set under a shell-like cover. Finally, Elvis came on.

Dixie was not surprised by Elvis's movements onstage. Some musicians keep time by tapping a foot. To keep time Elvis had a way of shaking his left leg, which somehow got amplified in the baggy, deeply pleated trousers he wore. The gospel quartets that she and Elvis heard at the all-night sings in Ellis Auditorium were also movers, gliders, and shakers, and they too brought large audiences to their feet shouting, swaying, and clapping in time. These were highly spiritual experiences, but they were also highly physical and sensual. It was a public venue in which good women had a license to move their bodies in ecstasy. For some people, it was also sexual. During an interview with a writer, one quartet member affirmed that gospel singers on tour had sexual relations with fans. "Sure," he replied with a wicked grin. "There's no ____ as good as Christian ____."

Dixie knew that the bass singer with Elvis's beloved Blackwood Brothers Quartet shook much like Elvis, and the women just loved it. He was called "Big Chief" because he had Indian blood. But what Dixie saw when the girls broke out at Overton Park was very different from what she saw at Ellis Auditorium. Elvis was not performing like a member of a quartet celebrating salvation and a "glory land" of eternal happiness "up there." Typically the four gospel singers would be in business suits and with this line would simultaneously point their right index fingers heavenward, smiling confidently and nodding their heads affirmatively. Whatever Elvis intended to convey to his audience, his performance was read by the girls as sexual, and they responded loudly, physically, and with striking sexuality.

Dixie was outraged. She wanted to leap to Elvis's defense and tell the girls to "shut up and leave him alone." She wanted to challenge them: "What do you think you are doing here?" Forty years later she looked back and saw that this was the beginning of the end of her dream of living her life with Elvis and bearing his children. "I felt like all of a sudden I was not a part of what he was doing. He was doing something so totally him that I was not a part of it," she recalled. "And he loved it."

Dixie was absolutely right. Elvis had revealed a large part of himself that she had not known before, and within weeks he began to construct a way of life that had no clear place for Dixie, nor, indeed, for any one woman. It was then that Elvis lost his capacity for loving one girl, one woman, and took up the mission of loving them all. It was then that he lost the wife and the children who would have been born every other year—Gladys had wanted to have three. He lost the secure position he would have had as, perhaps, a master electrician in the trades in growing Memphis, a predictable well-paid forty-hour workweek with a two-week vacation every summer—hopefully at the beach on the Gulf Shore. He also lost the pleasures of a three-bedroom, red-brick ranch house with a two-space carport in a solidly blue-collar Memphis suburb such as Whitehaven or Raleigh, singing with the choir in the new Assembly of God Church building on upscale McLemore Street on Sunday mornings, and dinner every Sunday after church with his parents, his wife, and at least one little Elvis in a white suit and one little Dixie in bright frills. This, more or less, was what always happened with his friends from the Courts and Humes High.

The breakup between Elvis and Dixie began at the Shell in July 1954, but it took fifteen months of increasing pain on both sides for both to fully recognize that they were not to spend their lives together. Dixie suffered from his absences; Elvis suffered from his suspicions that Dixie was intimate with other young men while he was gone. At first, on the surface, they carried on much as before. When Elvis was home they would go to the movies, eat hamburgers, drink milkshakes, and sit on her front porch at night and "spoon." Sometimes Dixie would go with Elvis to Scotty's brother's dry-cleaning plant on North McLean Street just beyond Overton Park and listen while the Blue Moon Boys rehearsed. Other times he would leave her and go hang out with Dewey Phillips, who would take him down to Beale Street to meet and listen to the black musicians, or home to his garage where he screened movies privately for himself and his male friends. The movies were perhaps sexual in nature.

Everywhere Elvis and Dixie went, girls vied shamelessly for his attention. She was outraged, but he seemed not to mind at all such loose, unladylike behavior. She was sure that there was no other girl for him, but she was aware of how only months before they had wondered if they would have the strength to wait until they married for the consummation of their love.

On the road, Elvis did not wait at all for sexual consummation. Out here were other girls for Elvis, and many of them. In particular, he was reinventing himself in and about Shreveport, Louisiana, where he was appearing on the *Louisiana Hayride* every Saturday night. He, Bill, and Scotty would hardly check into a motel or a hotel before the girls would begin to swarm around. Elvis loved the attention.

Scotty and Bill witnessed his behavior after one sexual event. Scotty thought that it was probably his first. They had checked into a Shreveport hotel, renting one room with two beds because that was all they could afford. In the wee hours of the night, Scotty and Bill sat in the lobby waiting for Elvis to finish whatever he was doing up in the room with a girl he had met earlier in the day. Finally Scotty looked up and saw Elvis and the girl coming down the stairs. After an awkward moment, Elvis took the girl over to a corner of the lobby, left her, and came back to them. He was very agitated.

"The rubber busted," he exclaimed. "What do I do now?"

They had cautioned Elvis about venereal diseases and possible pregnancies with girls on the road, but they had no advice to give him in this particular crisis and went on up to bed. The next day they asked Elvis what he had done. Nonchalantly he declared that he had taken the girl to the hospital emergency room.

"The emergency room!" Scotty and Bill were aghast.

"I got them to give her a douche," Elvis explained.

Scotty looked at Bill.

"I didn't know they did that" was all he could say.

Through all of this, Elvis telephoned home almost every night, often talking to Dixie, who would be visiting with Gladys. Sometimes he called Dixie separately, using her neighbor's phone. Again and again he expressed his great love for her. On one occasion when Elvis returned from touring in Texas, he brought her a sleeveless blouse and a pair of shorts in pale pink. He could hardly wait until she tried the outfit on. For Christmas, he gave her a suit. She put it on, and again his excitement ran high. Elvis dressed Dixie with an enthusiasm that few young men could have mustered in dressing their girlfriends, if indeed they dared attempt to dress them at all.

In January 1955, Elvis was gone for three weeks running. When he returned he and Dixie went to another all-night sing at Ellis Auditorium. Thereafter, for months, he was on the road almost constantly. The girls had claimed him as their own, a claim that came to a crescendo in the Jacksonville "riot" in May 1955.

Even as Elvis was busily involved with other girls on the road, he continued to call home nightly and check up on Dixie through his parents. He liked hearing that she was actually with them. When she was not, he questioned Gladys closely. "Has she been over?" he would ask. "Did she spend the night?" He was exceedingly possessive. "He didn't want to relinquish that control," Dixie thought, "regardless of how long he was gone or what he was doing." She was true to Elvis, and in his absences she got closer still to Gladys. They cooked and ate at Gladys's house. They took walks and shopped together. "When Elvis was out of town, I would go over and stay with them," she said. "I spent the nights lots of times and slept in his bed while he was gone."

Elvis escorted Dixie to her junior prom in the spring of 1955. He was marvelously attired in a white dress coat and shirt with a black bow tie, and she was so proud of him. By then, Elvis was renting a whole four-room house for his family on Lamar Avenue, a main thoroughfare on the south side of town. Neighboring kids would see Elvis and Dixie sitting on the front porch, talking and holding hands. Dixie saw that Elvis was changing, not only on the road but also in Memphis. He was developing a whole new set of friends, young men who were nothing at all like the friends he had had before. "They used horrible language, they all smoked, everybody had a drink," Dixie said. More and more he was with them, guys like George Klein and Red West. He flourished only when he was the center of attention, and they gave him a lot of attention.

Elvis pressured Dixie to have no one else in her life, especially boys and young men, no matter how innocent the relationship. He quizzed her relentlessly about who she was seeing when he was gone, where she was when he called and she wasn't there, and so on. Dixie, however, was not willing simply to sit at home while Elvis was away. She continued to go out with her friends—not dating anyone, but being with boys and girls from church and school. They would go to the Busy Betty on Lamar, to listen to the jukebox and dance. She told Elvis what she did, but he could not accept even these ordinary teenage pursuits. "That was the basis of every argument we ever had," she recalled. "He was very possessive and very jealous." Several times she gave him back his class ring. He would leave and within minutes be back again. They would sit on her front porch, cry together, and reconcile. Even though he would "run the women" through his hotel and motel rooms at a great rate while on the road, Elvis would not let Dixie go.

Finally, in October 1955, both Elvis and Dixie realized that it was over. Elvis never confessed that he had been unfaithful. Dixie, not Elvis, broke the news of her decision to end it to Gladys. The two women cried together and vowed to remain friends. Dixie's own mother was reluctant to accept the ending. She would say, "Well, what are you going to do if you meet somebody else and get married, and after you get married, Elvis comes back." Suppose Elvis said, "Hey, I made a mistake, and I want you to come and be my wife." Dixie was quick to respond. "Well, I'll just divorce whoever I'm married to and go live with him," she declared.

Soon Dixie did marry and begin her family. So, too, did the Elvis girls. Those hundreds of thousands of young women in his audiences in 1954, 1955, 1956, and 1957 matured, married, and had children. Even so, they maintained their affairs with Elvis at full strength and never felt the need to divorce their husbands and leave their families. One described neatly how she managed her ongoing and passionate love affair with Elvis. In her thirties, married and with a son, she said she had three men in her life: her husband, her son, and Elvis Presley. Every so often she would just have to be with Elvis. She would go off to attend a performance or visit Graceland or whatever. Her husband and son understood this and were not jealous. After her meeting with Elvis, she always returned to the other males in her life—a better wife and mother, and a happier woman.

PARADOX

Tightly woven into the Dixie story is the grand paradox in Elvis's life: he never found the woman who made his life whole. Millions of women loved him with their hearts, and they never deserted him. Several hundred loved him with their bodies, many for a few hours, some for months, and some for years. But it was not within him to be true to one woman alone, and like Dixie they all left him. It was always Elvis who was left alone, the one thing in the world he most feared. His sometime bedmates went on to more satisfying and lasting relationships while Elvis continued his fruitless search. It was he, not they, who suffered from unrequited love. It was he whom everybody knew and nobody understood. It was he who was doomed to loneliness, a loneliness that he fought, strangely and futilely, by striving always to have a girl in his bed when he went to sleep and when he awoke.

THE DEATH OF GLADYS

Gladys's health had begun to decline in the Courts. Perhaps her illnesses were fated by her genes. The Smiths were not very healthy people. Her father had died suddenly at about fifty, having no clearly visible previous illness. Her mother, Octavia, had tuberculosis and was an invalid virtually all of her adult life. Some of the Smith children and grandchildren seemed to be born physically and perhaps psychologically impaired. Several drank to excess. So had Gladys around her fortieth birthday, and the drinking was accompanied by wild mood swings.

As the money began to pour in during the spring of 1955, Elvis rented a brick house for the family at 2414 Lamar and "retired" (to use the word

he jokingly used) his father from the workforce. Their next-door neighbors, the Bakers, remembered Vernon spending time working on cars
in his yard when he felt like it and not much else. He hardly spoke and
was not very responsive when spoken to. The Presleys did not at first
have a phone and used the Bakers'. Vernon would walk into the house
without asking or even knocking to use the phone or borrow things,
forcing Mr. Baker to put a hook on the door. Mrs. Presley, on the other
hand, had the nicest manners but was a "nervous creature." She had
passed out on her bed on the night they moved in, and the Bakers had
had to call their doctor to come help her. They never understood clearly
why Gladys had collapsed.

Elvis was on tour when the Presleys moved into the house on Lamar,
but when he came home the Bakers found him to be the soul of good
manners and modesty. "He certainly didn't want any of us to treat him
like he was more important than any of us were," Sarah Baker, the
fourteen-year-old daughter, later recalled.

Soon the Presleys began to talk to the landlord about buying the
house. They thought about adding on a room for Minnie Mae, who
often visited. Vernon, however, felt that the owner was jacking up the
price on them. In a huff, the Presleys rented a much more attractive
and comfortable house around the corner at 1414 Getwell for $85 a
month.

As Elvis traveled more, Gladys drank more. Elvis worried about
her. In March 1956, he bought her a very comfortable three-bedroom
ranch house on upscale Audubon Drive near White Station, the very
white suburb on the east side of town. But Gladys was increasingly
frightened for his safety. Attending one of his performances in Florida,
she was horrified by what she saw as a physical attack by the girls in
the audience upon her son. She grabbed one of the girls.

"Why are you trying to kill my boy?" she demanded.

"I am not trying to kill him," the girl answered. "I just love him so.
I want to touch him."

Gladys begged Elvis to give up his career and stay home. It was the
one thing in the world that he could give her that he would not give
her. He was very blunt in telling his mother that she would have to get

used to his new life. "I told her," Elvis said to an interviewer in 1956, "'Mama, if you're going to feel that way, you'd better not come along to my shows because that stuff is going to keep right on happening.'" Then he added, "I hope."

As Elvis continued with his career, Gladys grew ever more anxious, and with good reason. There was a car wreck, another car that caught fire, two narrowly averted airplane crashes, the famous Jacksonville "riot" in May 1955, and riotous girls in general. Again and again, Gladys begged Elvis's bodyguards to take care of her "exhausted son" as Elvis left for another tour. Behind all her troubles, she felt, was the evil genius of the Colonel, manipulating and dominating everything. She hated the Colonel, and she hated what he was doing to her son. But she had virtually no control, and she drank more and more.

Elvis bought Graceland in 1957, and the move there in the spring did not help, even though the primary motive was to shield Gladys from the public that was always pressing around, some of them even threatening her and Vernon for having produced a son who was a monster and a menace to morality. The high, thick stone wall that stands across the front and up the sides of Graceland today—finished off for total enclosure all around the estate with a high, solid wooden fence—was built to protect Gladys, not Elvis. Moreover, he established a round-the-clock guard at the wide thick-iron double gates at the front. Within the bastion, he installed Gladys and Vernon in an upstairs bedroom just down the hall from his own.

Elvis also brought a raft-full of relatives to Graceland in the late 1950s and settled them in the house and in mobile homes and outbuildings behind it. He provided a neat, small, comfortable wooden house for Travis Smith, Gladys's brother, his wife, Lorene, and their two young sons, Billy and Bobby, in the northeast area on the back side of the estate. Everyone had a job of some sort and was on Elvis's payroll. Travis headed up the guards who worked out of a gatehouse at the main entrance to Graceland. Vernon's brother, Vester, married to Gladys's sister Clettes, was also a guard. Their daughter, Patsy, became Vernon's secretary, working in a small house behind the big house that Vernon had turned into his office. Patsy's husband, Gee Gee Gambill,

helped Earl Pritchett, who was the head groundskeeper and maintenance man at Graceland. Earl had married Elvis's aunt Nash. Delta,
Vernon's sister, stayed with their mother, Minnie Mae, eventually living
in quarters next to the kitchen on the first floor. Delta managed domestic services in the household, which were supplied by black cooks
and maids.

Gladys brought her beloved bevy of chickens from Audubon Drive
and turned them loose in the yard, where they clucked and strutted
about stiff-legged, scratching and pecking at the grounds of Graceland.
She derived great pleasure from feeding them every evening wherever
they happened to be, in back, beside, or in front of the elegant Georgian
mansion with a portico, two large stone lions crouched on either side
of the entrance, and four two-story-high white Corinthian columns. Finally, even this simple, nurturing joy was taken away from her. It was
decided—probably by Colonel Parker—that it was unseemly for the
mother of Elvis Presley to feed chickens, especially in the front yard
where the fans at the gate could easily see her. "They won't let me
see Elvis," Gladys would complain to Annie Presley, the wife of Sales
Presley, Vernon's cousin. "And now I can't even feed my chickens. It's
supposed to be bad for his image."

Gladys's distress mounted with Elvis's success. Vernon, on the other
hand, had no difficulty at all with Elvis's career and rapidly rising income.
He once announced loudly in the Sun studio that Sun Records, and
hence Sam Phillips, would be nothing without his son. At first he was
totally supportive of Elvis signing on with the Colonel, but he soon fret-
ted that the Colonel's share of Elvis's earnings was much too large. Elvis's
success went directly to Vernon's head. Elvis, for his part, sheltered his
father from all criticism. He made him his personal business manager,
soon paying him some $40,000 a year and eventually $75,000. Vernon
did not complain at all about Elvis's absences. When Elvis was gone,
Vernon was the lord of the manor at Graceland, sternly commanding a
staff of a dozen or more employees and counting every penny. At last, he
was getting the money and power that he had long known he deserved.
It was as if everything he had learned about command and control as a
convict in Parchman was coming into force within the walled community

of the estate and his true value was now recognized—that is, as long as Elvis was away.

Beginning in the fall of 1956, Elvis spent much time in Hollywood, leaving Vernon in charge in Memphis and Gladys bereft. When Elvis bought Graceland, she had imagined that she and he would have a glorious time together remodeling and furnishing the house. It was not to be. He came home from Hollywood between movies just as they were beginning the process. He made some quick choices, left some general instructions, and took off for the Gulf Coast with the guys to enjoy a couple of weeks of beach life and the adoration of the girls. What came out at Graceland was a decor that was some of Elvis, some of Gladys, and a lot of the interior decorator from Goldsmith's Department Store.

Vernon had little say in furnishing the house, but he must have thought that at last he had finally and fully arrived at his appropriate station in life when a beautiful blond Hollywood star came by for a visit while Elvis was out of town. It fell to Vernon to show her around Graceland first and then the whole city of Memphis. Gladys was upset by Vernon's giving the blonde too much attention, took him to task, and a row ensued. Gladys screamed while Vernon mumbled.

More and more Gladys felt isolated and powerless. Night after night she insisted that her oldest sister, Lillian, come stay with her after Lillian had worked all day as an inspector at Fashion Curtains downtown. Gladys was drinking more, now vodka instead of beer, since it was said not to leave a smell on your breath. Lillian said that Vernon, who simply wanted to keep Gladys quiet, supplied the vodka.

When Elvis was around, Gladys would rally and her spirits would rise. But he was seldom around. His induction into the army in March 1958 was the blow that finally broke her. While he was stationed in Texas at Fort Hood, she, Minnie Mae, Vernon, and Lamar Fike, one of Elvis's bodyguards, settled in a nearby town, Killeen, and maintained a home for him. In August 1958, a multiplicity of ailments brought her back to Memphis and immediate hospitalization. Elvis managed to arrive only hours before her death. The cause of her death was officially announced as "heart failure." In fact, she died of liver failure brought on by alcoholism. "It seems she drank too much," her attending physician said privately almost four decades later. She was forty-six years old.

Elvis fans can still detail the scene, Elvis and his father, sitting on the front steps of Graceland crying and consoling one another. They brought up a fond image of Gladys "feeding them chickens" in the yard.

Gladys's death brought the last meeting between Dixie and Elvis. She was married now and had a child. When she came to the National Funeral Home, he came right up to her. "Look, Dad," Elvis exclaimed to Vernon, "here's Dixie." He made her promise to come by Graceland that evening. He wanted to talk to her, he said. Dixie and her aunt sat near the back during the ceremony. Recurrently he was overcome and "would just cry out," one friend recalled. At Forest Hill Cemetery, after the service there and as the coffin was about to be sealed in a vault, Elvis surrendered totally to his grief. Crying uncontrollably, he leaned over the casket.

"Goodbye, darling," he wailed, "goodbye. I love you so much. You know how much I lived my whole life for you." It took four men to pull Elvis out to the limousine for his departure. Overcome, Elvis cried out again, "Oh, God! Everything I have is gone." In truth, of course, he had not lived his whole life just for her. He would not give up one iota of his career nor even a part of his two-week vacation on the Gulf Coast beach to stay with her.

Early that evening, Dixie drove down to Graceland to leave word at the gate that she could not come over to visit that night but would come the next day. She planned to leave her message at the gate and not go in. She was in shorts and her hair was up in curlers. Dixie parked at the gate and delivered her message to the guard, who called up to the house. She got in her car to leave, but the motor would not start. While she was sitting in the stalled car, one of Elvis's cousins came and said he was waiting for her at the house. Elvis met her at the door. He had shooed all the other guests away. He had the maid bring lemonade for them. They sat in the living room and talked, not a sound coming from the crowd of mourners who had disappeared toward the back of the house.

They talked about Gladys and their lives together. Elvis told about one of his backup singers who had given up the sin-filled world of show business to devote his life to the Lord. Dixie suggested that he could do the same. Elvis said no, it was too late. They went into the music room. Elvis played the piano and sang for her. One song was "I'm Walking Behind You on Your Wedding Day."

The next evening, "all dressed up," Dixie came and paid her respects to the whole family.

EUROPE

Elvis went to Europe on the USS *Randall* in September 1958. Another draftee, Charlie Hodge, was on the same ship. Charlie was a gospel singer who had met Elvis in 1955 backstage at Ellis Auditorium during one of those all-night sings that he so loved. Charlie sang with a gospel quartet, the Foggy River Boys. Short, animated, and eager to entertain, he often played the part of the country clown, joking and telling humorous stories. Charlie arranged to bunk just above Elvis during the voyage, and together they organized entertainment for the troops. Elvis only played the piano. He was never introduced, and he never spoke. Charlie later wrote a book, *Me 'n Elvis*, in which he said he comforted Elvis at night when he cried over the loss of his mother. He claimed he could hear Elvis thinking about his mother in his bunk even when Elvis was lying there silent.

Charlie clearly loved Elvis. Often he was jealous of the attention that Elvis gave to other guys, and sometimes he went away for a while. But always he came back. He was the only person from whom Elvis ever took anything resembling singing lessons. For all his natural talent, Elvis never had professional instruction in how to use his voice. Charlie had attended the Stamps-Baxter School of Music in Dallas, Texas. He taught Elvis to use some of the techniques he had learned. Toward the end of Elvis's life, when he was so weak he could no longer sustain certain notes, Charlie, who played rhythm guitar behind him, said that he sang them for him, blending in so smoothly that no one knew that it was Charlie, not Elvis, whom they heard. At least in those moments, Charlie was one with Elvis for the whole world to see. For twenty years, Charlie lived much of his life in Elvis's very household, as he later proudly declared. He never married, and in the final years he had a room in one of the buildings behind the mansion at Graceland.

THE ELVISIAN UNIVERSE

In Germany, after the ship docked in Bremerhaven, the soldiers mounted a train that took them south. Elvis soon set up a household in Bad Nauheim, close to the army base on which he was stationed. This began the curious ménage in which Elvis would live, with variations, for the rest of his life. Gladys was gone, and Elvis took her place at the center of the Presley home. He was the sun, and everyone else became planets and moons whose movements were determined by his gravity. Yet Elvis, without Gladys, was not a whole person. There was no steady core, no center of being, only fragments trapped somewhere in that beautiful voice and body that so many people adored. It was as if the sun itself—Elvis—was never at rest in the heavens, but rather always shifting about. After the demise of Gladys, in the Elvisian universe nothing was fixed, nothing was certain.

Elvis struggled earnestly and ceaselessly to pull himself together after his mother died. In doing so, he surrounded himself with certain chosen persons whom he required to perform for him in certain ways. All together, he used these people to wall away the outside world and create a protected space within which he lived and sought to define himself. In effect, he shaped three institutions in which many individuals came and went, but the institutions continued. Each of the three was already in his life in embryonic form before Gladys died. The first included certain family and clan members, Smiths and Presleys, that he chose to attach to himself. The second consisted of "the boys," "the guys," the men who eventually came to sometimes boast the title of "the Memphis Mafia." Finally, there were the girls who shared his bed.

The Presley and Smith families had come together in East Tupelo in the 1920s and 1930s when they, like millions of other rural Southerners, fled the depressed countryside. Some moved as families into Tupelo proper, and during and after World War II over to Memphis. When Elvis moved into Graceland, he virtually turned it into a Presley-Smith compound, a safe house, surrounded by walls and guards. While he was in the army, he left it intact, like a family bastion, under the guard and charge of his relatives. When he went to Germany, he took his father and his grandmother with him. Indeed, they flew in only three days after he debarked from the USS *Randall* in Bremerhaven, a port on the North Sea, on October 1, 1958. Had Gladys lived, he would have brought her to Germany too, and the house in Bad Nauheim would have been her home, her Graceland in Germany.

Elvis also brought two of his young men, Red West and Lamar Fike, into his household in Germany. For the rest of his life, "the boys" would always be with him, still called "the boys" when they were in their thirties, before they finally sometimes rose to the dubious dignity of being called "the guys." Almost all were on his payroll, and some he simply allowed to attach themselves to him. Strenuous denials to the contrary, most would hardly have given him the time of day were it not for his fame, his excessively generous gifts, and the leftover girls. Elvis knew this, and it pained him greatly to weigh the real extent and nature of his isolation. His greatest fear, he often confessed, was that his fans would desert him, he would have no money, and he would be alone.

Eventually he delighted in dubbing his guys "the Memphis Mafia," a term coined by a Las Vegas journalist. It suggested that they were "blood brothers," sworn to lifelong loyalty, secrecy, and whatever violence was necessary to protect "the boss" and promote his interests. Elvis liked that and he needed that. On one occasion he decided to dress the guys in identical dark mohair suits and sunglasses, and, later, to strike a medallion they all conspicuously displayed. The medallion featured a streak of jagged lightning and the letters *TCB*, standing for "Taking Care of Business." The idea of the lightning symbol might have been borrowed from the insignia of the Third Armored Division, the men who in 1944 and 1945 courageously faced the superior armor of the Panzer Corps and drove into Germany. As a soldier, Elvis belonged to the Third Armored Division, though his primary duty was to drive not a tank but the jeep in which his sergeant rode.

"Taking care of business" meant whatever business Elvis happened to have in mind at the moment—be it having a party in Las Vegas, Hawaii, or Colorado, a night at the movies, the amusement park, or the skating rink in Memphis, or protecting his body or his psyche from attack, real or imagined. "Mafia" suggested that his guys were capable of forceful, violent, and, if Elvis wanted, even illegal action.

Elvis's insistence that his guys were a "Mafia" worked directly to counter his fear of desertion. Their loyalty was to him above all others. He would even come before their wives, lovers, girlfriends, and children. Frequently, Elvis tested their dedication by making sudden, capricious, and outrageous demands upon them. For instance, after his engagement in Las Vegas was over he might decide to keep them there doing nothing until only hours before Christmas while their families and friends waited in Memphis with Christmas trees lit and presents wrapped, or suddenly whisk them away to Palm Springs on the spur of the moment, thus trashing any other plans the families might have. But nothing they did was ever enough to relieve his fears of desertion. Recurrently, he had evidence that some among those closest to him would betray him, just as he always feared.

"The boys"—"the Memphis Mafia," "the guys"—became an institution that persisted even as a dozen or so individuals came and went. Other people both in and out of the entertainment industry looked upon the Elvis entourage and its behavior as a strange phenomenon. For many, it seemed some sort of irritating hangover from an early and misguided adolescence, a view that gained credence from the guys' proclivity for low-level practical jokes and mock combat—water fights, cream-pie fights, roller-rink fights, fireworks wars in which they threw firecrackers and shot roman candles at each other, often with painful effect, and enthusiastic football games in which the boys dashed about and called excitedly to each other as the ball spun through the air. Elvis was always the quarterback on his team, and his team always won.

Jerry Leiber, coauthor along with Mike Stoller of "Hound Dog," "Jailhouse Rock," and many other Elvis hits, remembered one occasion at a studio in Hollywood when Elvis got control of the public address system and pretended to be an airline pilot. "This is your captain speaking," Elvis began, and continued with what he thought was a clever spiel. The guys thought this was hilarious.

Also, they thought it was great fun when they installed a two-way mirror in Elvis's house on Perugia Way in Bel Air, one of the houses in which he lived during his early movie years. This "peeping Tom" device enabled them to observe one—or perhaps two—of the guys having sex with one of the always available girls. By their own standards, they improved upon the idea in Elvis's next house on Bellagio Road. This time they put a two-way, five-foot-square mirror in the cabana by the swimming pool where the girls would change into their swimsuits. In order to arrive at the observation point, the guys had to crawl stealthily under a partition, a challenge they gleefully accepted as a part of this game. When Elvis was with the rising movie star Ann-Margret, they attempted to slide thin mirrors under his bedroom door so as to get a look at the highly talented, marvelously beautiful star unclothed and perhaps engaged in sexual exercises with the boss. Such "hijinks," as Elvis's biographer Peter Guralnick called their various amusements, were ordinary for the Elvis entourage.

Individual Mafiosos could be very mannerly, but together they were at best a menace to ordinary civility, and at worst like playground bullies insulting, intimidating, and physically hazardous to those unfortunate enough to be around them. The sum of their badness, it seems, was greater than its parts. The glue that held it all together, was, of course, Elvis himself.

Elvis, and Elvis alone, chose each particular member and created the Mafia. It was his monster, created to devour the monsters that would devour him. Elvis molded their collective character, set their agendas, and gave them whatever power they had as a group. Their central role in life was to please him. Most of all, he demanded that they simply be there whenever he wanted them there.

The guys therefore had two jobs. One job was to entertain Elvis, to perform for him wherever he was and at any time, day or night, just as he entertained his audiences. The other job was whatever.

Another job, no less vital, was to manifest visibly and palpably the extreme anger and rebelliousness that Elvis felt but dared not show publicly. For example, hijinks on the set were a way for Elvis to express his unhappiness with how the movie people were misusing what he considered to be his great talent as an actor. As he became increasingly unhappy, the Mafia became increasingly violent. They had the numbers, the muscle, the size, the will, and even an eagerness to intimidate. They cultivated the look, manner, and reputation of men who enjoyed beating people up. Often enough the violence was real, and the police looked the other way. In time, they would involve Elvis in lawsuits, not just for black eyes and bloody noses but for smashed teeth, broken bones, and at least one alleged concussion. Elvis's gang was decidedly juvenile, but it was also dangerous.

In time, each guy had some specific duty—bodyguard, managing food, wardrobes, housing, transportation, and entertainment—but they spent most of their time lounging around waiting to see what Elvis wanted them to do next. They joined in his games with unbridled enthusiasm, glared at his enemies, laughed at his jokes as if on cue, and called him "boss." Elvis so loved that title that he had a sign made for his desk in the office next to his bedroom in Graceland that read ELVIS PRESLEY— THE BOSS.

Occasionally, their mission astounded observers. For example, on location in Florida in 1961 to make the movie *Follow That Dream*, his director was having difficulty understanding Elvis's psyche. He thought he might get to know Elvis better and thus improve his performance by inviting him over for dinner. The Elvis camp was thrown into great consternation. Elvis did not accept dinner invitations. What would he say at the dinner table with intelligent, educated, and articulate people all around him? How would he know which fork or spoon to use? Finally, the reply came to the host that Elvis would come, but only if the guys were invited too.

The Memphis Mafia gave Elvis a sense of control over a part of his life, be that part ever so tiny. Seldom, almost never, did he venture out of that carefully constructed universe alone, and within it he monitored each person closely not only for behavior but also for attitude. At Graceland, he had surveillance cameras that fed a screen in his bedroom. His guys discovered that he sometimes listened silent and unseen at the top of the stairs to their conversations downstairs. When two of them talked privately within his sight but out of his hearing, he demanded to know what they were talking about. One time, Marty Lacker was in the swimming pool with Sonny West. When Elvis yelled out, "What are you guys talking about?" Marty said, "Nothing." Elvis replied, "No, dammit, what are you talking about?" Marty then gave him an answer that Elvis liked. Elvis kept them constantly on edge and at war with one another by specially favoring one person over others with his attention, or lavishing gifts on one and not the others.

Ironically, Elvis's own worst and most calculated cruelties were directed against individuals among the guys. In effect, he used members of the gang as whipping boys. Lamar Fike was a favorite target. Slightly younger than Elvis, Lamar weighed three hundred pounds and by his own description was "a character." He was also very bright and quickly articulate. As a child, he lived in Cleveland, Mississippi, with his Jewish mother and gentile father. In that small town in the Mississippi Delta, they were Presbyterians, but when they moved to Memphis, where his father became a relatively well-paid farm equipment salesman, his mom decided to join the elite St. John's Episcopal Church.

Lamar loved singing in the church choir. In fact, he loved anything that suggested show business. After his father died, he and his mother moved to Texas. Lamar did not last through his first semester at Texas Christian University and soon was back in Memphis. He dabbled in radio, flashed wads of money to get the attention of local radio celebrities, and got to know George Klein and Cliff Gleaves, both disc jockeys and close friends of Elvis. Through them, he met Elvis, and Elvis liked him right away.

Returning to Texas, Lamar lied himself into a job as a disc jockey, but soon found it too taxing—all those switches, records to find, play, and restore to their proper places, schedules to keep, entries in logs to make, and rules and regulations. One day, he was on the job alone in the radio station. He put a long-play record on the air, locked up the station, got into his car, and left. Listening to the station on his car radio as he drove away from town, he heard the *click—click—click* of the needle on the circling record in the deserted studio in the locked building. Lamar drove to Hollywood and straight to the Beverly Wilshire Hotel, where he knew Elvis and the guys were staying. He joined up with Elvis and stayed with him for the next five years—one year in the movies, two years in the army in Europe, and another two years in the movies.

At Elvis parties, because of a prejudice against sex with full-bodied men, Lamar found himself at the back of the line in the competition for leftover girls. He fought valiantly to survive emotionally in the swirling flood of feminine beauty and abundant sex, but Elvis was no help in the struggle. In Hollywood, Lamar fell in love with one of Elvis's lovers, the star Natalie Wood. When Lamar asked Elvis what she was like sexually, Elvis cruelly crushed his romantic fantasy by telling him that Natalie was deficient in feminine hygiene. Rather sadly, it usually fell to Lamar to drive the Elvis girl (or girls) of the evening home in the wee hours of the morning after Elvis had finished with her.

Lamar's love life might have sometimes languished, but he was not at all a pitiful creature. He was saved by a razor-sharp mind, a Falstaffian demeanor, and a truly amazing—given this maelstrom of fantasies—grasp of realities and absurdities. He was quick and accurate in his judgments about individual character and personal relations, and he was sometimes wickedly and acidly articulate. Of all the guys, including Elvis, he was probably the quickest of mind, and he was not slow in putting his thoughts into cutting language.

The Elvisian universe was a thing unto itself, but it still had somehow to find its way among other universes in the broader cultural cosmos of Memphis, Hollywood, New York, the United States, and beyond. It was compelled to respond to outside forces—particularly the army, the movie people, the record people, the television people, the Las Vegas and tour people, and the fans. Colonel Tom Parker mediated these responses very effectively. It was he who created the conditions that allowed Elvis to live as he did. He brought in the money without which there would have been no Elvisian universe, and he promoted and protected the marvelously beautiful images of Elvis that floated in the minds of Elvis's audiences everywhere—highly marketable commodities. By the Colonel's rule, Elvis never performed casually and for free. Even shows done ostensibly for charity were carefully calculated to increase Elvis's revenues. If the Mafia went too far in their hijinks, they would hear the Colonel's stern voice. If outside forces became too menacing, those forces would feel his power.

Elvis's image was precious, but it was vastly distant from the life that Elvis really lived. Lamar Fike sometimes chuckled over how good a job the insiders did in promoting the deception. It was a construct, a deception from which everyone derived "fun" and an income of a magnitude they would have had difficulty achieving elsewhere. Both the Colonel and Elvis established and stringently enforced the rule that no one in Elvis's private life should ever tell outsiders what it was really like.

The Colonel himself carefully stayed out of Elvis's personal affairs. He did not even live in Memphis, but rather in Madison, Tennessee, near Nashville and more than two hundred miles east of Graceland. Only when he feared that Elvis's public performances might be adversely impacted or his image tarnished did he intervene. For more than twenty years, Elvis was his only client, and altogether he served him well.

THE GIRLS IN GERMANY

After Elvis went to Germany, he and Anita Wood, a Memphis friend, talked about her coming over for a visit. She never did, but Elvis wrote to Anita for a year and a half, a uniquely long string of correspondence for him. He loved her as no one else in the whole world, he declared, and always would. He eagerly waited the time when they could marry and have "a little Elvis." He insisted that she remain "clean and wholesome," meaning virginal. In one letter he described himself as a "lonely little boy 5000 miles away." If Elvis was lonely, it was certainly not because he was alone. Almost immediately after he arrived in Germany, he was keeping company with a fifteen-year-old German girl, an aspiring model named Margit Buergin, whom he compared favorably to Brigitte Bardot. With this girl, he wrote one of his friends, it was "Grind City." Margit became pregnant and had to abort Elvis's child, an event, she later said, that left a scar on her psyche. Soon, he introduced another fifteen-year-old German girl, Heli Priemel, to his bed. He called her "Legs."

In Germany, the girls flocked to Elvis. Important among them was nineteen-year-old Elisabeth Stefaniak, a beautiful German girl whose father had deserted her and her mother during the war. After the war, her mother married an American army sergeant. She lived with her mother, her adoptive father, and a six-year-old half-sister on an army base near the Czech border where Elvis was stationed temporarily in

November and December 1958. She sought his autograph at the post theater, and he took to her immediately, inviting her to sit next to him during the movie and putting his arm around her shoulders, an act, with Elvis, of possession. He walked Elisabeth home and behaved in a considerate and gentlemanly manner. On Thanksgiving morning, he knocked on her door unannounced and spent a delightful day with her family. Elvis had found his target, and he was being his charming self.

Soon he hired Elisabeth to serve as his private secretary, given her command of both German and English. She would live in his household, have her own room, and be one of the family. He assured Elisabeth's parents that his father and grandmother would watch over her. On the very first night, however, Elvis let Elisabeth know in a matter-of-fact way that her job would be much more than secretarial. One of her duties was to sleep with him—every night when there was no other girl immediately available for his bed. Elvis explained that he would not have full intercourse with her. He did not do that, he said, with any girl "he was going to see on a regular basis" for fear of getting her pregnant.

Elisabeth did not find the nonsecretarial part of her job especially onerous. Indeed, she soon came to adore Elvis and would do willingly whatever he wanted. When they moved from a hotel into a house, she was given the room next to his.

The rub for Elisabeth was that Elvis continued his revolving-door routine with girls. Often the guys would recruit beautiful young women to offer Elvis. Sometimes he would do his own recruiting from the young women who swirled about the front of the house and bring them in where his bodyguards and other male hangers-on gathered every evening to talk, sing, and drink lemonade. Lemonade was usually the mandatory drink in Elvis's house after Gladys's terminal encounter with alcohol. After a while, Elvis would invite one of the girls up to his room for sex. In her bed next door, Elisabeth could hear them. When the tryst was over and Elvis had sent the girl away, he would lie on his bed and knock on the wall three times to signal to Elisabeth that she should come over. Many nights she crawled into Elvis's bed only minutes after the other girl had left, and she must have felt the lingering warmth of that girl's body. She consoled herself that the other girls came and went, but she was the one who stayed.

On or soon after Sunday, September 13, 1959, the girl who had just left was a fourteen-year-old ninth grader, Priscilla Beaulieu, whose father, an officer in the US Air Force, was stationed nearby in Wiesbaden. Priscilla had been recruited for Elvis by Currie Grant, an airman first class in the Air Force and an assistant manager of the Eagle Club, the military canteen in Wiesbaden, who had charmed his way into the group of young men surrounding Elvis. Though married and the father of two small children, he was, he confessed, a "sex addict," and his major aim in life was to seduce very young women; in fact he targeted very young girls, such as Priscilla.

During the summer of 1959 Currie had spotted Priscilla in the Eagle Club soon after she arrived in Europe. A stunning beauty, she had been elected the "Most Beautiful, Prettiest Eyes, Best Dressed" girl in her junior high school in Austin, Texas, that spring. He immediately engaged her in conversation. "Would you like to meet Elvis?" he asked. This was the ordinary bait used by men in Elvis's coterie. Bringing in pretty girls for Elvis was a very pleasant part of their job. It raised their stock with Elvis, and there were always girls left over after Elvis had taken his pick. Almost forty years later, Currie told the writer Suzanne Finstad that Priscilla had approached him about an introduction and he had exacted sex from the fourteen-year-old girl four times before delivering her up to Elvis. Priscilla finally demanded her due, he said, and he took her to Elvis. Everyone in the room saw that Elvis was smitten at first sight.

Priscilla vigorously denied that she had sex with Currie in order to meet Elvis. He had willingly invited her to meet Elvis, she said, and her parents had given permission only after questioning him closely. Her father was loving but very strict, she said. She was enthralled by Elvis from the first. Seemingly shy, Priscilla was actually merely quiet. She was observant and very smart. She had a gift for focusing intensely on what she wanted and getting it—sooner or later. For a dozen years, she wanted Elvis.

Elvis, as always, was skillful in the wooing process. When he wanted, he could make a girl—an audience of one—feel that she was the only one

in the whole world for him. For the moment, it was true. Elvis was a romantic; recurrently he felt that his dream was coming true. That evening
he showered attention on the doll-like girl wearing, as Lamar Fike said,
a "little blue-and-white sailor suit, and white socks." He talked to her,
played the piano for her, and—if not that night, within a few nights—
sent her up to his room, where, after a discreet interval, he joined her. He
made love to her in every way short of penetration. It was as if Priscilla's
virginity were another thing that Elvis strangely and sorely needed to
maintain.

Priscilla was in Elvis's bed in the house in Bad Nauheim practically
every night that he was at home during his six months in Germany. Elvis
taught her how to make love in various ways short of full intercourse,
and she proved an apt pupil. As she wrote candidly in her book, *Elvis
and Me*, every evening the pattern of ardent foreplay went on and on.
Again and again, she pled with Elvis for the consummation of their love,
but he steadfastly refused. It would spoil everything, he explained. Elvis
did with Priscilla what he had learned to do with many of those hundreds
of thousands of American girls who had followed him so passionately
onstage, on records, on television and in the movies. In lovemaking, as
in entertaining, Elvis's outstanding talent was oral. Leaving Priscilla frustrated but technically virginal, he flew back to America in March 1960.

THE OTHER GIRLS

Elvis had sex with other girls even while he only was having foreplay
with Priscilla. His relationship with Elisabeth was different from all the
others. She lived in his house and was Elvis's insurance that he would not
sleep alone. The girl in the bed, like Elisabeth and those who followed,
was different from all the other girls in that she had a degree of perma-
nence in her intimacy with Elvis—a year, two years or more, and sometimes even a possibility of marriage and, hence, presumed perpetuity.

In addition to the girl in the bed, there were hundreds of other
girls who had sex with Elvis. Lamar Fike, who lived in Elvis's various
houses and was almost glued to him from 1957 to 1962, said that his
seemingly endless desire for sex with huge numbers of girls and young

women came only after his mother's death in 1958. There had been a river of sex before; now there was a flood.

From the time of Gladys's death until his own in 1977, between the transients and the relatively permanent, Elvis would always have some girl or young woman in his bed—for petting, for companionship, for a sense of comfort and security, for sex, for affirmation of his masculinity, for a complex of reasons that defy complete understanding. Lamar said that "his sexual appetites were very, very strong...Really, the touching and the feeling and the patting and everything else meant more to Elvis than the actual act." Lamar summed up his description aptly. "I guess Elvis was the King of Foreplay," he concluded.

Other than simple availability, the only qualification for the young woman was that she be, by common consent among men, unusually attractive physically. Very often the girls were certified beauty queens, models, movie stars, or starlets. They always had to be women that other men would lust after, fantasize about, and envy him for. Never did his selection of a bedmate have to do with her intellectual prowess or strength of character.

The girl in the bed—along with his extended family and the guys—became the third vital institution in Elvis's personal life. It was as if he seized upon these ingredients and attempted to make the mix that would give him self-definition and a feeling of security after his mother's passing. The ingredients were obvious, yet the mix was complex. The girls in Elvis's bed, for example, related to the guys and his family in multifarious ways and evolved over time. But, clearly, the three-part pattern first took form in the household that Elvis created in Bad Nauheim in 1959 and 1960. On August 16, 1977, it was evident in the people who stood around his body on the bathroom floor at Graceland. One, Ginger Alden, had literally been the girl in the bed waiting for him at the very moment he died.

The Sins of the Father

In Bad Nauheim, Elisabeth Stefaniak bonded with Elvis's grandmother Minnie Mae, whom everyone called "Grandma." It was a relationship that Elvis encouraged. Indeed, it was virtually the only relationship that Elvis allowed her. Elisabeth and everyone else understood that she was hardly to look at any other man, much less become friendly with one. She was to keep her distance especially from the men in Elvis's coterie, which included several of his buddies from the army, most notably fellow draftees Charlie Hodge and Joe Esposito.

Elvis's jealousy and consequent suspicions were boundless. For example, in March 1959, Elisabeth was riding with Vernon in Elvis's Mercedes on the autobahn when Vernon lost control, flipped the car over several times, and put Elisabeth in the hospital. After first determining that his father was all right, Elvis went straight to Elisabeth's hospital room, where he found her heavily bandaged and in much pain. Without expressing any feeling at all for her plight, he immediately demanded to know if she and his father had "engaged in any advances toward each other" just before the wreck.

Elisabeth was aghast. What advances?! How could Elvis imagine such a shocking thing, his middle-aged father and his nineteen-year-old lover, contemplating sex together at all, much less engaging in such physical contact in a speeding car? She assured him that there were no advances. His father had always been a perfect gentleman to her, she said.

While Elvis was outrageously insensitive in his treatment of Elisabeth, he had good reason to be suspicious of his father. Recurrently, Gladys had been angry with Vernon because he spent too much time down at the gate, where the girls were always eager to talk to him. She was furious when a beautiful blond Hollywood star came to Graceland during Elvis's absence and Vernon rushed eagerly to play the host. There was no telling what Vernon had in mind, but the role could not have failed to inflate his manly ego. Gladys's sister Lillian, who spent a lot of time at Graceland during these months, said that such things were the only things that Gladys and Vernon fought over.

And they did fight. Billy Smith and Lamar Fike attested to that fact, and each was in a position to know. Billy was family, close family. He was Travis Smith's son and during his childhood had sometimes lived in the same house with the Presleys and always nearby. He was loyal to Elvis and his immediate family, and he never wrote his own tell-all-and-more book. Yet he was generous in talking to interviewers, who found him straightforward and forthcoming. His stories had consistency and credibility. He had thought deeply about his experiences with his cousin and Gladys and Vernon. Generously, he shared his hard-won perspectives.

Billy thought Vernon first started beating Gladys when Elvis went on the road. He picked times when Elvis was away and she was drinking and ill. Vernon would get mad at her. He himself drank, and "he got mean as a snake when he got drunk." Once Gladys "had a mark on her face, right this side of her eye, on the left temple." Billy's father told him that when Elvis saw the mark he said, "Daddy, you lay a hand on her again, and I'll kill you!"

Lamar Fike, who lived with Elvis almost constantly from the summer of 1958 to 1962, added to the accounts of Vernon abusing Gladys. Elvis frequently called home, he thought, in part to make sure that Vernon was not mistreating his mother. He lived with the Presleys while they were in Killeen, Texas, from mid-June to September 1958, when Elvis was stationed at Fort Hood. Gladys and Vernon would argue, he said, Gladys screaming and Vernon mumbling in response. Lamar and Elvis once heard them arguing in another room. "You steercotted [castrated] bastard!" Gladys shouted at Vernon. Lamar turned to Elvis and said, "That's the funniest line I've heard this year." On one occasion while Gladys was cooking, they got into another fight, and Gladys hit Vernon on the side of his head with a pot of navy beans. Lamar and Elvis rushed into the kitchen to find Vernon lying on the floor out cold, covered with beans.

"Vernon started jumping everything that moved the day after Gladys died," Lamar recalled. Right after they returned to Texas following Gladys's funeral, Vernon had picked up a blonde who came to the house. They drove away, and by the time they returned Elvis had come home. "Who is that?" he asked Lamar. He hardly needed to ask; he knew what was happening. When Vernon came in he said, "Daddy, I want to talk to you." They went into a back bedroom. Vernon hemmed and hawed, but Elvis's voice was clear. "Now look!" he said, "Mama ain't been in the ground a week! We're going to have some changes here!" When they got to Europe, Lamar said, Vernon got worse.

"Dee" Stanley was in her thirties, the mother of three boys, and the wife of army sergeant William Stanley. They lived near Elvis, and Dee took it upon herself in November 1958 to call Elvis, express condolences on the loss of his mother, and welcome him to Germany. The personal connection that justified such hospitality, she seemed to think, was that she too was a Southerner. Possibly she intended to engage Elvis in a romantic way, but he dodged the bullet by passing her invitation on to Vernon to deal with while he was away with the army on maneuvers. Vernon invited Dee to coffee in the restaurant in the hotel where the Presleys were then staying. In return, she invited him home to meet her husband. Coffee gave way to liquor, and liquor gave way to sex between Vernon and Dee, right under her husband's nose. The sergeant was a heavy drinker and seemed not to notice. Even so, Elvis's bodyguards, Lamar Fike and Red West, were alarmed. How could the husband not know? William Stanley had been one of General George Patton's bodyguards, and he might get physical with Vernon.

Soon Vernon grew even bolder. He started bringing Dee to the house in Bad Nauheim. He would take her into his room, just off the living room. Dee was very audible in her lovemaking, and her cries of ecstasy could be heard all over the house. Lamar recalled that "Vernon would come out of the room about twenty minutes later, and be real cocky, and he'd sit there." Soon it got worse. "One time, they spent over an hour in there, and Elvis had about fifteen people in the house." When "Dee started to holler, Elvis got up and started playing the piano so loud it made Liberace sound like a paraplegic." Vernon's romance with Dee was still in full blossom when Elvis suspected his father of making advances on Elisabeth. It was a bit too much.

Elisabeth soon concluded that Elvis was jealous of any personal relationship that did not revolve around him, not just sexual relationships. He invested heavily and successfully in building up his connection with each person he brought into the circle. "He had a way of making anyone feel they were the most important person in the world to him," she said. Once they were hooked, he demanded total and absolute loyalty.

Violators were threatened with immediate expulsion, especially males, she thought. Lamar laughingly estimated that Elvis fired him 150 times, and even Billy Smith racked up several dismissals. Often the firing required what the participants considered clever dialogue.

"You're fired," Elvis would yell.

"You can't fire me, I quit," the other would yell back.

The firings seldom lasted long.

Elisabeth was enthralled by Elvis. She willingly accepted the limits he imposed upon her and even forgave his sudden, emotionally violent, and cruel rages over the most trivial things. On one occasion, they were shopping at the Post Exchange. He wanted to buy another wastebasket for his room. Elisabeth suggested that he did not need another wastebasket.

"Don't ever...," Elvis exploded and warned her never to challenge him. Never.

When displeased, he did this with everyone in his circle. Lamar said he would kill a fly with a sledgehammer. Sometimes he would show great anger at one person while he winked at another as if to assure him that he was especially favored. Such performances, of course, were just another way of maintaining control over his coterie.

In time, Elisabeth came to follow her feelings for one of the young men among Elvis's guys, Rex Mansfield. He returned her sentiments in full measure. Rex, like Elvis, was a draftee and had served with him from the day both left the induction center in Memphis for Fort Hood in Texas. He was intelligent, clean-cut, and handsome. Elvis was very fond of him and called him "Rexadus." Rex could attract girls without Elvis's help. His superiors made him a tank commander while Elvis was still driving a jeep for his sergeant. Rex's success caused some resentment on Elvis's part, but Rex was impossible to hate. Elvis decided that the army favored Rex because Rex was his friend. Elvis took Rex on junkets to Munich and Paris, where the boys eschewed all the famous sights—no Louvre, no Eiffel Tower—slept all day, enjoyed the clubs all night, and brought girls back to their hotel.

All during his European stay, Elvis was obviously nonplussed by a European attitude that sex outside of marriage could be something less than a cardinal sin. Indeed, the clubs in Munich and Paris seemed to celebrate sex as if it were a thing unto itself and had nothing at all to do with social propriety, morality, or religion. These people appeared to feel no guilt at all about any kind of sex, homo or hetero, solo or group, masochistic or sadistic. Elvis tried hard, but he never quite knew what to do with it all. There are photographs of him with the girls in the Moulin Rouge in Munich in which he looks like a man who does not know how to perform with them in an appropriate way. His whole body seems limp. He had exhausted himself and could do no more among these women who seem so worldly-wise and so physically feminine. Perhaps, among other things, he had caught a glimpse of the erotic and exciting possibilities of mixing sex and pain.

What Elvis saw in the nightclubs of Europe was so unlike American sex, so unlike back-seat, drive-in-movie love-making, so unlike Tupelo and Memphis and even Las Vegas, that he seemed staggered. In America, he was broadly recognized as the king of sex; his girlfriends had applauded his performances often enough to convince him that he was highly talented. But here he was not even a prince, much less the king. In Europe, apparently, men often rose to heights he had never achieved in America. Moreover, they did it in ways that he had never dreamed of. Europeans did it all more honestly, more gracefully, with less fumbling, and with variations that he could hardly imagine. If European men did what a man should do, Elvis was still a teenage boy.

In Europe, Elvis protected himself successfully from European influence. He took not the slightest interest in its art and architecture. He learned nothing of its history and culture. He lived in Germany for a year and a half and seemed not to have absorbed even a respectful smattering of the German language. Instead, he constructed and lived within his small, tight Elvisian universe. In Germany, Minnie Mae cooked for him the fat-laden Southern meals he found so satisfying. He surrounded himself with guys, all Americans and young, who shared his values and inflated his ego. He took refuge in a domestic construct in which he could entertain the girls and did not feel threatened. After a year in Europe, Elvis was still sexually at sea. It was a sea that he did not understand. It confused and threatened him. In the crisis, Priscilla

Beaulieu, a purely American girl, came to him like a gift from heaven. She was absolutely, almost miraculously, the perfect solution for him in his time of great need. In September 1959, she was barely fourteen years old and already a stunning—though miniature—beauty. She was very young, a child really, and totally malleable. She became Elvis's willing clay.

BACK TO ELISABETH

Elisabeth Stefaniak shared the secret of her love for Rex Mansfield with "Grandma" Presley, who encouraged the relationship. When Elvis returned to America, Elisabeth came with him, ostensibly slated to continue her service as his private secretary. She rode around Memphis with Elvis on his motorcycle, sitting behind him, her arms wrapped around his middle. He gave her a new yellow Lincoln and lessons on how to drive it. After a week, amazingly, he told her she could date other men. She immediately called Rex, who had returned to his hometown to work for the company he had left two years before. He had turned down an offer from Elvis to work for him as a kind of "foreman" of the guys, a job that soon fell to Joe Esposito, another of Elvis's army buddies.

Rex appeared at Graceland just in time to help Elvis dress for a night at the movies. With great trepidation—as he was helping Elvis adjust his suspenders—Rex said that he would like to go out with Elisabeth that evening, somewhere where they could be alone. Elvis fell silent for a long moment while Rex waited. Finally, he responded. "Rexadus, you know Elisabeth will never love anybody but me," he said, looking at himself in the mirror and striking an admiring pose. Rex replied that he just thought Elisabeth needed a break. Elvis said he was glad that Rex was taking her out because he knew that he would always treat Elisabeth like a lady. He meant there would be no sex.

The next day, Elisabeth was sitting in a car in front of Graceland about to flee from Elvis and rejoin Rex. Elisabeth had put out the story that she was going to see her parents, who were visiting in Florida and in the process of relocating in America. At the last moment, Elvis came running out of the house and brought her back inside. As usual, one of the guys had ratted on her to make points with the boss. Looking her straight in the eye, she recalled, Elvis asked her if she was going to meet Rex. She lied convincingly, and Elvis let her go. Elisabeth and Rex married within three months, sending Elvis an invitation to the wedding that went unanswered. Except for receiving one of the stock autographed photos sent out the next Christmas by the staff, they never heard from Elvis again.

ANITA WOOD

Elvis could let Elisabeth Stefaniak go because he had Anita Wood ready and waiting in Memphis. Anita had been waiting, in fact, for the two years that Elvis was in the army. She was a crowned beauty queen from Jackson, Tennessee, who aspired to make a career for herself as a singer. In July 1957, at nineteen, she was cohost on a Memphis television show, the *Top Ten Dance Party*. Elvis saw her on the TV screen and got George Klein to bring her out to his new home, Graceland. He began a serious courtship immediately. They drove downtown to see a giant cut-out of Elvis at the theater where his first movie, *Loving You,* was about to premiere. Then he took her to a drive-in restaurant where they always served Elvis in a private dining room inside. Then he showed her Graceland room by room, talking all the time. When Anita told him she did not feel comfortable lingering in his bedroom (with the nine-foot-square bed), they descended to the living room and spent the evening talking and singing at the piano. In the end, Elvis himself, not Lamar Fike or another of the guys, drove her to her rooming house, a proper establishment run by Mrs. J. B. Patty. As they parted, Elvis received a chaste kiss. Anita Wood, it seems, was Dixie Locke's successor as a potential wife.

The courtship of Anita during the summer of 1957 was strikingly classic, including her meeting his parents under the most favorable conditions Elvis could imagine. It also included the usual confessional in which he charmingly revealed his human vulnerabilities despite his greatness. Elvis took Anita and his parents together to a private showing of *Loving You*. He drove her about Memphis in a panel truck—such as he had driven for Crown Electric—to see all the places he had lived and frequented, including the route he had walked between one of his homes and the grocery store. The panel truck allowed them to move about the city unrecognized and without his usual entourage of young men. He told her everything about himself from infancy on. He confessed his great dread of entering the army, an emotion he could not express in public without contradicting the perfectly patriotic image that he and the Colonel were carefully projecting. He gave her a pet name, "Little," inspired by the size of her feet. He greatly admired his mother's small feet, and he and Anita began to talk baby talk to each other as he and Gladys did.

Gladys liked Anita a lot, seeing in her a likely lifelong mate for her son. Elvis would marry Anita, she decided, settle down, and begin a family. "I just can't wait," she told Anita, "to see that little ol' baby walking up and down the driveway." Anita was frequently at Graceland, and she noticed that Gladys was often sick and stayed in her room. Her ankles and legs were swollen, she was overweight, and she had heart trouble. "She never ceased to worry about Elvis," Anita recalled, but she never suspected that Gladys had a problem with alcohol.

Unlike Dixie, Anita happily joined Elvis's all-male Memphis gang. The boys swirled around her and Elvis as if they were the golden couple in a high school senior class. They all went to the movies, the drive-in, the roller rink, the amusement park, McKellar Lake. Now and again, Elvis would take advantage of Anita's innocence to amuse the boys. Riding in the back seat of the car with the gang all around them, he would have her call out, "My cunt hurts," without knowing what she was saying. The boys thought it was hilarious.

Lamar Fike was glued to Elvis by then. George Klein continued to balance his disc-jockeying career with adhering to Elvis as closely as he could. In 1956, George brought Cliff Gleaves to Elvis. Cliff was a young man, a disc jockey in the region, and an entertainer who imitated the voices of famous people. He was always desperately seeking some way to break into the big time. Cliff sensed that Elvis was his ticket to success and hung around in Memphis until he met Elvis, who liked him immediately. On the very same day that Elvis first had Cliff out to his house for a visit, he had him move out of his room in the Memphis YMCA and into one of the three bedrooms in the Presley house on Audubon Drive.

George Klein also brought in Alan Fortas. Part of Memphis's affluent and cultured Jewish community, Alan had been an All-City Tackle at Central High School, and Elvis had seen him play. Afterward, he had attended first Vanderbilt University and then Southwestern College in Memphis, but dropped out finally to work in his uncle's junkyard, where, happily for Elvis biographers, he happened to find Elvis's high school report cards and preserve them. Unlike Cliff, Alan did not plot to meet Elvis. His opportunity came because his friend George Klein could not drive a car. George always needed a ride, and often he needed a ride to Graceland. One day he asked Alan if he would like to meet Elvis. Elvis took to Alan right away and invited him back. Alan became one of "the guys," dubbed "Hog Ears" by Elvis.

By the fall of 1957, everyone understood that Anita was Elvis's girl and assumed that she and Elvis would someday marry. But, as the guys knew, there were many other girls and young women for Elvis on the road and even at Graceland—under Anita's nose. Elvis had seen disc jockey Betty Maddox on local television and had her over from time to time. If Anita called while she was there, he would have one of the guys say that he was tied up for the evening. Venetia Stevenson, a movie star, also came for a visit. Compared to what came later, Elvis was discreet about these affairs, since Graceland was still Gladys's home. Gladys had laid down the law: there would be no "slut parties" at Graceland while she lived there.

There was one very odd kind of party that Elvis recurrently had at Graceland that was not forbidden by Gladys. On occasional evenings, Elvis had a trio of fourteen-year-old girls join him in his bedroom for pillow fights, tickling, kissing, and cuddling. If one of the girls got nervous while wrestling with the twenty-two-year-old, 180-pound Presley, one of the girls later recalled, "all you'd have to say is 'Stop!' and he'd roll over and quit." It fell to Lamar to drive these girls home at the end of the evening. Actually, these games had begun a year before when the girls were thirteen and visited Elvis on Audubon Drive for the same kind of fun. Elvis knew them because the father of one ran an auto repair shop that Vernon patronized. Somehow, this made everything all right.

Anita seemed unaware of the magnitude of Elvis's interest in other girls and young women, and their romance seemed to flower. By the end of August 1957, Elvis was telling reporters that "Anita is number one with me—strictly tops." As his train left Memphis for his return to Hollywood, the local press reported that Anita "burst into tears and Mrs. Presley put her arms around her." Soon Anita visited him in Hollywood, and he gave her a "very expensive" diamond and sapphire ring. Just before he went into the army, he gave her a car, and on the last night they and the boys went to a drive-in movie and the skating rink. Before he finally left the rink, Elvis got in and out of the car three times, so reluctant was he to surrender the pleasant diversions he had enjoyed over the last few years.

Anita visited Elvis and the Presleys in Texas while Elvis was in training. It was as if she were already one of the family. When Gladys died, she was in New York preparing to appear on *The Andy Williams Show*, a major event in her rising career as a singer. Immediately after the show, she flew to Memphis, arriving at Graceland at 2:30 a.m. to find Elvis and Vernon sitting on the front steps. Elvis brought her in to see the body. "Look at her little sooties [feet], Little," he urged. "Look at her little sooties, she's so precious."

Home again in Memphis in the spring of 1960, Elvis let Elisabeth Stefaniak go and resumed his relationship with the virginal Anita. Anita was taken aback by her first sight of Elisabeth. She had been led to believe that Elisabeth was a drab secretarial type, the opposite of the very attractive young woman she was. But Elvis showered Anita with attention, and they were soon back where they had left off. The whole world assumed that she and Elvis would marry, and so did she.

Over the months, Anita slowly began to realize that there were other women in Elvis's life and at least one of those relationships was serious. During one trip to Hollywood, she discovered a letter from Priscilla Beaulieu begging Elvis to bring her over for a visit. In March 1960, she had seen the girl in a photograph in *Life* magazine, a tearful young teenager crying after Elvis as he boarded the plane to fly home. Elvis explained to Anita that the child simply had a crush on him. He continued that story as well as concocting other stories to explain all the women circling about. Finally, Anita realized that Elvis would not marry her in the foreseeable future, if ever, and she was eager to marry and begin a family.

It was time to end the relationship, she decided. In August she invited Elvis and Vernon to sit down with her at the table in the dining room at Graceland and gave them the news. It's over, Anita said. Both Vernon and Elvis expressed their regret at her decision. Elvis expressed his a bit too easily. He announced his hope that he was doing the right thing in letting her go. Then he did let her go. Anita arranged for her brother to come and pick up her things. Unlike Elisabeth, it seems that Anita did not sleep with Elvis. Nor did she have sex with him. She exited his life as she had entered it—virginal.

Anita went back to her hometown, Jackson, Tennessee. She had invested heavily in Elvis and lost. She lost a year and a half before Elvis went overseas, a year and a half while he was overseas in the army, and then two years after he came back. Five years was a long time to wait for him. When she recovered, she married a man who played baseball with the Cleveland Indians.

Priscilla: The Feminine Elvis

Elvis could let the virginal Anita go because now he had the virginal Priscilla. They had stayed in touch since his departure from Germany. She wrote him on stand-out pink stationery that allowed Joe Esposito to pluck her letters out from the great piles of fan mail. Finally, Elvis persuaded Priscilla's father, Captain Beaulieu, to allow him to bring her over for a two-week visit in Hollywood at the end of June 1962. The captain accepted a story that Elvis concocted. She was to stay at the home of the man who customized vehicles for Elvis and be chaperoned by the man and his wife. Of course, Priscilla, now seventeen, was with Elvis the whole time after the first night, most of it in Las Vegas, not Hollywood. Anita, meanwhile, was back at Graceland.

On August 6, within weeks of Priscilla's visit, Anita announced her breakup with Elvis in the *Memphis Press-Scimitar*. Elvis was now totally free. He barraged Priscilla's father with phone calls asking him to let her return for Christmas. Again, he prevailed. She came for three weeks, beginning just before Christmas and staying into the New Year, 1963. He showed Priscilla Graceland and his favorite spots around town. As the time neared for her return, he called Captain Beaulieu begging for permission to extend her stay. The captain was unmoved and Elvis was furious.

After Priscilla flew back to Europe, Elvis mounted the campaign for her return. This time the pitch to her parents was that she would come to America to complete her education in Memphis in the highly respected Catholic high school for girls, Immaculate Conception, thereby facilitating the expected return of the Beaulieu family from Germany when the captain was reassigned in America. Her tenure at Immaculate Conception would not be long, less than three months, since graduation would occur in May. Elvis assured Priscilla's parents that she would live with and be chaperoned by his father and his father's new wife, Dee Stanley. Elvis hated Dee, and he hated that his father had taken up with her so soon after Gladys's death. But now that she had divorced the army sergeant and married Vernon, he painted them as a happy, settled couple successfully engaged in rearing three sterling young boys from Dee's previous marriage, Billy, David, and Ricky.

Captain and Mrs. Beaulieu bought the con. By early March, the captain had brought Priscilla to Los Angeles, where they met Elvis, and then took her to Memphis, where she settled in with the Presleys and matriculated at Immaculate Conception High School. As soon as Elvis finished the film he was working on, *Fun in Acapulco*, he returned to Memphis. Priscilla promptly moved into Graceland and into his bed.

Priscilla staggered through school days at Immaculate Conception after nights spent with Elvis. He supplied her with all the necessary drugs to survive, especially uppers. Elvis had been exploring them for himself ever since his days in the army. She had to cheat to pass her math exam, but she nevertheless graduated as planned on May 29, 1963. Elvis waited in his car during the ceremony so as to cause no disruption. Afterward, he threw a graduation party for her, and they had a month together at Graceland, much of it spent on his huge square bed in his bedroom with blackout windows.

Thereafter, year after year, Priscilla slept in Elvis's bed. Almost anybody who cared to know about it could know about it, but it never became a news item. No outsider knows why the Beaulieus allowed their barely fourteen-year-old daughter to become so deeply involved with America's sex idol, ten years her senior. In Germany, she was with him almost nightly for six months and stayed so late that in the morning she had to drag herself out of her bed to go to school. Two years later, after her graduation from high school, they allowed her to move into Graceland to live with him for an undetermined length of time in an undefined relationship.

In *Elvis and Me*, Priscilla attempted to answer the question concerning her parents' possible lack of responsibility and put the matter to rest. She vigorously asserted that she herself shielded her parents from knowledge of the depth of her physical intimacy with Elvis. For some time, she managed to keep her family away from Graceland entirely. Then, when they insisted on a visit, she made a great show of demonstrating that she did not sleep in Elvis's bed or share his room. She had her own bedroom at Graceland. When it became clear that she would have to give them a tour of the whole house, she hastily moved her things to Charlie Hodge's room down the hall. Only when she was showing them Elvis's room did she notice that she had left one of her shoes next to the big bed. She barely managed to kick it out of sight under the bed before they saw that display of intimacy.

Lamar Fike, Billy Smith, and others argued that Captain and Mrs. Beaulieu knew full well that their very young daughter was sleeping with a man who used her sexually, but they guessed that the captain had made a deal with Elvis. He would marry Priscilla at some later point in time when his career would allow him to give up his highly marketable bachelor image. With that marriage, their daughter, and they too, would be well set for life, emotionally and materially. That made the game worth the gamble. Suzanne Finstad, in her thoroughly researched *Child Bride*, argued that not only did Priscilla's parents know what was going on, but Priscilla and her mother had plotted the marriage from the beginning.

Such interpretations are persuasive but perhaps underestimate Priscilla's passion for Elvis and her determination to control her own life. In fact, she had just turned eighteen when she graduated from Immaculate Conception, and she was legally free to marry. Her parents might have wanted her to find and marry a man closer to her own age, but the choice ultimately was not theirs to make. Priscilla loved Elvis body and soul. She was exactly where she wanted to be. She did not care about school or an ordinary teenage life. She was not bothered by his age, and gave every evidence that she could keep up with his sexual appetite and performance. Indeed, her complaints were that she did not have more time with her lover and that he refused to have intercourse with her. Elvis was simply the great love of her youth. When she grew older, she moved on.

With Priscilla now safely attached to him and free from outside influences, Elvis proceeded to the consummation of his ideal. He recreated her in his image. He chose her clothes and shaped her looks in closest detail—hair, eyes, lips—as carefully as his own. He had her hair dyed a deep black, just like his. He darkened her eyes, as he had come to do very early in his show business career, wearing the dark makeup offstage as well as on. He put her in high heels, just as he put lifts in his own shoes to give the appearance of height. Some have speculated that Priscilla looked like Gladys, hence Elvis's obsession with her. It may be more accurate to speculate that Priscilla looked like Elvis himself, certainly after he completed his remodeling of her appearance. She was, in her looks and in her behavior, exactly what he wanted her to be. She was the girl he would have been were he a girl.

Elvis appropriated Priscilla's femininity just as he appropriated other people's songs. In her, he found a deeply feminine presence that was inherently beautiful, and he made it his own. He saw in her the beauty that he wanted for himself. Certainly he wanted the looks and the body, but it went much deeper than that. Priscilla was by her nature a superbly feminine creature, a phenomenon that people recognized on sight. He used the considerable means at his disposal to gain nearly total control over her—the walled compound of Graceland to confine her and a host of people on his payroll to guard her—and then he proceeded to possess what she possessed, in a sense to meld himself with her and somehow become whole, the feminine Elvis.

Sex Games at Graceland

Elvis still refused to have intercourse with Priscilla, but within the privacy of his quarters at Graceland they improved marvelously upon the sex play they had enjoyed in Germany. They invented sex games in which Priscilla might play the part of the teacher and Elvis would be her pupil, a very young boy susceptible to seduction. Or Elvis might be the patient and Priscilla the nurse, handling, fingering, and probing his body seeking to discover his malady and find a cure. At times, Elvis introduced another girl into the sex scene in his bedroom. In this play, Elvis had Priscilla and the girl pretend to make love while he watched, videotaped, and sometimes joined in.

They also got into the game of photographing themselves in various poses and scenes using a Polaroid camera, a handy new invention. Elvis and Priscilla could photograph the most private things, and no one else need ever see the picture. They became avid photographers, and they needed great quantities of fresh film. It was Priscilla's job to buy it, usually at a local drugstore. In time, clerks began to look askance at this girl who seemed to need so much Polaroid film. Priscilla was embarrassed and felt she had to explain herself. "I lost the last batch," she would say, or offer other white lies. The couple built a collection and kept it in a silver suitcase. Now and again the guys saw some of the photographs, and probably stole some. After Elvis's death, the silver suitcase was brought down from the attic in Graceland and delivered over to Priscilla.

The Movies

Elvis would make a lot of movies in the 1960s, twenty-seven of them in eight years, and his movies would earn him and the Colonel a lot of money. Elvis kept hoping for a great script and a great film. He told one young starlet with whom he was sleeping that he was offered the part of Val Xavier in a film based on Tennessee Williams's play *The Fugitive Kind* (1959). As it happened, Marlon Brando got the part of Val, the young singer with the guitar and the snakeskin jacket who grew tired of offering his body to homosexuals for money on a street corner in New Orleans and hit the road. In the story, Val drifted into disaster in a little town in the Mississippi Delta. After seeing Brando in the role, it is hard to imagine Elvis playing the part. It is also hard to imagine that the Colonel would allow his boy to play the part of a prostitute to male homosexuals. Interestingly, the starlet, twenty-two-year-old Annie Helm, thought that he would have been perfect for the part; "it was almost written for Elvis," she said.

Elvis had hardly launched his post-army career as a movie star before the light in his eyes began to dim. He did best when he played himself, a talented but striving singer, as in *Viva Las Vegas*. His next film, *Kissin' Cousins*, was more typical. It was made in seventeen days, and at that it was two days over the time allowed by the studio. It was produced by Sam Katzman, who was well known for his ability to turn out movies at minimal cost. The Colonel liked Katzman's style for giving only a little in the art of filmmaking and getting a lot back in money. Under the contract, Elvis was paid $500,000 plus half of the proceeds after the costs of production were met.

Only a few years into his film career, Elvis was rolling in money, but he was artistically bankrupt. Cheap movies included cheap songs, and RCA put them out as records. Director Gene Nelson thought that Elvis could have done better as an actor, but "he wasn't adventuresome, he didn't really want to learn." But then, he didn't have to. "Mostly he would just be his charming self and get away with it—because he was Elvis Presley."

Nelson puzzled, as almost everyone did, over Elvis's relations with the boys. "Why would he isolate himself with this bunch of idiots?" The trouble, Nelson concluded, was that Elvis "suffered an acute lack of self-esteem as a human being." He thought that "he felt that he was uneducated and had nothing to contribute to a conversation."

In Hollywood, Elvis also made a minor and successful career out of having sex with his female costars. He privately boasted of his conquests, and once allegedly said that he had slept with every female costar except Mary Tyler Moore. Some of the women with whom he had affairs, such as Juliet Prowse and Ann-Margret, were powerful personalities, who were more than a match for Elvis and used him more fully than he used them. Ann-Margret, for example, got some priceless publicity by practically announcing from the relatively safe distance of Great Britain that she and Elvis were to marry. Elvis had no such idea and had to scramble to set the record straight, not only with the public but with Priscilla.

Some other movie-set affairs were simply pitiful. For example, on location in Florida, his leading lady became his sex partner, but she finally had to give up on it. She said that things got very confused with all the guys hanging around all the time.

One of Elvis's brief lovers was Donna Douglas, who later became America's darling as Elly May Clampett on the tremendously popular television show *The Beverly Hillbillies*. Donna was a beauty queen, Miss New Orleans, propelled out of the South and onto the stage. By the time she gained recognition in Hollywood, she was a single mother with a small child. She was not at first highly successful, but in 1965 she won the female lead in an Elvis movie, *Frankie and Johnny*. On the set, Donna and Elvis soon realized that they shared a huge interest in spiritual matters, especially Eastern religion. Donna could hold her own in any discussion. She was very bright and well informed. Off-camera, they would spend hours together poring over Elvis's heavily underlined and annotated books on the subject, and off the set they spent a lot of time in bed. Donna really believed that Elvis loved her and would marry her. Then, just as the filming was completed, it all dissolved, and Donna was heartbroken. It was a disappointment she never quite got over and later publicly lamented.

Elvis explained away news reports of his movie affairs to Priscilla as Hollywood hype concocted to sell films. Priscilla was never at ease with all of this, but she was also unwilling to leave Elvis. It was the Colonel who came to her rescue. He finally decided that it was time to change gears. Elvis and Priscilla needed to marry. In *Elvis and Me*, Priscilla insisted that Elvis himself decided that they should wed. Just before Christmas 1966, he knelt down before her in Graceland, made his proposal, and gave her an engagement ring. On May 1, 1967, they were married in Las Vegas in a quick civil ceremony in a relatively small space in the Aladdin Hotel, with few witnesses, had a small reception, posed for the news people alerted to the event only hours before, and then retreated quickly to Elvis's less than elegant Palm Springs house while the world absorbed the news.

Colonel Parker, of course, could not allow the world to know that his boy had been playing sex games with this young woman since she was barely fourteen years old and had kept her in his bed at Graceland for the last four years. The world accepted the marriage as the consummation of a beautifully romantic relationship. Again, it was a brilliant public relations coup for the Colonel. A year later Elvis's marriage had become a disaster, and his career was approaching the same end.

Elvis Presley's birth home in Tupelo, Mississippi. Photograph in the Carol M. Highsmith Archive, Library of Congress, Prints and Photographs Division.

Elvis with his parents, Gladys and Vernon Presley, c. 1938. Joseph A. Tunzi/ JAT Publishing.

Elvis with his parents, 1950. Joseph A. Tunzi/ JAT Publishing.

Elvis on stage with the Blue Moon Boys, 1954. Joseph A. Tunzi/ JAT Publishing.

Publicity photo of the Blue Moon Boys: Scotty Moore, Elvis Presley, and Bill Black, c. 1955. Joseph A. Tunzi/ JAT Publishing.

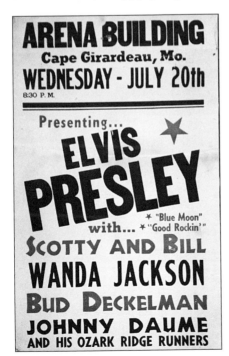

Elvis Presley with Scotty and Bill poster, Cape Girardeau, Mo., July 1955. Taken at the Country Music Hall of Fame in Nashville, Tennessee. Thomas Hawk, photographer, Flikr.

Elvis on his way to fame at the *Louisiana Hayride*, 1954. Louisiana State University-Shreveport Archives and Special Collections.

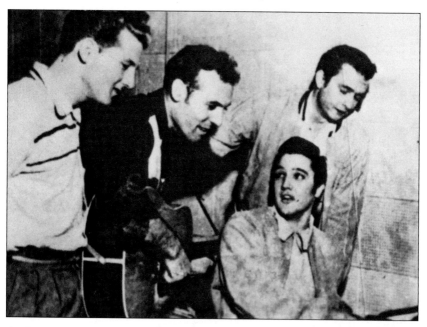

An impromptu session with Jerry Lee Lewis, Carl Perkins, Elvis Presley, and Johnny Cash at the Sun Record Studios in Memphis, Tennessee, on December 4, 1956. Originally published in the *Memphis Press-Scimitar*. Courtesy of the Memphis and Shelby County Room, Memphis Public Library & Information Center.

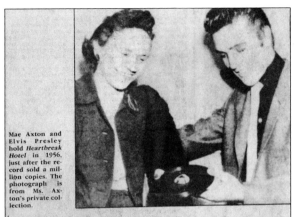

Mae Axton and Elvis Presley hold *Heartbreak Hotel* in 1956, just after the record sold a million copies. The photograph is from Ms. Axton's private collection.

'Heartbreak' duo helped take Elvis off a lonely street

Headline and 1956 photo from article on Elvis and Mae Axton, who wrote "Heartbreak Hotel," just after the record sold 1 million copies, 1956. Published in the Memphis *Commercial Appeal.* Courtesy of the Memphis and Shelby County Room, Memphis Public Library & Information Center.

Portrait of a young Elvis. Memphis and Shelby County Room, Memphis Public Library & Information Center.

Elvis rehearsing with band, swiveling hips, on *The Ed Sullivan Show*, September 9, 1956. Joseph A. Tunzi/ JAT Publishing.

Elvis with crowd in Florida, 1956. Joseph A. Tunzi/ JAT Publishing Publishing.

Teenage girls add graffiti to the bottom of an Elvis movie poster, 1956. World Telegram & Sun photo by Phil Stanziola. Library of Congress LC-USZ62-114912.

Elvis in a matinee performance at the Alabama Fair and Dairy Show, Tupelo, Mississippi, September 26, 1956. Joseph A. Tunzi/ JAT Publishing.

"Jailhouse Rock" (1957). Joseph A. Tunzi/ JAT Publishing.

Last photo of Elvis with his parents, March 24, 1958. Memphis and Shelby County Room, Memphis Public Library & Information Center.

Elvis Presley was stationed in Grafenwoehr, Germany, in 1958. Courtesy of U.S. Army Garrison Grafenwoehr.

Colonel Tom Parker (far left) with Elvis on his return from Germany, 1960. Memphis and Shelby County Room, Memphis Public Library & Information Center.

The façade of Graceland in the late 1950s or early 1960s.

Elvis posing with a car in front of Graceland. Photographed by Charles A. Nicholas for the Memphis *Commercial Appeal*. Memphis and Shelby County Room, Memphis Public Library & Information Center.

Elvis and Priscilla's
wedding at the Aladdin
Hotel, Las Vegas,
May 1, 1967.

Elvis during
his '68 Come-
back Special on
NBC. Joseph
A. Tunzi/ JAT
Publishing.

Elvis, Priscilla, and
Lisa Marie, December
1970. Joseph A. Tunzi/
JAT Publishing.

Priscilla and Elvis at a
Jaycees event honoring
him as one of Ten
Outstanding Young Men
of the Nation, January
1971. Memphis and
Shelby County Room,
Memphis Public Library
& Information Center.

Elvis after a performance
in Las Vegas, January or
February 1970. Joseph A.
Tunzi/ JAT Publishing.

Elvis rehearsing in Las Vegas for his 1970 documentary, "Elvis: That's the Way It Is." Joseph A. Tunzi/ JAT Publishing.

Elvis Presley meets President Richard Nixon on December 21, 1970. White House Chief Photographer Oliver F. Atkins. General Services Administration. National Archives and Records Service. Office of Presidential Libraries. Office of Presidential Papers. Collection RN-WHPO: White House Photo Office Collection (Nixon Administration), 01/20/1969–08/09/1974.

Marquee of the International Hotel, Las Vegas, 1971. Joseph A. Tunzi/ JAT Publishing.

Elvis at
Madison
Square Garden,
1972. Joseph
A. Tunzi/ JAT
Publishing.

"Elvis' Personal Brand of Fireworks Lights the Night for Homecoming."
Article and photo covering the Elvis Concert at the Coliseum, Memphis,
Tennessee, over the Bicentennial weekend, July 6, 1976. Staff photo by
Ken Ross. Published in the *Memphis Press-Scimitar*. Memphis and Shelby
County Room, Memphis Public Library & Information Center.

Elvis and Ginger Alden on vacation in Hawaii, March 1977. Joseph A. Tunzi/ JAT Publishing.

Mourners gather at the gates at Graceland on the day Elvis died, August 16, 1977. Photographed by Saul Brown. Memphis and Shelby County Room, Memphis Public Library & Information Center.

Crying for the King. One woman consoles another in the crowd at Graceland on the day Elvis died. Photographed by Saul Brown. Memphis and Shelby County Room, Memphis Public Library & Information Center.

138th Year   No. 229   Memphis, Tenn., Wednesday Morning, August 17, 1977

Death Captures Crown Of Rock And Roll
—Elvis Dies Apparently After Heart Attack

By LAWRENCE BUSER

Elvis Presley died Tuesday, apparently after a heart attack, at Graceland Mansion. The 42-year-old 'king of rock and roll' was found unconscious in his night clothes at 2:30 p.m.

Presley was found by his road manager, Joe Esposito, and was taken by ambulance to Baptist Hospital's emergency room where he was pronounced dead at 3:30 p.m., police said. Hospital officials announced the death at 4 p.m.

Esposito told authorities he could find no sign that Presley was breathing or could not detect a heartbeat. He began emergency resuscitation efforts and called Memphis Fire Department ambulance.

Shelby County Medical Examiner Jerry Francisco, who performed an autopsy, said the death was due to "an erratic heartbeat" but added that the exact cause of death may never be determined.

"There was severe cardiovascular disease present," Dr. Francisco told newsmen Tuesday night after the autopsy was performed. "He had a history of mild hypertension and some coronary artery disease. These two diseases may be responsible for cardiac arrythmia, but the precise cause was not determined. Basically it was a natural death. The precise cause of death may never be discovered."

Initial police reports yesterday said homicide officers were investigating the possibility of death from a heart attack or from an accidental overdose of drugs.

Francisco said, however, there was "no indication of any drug abuse of any kind." He said the only evidence of drugs involved those Presley was taking for his physical condition — mild hypertension and a colon problem.

Francisco said there would have been evidence of needle tracks in his arms or other parts of his body if illegal drugs were involved. He said there would have been evidence in or on his nose if cocaine had been involved.

He said death occurred between 9 a.m.

and 2 p.m. "There's no way to be more precise than that," Francisco said.

Dr. George Nichopoulos, Presley's personal physician, said last night he was not aware of "anything he did unusual yesterday (Monday)" and said "his fiancee — Ginger Alden" was the last person to see Presley before his body was found about 2:15 p.m. or 2:30 p.m.

As news of Presley's death spread, telegrams and phone calls began pouring into Memphis from mourners and newsmen throughout the world wishing to either express condolences to Presley's survivors or to arrange lodging to attend the funeral, or both. Radio stations began playing Elvis music and record stores in Memphis and

other parts of the country reported a run on Elvis records.

Memphis Mayor Wyeth Chandler said flags on all city buildings would be flown at half staff until the funeral.

Police said they were told Presley had played racketball at his home early Tuesday and quit about 6 a.m. when he told friends he was going to read.

Esposito found Presley in his night clothes in his second-floor bathroom. He said he could find no sign of breathing or heartbeat and immediately summoned an ambulance.

Nichopoulos was performing cardio-pulmonary resuscitation when the ambulance

arrived shortly after 2:30 p.m.

A Memphis Fire Department ambulance from Engine House 29 at 2147 Elvis Presley Boulevard responded to the call at 2:33 p.m. and by 2:56 p.m. had taken Presley to the emergency room at Baptist Hospital in Midtown from his Whitehaven home seven miles away.

Martin Davis of Chattanooga, a construction projects engineer with K-Mart Discount Stores, said he was driving south on Elvis Presley Boulevard when an ambulance almost hit him as it turned into the driveway at Graceland.

"The ambulance damn near ran over me," he said. "It hit the gate as it was (Continued on Page 12)

Elvis Went From Rags To Riches

By WILLIAM THOMAS

He was born in a two-room house in Tupelo, Miss., on Jan. 8, 1935, a nobody with a somebody destiny.

He was the twin who lived — the son of Vernon and Gladys Presley, who had been married two years earlier in Verona, Miss., amidst the Great Depression.

"We matched their names," his mother recalled later, "Jesse Garon and Elvis Aron. Jesse died at birth. Maybe that is why Elvis is so dear to us."

For the next 13 years, the Presleys struggled for survival in Mississippi. Vernon Presley farmed while his wife toiled in shirt and dress factories. They moved to Memphis in 1948, but things didn't get better — at least not right away.

Mrs. Presley worked as a nurses' aide at St. Joseph Hospital. Elvis enrolled in L.O. Homes High School and worked as an usher in a movie theater.

Briefly, he went out for the football team but had to quit in order to go to work.

Although the family was so poor that they had to accept a charity Christmas basket during the holidays, Presley man-

Hearse Takes Body Of Elvis Presley From Baptist Hospital   By Fred Griffith

'Are You Sure There's No Mistake?'
—The Desired Answer Never Came

By TERRY KEETER   announcement that earlier reports had tied other emergency cases into the hospi-

The front page of the *Commercial Appeal* announcing Elvis's death, August 17, 1977. Memphis and Shelby County Room, Memphis Public Library & Information Center.

Graceland Meditation Garden. Gravestones (from the left) of Elvis's grandmother, Minnie Mae Presley; Elvis Aaron Presley; Vernon Elvis Presley; and Gladys Love Smith Presley. A. Lee Bennett Jr/ Flickr https://flic.kr/p/e51p3F

PART III

COMEBACK AND DIE

CHAPTER EIGHT

THE COMEBACK SPECIAL

The sixties were mostly the movie years for Elvis. After his television appearance with Frank Sinatra in May 1960, he did not perform on TV again for eight years, until *Elvis*, his "Comeback Special" in 1968. Instead, he made one more or less bad but very lucrative movie after another. They were lucrative because so little money was invested in producing the films and so much was paid to Elvis and the Colonel.

Elvis produced no hit records during most of this period. His last No. 1 hit was "Good Luck Charm," which came out in February 1962. Even though that record reached the top in singles sales, it sold fewer than eight hundred thousand copies, nearly half a million fewer than his previous hit, "Can't Help Falling in Love" (1961). The songs that he did for the movies, such as "Do the Clam" from *Girl Happy* (1965), were often given to RCA to fulfill his recording commitments. They were mediocre precisely because no substantial effort was made to achieve quality. Over time, Elvis came to hate moviemaking, and he became less and less interested in producing records.

Nonetheless, Colonel Parker concocted schemes to strike ever more spectacular, highly publicized deals to make ever more money. He very much wanted Elvis to get a salary of at least a million dollars for a movie. In November 1967, he had negotiated a contract for a film, *Charro!*, for which Elvis would be paid $850,000 and half the profits. That seemed pretty good, but the profits from Elvis's movies were evaporating as the movies got worse. The Colonel and his Hollywood partners were constantly cutting the budget to meet Elvis's salary (more than half of the total cost), and the quality of the films had deteriorated so much that people were increasingly unwilling to pay money to see them. No moviemaker was stepping up with a million-dollar salary offer, and the possibility arose that there might come a time when there would be no acceptable offer at all.

In the looming financial crisis, the Colonel moved adeptly. Ultimately, he negotiated an arrangement with NBC whereby the network would put up $850,000 for another Elvis movie, plus $250,000 for a television Christmas special, plus $125,000 more for another airing of the special in 1969, plus some extras to bring the total up to $1,250,000. NBC brought in the Singer Company (the maker of sewing machines) to sponsor the show. In January 1968, immediately after the deal was closed, Parker organized a press conference in which he boasted to the world that he had just negotiated a contract in which his client would receive for his work well over a million dollars, unprecedented in show business. The Christmas show was scheduled to be recorded in NBC's studios in Los Angeles in June 1968 to air on December 3.

CAST AND CREW

What finally came out of the Colonel's deal was not at all the trite, homey, Perry Como–style, Christmas-by-the-fireside kind of presentation that he had projected. Steve Binder, the thirty-two-year-old director chosen by NBC producer Bob Finkel to do the show, had another vision. Among his recent credits was a breakthrough television special he had built around the young, beautiful English singer Petula Clark. It was bright, bouncy, dynamic, and almost flashy, virtually the opposite of the carefully casual, snap-your-fingers, bend-your-knees-and-sway productions that were then standard for pop singers. The Petula Clark show also became highly controversial for its racial content. Onstage and right in front of the cameras for all of America to see, a very handsome black man, singer Harry Belafonte, notorious among whites as a civil rights activist, had touched Petula's arm. Steve Binder had suggested that it was a good idea that they get "close" on camera, and the two stars had willingly obliged. In spite of all the progress made on civil rights, America was still not at all comfortable with suggestions of interracial intimacy between men and women, especially when one of the parties was white, female, young, blond, and beautiful. Some Southern affiliates of the network refused to air the show as originally taped.

Steve thought that a lively production built around Elvis in the same style as the Petula Clark show could have great cultural significance, a marker for the revolution in musical entertainment in America that was then under way. In his initial meeting with Elvis in his office on Sunset Boulevard, Steve gave him the hard sell. It was a marvelous opportunity, he urged, for Elvis to show the world "who he really was" by telling his life story through his music. Steve's proposal offered the prospect of an answer to Elvis's most ardent prayer. His great sorrow, he often lamented, was that nobody understood him, nobody knew who he really was. Now he had a chance to tell the world who he was, through his own medium, music. When Steve asked Elvis what he thought of the idea, Elvis replied that he was "scared to death."

While Elvis went off to Hawaii in mid-May for a two-week vacation, Steve worked out the storyline for the show. The theme would be that Elvis was a poor boy who gained fame and fortune through a great gift that was there all the time just waiting for recognition—his amazing talent for music. The discovery of his gift in Sam Phillips's studio was a miracle, and Elvis's music over time, it declared, revealed the real Elvis. The theme song would be "Guitar Man," a recent hit by singer, songwriter, and dynamic showman Jerry Reed. Elvis would be the Guitar Man.

When Elvis returned from Hawaii, Steve laid out the full package for him. Steve was increasingly excited by the prospect of creating a significant cultural event, and he presented the program with great enthusiasm. If Elvis did the conventional show that the Colonel and the bigwigs at the network wanted, he would end up riding off into the sunset and obscurity. If he took the highly creative chance being offered, he could be reborn as a star. As Steve concluded his pitch, he was afraid that Elvis might flee from the daring project he had already detailed. He hastened to add that anything could be changed to suit Elvis. Elvis did not hesitate a moment. "No, I like it all," he said.

Steve, his associate Bones Howe, Elvis, and the writers began to meet in Steve's offices every afternoon at three o'clock. Bones was a recording engineer, a master at using the newest technology to put performances on tape and preparing them for replaying as records, films, and television shows. Bones was on top of the revolutionary new technologies, and his work on the Comeback Special contributed significantly to its success.

The team had hardly begun its work when they were seriously distracted. On June 5, presidential candidate Robert Kennedy was shot and killed in the basement of the Ambassador Hotel in downtown Los Angeles, only a few miles away from Steve's office. Steve later said that Elvis was very upset. He said that Elvis couldn't talk about anything else. He talked a lot about what he considered to be a conspiracy against the Kennedys, linking the shooting of Robert Kennedy to the shooting of President John Kennedy in Dallas five years before. He was also concerned about the assassination of Martin Luther King Jr. in Memphis only two months earlier, just blocks away from where Elvis had lived as a teenager. The murder of King in Memphis was especially awful, Elvis said, because it confirmed bad feelings that people had about the South.

Steve was surprised and delighted by what he saw as Elvis's lack of prejudice. He concluded that Elvis transcended the racism of his native region. Those prejudices had become shockingly visual on television news all during the early 1960s as mean-faced and burly Southern white policemen attacked peacefully protesting African Americans with billy clubs, fire hoses, and snarling police dogs. The nation watched as Ku Klux Klansmen bombed a black church in Birmingham, Alabama, in 1963, killing four young girls. It looked on as Klansmen killed three civil rights workers in Philadelphia, Mississippi, in the summer of 1964. Understandably, non-Southerners came to think of the South, particularly the Deep South of which Elvis was a native, as filled with ignorant "white trash" Klansmen and quasi-Klansmen, implicitly authorized by local white communities to brutalize and kill not only blacks but also whites who sided with blacks.

In August 1965, a massive riot broke out among African Americans in the Watts area of Los Angeles. From that summer into 1968, in virtually every major city in America—Los Angeles, New York, Detroit—smoke plumes rose over black ghettoes as testimony that not all unhappy African Americans lived in the South.

Whites in the North and West grossly misunderstood the nature of race relations both in the South and at home. For the South, they assumed that federal legislation putting black people physically next to white people in public places and at the polls would solve the problem soon enough. Bad race relations in America, they thought, was a Southern matter. They were sure they would be eradicated by the Civil Rights Act of 1964, which prohibited segregation in public facilities and racial discrimination in education and employment, and the Voting Rights Act of 1965 that prohibited discrimination against blacks at the polls. They were simply unaware of the seething anger of blacks in their midst until the burning, looting, beatings, and killings broke out. By the summer of 1968, when Steve, Elvis, and the others were conceiving and creating the Singer Christmas special, white Americans were signaling their anger at the rioters and their absolute determination that such demonstrations would end or be met with crushing violence. Former vice president Richard Nixon of California was running for the presidency on a platform of "law and order," essentially advocating using whatever force was necessary to stop rioting blacks. He was running against George Wallace, an Alabama third party candidate for president who openly waved the banner of white supremacy across the nation and eventually gained half of his ten million votes from outside the South.

The Comeback Special as a Liberal Crusade

In the midst of rampant racism and national turmoil, it was a small wonder that Steve was delighted to see that the star of his television special was unprejudiced in spite of his lower-class Southern roots, lack of sophistication, and limited education—shortcomings indicated by his unflagging but marvelously creative, even poetic, use of double negatives and improper contractions such as "ain't no."

For two weeks, Elvis, Steve, and the writers met every day for hours on end and worked out a script for the show. Every day they drank

Pepsis, smoked cigars, and encouraged Elvis to say whatever he wanted to say. Elvis talked freely about his life, and he poured himself into the creation of the show. In the process, Steve came to see a truly noble Elvis. Not only was he not prejudiced against blacks, he was simply a great human being. Steve saw his own mission in this matter with crystal clarity. "I wanted to let the world know that here was a guy who was not prejudiced, who was raised in the heart of prejudice, but who was really above all that," he said. "Part of the strength that I wanted to bring to the show was [that sense of] compassion, that this was somebody to look up to and admire." If Elvis could do it, the whole white South could do it.

Soon Steve came to see the show as not only a celebration of Elvis but also a manifestation of the great American democratic dream. Elvis was not only a poor boy who reaped the just reward for his talents and virtues in an open, free society; he was a force for unity in a deeply troubled and divided nation. "All of a sudden I realized," he later recalled, "I've got Elvis Presley, Colonel Parker, Confederate flags, a black choreographer, a Puerto Rican choreographer, and a Jewish director! Everything in the show was integrated—behind the scenes, and in front of the camera [with] Elvis singing along with the Blossoms [a black female group], the dance sections black and white and—you know—purple." Steve was inspired. "We were all one big happy family," he exulted.

NOT ONE BIG HAPPY FAMILY

In truth, in the beginning the cast and crew of the Singer special were very far from being one big happy family. For one thing, there was a wide cultural gap between Elvis and his people on one side and Steve and his people on the other. Culturally speaking, they came from different worlds.

Steve chose Billy Goldenberg to be the musical director for the production. Billy had graduated from Columbia University in 1957 and apprenticed under the Broadway composer Frank Loesser, famous for *Guys and Dolls* and *How to Succeed in Business Without Really*

Trying. Previously, he had had no interest at all in Elvis Presley or his music. But he did have great respect for Steve Binder and came to share his belief that this show could be made into a cultural milestone. Getting there, however, required that Elvis change his style of performance. No more simply breaking into hokey simpering songs amidst adoring young women as he had in his movies; no more wiggling around behind a microphone and in front of a handful of countrified musicians as he had onstage.

Achieving the transformation to a more sophisticated performance in a television format proved to be a hard, almost desperate struggle. The great difficulty came from Colonel Parker and the people in Elvis's coterie who seemed determined that they were simply not going to let him change his style. Parker himself kept reminding Steve and the production staff that this was a Christmas show, and it should feature the traditional Christmas songs. After all, the sponsor was the Singer Company, which was not exactly a "rock and roll" outfit.

As usual, the Colonel sent in his own minions to make sure of the purity of the "product," as he called Elvis's productions. One of these was Billy Strange, a songwriter and arranger who had worked with Elvis on his most recent movies. Parker made Strange the "personal music director" for Elvis for the show, thus presumably assuring continuity with his latest performances. Day after day, dressed in cowboy hat and boots, Strange drifted in for what were supposed to be rehearsals but did nothing at all with the proposed music. He sat around and talked and seemed to think that he was merely making a social call. People in the business knew that this was typical behavior for Strange. Steve and Billy Goldenberg grew increasingly anxious as the time drew near for actually going into the studio with musicians and taping what they had prepared. Elvis's people were thinking that when that time came he would simply go onstage and sing "Jingle Bells," "I'll Be Home for Christmas," and a dozen or so other numbers, form-fitting his mood to the message of each song with his usual emotive brilliance. Hence no special preparation was required.

This was not what Steve and Billy had in mind. Among other things, the projected script called for a long segment in which Elvis would appear onstage with a large orchestra behind him and tell the story of his career by singing a series of his most famous songs. Again Elvis's people were dragging their feet and nothing was being done, no sheet music written, no orchestra made ready, no carefully scripted rehearsals. Furthermore, Joe Esposito, Elvis's right-hand man, who often spoke for the Colonel, began phoning Billy Goldenberg. "We don't like orchestras," he would say. "Elvis works well with guitars." Billy pointed out that the music contemplated was not just guitar music. It was very complex, he explained, a "lot of conceptual stuff."

"I don't know if that's gonna do, sonny," Joe responded threateningly.

Finally, Billy told the producer that he needed to work with Elvis directly. He did not like, he said, "being called by people and having to worry about whether I'm going to be killed for writing a dominant seventh." He won. Billy Strange was fired from the show, Joe Esposito's menacing calls ceased, and Billy Goldenberg gained access to Elvis.

Still, Billy had to deal with the guys, who were almost always hanging around. He walked into the studio one day to find Elvis alone at the piano playing the first part of Beethoven's "Moonlight Sonata." When Billy expressed his interest, Elvis responded eagerly. "Oh, do you know this?" and played the first part again. Billy sat down beside him and played the rest. Elvis was impressed. They spent the remainder of that session "learning," as Billy described the process, the first movement of the piece. Thereafter, every night they did a little Beethoven on the piano together. Billy liked Elvis and thought that he was a quick study. Elvis also liked Billy. Soon Billy was amazed to find even Colonel Parker becoming friendly toward him.

"My boy likes you a lot," the Colonel declared genially.

One night Elvis was playing the "Moonlight Sonata" when two or three of his guys came in. "Immediately he picked his hands up from the keyboard, as if some strange, dark shadow had come over the place," Billy recalled.

"What the fuck is that?" they said.

"Oh, it's just something we were doing," Elvis answered.

"Oh, it's awful," they said.

Elvis made no comment but simply picked up his guitar and began to play "those old E-major chords again." Again Billy called the producer, and the guys stopped coming to their sessions. Elvis, he said, "couldn't wait to continue."

Billy Goldenberg liked Elvis, but he did not see the purely noble Elvis that Steve Binder saw. "The one thing I've always felt about Elvis is that there was something very raw and basically sexual and mean," he told the writer Jerry Hopkins as he was researching his 1971 biography of Elvis. "There's a cruelty involved, there's a meanness, there's a basic sadistic quality about what he does, which is attractive," he said. "Most of Elvis's movies have shown him as the nice guy, the hero, but really that is not where he shines best. He's excited by certain kinds of violent things...I thought, if there was a way we could get this feeling in the music..."

A generation after the Comeback Special Billy Goldenberg had not changed his mind about a dark and deeply sexual Elvis. He "tuned in to the darkness, to the wild, untamed, animalistic things," he told Peter Guralnick. "That was [such] a big part of Elvis," he said. "He did not make his statement by being sweet. He was blatantly sexual and that was something I wanted in the music. And if I could get that, I felt I was getting closer to the raw Elvis. Not the Elvis that came in the room to talk to you, because he was the sweetest person in the world, I mean, he was [the] good son—I think that was a lot of Elvis' problem."

Another highly creative artist on the staff who had his own special sense of Elvis's essence was the designer Steve Binder had chosen to create Elvis's costumes for the show, Bill Belew. As Bill said, the one word that came to his mind the moment he first saw Elvis was "Napoleonic." Bill associated Elvis not with the ideal of American democracy but rather with raw power, the French emperor who inspired total loyalty from millions of people.

Bill told Elvis that his costumes should have high collars that framed his face. He should wear soft silk shirts and scarves and never neckties. He could conceive of grown men wearing V-necked silk shirts, the V dipping down toward the waist and threatening not to stop there. He liked tight-bottomed creaseless cuffless pants with legs ballooning below the knees, the looseness of which emphasized the tight bottom and the cleavage of male buttock above. Any decent person would have called such outfits obscene, if not outright immoral. Elvis could not even wear underwear under some of the costumes Bill made for him because the lines would show. Among other attire, Bill created the black leather, tight-all-over suit that Elvis wore for some segments of the Comeback Special. He was surprised and delighted that Elvis so readily adopted his most flamboyant suggestions.

Free at Last

As Steve, Billy, and Bill gained control, everyone was amazed at how cooperative Elvis was. They had expected him to use his "star power" and manifest a lot of "artistic temperament." Instead, as they began to rehearse various segments of the show, he became increasingly enthusiastic, accepting direction readily and involving himself creatively in developing details.

What came to be called the "informal" segment in the Comeback Special was inspired by Elvis's long-standing love of casual sessions offstage with his friends when they would sit around, talk, play the piano, pick guitars, and sing whatever came to mind. It was the kind of male gathering, although without music, that Elvis must have seen in barber shops, gas stations, and cafes in East Tupelo and Tupelo when he was a boy—all men, hanging out, joking, bantering, showing their wit to one another in amiable, low-key exchanges. Billy Goldenberg witnessed Elvis enjoying such sessions with the guys as they began to work on the show. He was intrigued. He said that Elvis could sing ninety-five choruses of "Jingle Bells" without tiring, switch to another song for a time, then go back and do ninety-five more choruses of "Jingle Bells." All the time the guys would whoop and holler encouragement. As Elvis played and sang the same words over and over, the intensity would grow to a climax and end in some sort of jubilation. Steve Binder also saw how Elvis came alive in these sessions, and he used that insight to create what became for many the most appealing part of the show.

This "informal" segment (shot in four performances on June 27 and 29) had Elvis and some of "the guys" exposed on all sides on a high fifteen-foot-square glistening white stage trimmed in bright red. It was like a small boxing ring without ropes or posts. Elvis was zippered into the skintight black leather outfit that Bill Belew had made for him. It was, his biographer Albert Goldman wrote, "a fabulous black leather motorcycle jacket with a stand-up collar, heavy welts along the seams and a broad, double-buckled strap around each wrist." The effect was not cheapened by metal studs or ornaments. Elvis's guys were seated casually and closely around him on the tiny stage. Charlie Hodge, who dearly loved the extravagance of all this, was there with his electric guitar, very excited, and exceedingly alert to every move that Elvis made. Alan Fortas, who projected a sort of teddy bear affability and had virtually no musical ability, was given a guitar case to lean on. Lance LeGault, Elvis's choreographer and sometimes stunt double, who was not one of the guys but was deeply loyal and had worked on a number of his movies, had a tambourine.

Appropriate to the storyline, Steve Binder wanted to put Elvis's very first backup group, the Blue Moon Boys, on the stage with him. Two of them were there, Scotty Moore with his guitar, and D. J. Fontana with his drumsticks and a top-down guitar case in his lap serving as an impromptu drum. Bill Black, who had played bass fiddle with the Blue Moon Boys, had died of a brain tumor in 1965. Even if he had been alive, he might have refused the invitation. Up until his death, he was very bitter over his dismissal in 1957—with only two weeks' salary—by Elvis.

Elvis had not shared the wealth with the musicians who had done so much to launch his career. He paid each a flat $200 a week when working and a pitifully small retainer of $100 when not. Scotty and Bill demanded a raise of $50 a week and the right to work elsewhere when Elvis laid them off. D. J. decided not to ask for more, saying he had not expected more. To press their case, Scotty and Bill handed in their resignations and complained of their treatment to the local papers. Immediately, an angry Elvis responded in the press. He declared that he accepted their resignations with no sense of loss. "It may take a while," he told a reporter, "but it's not impossible to pick replacements." Vernon promptly sent Scotty a curt "notice of separation" and a check "in the amount of $86.25, representing payment in full for all services rendered for us prior to September 21, 1957." But in 1968 Bill was dead and Scotty was forgiving. The men on the platform were totally joyous.

The scene onstage was supposed to appear spontaneous, but a script and cue cards had to be placed within Elvis's line of vision. He was to seem to talk casually about his past, pointedly emphasizing his humble beginnings and depicting a pure young man entering a selfish and sinful world. The guys were to make sympathetic noises and appropriate comments—"Amens," as it were. Elvis had hardly begun before he lost his place in the script and appealed to the audience for help.

"What do I do now, folks?" he asked. As always, they loved his confession of helplessness and showered him with expressions of their love and affection. Elvis reciprocated and rambled about charmingly until he found out what they wanted to hear. Thereafter, he talked, played, and sang exuberantly. The boys whooped it up accordingly. Elvis was rising again, buoyed as always by a live and warmly responsive audience.

Actually the producer and Colonel Parker had been negligent in not having carefully selected beforehand an audience for the performance, one that could be counted on to be enthusiastic. The special, of course, was a collection of various performances. In the last hours, they virtually brought people in off the street. Even so, the Colonel quickly came up to speed. "Who loves Elvis?" he called out to the gathering audience. He chose the youngest and most attractive women from among the respondents and planted them up front where the cameras would catch them. It worked. Elvis, tanned and trim after his Hawaiian vacation, was gorgeous in his black leather suit. He exuded the animal sexuality that Billy Goldenberg thought he could manifest onstage. It was not the 1950s all over again; it was better. Elvis was older, and the girls were women. The sex-play was riper, relaxed, and richer. It was savored and relished by the audience.

During a part of the "informal" segment, several women were drawn up from the front of the audience to sit on the edge of the small stage on either side of the stairs. They are in their late twenties or early thirties, attractively and comfortably dressed. Elvis performs standing above them.

214

After he does "Tiger Man," one of the women hands him a Kleenex. He wipes the sweat from his face and gives it back to her. She puts the damp tissue carefully away in her purse. A tittering stir moves through the audience as it relishes the depth of the exchange. Elvis then swings into a steamy "To Spend One Night with You."

Next comes one of Elvis's finest moments ever onstage. He settles down between the two women who were seated on either side of the stairs leading up to the stage. He sits with his feet on one of the stairs, and the women move close to him. Their bodies close to his, their feet also on the stairs with his. Both are about thirty, mature and knowing, attractive. One is white skinned with dark hair piled high in a bouffant. The other is slightly dark, Hispanic or Asian. She leans toward Elvis, her legs tucked neatly under her, rounded knees together. Elvis sings "Memories," while the two women listen and watch him. The deep feelings—the warm and knowing intimacy—that passed between those women and Elvis was palpable, compelling even now, as one watches a film of the show.

The original script called for Elvis to close with a Christmas song and a monologue, a token tossed to the culturally conservative sponsors and the Colonel. Compared to the excitement they were generating, Christmas now seemed a dull passion. Steve Binder thought he had a better idea. He asked his vocal arranger, Earl Brown, an African American, to compose a song especially for the ending, one that would define what Steve thought the show was all about. Overnight, Brown came up with "If I Can Dream." Elvis just loved it. Singing the words before a studio audience, he preached love to a nation; he was the great unifier that Steve had imagined him to be. Elvis threw himself into the song:

> *There must be lights burning brighter somewhere*
> *Got to be birds flying higher in a sky more blue*
> *If I can dream of a better land*
> *Where all my brothers walk hand in hand*
> *Tell me why, oh why, oh why can't my dream come true*

In the next verse, he thought that "there must be peace and understanding sometime" and that strong "winds of promise" would blow away all "doubt and fear." In the third verse, he declared, "We're lost in a cloud with too much rain" and "trapped in a world that's troubled with pain." But as long as mankind can dream, "he can redeem his soul and fly." In the final verse, he was "sure that the answer's gonna come somehow." He then sang, "In the dark, there's a beckoning candle." While he can think, talk, stand, walk, and dream, "let my dream come true, right now," he pleaded.

"Let it come true right now," he repeated. "Oh ye-e-a h."

The message was, of course, a melodramatic but watered down and musically overblown version of Martin Luther King's 1963 "I Have a Dream" speech, but the whole thing somehow brings to mind Judy Garland singing "Somewhere over the Rainbow." Shallow as the song was, with Elvis singing, it sounded good. Elvis did the song backed by a full orchestra conducted by Billy Goldenberg, and he sang in his risingly emotional, over-the-top, climactic style, falling in the end to an anguished and tremulous plea. With Elvis, the medium—himself—was the message, not the words.

Two days later Elvis did another part of the show before another live audience. This was the "stand-up" segment that took him through the great hits of his career. Billy Goldenberg arranged the music and led the orchestra. Again Elvis was in the black leather suit, but now he was all over a full-sized stage, slinking like a panther, sliding down to his knees on "Hound Dog," pacing, panting, jerking, strands of jet black hair falling excitingly across his face, giving out handkerchiefs drenched with his sweat to the audience. The wet handkerchief bit was a trick he had copied from singer Tom Jones.

The "informal" and "stand-up" segments had been done with live audiences. The third major segment, "Guitar Man," was done with no audience. It opened with one hundred guitar players playing "Guitar Man" for a minute and a half on a large stage with huge lit-up three-dimensional letters that spelled out E L V I S. As the sequence proceeded, at times there were as many as eighty musicians, singers, and dancers on the stage at once, throwing themselves about, singing, swaying, and shouting with seemingly total abandon. It was an extravaganza, huge and costly, far beyond the original budget, but by this time

NBC saw high ratings for this show and paid willingly. In effect, Steve and Billy had put Elvis into an extravagant Broadway production.

The Guitar Man was Elvis, an innocent and highly talented young man who set out from home into a selfish and sinful world. Originally, Steve had begun the segment with Elvis going into a room full of women ("It did not say whorehouse," Binder later emphasized), where he gravitates toward a girl named Purity and sings and dances amid a score of others before the police raid the place and drive him out into the world again. When Steve made the mistake of confessing to NBC that the scene actually took place in a brothel, the sponsors pressured him into cutting it out of the final tape. "People would have remembered it for years," he lamented to the writer Jerry Hopkins.

The Singer Sewing Machine Company, NBC, Steve Binder, and the superbly creative artists that Steve gathered around him in June 1968 created the mold that Elvis and his company would fill with their performances in hotel showrooms and tour venues all over America during the last eight years of his life. It was a stage full to overflowing with performers, a band of several carefully chosen musicians (piano, drums, and guitars, one of which was always played by Charlie Hodge), a full orchestra, a black presence, a female presence, and a gospel quartet or quintet (a religious presence representative of the working class South).

The Comeback Special was light-years away from "Jingle Bells" and "A Blue Christmas." It was a Broadway musical extravaganza. It created a stage filled with Elvis and his people. At a get-acquainted party before rehearsals started, there were thirty-six dancers and thirty-five musicians. There were eighty performers in the opening scene of "Guitar Man," all in motion—backup singers black and white, male and female, a quartet, a trio, a high soprano, a full orchestra, virtuoso musicians on drums, guitars, and piano from country, pop, soul, Nashville, Los Angeles, and Muscle Shoals, Alabama. He changed his costumes three times in one scene. He wore a dozen or more different costumes during the show, each of them bold in the Bill Belew mode, daring but strikingly appropriate to the performance.

The Comeback Special was drenched in black culture. It was as if Steve, Billy, Bill, and Lance LeGault had taken Elvis up and out of the

Snow White world of Hollywood movies, dunked him into the current broad-flowing stream of black culture in America, and put him back onstage again. The change is striking in a scene in the "Guitar Man" segment that opens with a black male dancer very still in a crouching position forehead down on the stage floor. Slowly, he unfolds himself to a mournful rendition by orchestra and singers of "Sometimes I Feel like a Motherless Child." The scene soon builds to a joyous, jumping, triumphal, shouting, double-clapping "Where could I go but to the Lord?" All the while, black and white dancers, girls dressed in white, boys dressed in black, are throwing themselves around the stage. The Blossoms (three black women) and Darlene Love (also black and a high soprano) are doing music and motion that no whites, no men, and few women of any color could do. Elvis, dressed in a smart-cut purple suit, a white shirt with a wide collar, and a red bandanna around his neck, singing and dancing, melts easily into the flow. Elvis scorns no music.

Finally, all during the Comeback Special there was Elvis himself, resplendent in outré costumes, doing karate moves, slides, kneels, and, metaphorically speaking, cartwheels and somersaults, bantering onstage with his friends, and talking to his audience. No longer did he merely jiggle his leg or move through carefully choreographed scenes. With Lance Le-Gault's help, he developed relatively graceful and flowing movements and began striking statue-like poses. He delivered rambling monologues, especially one in which he repeatedly depicted himself as a poor boy in Memphis, who had only wanted to make a vanity record for his mother during his lunch-hour break from his job driving a delivery truck for an electric company. This was not a true story but an Elvis myth that he himself loved to tell. It was an imagined and highly romantic tale that worked for him and left out many things.

The taping of the whole production was completed before the end of June 1968. As Steve edited hours of tape down to the one-hour show that would be aired in December, he knew that he had done it right. Elvis had burst forth in all his natural beauty. "All of a sudden you could see the metamorphosis," he said. "All of a sudden the confidence started swelling." Guided by his managers, Elvis had discovered himself anew. Again he found himself rising up to meet the applause of live audiences while performing onstage—as he had in the Shell in Overton Park in Memphis in July 1954, and yet again when he appeared with Milton Berle on the flight deck of the carrier *Hancock* in San Diego Bay in April 1956. Elvis was now fully mature, darkly sexual, and imperiously commanding.

"They still like me!" Elvis exclaimed as he came off the stage after his second run at the stand-up performance before a live audience. It was as if he had achieved once again the much-needed affirmation that he got from the enthusiastic applause of the audience in the talent contest at Humes High fifteen years before. Now, he had become what a studio audience in 1968 wanted him to be.

Elvis sent someone to ask the Colonel to come to his dressing room. "I want to tour again," he told his manager. "I want to go out and work with a live audience."

COLONEL PARKER RE-CREATES THE ELVIS VENUE

Colonel Parker, having caught the vision of an Elvis bankruptcy, was ready for a change too. In the mid-1950s, he had moved Elvis from the stage to television and then to the movies. A decade later, he moved him back from the movies to television and then to the stage again, in Las Vegas and then into widening streams of touring. The Colonel moved quickly to totally finish off Elvis's movie career, get him back into the recording studio, and book him for live shows.

Elvis's movies never took long. Within a year, he was done with the three films already contracted: *Charro!* in July and August 1968, *The Trouble with Girls (And How to Get into It)* from late October to mid-December, and *Change of Habit* in seven weeks during March and April 1969.

Meanwhile, in January and February 1969, Elvis returned to the recording studio with a passion he had not shown in years. The studio he chose was not in Nashville, New York, or Los Angeles. It was in Memphis. There, American Sound Studio was heavily involved with "the Memphis Sound," a genre that was rivaling the highly popular Detroit "Motown Sound" in the late sixties. It had produced a phenomenal ninety-seven hits on the charts in twenty-eight months. The studio was located, appropriately, on the black side of the city, in a run-down building at 827 Thomas Street. The guiding genius was Lincoln Wayne "Chips" Moman, who was born in La Grange, Georgia, in 1936, hitch-hiked to Memphis at age fourteen, and entered the music business as a guitarist. Chips had gathered a talented assemblage of musicians to play backup in his studio, some of whom Elvis had known from his early years. These Memphians had absorbed what black musicians were doing in Memphis and elsewhere in the 1960s and played what people wanted to hear in the way they wanted to hear it. Chips's stars were black and white, male and female, singles and groups, country, rock, pop, and soul. One of his successes was Dionne Warwick.

Elvis chose the right place. In ten days, he cut thirty-six songs. In both art and numbers, it was, arguably, his most productive recording session ever. Among the hits that emerged were "In the Ghetto (The Vicious Circle)," carrying the sad and simple message that a baby born in the ghetto probably could never get out and would probably die a violent death, and "Suspicious Minds," which carried a theme that Elvis took very personally, which is honesty and simple purity in important relationships. Priscilla, rejected sexually by Elvis after the birth of Lisa Marie, had already had an affair with her dance instructor and was developing interests in other men. Elvis suspected, erroneously, that she was having—or about to have—an affair with Jerry Schilling, probably the most sensitive, honorable, handsome, and gentlemanly of his male associates and certainly the best educated.

At first, Elvis had doubts about recording "In the Ghetto" because the race element might antagonize some of his fans. The Colonel had always told him to stay away from socially sensitive issues and politics. Elvis had never given the public the slightest hint of where he stood on the civil rights movement or the war in Vietnam, and there is no readily available evidence that he ever voted. But Elvis liked the ghetto song for its feeling and, as usual, melted himself into the appropriate emotion.

His pursuit of the racial theme continued in an innocuous vein in the film *Change of Habit*, in which he played an idealistic young doctor, John Carpenter, who ministered to black youth in the ghetto with the aid of nuns who had temporarily dropped their habits for secular clothing. The movie was upgraded substantially for thespian quality and convincing moral tone by his costar, Mary Tyler Moore, who played Sister Michelle Gallagher, sworn to perpetual purity and virginity no matter how sexy Dr. Carpenter seemed to be as he swiveled his hips around the neighborhood.

Elvis's record from the Singer special, "If I Can Dream," came out in October 1968, rose to No. 12 on the charts, and eventually sold eight hundred thousand copies, a height Elvis had not achieved since 1965. That score was dwarfed by what came out of his recordings in Memphis in the American Sound Studio. The January–February sessions produced three records and two albums that sold more than a million copies each. "In the Ghetto" reached No. 3 on the best-seller charts, and "Suspicious Minds" became No. 1, his first since 1962. Elvis was into his music again. He was getting better material to work with, and it showed in a broad popular reception of his records and increased sales.

LAS VEGAS

Elvis was on a roll, and so too was Colonel Parker. He booked Elvis into the brand-new two-thousand-seat Showroom Internationale of the International Hotel in Las Vegas for four weeks beginning Thursday, July 31, 1969. Opening night was attended by a huge and enthusiastic crowd of invited celebrities and critics. The Colonel immediately re-negotiated an increase in Elvis's salary from $100,000 to $125,000 a week. Further, he signed Elvis up for two shows a night for four weeks each January and August for the next five years for $1 million a year plus benefits—such as luxury suites for himself and Elvis in the hotel. Elvis's suite was, at first, on the top floor, the twenty-ninth. Later, the hotel built a penthouse suite on the thirtieth level that he used. During his first run in Las Vegas and ever after, including his last engagement in December 1976, Elvis filled every seat in the Showroom every night.

Steve and his people had built the Comeback Special, but Elvis himself put together his first Las Vegas show, filling the forms onstage that were developed in the special. He carefully considered virtually every singer and musician he knew, and he consulted personally with many of them before making his choices. He selected each artist, he chose the songs and arrangements, and in exhaustive rehearsals he tuned them all together up to perfection.

As in the Comeback Special, the very singers and musicians that Elvis chose to bring to his stage celebrated simultaneously American diversity and American harmony. He had heard but never seen the Sweet Inspirations, a black female group that had sung backup for some of the leading black female singers in the nation, most notably Aretha Franklin. He loved their sound, and he was not at all disappointed by their looks when he saw them. Later, for a brief time, Elvis also added high soprano Millie Kirkham to the troupe. When Millie dropped out to pursue her career in Nashville where she could be with her husband and two children, Elvis replaced her with thirty-five-year-old Kathy Westmoreland. Kathy was a highly trained and sophisticated white musician whose talents were in great demand in recording studios and on television in Los Angeles and elsewhere. She was a perfect complement to the Sweets.

Elvis also brought Southern gospel to Las Vegas. Before he came to Sam Phillips, his great musical ambition was to sing with a gospel quartet. Now, he brought a gospel quartet to "Sin City" to sing with him. He chose the Imperials, a group out of Atlanta he had worked with before. Later he would bring J. D. Sumner, who could sing in a phenomenally low key as a result of a childhood illness, and his Stamps Quartet onto the stage. Elvis relished high voices, such as Kathy's, and low voices, such as J. D.'s.

Thus, Elvis onstage came to be backed by nine singers: five men and four women, six whites and three blacks. They could sing gospel, blues, and opera, but onstage with Elvis they sang everything. Elvis picked his band of five men from among the best studio musicians in America— piano, drums, and guitars. Always with him was Charlie Hodge, playing rhythm guitar, handing Elvis glasses of water and scarves, holding his hand mike for him, and doing whatever he needed in a manner that showed his boundless affection and admiration. Elvis was also backed by the newly formed twenty-six-member International Hotel orchestra. As Vegas musicians, they were accustomed to playing behind whichever performer happened to be in front of them. Elvis soon tuned them up to his liking, demanding that they be ready to swing into any one of the couple of hundred tunes he had mastered in his career.

Elvis attempted to persuade Billy Goldenberg to come to Las Vegas to conduct the International Hotel orchestra for his shows. Billy, however, wanted to continue with his career in Los Angeles and New York, and eventually returned to Broadway.

Bill Belew stuck with Elvis. He continued to design and construct striking costumes, skintight suits that struggled with an intriguing lack of success to contain Elvis's imagined sexuality, karate outfits, the high-collared, wide cape that became a favorite, and, in his later years, loose clothes to hide his obesity. An invoice dated January 19, 1970, for some of Elvis's costumes for the second Las Vegas run shows Bill's exquisite aesthetic still at work. It lists four "Silk Crepe Shirts" at $100 each, "28 China Silk Scarfs" at $10 each (to be made moist with Elvis's ever-flowing bodily fluids and thrown to women reaching up from the audience), 2 white jumpsuits, 2 black jumpsuits, 1 white mohair suit, and 1 white jumpsuit with a Cossack top. The total cost came to $3,030. In the final dress rehearsal for the opening show, Elvis wore one of Bill's "Cossack suits," complemented with a "dangling macramé belt." Bill, who always came to Elvis's Vegas openings, attended a later opening with a woman who leaned over and said to him what he already knew. "You can feel the sensuality and the sex oozing from that man," she said.

In spite of Tom Parker's reputation for driving hard bargains, the International Hotel was not taken advantage of by the Colonel. Anyone could have done the math, and the hotel did. A $15 minimum charge for each patron in full houses would bring in more than $1.5 million over four weeks. In fact, the first engagement itself grossed over $1.6 million for the hotel.

At first, Elvis's show was the only major show in Las Vegas that made a profit, and it set a new standard of success in that business. Previously, hotels booked shows only to attract people who would gamble, and they accepted related losses because of the tremendous profits they reaped for the casinos. Elvis's sold-out performances proved that a hotel's showroom itself could be another money maker. Also, Elvis doing two shows a night seven days a week broke precedent, since performers ordinarily demanded one or two nights off a week during a long engagement. Not Elvis. He wanted total exposure. He could not see himself sitting around twiddling his thumbs one whole night when he could be basking in the adulation of his fans.

TOURING

Even while Elvis was performing in Las Vegas in August 1969, Tom Parker signed him up for six performances over three days in February 1970, in the 50,000-seat Astrodome in Houston during the Annual Texas Livestock Show. His first performance in the first afternoon show did not go well. The sound system was bad, and Elvis was sandwiched in between the chuck wagon race and the calf-roping event. Only some 16,000 people attended, 4,000 of whom were handicapped children specially invited. After the performance, Elvis confessed to one of his entourage that he feared his career was over. Depressed, he went to bed. In the evening, the sound was improved, the performance drew more than 36,000 people, and they liked him. Elvis was elated. On Saturday evening, attendance soared to 43,614, the largest ever for a show in such a venue. In three days, more than 200,000 people saw Elvis perform live in Houston.

By then, the Colonel had put together Elvis's first road tour since 1957. Both Elvis and the Colonel realized soon after its opening that the Vegas show could go, ready-made, on the road and reap a handsome profit. On September 7, 1970, Elvis rolled out of a four-week run in Las Vegas, and two days later he began a six-day tour in Phoenix, proceeding on to St. Louis, Detroit, Miami, and Tampa, before ending in Mobile. The tour was a tremendous success. It generated wildly enthusiastic audiences for Elvis, boosted his self-confidence, and yielded quick cash. Sold-out performances in each city brought Elvis $175,000 for the six days. Six days on the road brought Elvis even more cash than a week in Vegas.

After the Astrodome and the six-day tour that began in Phoenix, the troupe hit the road every year, hip-hopping over all of America, from the Von Braun Civic Center in Huntsville, Alabama, to the Pershing Memorial Auditorium in Lincoln, Nebraska, from the Sports Arena in San Diego to the Civic Center in Baltimore. In 1972 and 1973, he did six tours over a total of sixty-eight days. In 1974, he did four tours lasting fifty-five days. In that year, he did 152 shows, counting his tours, two runs in Las Vegas, and one run in Lake Tahoe. In 1975, he did three tours lasting forty-one days. And then in 1976, he did nine tours over a total of 87 days, more than twice the number of days he had spent on the road the year before. In the first half of 1977, Elvis did five tours lasting fifty-six days. If he had lived just one more day, he would have died on tour.

The form of an Elvis show remained the same in Vegas, Tahoe, or on the road. But the specific content, the living art that Elvis and his troupe poured into the form, was constantly changing. The wimpy "If I Can Dream" was dropped, and, to end the show, "An American Trilogy" was added. The Trilogy began with a rather mournful rendition of "Dixie"—as if the South were dying a sad but necessary and lovely death. It then passed into a hardly less mournful black song, "All My Trials"—as if to acknowledge that African Americans had once had a hard time. But the mood of the Trilogy suddenly switched to end with a rousing rendition of "The Battle Hymn of the Republic" in which God will save America to enjoy a surely glorious but unspecified future. His truth goes marching inexorably on with band blaring, chorus in full voice, drums rolling, and Elvis standing spread-eagle, cape held wide, singing with all his might. As the show closed, there was no room in the air for anything else—to breathe the air in that space was to breathe in Elvis's air and absorb his performance.

Elvis's show was changed to end with a blast; it was also changed to begin with a blast. In 1971, Joe Guercio became the conductor of the International Hotel orchestra. Joe was a veteran Las Vegas music man and not worshipful of the stars behind whom he led his band. Virtually from their first rehearsal, however, he developed a great respect for Elvis's talent as an entertainer. Following a suggestion from his wife, Corky, and with approval from Elvis, Guercio developed the idea of opening the show with Richard Strauss's powerful composition *Thus Spake Zarathustra*. He arranged the piece brilliantly for maximum dramatic effect. First, his band filled the theater to bursting with sound. As his timpanist came down with the last eight notes, Elvis's drummer began a roll that would bring Elvis striding onto the stage, fantastically costumed, striking a series of dramatic poses, while the audience applauded wildly. Guercio caught Elvis's ambition perfectly in a single sentence: "He wanted to be a god."

Guercio thus described succinctly a real change in Elvis after the Comeback Special and a change in the tone of his show. Elvis had come to see that his role in life, on stage and off, was to save mankind. He had been chosen from among many. His repertoire came to include various songs working on the vision theme—"If I Can Dream," for example. He began to give melodramatic readings of "How Great Thou Art." His costumes increasingly came to suggest some sort of divinity. When he ended his show with "The Battle Hymn of the Republic," the spotlight shining fully upon him, he would hold his flowing golden cloak out to extremes like angel's wings and lift his rapt face heavenward, eyes closed as if transported.

FINANCES

With hotel engagements, tours, and increased record sales, Elvis's income swelled dramatically during the next four years. In 1969, he netted only $1.325 million after income taxes. In 1970, he netted $2.4 million after taxes. In 1971, his net income approached $3 million, and in 1972 it swelled to nearly $4 million. The vast increase in Elvis's income then and later came mostly from live performances, especially from touring.

Elvis did not, however, become rich. His performances grossed on average about $5 million a year during the last several years of his life, but at his death his total assets probably amounted to substantially less than $3 million. Like his parents, Elvis apparently never thought about saving any money for a rainy day. He never bought stocks, corporate bonds, or rental property for investment and income. The final inventory of his possessions filed in the court records of Shelby County show that he did buy a $10,000 US government bond. He probably forgot he had it. He practically never invested in anything he could not eat, wear, ride, or live in. Such scattered investments as he did make—for example, buying and selling airplanes—lost money.

A large part of Elvis's income went toward keeping more than twenty people on his regular payroll, including a staff at Graceland, his "guys," and his father, Vernon, whom he eventually paid $75,000 a year. Marty Lacker estimated that Elvis's payroll ran to about $100,000 a month. Also, he was famous for his gifts to friends and strangers—new cars being a favored item. In all, he gave away about 275 "luxury cars" worth well over $3 million, almost all of these in the last ten years of his life. The gifts often came in batches. In one spree, he gave away ten cars worth about $10,000 each in a few days. Another came when he was stocking his Circle G Ranch south of Graceland, buying trucks, mobile homes, horses, boots, and cowboy outfits for everyone. In one day, he bought twenty-two trucks. Vernon could hardly stand it. That night he came out of his office at the Circle G carrying a tape from an adding machine in his hand.

"Marty, look at this!" he exclaimed, shaking the tape. "He's spent $98,000 on trucks and given them away."

Marty had no sympathy for Vernon in his distress. "What do you want me to do?" he said. "He's your son."

Elvis spared no expense in maintaining and running Graceland. It housed or supported more than a dozen of his relatives at various times, and it operated as a sort of all-expenses-paid club for the guys with its television room, pool room, and swimming pool. The guys' girls were also welcomed. Priscilla said that it was like a "breeding ground." The kitchen was fully stocked with food and drinks, open twenty-four hours a day, and staffed with a cook ready to serve up whatever the guys ordered. All of the cooks and maids were black women—the only African Americans in Elvis's employ. Marty thought that running Graceland cost about $40,000 a month.

Unlike many other high-income Americans, Elvis never took advantage of available tax shelters. Medical doctors, for instance, in the 1960s and 1970s, reaped unprecedented profits due to a relative shortage of physicians to meet the swelling "baby boomer" population, noncompetitive pricing, and the cash cows generated by Medicare, Medicaid, and health insurance companies. Seeking to escape from federal income taxes that might take away a third or more of their income, doctors bought farms, which provided tax shelters legitimated by Congress to meet an American desire to protect those who tilled the earth. Often physicians—as farmers—turned their farms into ranches to raise cattle or horses, which required relatively little labor, equipment, and expense. If they moved, their well-kept farms could be turned into ready cash. When they retired, they could live comfortably on their country estates, where some had already become "gentleman riders," elegantly dressed in riding outfits, handsomely mounted, riding to the sound of horn and hound, chasing the tiny but wily fox.

Elvis did keep horses and sometimes rode, but he rejected the elite's fiscal model. He spent all that he made as fast as he made it—like almost all of the people who worked for him, like almost all of his relatives, like he himself would have done had he become an electrician rather than a star entertainer, like the great majority of the fans who came to see him in Las Vegas or Tahoe, Buffalo, Little Rock, or Wichita. Elvis shared totally the material world view of his people, that is, enjoy to the fullest the fruits of one's labor now before the boss or the bank or the government snatches it away from you.

TOURS AND SHOWROOMS

With his initial and highly successful tour in September 1970, the pattern for Elvis's performance venues for the rest of his life was set. Appearances in the Showroom in Las Vegas (and, beginning in July 1971, at the Sahara Tahoe Hotel in northern Nevada near Reno), punctuated a continuous stream of tours, each lasting from about ten to twenty days. At first, the Colonel got RCA and a professional management company to underwrite the tours and share in any profits. But soon he decided to manage the tours himself and take as his commission one-third of the profits, an arrangement that Elvis easily accepted as fair.

The Colonel was indeed a superb tour manager and soon developed a process whereby he would arrive in the venue the day before Elvis, to make certain that Elvis's coming was hyped to the maximum, all seats sold, and conditions optimal down to the finest detail. He would fly out to the next venue as Elvis and the company of some thirty-five musicians, singers, helpers, and bodyguards flew in. Later, the number in the troupe swelled to more than fifty.

It was as if Tom Parker were back in the carnival where he had begun in show business, striking the tent after midnight in one town, only to raise it in another town the next day with great hoopla, as if nothing so great as this had ever happened before anywhere on the face of the earth. At first, they leased planes for their tours. But in 1975, Elvis had a retired Delta Airlines Convair jet revamped for his own use. He began crisscrossing the country at will, sometimes on tour with the most favored members of his troupe and often on a mere whim and with whomever he chose. He named the plane the *Lisa Marie* after his seven-year-old daughter.

Keeping the *Lisa Marie* in the air was an expensive proposition. On one occasion, they touched down to refuel in El Paso, Texas, where gas was relatively cheap. Joe Esposito had forgotten to bring Elvis's credit card and had to borrow Lamar Fike's. The charge for gas to fill the tanks was $5,000—pocket change for Elvis, a small fortune for Lamar. The crew cost money too. The *Lisa Marie*'s perfectly-named pilot, Milo High, or a substitute, was always on call, along with a roster of copilots and engineers.

Parker loved his work in Las Vegas and on the road. By this time he needed all the money he could get. In Las Vegas, he became addicted to gambling. He was often at the tables wagering staggering sums on a roll of the dice or a spin of the roulette wheel. Knowledgeable persons thought that he was losing money at the rate of about a million dollars a year, and many thought that the International Hotel in Las Vegas—which was acquired by Conrad Hilton in 1971 and renamed the Hilton International Hotel—held his markers for large sums and dangled those over his head to keep Elvis performing at a killing pace and to squeeze more profit for themselves out of Elvis's labor. Whatever the case, Elvis continued to perform at the Hilton after the five-year contract had expired.

CREATING THE IMAGE

During the first few years of Elvis's career, Sam Phillips and the girls in Elvis's audience did not fully know what they did, while Elvis himself sometimes asked, with genuine wonder, "What did I do?" But clearly, they all moved within the context of Southern white culture in the mid-twentieth century. One great irony of the Comeback Special was that its stage forms were created by people who felt that they knew very well what they were doing, and they did not move within the context of Southern white culture. To the contrary, the creators of the special were distinctly non-Southern. Steve Binder, Billy Goldenberg, and Bill Belew, in their roots and values, sprang from virtually the opposite end of the cultural spectrum. Elvis's people had been in America and in the South for centuries, living and working on the land as farmers. The Binders, Goldenbergs, and Belews were new, national, and urban.

Elvis became urban, but never urbane. He eschewed New York, and he never "went Hollywood." In Los Angeles, he was practically never in the nightclubs, never at the Oscars, never in the homes of the famous for dinners or social events. Rather, he walled himself up in one of his mansions with the guys. His regular guests, even if famous, were female, young, and not there for dinner. Anyone who wanted to socialize with Elvis had to come to his house. Like other Americans, he partied in Las Vegas and retreated to Palm Springs, but home was home.

Steve, Billy, and Bill each saw a different Elvis, and each projected his own image of Elvis onto Elvis. Those images were often incongruous and even contradictory. Steve saw him as an ideal American, a warm and generous person, modest, miraculously pure, not prejudiced against blacks, Jews, or Catholics, a poor boy who had made good by a gift for music, but whose success had not made him pretentious or arrogant. Billy saw him as a super-sexual creature, a good person who was nevertheless at bottom animalistic, wild, dark, rapacious, and even sadistic. Bill saw him as imperious, commanding, dominating—

almost with whip in hand. Just as Elvis read each audience and gave them what they wanted, he read Steve, Billy, and Bill and gave each what he wanted. Insecurity seeks adoration. Such was the nature of Elvis's genius. In the Comeback Special, Steve and his associates built the mold and Elvis poured himself into the spaces created for him to make a work of art that was, after all, embodied in him and essentially his own. Elvis played brilliantly to their perceptions of him.

ON TOUR: THE THIRD ELVIS

The first great Elvis image—the "Bad Elvis"—was launched by the young women at the Shell in Overton Park in July 1954. The second Elvis image—the "Good Elvis"—was the creature of the Cold War. It was clearly visible on the flight deck of the USS *Hancock* in San Diego Bay in April 1956, then sanctified by Ed Sullivan on his show in January 1957.

The third and final Elvis image, much more complex than the first two, brought back the bad Elvis in another mutation. Now Elvis was "bad" in the sense that bad meant "good," even "the best." Now clearly an adult, he is free and independent. Liberate yourself and have fun, he urges white Americans tired of black civil rights activists, Communist confrontations, and a demoralizing war in Vietnam. He is self-confident, neither giving nor accepting abuse, indicting his enemies, joyous, loving life, hedonistic but harmless. The image was hatched with the Comeback Special and achieved full flight during his first engagement at the International Hotel in Las Vegas in August 1969. It continued through his tours and hotel showroom appearances until his death in 1977. It was the image that his audiences needed and wanted; it was the spirit that they would travel from afar to be near and share.

Las Vegas, America's premier "Sin City," was the perfect place to launch and sustain the "bad" Elvis. From July 1969, through December 1976, he played fifteen engagements in the Showroom of the International Hotel. In Las Vegas, drinking was encouraged, prostitution was openly practiced, gambling was virtually mandatory, and no-fault sex pulsated through the air. All sorts of things forbidden in conventional

American life were smiled upon there. Physically, the city was literally an oasis in a desert; morally, it was an enclave of sin in a puritanical nation. For those who came to play, it was Mardi Gras without masks. Lent could come later, when they got back home with family, friends, and neighbors, work, and church.

Elvis loved Las Vegas. He often stayed there in the Imperial Suite in the International Hotel even when not playing in the Showroom. He loved the audiences he attracted night after night, first to a dinner show in the evening and then a later show that often went on past midnight. He threw his sweat-drenched scarves into the audience just as the first bad Elvis had thrown his spit-wet chewing gum to the girls. Women loved it. They threw bras, slips, panties, and keys—marked with their room numbers—back at him, women both young and middle-aged. It was the bubble again, but riper and richer with age.

In Las Vegas, Elvis the rebel burst forth. Rising resentment erupted upon what had seemed to be a smooth, even-tempered surface. No one was ever going to mess with him again. In rambling monologues, he depicted how other boys in his high school had not liked him and wanted to beat him up. He was like a "squirrel" they had spotted in a tree, he said, and the cry went up to "get him." The seething anger that he had long felt over his treatment by Ed Sullivan and Steve Allen on national television and movie moguls in Hollywood poured out onstage like so much bile—Elvis's revenge.

Elvis was now ready to do violence to his persecutors, past, present, and future, as he demonstrated onstage by aggressive karate chops and kicks. He was himself prepared for combat, physical and otherwise. Also he had his own gang, strong unsmiling men ready to inflict whatever pain upon others he desired. Now, he would "get them."

His arsenal included his live audiences, always in close support. They never lost their love and affection for him. They raised him up. They did, in truth, think of him as "the King."

CHAPTER NINE

GIRLS AND GUNS

PRISCILLA

Even though Elvis had wanted to keep Priscilla in his bed, he had not wanted to marry her. After he learned of her pregnancy, he rued to Lamar Fike that he "didn't pull out in time." As Priscilla's pregnancy progressed, he bought a farm and created the Circle G Ranch. He settled Priscilla and himself in a cozy little house on the ranch, and for a time he romanticized his life with her there. Happily, they waited for the arrival of the baby. In the seventh month of her pregnancy, however, Elvis suddenly proposed "a trial separation," a phrase for a phase in a declining marriage that usually ended in divorce. She was shocked, hurt, and confused, but he quickly dropped the idea and never brought it up again. The baby, Lisa Marie, came on February 1, 1968. He beamed over his little family for a while, but he stopped having sex with Priscilla immediately after the birth. She tried everything, including donning a black negligee and cuddling up to him in bed, but her best efforts only ended in her own humiliation.

In spite of her frustration in the bedroom, Priscilla behaved very much as a wife and mother should. She attempted with some success to take over the management of the household at Graceland, establishing regular meal times and regular routines. She also attempted to improve the decor, not at all a difficult task. Even so, one staffer at Graceland remembered that most of the new furniture came from Sears. In November 1967, Priscilla persuaded Elvis to buy a house in Beverly Hills for their family at 1174 Hillcrest Road, a house with space for guests but no space for "the guys." No more two-way mirrors, no more sex parties, no more "fun."

Elvis countered Priscilla's push for domesticity by reinventing his Palm Springs house, the house where he and Priscilla had spent their honeymoon. He turned the place into a poor-boy's version of Hugh Hefner's Playboy Mansion for himself and the guys. They spent virtually every weekend there and as much time otherwise as they could manage. Invited showgirls provided a ready and willing reservoir upon which they could draw for sex. The place boasted a patio with a large swimming pool where the boys and girls played.

In the early 1980s, Priscilla and her companion, Mike Edwards, a well-known male model, visited the place. It had been locked up and empty since Elvis's death in 1977 and was just as he had last left it. Mike had adored Elvis, and he was eager to get an intimate sense of him in his retreat there. He pulled down cans of Vienna sausage and pork-and-beans from the kitchen cabinet and examined the dishes, which were "plastic and mismatched, some cream-colored and others with little green leaves printed around the rims." He saw a cracked Frisbee lying in the corner of the patio where it had last fallen. He sat down, as Elvis often must have, on the oversized couch in the recreation room, which contained a giant video screen, a pool table, and a jukebox filled with records. In the bathroom, he found a couple of used syringes, small bars of motel soap, and a bottle of Brut. Priscilla called out, "I want to leave." Riding back to Los Angeles in Elvis's 280SL while Mike drove, Priscilla leaned her head out of the car window to let the hot desert air blow through her hair.

"What really happened between you two?" Mike asked.

"I grew up," Priscilla replied.

Wives and serious girlfriends were strictly excluded from the Palm Springs place; groupies were welcomed wholesale, and often carefully selected Las Vegas dancers were invited to swim naked in the pool and pair off with the guys in the bedrooms arranged around the patio like a motel. Elvis liked especially to retire to his room with a number of the girls along with a very special Vegas showgirl who was a lesbian.

During the summer of 1971, Priscilla and Joanie Esposito, Joe's wife, had raided the place while the boys were away. In the mailbox, Priscilla found a highly appreciative thank-you note to Elvis from a recent female guest. Another guest had written a note to Sonny West in which she had fondly referred to him as "Lizard Tongue." Furious, Priscilla phoned Elvis in Las Vegas. He pled total innocence. He could not control the fantasies of his fans, he said. Furthermore, how dare she bother him for no good reason when he was about to go onstage in the Showroom. Priscilla ended up apologizing to Elvis. The guys saw great humor in the boss's clever handling of the situation. Priscilla was not deceived.

Neither were Joanie and the other wives. For a time, marriage had been the fashion among the guys; now divorce crashed through the Elvis coterie. After Elvis hung up the phone in Las Vegas, Lamar Fike quipped that maybe the boys could get a "group rate" from a divorce lawyer. "That little liaison," he said, "eventually cost Joe his wife, cost me my wife, and cost Elvis his."

Seeking relief from her demands, Elvis encouraged Priscilla to get out into the world more. She took dance lessons and had an affair with her middle-aged instructor, her first short run at adultery. She next became interested in karate, and Elvis, busy elsewhere, encouraged her to take up the art. She did so with a passion, hanging out with fellow students, attending tournaments, and visiting local karate schools, including that of Chuck Norris. In the swirl of supple male bodies clad in white pajamas with black belts, she encountered Mike Stone. Mike was part native Hawaiian, the world karate champion in 1964 and 1965, and very muscular. Priscilla pursued Mike steadily even though he was married, with a four-year-old daughter and a baby on the way. Soon, they became secret and passionate lovers. He provided the bridge, she said, over which she crossed from girl to woman. She was then twenty-six.

Two Virgins and Barbara Leigh

Meanwhile, Elvis was getting high on the Comeback Special and its sequels, and he was even needier sexually than usual. One of his aides said they fed him a steady stream of women to keep his confidence up. In August 1970, he suddenly stumbled into an incredible triangle of ravishingly beautiful young women. Two of them were twenty-five years old and self-proclaimed virgins—an impossible dream for Elvis, who was obsessed with virginity—and the other was about as far from virginity as a girl could get.

Joyce Bova was one of the virgins. She worked for the House Armed Services Committee on Capitol Hill in Washington. In August 1969, she had felt the need to take a break from her tedious work of sorting papers and flew out to Las Vegas. She was waiting for an Elvis performance when one of Elvis's greeters invited her backstage. In Joyce's meeting with Elvis, he invited her up to his suite after the show for a private dinner. He was much taken with her. She enjoyed the visit; he was so sweet and gentle. But she declined to stay the night.

After Joyce returned to Washington, Elvis kept calling her, inviting her out to California. She was hesitant. She was a devout Catholic, and Elvis was married. She believed that sex outside of marriage was wrong and adultery a sin. Nevertheless, she was intrigued and finally accepted his invitation to come to Las Vegas during his August 1970 engagement, arriving in time to attend the postshow gathering backstage on Sunday, August 30.

Death Threat

Life had not been easy for Elvis over the previous three weeks. He had begun his third Las Vegas engagement on August 10. As always with Elvis, the thrill of a new beginning had rapidly diminished. By the end of the month, he was bored and not as good onstage as he should have been, which professional critics noticed and his audiences as usual ignored. On Friday, August 14, Patricia Ann Parker, a twenty-three-year-old waitress in North Hollywood, had filed a paternity suit against Elvis, claiming that he had gotten her pregnant during his second Las Vegas engagement. Patricia Parker had given birth to a baby boy she named Jason Peter Presley. Insult was added to injury when the person who served the court papers on Elvis pretended to be another adoring fan seeking an autograph, then shoved the documents into his hand. Elvis was outraged. "How can anyone do this to me?" he wailed to his audience during one performance. "I am completely innocent." In the end the paternity suit was dropped.

The real possibility of giving Lisa Marie a well-publicized illegitimate half-sibling was bad, but much worse was about to come. On Wednesday, August 26, an anonymous caller informed hotel security that there was a plot to kidnap Elvis. The next day the Colonel got a similar call. That Friday, Joe Esposito's wife, Joanie, received a call from a man who said that Elvis was to be killed during the show on Saturday night. Less than an hour later, he called again to say that for $50,000 he would identify the killer.

The authorities acted immediately to protect Elvis. The FBI, the local police, and hotel security all rushed in. Elvis called in all of his friends, including even the diminutive disc jockey George Klein, from Memphis, to shield him with their bodies from the assassin's bullet. For years, he had demanded that his bodyguards and close friends promise to throw themselves in front of any bullet meant for him. Some did promise, but his cousin Billy Smith would not. "Hey, my life's important to me too," he responded. "I ain't stopping no damn bullet for nobody."

Backstage on Saturday night before he went on for the first show, Elvis went from person to person, tearfully saying good-bye. Then he went onstage with a pistol in each boot. During the performance, a man in the balcony shouted out, "Elvis!" Everyone froze. But the man only wanted to ask Elvis to sing a favorite song. No killer emerged during that show or the next one.

After Sunday's show, a slew of friends and well-wishers were with Elvis backstage. The threat was a hoax. Everyone was exuberant with relief. Elvis was playing the charming host. Among other famous guests, he greeted Ricky Nelson and his wife, and Jim Aubrey, the head of MGM and his date, Barbara Leigh, a dark-haired twenty-three-year-old starlet. When Aubrey became separated from her for a time, Elvis got Barbara's phone number. Apparently to avoid any confusion on his part as to whose number this was, she also wrote out her name on the slip of paper.

Joyce Bova arrived from Washington just in time to join that gathering. After a year of entreating phone calls from Elvis and ambivalence on her part, she had decided to come to Vegas to determine if she and Elvis had a future together. She saw that he was very excited. One leg shook constantly. He could not stop talking about the assassination threat. He was boastful, bragging about his courage in the face of the threat of a murderous attack. He acted as if he had not been afraid the previous night, but his bodyguards and friends had been quivering with fear. "You guys were really scared, weren't you?" he challenged.

For Joyce, Elvis was so different this time, arrogant, showing off in front of everyone, putting the guys down. He was not the sensitive and gentle man she had met the year before. Even so, she agreed to spend the night with him to see if they had a future. When they were alone in his suite, she tried to find out why he seemed so different. As she probed, he grew increasingly angry. "You can't always be questioning me, Joyce," he said. "I'm tired of people telling me how I am, or how I'm not. How they think I'm different, how they think I change from one time to another." She had to trust him, he insisted, and join in his vision of them together. Angered, Joyce hit him where it hurt. During those phone calls inviting her out to California, she repeatedly irritated him by raising the subject of his marriage to Priscilla. Now she indicated yet again that he was still a married man. What vision of them together was possible?

Elvis blew up. He had already explained that, he raged. He and Priscilla had an open marriage. "If you're going to stay, then stay," he said, flinging a black silk pajama top at her. In his mind, obviously, this was her whole costume for the evening. Joyce slammed the door as she left.

The next day Elvis called Barbara Leigh in Los Angeles. He reached her just as she got home from her trip to Vegas. He wanted her to come see him on Wednesday. She couldn't. She had a date to go on a cruise with Jim Aubrey on his yacht. Well, Elvis said, just come up tonight. She flew up. One of the guys picked her up at the airport, and she spent the night with Elvis. She had "the best time," she said. So good that Aubrey had to wait for her tardy return to Los Angeles.

On the same Monday that an eager Barbara Leigh flew into Las Vegas, an angry Joyce Bova flew out. Priscilla also flew in that day, bringing with her two-and-a-half-year-old Lisa Marie. It was the sort of juggling act with women and sex that Elvis relished. With Joyce barely gone, he managed to have sex with Barbara, even while his wife and daughter were arriving.

KATHY WESTMORELAND

In addition to Joyce, Barbara, and Priscilla, Elvis had another dark-haired beauty on the line. He was pursuing his second virgin of the season, twenty-five-year-old Kathy Westmoreland, the high soprano he had added to the company to replace Millie Kirkham a week after the August 10, 1969, opening in Vegas.

Soon after Kathy joined the show, she had been invited to a party in Elvis's suite. Virtually from the moment Elvis entered the room "looking gorgeous," she was enthralled by him. "He just looked beautiful in this black velour-type suit with the high collar, laced so his chest showed," she recalled years later. He walked straight over, sat down beside her, put his arm around her, and started talking to her again. "He told me how much he cared about me, you know, that he was interested in me and liked me, and when he kissed me, I crossed my eyes," Kathy said. She could not believe that Elvis would choose her over all the glamorous young women who hovered about. Then they began talking about their common interest in matters of the spirit. Kathy told him she was a virgin. Elvis liked that. He explained that he and Priscilla had an open marriage, but hastened to assure her there would be no sex unless she wanted it. Then he walked her back to her room. As in the initial meeting with Joyce, he was the perfect gentleman.

Before the August 1970 engagement was over, Kathy was sleeping with Elvis. But there was no sex. He told her that he feared being alone, having had nightmares as a result of the assassination threat and all. She knew that other women slept with Elvis, but when no one else was available she was happy to share his bed and assuage his fears.

When they all flew to Phoenix to begin the tour on September 9, Elvis made certain that Kathy flew with him and not with the rest of the troupe on another plane. It was another signal, especially to the guys, who must now keep their hands off Kathy, that Elvis had chosen her. She was still a viable candidate for a relatively permanent position in his bed.

The show in Phoenix was a tremendous success. One critic noted that "the crowd that filled the house was young." It was "screaming and stamping whenever he posed, pointed, stabbed and sprawled."

They wanted to hear the old songs. Elvis was back in the saddle again, both in Vegas and on the road.

Kathy continued to sleep with Elvis in Phoenix and after. In Detroit, on September 11, it seemed to her that he was committing himself to her. However, as they headed south for Miami the next day, Elvis had Kathy moved into another room. His relatives would be coming for a visit, he explained. Kathy said that she understood, but she was confused and hurt.

In truth, Elvis was flying Barbara Leigh in from Los Angeles, not relatives. Barbara had no trouble having sex with Elvis, married or not. But she did not get along with the guys. "They kind of got the leftovers," she said with her usual candor in such matters, "and I stopped all the girls from coming around whenever I was around." The downside for Barbara was that Elvis was always demanding attention. The game, she felt, was barely worth the trouble.

After the September 1970 tour, Elvis spent a lot of time in Palm Springs with the guys. In late October, he persuaded Kathy to join him there for a weekend. Just as she walked in the door, he was on the phone with Priscilla explaining why he could not come back to join his wife and child in Los Angeles right then. Elvis read poetry to Kathy, read to her from his books on spirituality, and lamented the death of his pet chimpanzee so emotionally that tears came to her eyes. As they entered the dining room in the afternoon of the next day for breakfast, the guys were already gathered around the table.

"Hey, boys, you know what?" Elvis exclaimed. "Our Kathy is still a virgin."

Humiliated, Kathy retreated to the bedroom, intending to pack her things and flee. Elvis came in, almost started up his little-boy act, then saw her fury. He pulled her close.

"Honey, I wasn't trying to shame you. I'm proud of your being a virgin. Not many girls could hold out this long," he said. "I wouldn't hurt your feelings for the world."

That night, they had sex. The following night, he advised her to go on the pill.

Kathy had to go back to Los Angeles to meet television and recording commitments, which Elvis urged her to cancel. "I'll always take care of you," he said. Kathy promised to come back the next weekend.

Meanwhile, Barbara Leigh was in and out of Palm Springs. Elvis told her his life's story, including how when he was a boy he had caught a glimpse of a girl's panties while he was wrestling with her and how he was victimized at school. He also tried unsuccessfully to interest her in spiritual matters, but Barbara was into other things. "In those days I had so many boyfriends and guys pursuing me—I think I was oblivious to right and wrong," she said. She began to lose interest in Elvis. "Get this. Get that," he was always ordering. There was a lot of sex at first. He was a great kisser and very sweet, but not the stud she had expected. She ascribed the difficulty to the drugs he was taking. "It was hard for him to be a natural man," she said.

Kathy Westmoreland came back the next weekend. She found Elvis to be plenty natural—by her standards. "But that night, in the quiet stillness of each other's arms after a flurry of passion, things began to go topsy turvy," she said. She told him that even love was no excuse for adultery. When Elvis was not able to talk her into easily accepting their physical relationship, he was furious. "Does that mean I have to get someone else, train them just like I want them?" he demanded. Kathy was outraged. "Am I some kind of dog or puppy that you housebreak?" she responded. "I'm a woman, a human being." In the end they made up, but thereafter everything was strange to Kathy. On the surface, things seemed fine, but underneath there was always a tension. Kathy had just lost not only her virginity but also her chance at becoming Elvis's relatively permanent bedmate. The troupe began another tour in November. Kathy started out sleeping with Elvis, but on the fourth night, when they played San Francisco, he moved her out of his bedroom. She knew her place was filled by another woman. Onstage that evening he boasted about his records, fifty-six gold singles and fourteen gold albums, as if those trophies ought to free him from his troubles. "I've outsold the Beatles, the Stones, Tom Jones—all of them put together," he bragged.

BADGES, GUNS, AND POLICEMEN

In the fall of 1970, Elvis was falling apart. He became obsessed with obtaining police badges. When his show played Denver, he wooed the city police and got them to promise him a real police badge. Shortly after, he flew back to Denver especially to collect his badge. Almost immediately, he cultivated particularly close friendships with several members of the Denver Police Department, buying each of his new friends a Lincoln Continental Mark IV at $13,000 each. He also got badges from ranking police officers in Memphis and Tupelo. In Los Angeles, he secured a gold police commissioner's badge after making a $7,000 donation to a police fund.

During the same time, Elvis developed an obsession with guns. In December, over a period of three days in Los Angeles he bought $20,000 worth of guns in one store. He kept four salesmen busy as he bought guns for himself, his friends, and people who just happened to walk in off the street. In his application for a permit to carry a handgun, Elvis gave "self-protection" as his reason. He also indicated that his weight was 160 pounds, which it probably was not, and he gave his height as six-one—which it definitely was not if he took the lifts out of his shoes. Back in Memphis, he got gun permits for both himself and his father. Soon he developed a huge and growing arsenal, including a .357 Magnum, a gold-plated .45 automatic pistol, a .22 caliber Savage revolver, a pocket-sized Derringer, an AK-47 carbine, and a Thompson submachine gun.

Elvis also became obsessed with men who possessed extraordinary powers of command. He had seen the film *Patton* (1970) several times, and he had memorized Patton's grandiose patriotic speech as compellingly rendered in the movie by the full-chested actor George C. Scott. He would recite it often and with manly gusto. Later he also liked to watch the 1977 movie *MacArthur*. Before his death Elvis could recite the general's farewell address before the US Congress verbatim and with feeling—"Old soldiers never die, they just fade away..." When he had learned that World War II general Omar Bradley lived in Beverly Hills, he visited him several times. The dignified and low-key general was no doubt amused by the bizarre costumes his visitor wore—offstage now as well as on.

Elvis also looked up Vice President Spiro Agnew in Palm Springs, where Agnew was a frequent visitor. He tried to give the vice president a gun, too, but Agnew explained that he could not accept a gift at that time. Elvis promised to keep it for him.

RICHARD NIXON

As the year 1970 came to an end, Elvis began spending money like water. He bought jewelry for everyone, expensive cars for several of his guys and Barbara Leigh, put down a $10,000 deposit on a new home for Joe and Joanie Esposito, and financed weddings, including that of Dick Grob, a sergeant and weapons training specialist on the Palm Springs police force.

Elvis was making a lot of money then, but the previous year, 1969, he had come dangerously close to bankruptcy. His wife and his father, his personal money manager (for whom he had just bought a new Mercedes), were exceedingly money conscious, some would even say miserly. Alarmed by Elvis's manic spending, they consulted with the Colonel and got what they wanted—his advice, to be shared with Elvis and explicitly stated to be his advice, that he must curb his spending. One might as well tell the sun not to set or the moon not to rise.

On Saturday, December 19, Priscilla and Vernon sat down with Elvis at the dining room table in Graceland and began to lecture him on what he had to do. Elvis could not believe what he was hearing. With exceedingly strong language, he pointed out whose money they were talking about and stormed out of the house. He got into his car, roared off to the airport, and took a plane to Washington. He checked into the Hotel Washington using one of his favorite aliases, Jon Burrows. The desk clerk wrote down the name of the guest as Jon Burrowe.

Elvis wanted to find Joyce Bova, but he only knew that she worked on Capitol Hill. He seemed unaware that there would be a multitude of government offices on the Hill and that they might not be open on a Saturday. Elvis was not able to locate Joyce by phone. His dialing skills were minimal; other people always did that for him. "Elvis wants to talk to you," they would say when the desired party came on the line.

Frustrated, Elvis flew to Los Angeles, having phoned Jerry Schilling to meet him at the airport when his plane arrived at 2:17 a.m. Jerry was alarmed to see Elvis enter the terminal with his face hugely swollen and covered with a rash. In the wee hours of the morning, having dropped off the two stewardesses to whom Elvis had offered a ride home in his limo, they got a doctor. Elvis told the doctor that his condition arose from eating chocolate on the plane. The doctor treated him and suggested that he eat no more chocolate. More plausibly, he was having a reaction to drugs and had come to California in part to replenish his drug supply.

Jerry was trying hard to build a career for himself working as a Hollywood film editor, but he agreed to escort Elvis back to Washington to help find Joyce Bova. Elvis had Jerry call Sonny West in Memphis, instructing him to meet them at the hotel in Washington, and allowed him to tell Vernon and Priscilla not to worry, but not where he was or where he was going.

On the plane to Washington, Elvis learned that California senator George Murphy was also aboard. He walked back to the main cabin from the first class cabin to talk to the senator. He expressed his admiration for the senator's patriotism and said that he too wanted to serve his country. In particular, he thought he could help the nation with its drug problem, since he had some influence with young people. He persuaded Murphy to contact the Bureau of Narcotics and Dangerous Drugs and the FBI to arrange for Elvis to talk to officials in each agency.

Elvis wanted more badges. He wanted to be appointed an undercover officer for the two agencies. Murphy suggested that Elvis also contact the White House.

Returning to his seat, Elvis penciled a letter to President Nixon on American Airlines stationery expressing his desire to talk to him about helping out the country. Jerry was aghast, but he helped Elvis find the language for his message to the president.

"Dear Mr. President," Elvis wrote.

He was concerned about the country, he said. He could help because he could reach people in subtle ways. "The Drug Culture, the Hippie elements, the SDS, Black Panthers, etc. do not consider me as their enemy or as they call it The Establishment. I call it America and I love it. Sir I can and will be of any service that I can to help the country out," he said. Elvis was thinking that he would work covertly. "I wish not to be given a title or an appointed position. I can and will do more good if I were made a Federal agent at Large, and I will help but by doing it my way through my communications with people of all ages. First and foremost I am an entertainer but all I need is the Federal credentials."

Elvis explained to President Nixon that he had prepared himself carefully for this labor. He had done "an in depth study of Drug Abuse and Communist Brainwashing techniques." He shared with the president the news that he was about to be named one of the year's "ten most outstanding young men" in America, an honor he thought the president himself had once received. "I would love to meet you just to say hello if you're not too busy," he said. In a "p.s." Elvis told President Nixon that he had a gift for him. On Monday morning about 6:00 a.m., Elvis and Jerry took a limousine to the White House, where Elvis gave his letter to a startled guard. After recognizing the man in bizarre garb as Elvis Presley, the young man promised that it would be delivered to a member of the president's staff. Elvis and Jerry went on to the Washington Hotel and up to the suite of rooms Elvis had rented on the fifth floor. Elvis's face was swollen, and the rash had broken out again. A doctor was summoned, and Elvis told the chocolate story again. The doctor prescribed some medication, told him not to eat chocolate, and charged $100 for his visit.

Elvis proceeded to the Bureau of Narcotics and Dangerous Drugs, where, as arranged by Senator Murphy, he was greeted by Deputy Director John Finlator. Elvis pushed every possible button to get the Bureau to give him a badge, including his strong desire to make a cash donation to the Bureau. All to no avail. They did not take donations or give out badges. Just as failure seemed imminent, Jerry called from the hotel. They were expected at the White House in forty-five minutes to meet Egil "Bud" Krogh, a member of the president's staff.

Sonny West arrived at the hotel just as Elvis came by to pick up Jerry. All three went to the White House and to Krogh's office. Krogh had passed Elvis's note, along with his recommendation that the president receive Elvis, to his boss, H. R. Haldeman, Nixon's chief of staff. Haldeman had written on the margin of the memo: "You must be kidding?" Nevertheless, he approved, and at 12:30 p.m. Krogh, having convinced himself that Elvis was not dangerous, and having relieved him of the pistol that he intended to give the president, ushered him into the Oval Office.

Richard Nixon needed all the help he could get in coping with young Americans in 1970 with the Vietnam War still ongoing. He quickly understood that Elvis might help him deal with a very specific problem—the young people of America who were burning Old Glory and protesting against this bloody and futile war against Communism in Vietnam, even around the sacred buildings of the nation's capital. In April 1970, he had ordered the invasion of Cambodia from Vietnam. He was in the War Room of the White House as the invasion was launched and took the occasion to praise the brave young men engaged in that action and to condemn the treasonous protests of the young people at home—predominantly students—who demonstrated so vigorously against the war. When he revealed plans to draft another 150,000 young men into the service, student protests broke out all over America; some five hundred colleges and universities were either shut down or severely impacted. At Kent State University in Ohio, twenty-eight National Guardsmen opened fire on student demonstrators, killing four and wounding nine. There was no higher authorization for such, but many drew a direct line from Nixon's virulent condemnation of the students to this massacre. The whole student movement was a tribulation to Nixon, but he struggled to understand it.

Richard Nixon had an image problem with young people, and Elvis Presley could help him. The president knew what he wanted from Elvis, but communication with the entertainer proved exceedingly difficult. To begin with, it was a shock to see a man who looked like this outside of a Halloween party or off a movie set, much less in the Oval Office. He looked like an actor in a horror story. He somehow seemed larger than life, tall, heavy-set, with long, jet black hair and low-reaching sideburns. He was still wearing his heavily ornamented large-lensed sunglasses as he approached the president. His lengthy Edwardian jacket was draped casually, European-style, around his shoulders, sleeves dangling. Beneath the coat one could see a purple tunic partially covering a shirt that was widely V-necked and parted down toward his navel, exposing an expanse of his hairy chest. Around his neck, he wore his "Tree of Life" necklace bearing the names of all the guys on its roots and branches, and a huge gold pendant in the shape of a lion's head rested against his chest. Around his waist, Elvis wore the wide, thick, gold, and sparkly belt given him by the International Hotel for breaking attendance records. As he strode forward to shake the hand of the president, Krogh noticed that in his left hand he was carrying a cluster of badges—his treasure trove of police badges.

As the two men groped toward a conversation, Elvis spread his badges out on the presidential desk, removed his sunglasses, and laid them down beside the badges. He had also brought photographs of himself that he showed to the president. He explained that he got the belt he was wearing for performing in Las Vegas. The president quipped that he himself knew how hard it was to play Vegas. Indeed, he had once charmingly and with a comfortable sense of humor played the piano there onstage with Liberace. Elvis, apparently, did not catch the president's humor. But while he had the floor for a moment, Nixon quickly offered the idea that he thought Elvis could reach young people. Elvis quickly agreed, but added that he must work only in his own way.

Elvis overwhelmed Nixon with his intensity. The president struggled to keep up but lost Elvis's train of thought when he launched into an attack on the Beatles. They were a center of anti-Americanism, Elvis charged vehemently, having come to America to make a lot of money, then going back to England and slandering America. How in the world could the president of the United States respond to that? Finally, the president relented and gave the man what he wanted. He told Krogh to order the Bureau of Narcotics to give Elvis a badge.

Elvis was elated. He threw his arm around the presidential shoulder and boldly asked Nixon to invite his friends Sonny and Jerry into the Oval Office, which the president did. Elvis was exercising control again—this time over the White House. After some chitchat and photos by the presidential photographer, Nixon decided to give these people some mementos of their visit to the White House and let them go. The president fumbled in his desk drawer for presidential cufflinks for his guests. As he approached the end of his supply, Elvis informed Nixon that these guys had wives too. The president again dived into his drawer to pull out presidential pins appropriate for women. Finally, the visitors, having pocketed their loot, left the office for a White House tour and a White House lunch.

Later, Elvis flatly refused to believe that President Nixon had been involved in the Watergate scandal in any way. However, when Vice President Spiro Agnew was forced to resign for having evaded his income taxes, Elvis blew up. "I want my goddamn guns back," he fumed.

Elvis dropped Jerry off at the airport. He and Sonny returned to the hotel, where Sonny had managed to contact Joyce. Both Joyce and her identical twin sister appeared at the hotel that evening. Elvis amazed everyone by immediately identifying which twin was Joyce. He and Sonny double-dated the Bova twins for the night.

That night, at last, Joyce went to bed with Elvis. Before they lay down, he told her that she was beautiful. "You're a pure little girl too, aren't you?" he said. "Even though it had not happened for me," Joyce said later, "I knew he could make it happen." She was surprised by his mode of proceeding. "The fervid sex that had made him famous had, in reality, been gentler, a sweet and tender passion." Joyce was surprised to discover what virtually all of Elvis's sex-mates were surprised to discover; he was not a tiger in bed after all.

The next morning they had breakfast together, probably the $18 restaurant charge that showed up on Elvis's hotel bill. Elvis and his party had occupied rooms 505, 506, 507, and 508. The whole bill amounted to $1,424.76. Elvis signed the statement in the hotel that morning, not as Jon Burrows, the name typed in at the head of the document, but as Elvis Presley and with a flourish. He was on a roll, and he was no longer working under cover. Further, his value to the nation had just been recognized by the president, and he'd had sex with yet another beautiful young virgin.

Elvis had the hotel send the bill to Vernon Presley at 3764 Highway 51 South in Memphis, Tennessee. For once, perhaps, Vernon thought that an expense was justified. His son had visited the president of the United States at the White House. There had to be some sort of reflected glory for him in that.

HOMECOMING

Elvis returned home with presents for everyone and boastful tales about his exploits. The contretemps in the dining room that had caused his angry departure only three days before was totally erased. On the day before Christmas, he gave a Mercedes each to Dr. Nick, his physician, and to Sonny West, who had helped him out in Washington and was about to be married in a wedding that Elvis had arranged and was paying for. Another was given to Bill Morris, recently the county sheriff, who had managed to give Elvis and virtually all of his guys in Memphis real deputy sheriff badges that, coincidentally, allowed them to carry guns legally. Elvis's male entourage became a walking arsenal. Anyone who attempted to assassinate Elvis Presley would be riddled with bullets. In the wee hours of Christmas morning, Elvis went down to the Memphis city police station "to say Hello" to the men in blue.

On the day after Christmas 1970, he drove downtown to buy some more guns, and on Monday, December 28, he attended Sonny's wedding wearing an extra belt bearing his new Shelby County deputy's badge (number 6), two guns in shoulder holsters, two pearl-handled pistols stuck in the waistband of his pants, a derringer in his boot, and a fifteen-inch police flashlight. Elvis was the best man, but the dignity of the ceremony was threatened by his reluctance to give up even the flashlight before going to the altar alongside the groom. "It won't look good," urged Marty Lacker, who had carefully organized the event.

After the minister had married the couple, Marty was unable to dissuade Elvis from moving the reception from the church to Graceland. This was the night when Elvis, all of the guys, Dr. Nick, and the present and past sheriffs of Shelby County, all dressed up for the wedding, posed for their semifamous group photograph proudly presenting their badges. Elvis was in the front row center, of course, and seated like a king in his court. His men either stood behind or kneeled beside him. Later that night, he insisted that everyone, including the bride and groom, go with him to the Memphian to see a movie.

On Wednesday, Elvis and eight friends traveled to Washington with Memphis ex-sheriff Bill Morris to tour the headquarters of the National Sheriffs' Association. Elvis also arranged a visit to the FBI headquarters in Washington for himself and his coterie on New Year's Eve day. As he leaned over to drink from a water fountain, a derringer fell out of his clothing. While he was in a stall in the men's restroom, a .25 automatic fell noisily to the floor. The FBI agents giving them the tour hardly knew what to do after the pistol went clattering across the tiles.

While he was there, Elvis offered to go undercover for the FBI as well as the Bureau of Narcotics. Director J. Edgar Hoover was not available at the time of the visit, but Elvis told the agents who met him that he considered Mr. Hoover to be "the greatest living American." He also shared with them his opinion that "the Beatles laid the groundwork for many of the problems we are having with young people by their filthy unkempt appearances and suggestive music." He also opined that the Smothers Brothers, Jane Fonda, and other antiwar entertainers "have a lot to answer for in the hereafter for the way they have poisoned young minds by disparaging the United States in their public statements and unsavory activities." On January 4, Hoover wrote Elvis a letter thanking him for his "generous comments" and assuring him that "we will keep in mind your offer to be of assistance," but offering no badge.

THE BEST MEN

Saturday, January 16, 1971, was one of the proudest days in Elvis's life. He was given an award by the nation's Junior Chamber of Commerce as one of America's Ten Outstanding Young Men of the Year. That morning, he attended the Jaycee prayer breakfast at the Riverview Holiday Inn in Memphis on a cliff high above the Mississippi River. At lunch, he heard the US ambassador to the United Nations, George H. W. Bush, urge cooperation between business and government.

That evening in Ellis Auditorium, along with the other winners, he gave his acceptance speech. He had been a dreamer since childhood, he said, and each dream had "come true a hundred times." This hardly seemed the case with his movie career, but he went on. He suggested that "these gentlemen over here" might well "be building the kingdom." That statement did not square well with reality either. The *Memphis Commercial Appeal* found that six or seven of the ten outstanding young men did not even belong to a church and indeed "felt a certain hypocrisy about organized religion." Elvis closed by quoting the words of a song, as he often did in seeking to convey his perception of some essence. "Without a song," he said, "the day would never end, a man ain't got a friend, and the road would never bend. So I keep singing a song," he concluded. "Good night. Thank you."

Elvis and Priscilla had flown to Memphis the night before, and Elvis had sat in his office on the second floor of Graceland composing his speech. He called Priscilla in to critique his work. She was amazed. "He shocked me with the eloquence of his speech," she said. She suspected him of lifting it from somewhere, "clever as he was."

Then Elvis was off to Las Vegas for another four-week run in the Showroom of the Hilton. With everyone gathered in his suite, he began showing off his guns and badges. At one point when he wanted everyone's attention, he pointed a pistol at the chandelier, aimed, and pulled the trigger. The gun snapped. Everyone watched in stunned silence. But the gun was not loaded, and Elvis doubled over with laughter. A moment later all the guys doubled over with laughter too. On another occasion, he blasted an image of Robert Goulet on his television screen with his turquoise-handled Colt .45. This time he did not laugh. They didn't laugh either. The pistol was loaded.

By early March, Elvis was writing an anxious and insistent letter to John Finlator to make sure that the Narco deputy chief got his commission papers in proper order. "Would you please make the credentials to read 'Agent at Large,' as I may be going overseas at any time on a concert tour," he wrote. "The credentials are of the utmost secrecy and importance," he declared. Again, he asserted that he had studied on his own and in depth "drug abuse, communist psychological brainwashing techniques, etc." He blamed motion pictures and rock music "for much of the confusion in this country." Because he was directly in the middle of both, his "status as a government agent would have to be kept secret as I would lose them to say the least." Elvis closed by saying he would contact the deputy director "from time to time to say hello" and inviting him to his home "in Memphis or Los Angeles to spend an evening with myself and my family."

TALES OF BOCCACCIO

Throughout 1971, it was guns, badges, policemen, and a rising messianic complex, all mixed in with road shows and hotel performances, recording sessions, and shuffling Joyce and Barbara, and presumably Priscilla, in and out of Elvis's bed. Kathy Westmoreland, having surrendered her virginity to no avail, retired from the rotation. The moving of girls and young women in and out of Elvis's arms was, like Boccaccio's tales, both sad and hilarious. It was a sickness that led to bizarre situations.

In March, while recording in Nashville, Elvis developed a severe eye infection, probably from hair dye and eye makeup mixed with sweat getting into his eye. Priscilla was in California putting the finishing touches on their new house, so he brought in Barbara Leigh. He persuaded her not only to stay in the hospital with him but also to share his hospital bed. There is no record of what attending physicians, nurses, and aides thought when they came into the room of the ailing Elvis and saw this rising television and Hollywood movie star propped up in the high white bed with him.

Barbara had to return to California, so Elvis flew Joyce down from Washington. As Vernon helped his ailing son up the stairs toward his bedroom at Graceland, she followed behind. She was touched by that father-son scene but then was shocked to see Priscilla in front of her. Actually, it was a full-sized portrait of Priscilla, with Elvis standing beside her, hanging on the wall in the stairwell. They looked "almost like brother and sister," she said, "both in facial structure and expression." Joyce stayed for a few days, nursing Elvis.

It was an intimate time for Joyce, stuffed away with him in his bedroom. But it was also strange. She felt hemmed in by the "velvet harem-like drapes" covering the windows, bulky "dark wood furniture," and "a red-and-black color scheme." His books on religion and philosophy lay all around, and she read to him from *The Impersonal Life*, his current favorite. During the previous winter in Las Vegas, he had persuaded her to take pills before having sex. Before long, Placidyl was her drug. When she left Graceland she asked Elvis for a supply to take with her.

Joyce was back within three weeks. This time, Elvis took her downstairs to meet his grandmother Minnie Mae. They engaged intensely right away because, as Joyce said, they talked about "the man we both adored." Minnie Mae was amazingly quick to embrace anyone in the endless sequence of Elvis's young women who happened by, and thereafter each could imagine that she was truly the only woman in Elvis's life. Joyce was favorably impressed by it all. That weekend she saw a beautiful Elvis, but she did not know how to respond when he suggested that she move into Graceland. There was, after all, his wife, Priscilla, to consider.

In late May 1971, Joyce was again back in the studio in Nashville with Elvis. The producers were having trouble finishing this recording session, in part because the musicians kept going outside to the parking lot, where they gathered in a van and smoked marijuana. They excused themselves from the studio, asserting that it was so crowded with all the guys in the Elvis entourage and all the talent that there was no place left for them to sit or stand. They were so far gone on "grass" that they thought Joyce was Priscilla.

To bring the musicians to sobriety and back to work, the security guards, who were Nashville policemen off duty, fed them "speed," amphetamines they had taken off a pusher they had just jailed. Elvis, for his part, attempted to bring them to a proper sense of their responsibilities by showing them his Narco badge and giving them a speech denouncing rock groups known to have drug problems. The musicians thought it hilarious that they should hear such preaching from a guy who was himself stoned. Joyce again went back to Memphis with Elvis. This time she inquired about the possibility of Dr. Nick writing her a prescription for her own bottle of Placidyl.

In mid-June, when Priscilla left Memphis for California to work on decorating their house, Elvis immediately brought Joyce back to Graceland. Two months later she joined him in Las Vegas, and she had big news.

She was pregnant. She had become pregnant at Graceland during her last visit. Joyce was determined to tell Elvis. She took her Catholicism seriously. Sexual relations outside of marriage and adultery were bad enough; abortion was beyond endurance. Alone in his room on the twenty-ninth floor of the hotel, she began to break the news gently by asking Elvis about his daughter. After he answered, she intended to announce that he was about to become the father of another child. She thought Elvis sensed what was coming and tried to avoid the issue by talking nonstop about how sacred motherhood was and how mothers should not try to be sexy. The message seemed to be that if she had a baby it would be her fault and sex between them would cease. Joyce asserted that sexuality was a part of life. Elvis waved her away. "Trust me on this, Joyce," he said, "I know I'm right." She gave up. Three weeks later she had her abortion and never told him.

On November 5 and 6, Saturday and Sunday, Joyce joined Elvis as he performed in Cleveland and Louisville. She observed that there were no "high rollers" in the audience such as she had seen in his audiences in Las Vegas. These huge crowds were true believers. Increasingly, Elvis was seeing himself as the messiah to the masses. His mission in life, he kept telling her, was to make people's dreams come true. She saw guns and books scattered about in his hotel room, and he always carried his Jaycees award and his badge from the Bureau of Narcotics.

ALL FALL DOWN

In 1972 Elvis wrote:

> *Philosophy for a happy life.*
> *Someone to love*
> *Something to look forward to*
> *And something to do.*
> E. P. 1972

After the November tour, Elvis flew to Memphis, then to California, and then back to Memphis where on Saturday night, December 11, 1971, he took Joyce Bova to a private screening at the Crosstown Theater. Increasingly, Elvis talked to Joyce about moving into Graceland with him, but she worried about his rapid mood swings—and the pills they both were taking. Plus, he was still married to Priscilla. On Sunday, he and Joyce flew to Washington and checked into the hotel where they had first consummated their love. On Tuesday, he flew back to Memphis and on Saturday Priscilla and Lisa Marie arrived from California. Now it was Priscilla who had some news for Elvis.

Priscilla told Elvis that she did not love him anymore and was separating from him. She and Lisa stayed for Christmas but flew out the night before New Year's Eve. With a dramatic flair that seemed to please him, Elvis gathered together an assembly of his people at Graceland and announced that Priscilla was leaving him. She had not told him why, he whined to everyone who would listen—in groups, in person, and by phone. Elvis was clueless as to the cause of her desertion.

Joyce was back at Graceland for Elvis's thirty-seventh birthday on January 8, 1972. She saw no great change in him. But he did say to her that he was past the age that Christ was when he was crucified—thirty-three. He needed, he said, to "plan the rest of my life's work."

Later that month Elvis opened again in Vegas. He added "An American Trilogy" to the show. He also added "You Gave Me a Mountain," in which the singer cries that his wife has deserted him and, most grievously, taken away "his reason for living," which was their "small, baby boy." Although some people liked to think that Elvis was expressing his own real grief, he denied this.

Joyce flew to Vegas for what turned out to be her last meeting with Elvis. Somehow, in a ladies' restroom in the hotel, she fell into a conversation with two young women, probably prostitutes. They talked enthusiastically about how they had recently performed for Elvis in his suite by making love to one another. When she confronted Elvis with the story, he just laughed it off. "Honey, I never touched those girls," he said. "I just watched." It was, he said, just "innocent fun."

Before she left, Joyce tried again to talk to him about his drug use. The drugs were a part of his mission, he said. The drugs were to gain "silence." "Silence is the resting place of the soul," he said. "It's sacred.

255

And necessary for new thoughts to be born. That's what my pills are for...to get as close as possible to that silence," he explained. Presumably, a drug-induced silence, not sober meditation, was bringing him closer to the divine spirit. "We all have divinity inside us," he declared. "Some of us just understand it more." People listened to him because of his understanding, he said. He knew what they wanted and needed. Some day they would all listen to him. Seemingly, a new messiah was in view, rising from Las Vegas and visiting stages all over America.

Joyce left the next morning while Elvis was still sleeping. "What a small, dull, shitty way for it to end," she thought.

THE GIRLS ARE GONE

Some days later, just at the end of the engagement, Priscilla traveled to Las Vegas. She not only wanted to leave Elvis, she wanted to live openly with Mike Stone. Elvis, a karate enthusiast, had idolized Mike. In August 1971, he had proudly introduced him from the stage in Vegas as having been the Grand International Champion for two years. "The best in the world," he declared. "My god, he will dissect you," he said in awe and admiration.

Losing Priscilla to no one in particular was one thing; losing Priscilla in a competition with another man who was famously masculine and virile was something else. Elvis flew into a rage. "He grabbed me," Priscilla wrote in *Elvis and Me*, "and forcefully made love to me. It was uncomfortable and unlike any other time he'd ever made love to me before." He told her that "this is how a real man makes love to his woman." Thus, the love affair between Elvis and Priscilla ended, ignominiously, with spousal rape.

Joyce was gone. Kathy had left. Barbara was living with Steve McQueen. Priscilla was having an affair with Mike Stone. Elvis was in a daze. He could not understand how these women could have deserted him. His search for new bedmates went on, as the guys went trolling for girls for Elvis in Los Angeles, in Las Vegas, in Memphis. The spring of 1972 passed, and he was still adrift.

THE DOCUMENTARY: *ELVIS ON TOUR*

While Elvis was thus bereft, the Colonel arranged for a documentary film—eventually called *Elvis on Tour*—to be made during the April 1972 tour. It was financed by MGM and produced by Bob Abel and Pierre Adidge, whose previous documentaries, including *Mad Dogs and Englishmen*, had won high praise. This film caught beautifully the magical quality of the rapport between Elvis and his audiences in performances in Buffalo, Hampton Roads, Richmond, and Jacksonville. In taped interviews, it also caught Elvis's thinking with an intimacy that no outsider had ever achieved before. In these, he did not always sound like the happy, upbeat, and healthy man he had always projected publicly. Instead, he took the occasion to run the litany of his torments and tormentors, including the "squirrel-get-him" analogy from high school and the trauma of having to dress in a tuxedo and sing to a dog dressed in a tie and top hat on *The Steve Allen Show*. He complained bitterly about the movie business, which he had thought would give him "a chance to show some kind of acting ability or do a very interesting story." But no, he said, and he became discouraged.

"They couldn't have paid me no amount of money in the world to make me feel self-satisfaction inside," he declared.

"But you still did them," Pierre Adidge pressed.

"I had to. I had to," Elvis responded with expiring breath.

So many abuses, so much humiliation—on television and in the movies. "I really took it as long as I could," he said. "Physically, emotionally, and everything."

When the Colonel saw the tape and heard what Elvis had been saying in the interview for the documentary, he was very upset. They could never admit that Elvis's movies were bad or that he was in any way lacking in talent. Parker remonstrated with MGM and achieved some adjustments. Nevertheless, a deeply troubled Elvis came through on the film.

Onscreen Elvis conveyed how he worked much too hard trying to convince the guys in his entourage that he was fully and excitingly engaged sexually.

Elvis's perennial search for a possibly permanent bedmate experienced an uptick in quality during the summer of 1972 when Cybill Shepherd came home to Memphis from Hollywood for a month of rest and rehabilitation. Cybill had been Miss Teenage Memphis before going west to pursue an acting career and had turned in compelling performances in *The Last Picture Show* and *The Heartbreak Kid*. She was also taking a leave of absence from her current lover, director Peter Bogdanovich. Years later, she told an interviewer that during this interlude she had taken the macho out of Elvis. What she had really done was merely discover what numerous other girls and women had already discovered about Elvis's lovemaking, that it was not very macho anyway.

LINDA THOMPSON

On July 6, 1972, eighteen years to the day after he had suddenly broken out singing "That's All Right" in Sam Phillips's studio, Linda Thompson came to him like a gift from heaven. Linda was the current Miss Tennessee in the Miss USA contest, twenty-two years old, and a senior at Memphis State University majoring in theater and English. She had a gift for engaging new people instantly and making them feel comfortable. George Klein brought Linda to the Memphian Theater one night while Elvis was enjoying one of his beloved midnight screenings. Elvis approved the introduction after cleverly scoping Linda out on his way to the men's room. The attraction was immediate.

Elvis had her sit beside him. As he usually did in such situations, he managed, seemingly casually, to throw his right arm across the back of her seat. He hastened to assure her that he was no longer married. In truth, his divorce was still a few weeks away.

Linda had brought along a visiting friend, Jeanne LeMay, the reigning Miss Rhode Island. When they got home in the wee hours of the next morning, Jeannie reported to Linda's aunt, with whom they were staying, that her niece and Elvis had been sitting in the theater kissing. Just then, as if on cue, the phone rang. It was Elvis for Linda. "Where have you been all my life?" he asked. The full-court press was on. Linda noticed that his voice was strangely slurred. She thought he might have been drinking.

Elvis invited Linda and Jeannie to the movies again the next night, and afterward out to Graceland. Linda fit right in. She rode around the grounds of Graceland with the gang in golf carts, and then she went with Elvis up to his bedroom. "We kissed, we made out—which was wonderful—and then we read the Bible," she told Peter Guralnick. "We felt as if we'd known each other all our lives—we kind of did [through knowing] how the other person was brought up."

Indeed, both came out of the same Southern white working-class culture. The Thompsons, like the Smiths and the Presleys, were country-come-to-town people. They worked hard all week to collect their pay on Saturday and ordinarily went to church on Sunday. Linda's father drove a truck for a trucking firm. The Thompsons honored and relished very close clan and family ties. They had struggled through the Great Depression but had prospered, relatively speaking, in postwar Memphis.

Linda's background was similar to that of Elvis's teenage sweetheart Dixie Locke, but Linda, like Elvis, was determined to succeed in a striking way in the world. Attending Memphis State University was an indicator that she was ambitious. Winning beauty contests was another way up for her, as it was for many Southern girls who had no special advantages by dint of their parents' affluence or social position. Linda made the most of her talents and looks, just as Elvis had. Elvis had to mold Priscilla into the woman he wanted; Linda was born and bred that way. Gladys would have loved Linda right away.

Linda recognized her kinship with Elvis virtually within minutes of their meeting and made the most of it. As they settled into their seats in the Memphian Theater, Elvis had explained that he had been separated from his wife since January. "I'm really sorry to hear that," she replied, "but I could have told you a long time ago, you should have married a Memphis girl." Elvis immediately grasped the sharp truth in her observation and laughed. After months of fruitless searching, he had found the girl he needed.

On the morning after their second night together, Linda went off to the beach with her family for three weeks. Elvis tried repeatedly to contact her, or at least his minions did. The phone was "ringing off the hook" when she got home. It was Elvis, inviting her to fly to Las Vegas with him. She accepted without hesitation even though, as she later said, she was still a virgin and took her religion seriously.

Elvis was a way up for Linda. Even though she only needed twelve more hours of course work to graduate from Memphis State, she really didn't want to go back to school that fall. Already she had thought about going to Los Angeles to start her acting career, going to New York to be a model, or becoming an airline stewardess. This was a marvelous opportunity to jump-start her search for a career, and she took it.

In the beginning it was, for her, also a lover's idyll. In his luxury suite on the twenty-ninth floor of the Hilton in Las Vegas, Elvis was "so loving and affectionate," everyone was so nice to her, and Las Vegas was so exciting. Early on, she saw that he sometimes staggered a bit and his speech was slurred. Within a few weeks, she realized that drugs were a major problem.

From the first Elvis must have sensed that Linda was the next one, another beautiful virgin to follow Elisabeth, Priscilla, Kathy, and Joyce. She was another girl whom he could initiate and train to his taste sexually, who would be devoted to him far and above all other men and faithfully share his bed—day and night. And so it was. Linda moved into Graceland and like no one ever before or after was with him constantly for more than four years—in Graceland, Los Angeles, Palm Springs, Las Vegas, and Tahoe, on tour, and on vacations in Hawaii and Colorado.

At home in Graceland, they would lounge together for days on the huge bed in his cavelike bedroom watching television, reading, eating, and talking. Linda would call him "Baby Bunting" and he would call her "Mommy." She would talk baby talk to him, and soon they developed a language with code words that they had made up, walling themselves into their tiny little world.

Linda flowed easily into Elvis's family, clan, and coterie. In November, she flew to Hawaii with Elvis and Lisa Marie to begin preparations for a television show that would be carried worldwide via satellite. During Christmas 1972, she shared festivities with the family, and Elvis gave her a mink coat.

A year or so after they met, Linda helped Elvis redecorate Graceland, moving away from the blue, white, and gold that Priscilla had used and into the dark red that Elvis chose. "It was red crushed-velvet every-thing, and red satin drapes, and red shag carpet," said Marty Lacker, one of the guys who prided himself on his aesthetic sense. Marty's sister and brother-in-law, home designers and decorators, had redone much of Graceland in the 1960s, including creating the Meditation Garden. Linda had tried to tone things down, he said. "Oh, yeah. That's pretty," she would say to Elvis. "Let me show you this, let me show you that."

"Let's face it—Elvis' taste sucked," Lamar Fike snorted. "If some-thing wasn't overdone, it was abnormal to Elvis."

Lamar said that at first the guys thought that Linda could not "chew gum and walk at the same time." Soon, however, they reversed their opinion. She was "as smart as they come," a "lady," and "a lot of fun." The guys not only accepted Linda; they positively liked her and soon came to respect her. Linda relieved them of a lot of work and stress. She took excellent care of Elvis whether he was asleep or awake. They had confidence in her vigilance and her capacity to act. As his drug intake increased, he would sometimes fall asleep with food in his mouth. Linda would dig the food out with her fingers to save him from choking to death. There were times when he was so drugged up that he almost stopped breathing, and Linda was there to call the doctor. Marty Lacker asserted that she was "like a mother, a sister, a wife, a lover, and a nurse."

She was also like one of the guys. One time, she parodied her own beauty-queen image by dressing up in her Miss Tennessee outfit, de-scending the stairs at Graceland with appropriate music to present her-self for the admiration of the gang, and breaking into a big smile with one of her front teeth blacked out. Like Ann-Margret, the other girl in Elvis's life whom they respected and truly liked, Linda knew who she was and did not feel threatened in the Elvisian universe. She was one of the guys, but they were also very much aware that she was an attractive young woman. Billy Smith captured that quality: "She was pretty," he said, "but her personality made her beautiful."

Decades later, Lamar Fike observed that Linda sometimes played "the dumb role, and acted subservient to a degree, but she'd get what she wanted." One might well add that she earned her pay from Elvis and spent it on what she wanted. Billy Smith said Linda "saved his life at least three times." She worked hard but unsuccessfully to get Elvis to change his drug habits, but outside of that she accepted him as he was. She helped him as well as she could for as long as she could. She wanted a career in show business and a measure of financial support until she got it. Elvis helped her move toward a career, and he was very generous to her in a material way.

THE GIRLS WHO CAME AND WENT

The number of girls streaming in and out of Elvis's bed diminished while Linda stayed with him, but not to zero. Elvis and the guys had developed the art and craft of waving girls into and out of Elvis's bed with the skill of air traffic controllers. They would pick up the incoming girl on the radar as she approached and clear the field for her landing. After being delivered to Elvis, she would taxi out onto the runway again, the field would be cleared for her departure, and she would take off. Rarely were two planes on the tarmac at the same time. Some returned from time to time, but sooner or later all flew away and never came back. Linda, of course, was well aware of what went on, but she knew that there was virtually nothing she could do about it. If she had forced Elvis to choose, he would have opted for the girls.

During his Las Vegas run in January and February 1974, Linda had gone off to do some modeling, and Elvis brought in, sequentially, two other young women, Ann Pennington and Sheila Ryan.

Ann was a twenty-three-year-old model and the single mother of a three-year-old daughter named Adriane. Ann had first bedded down with Elvis in Palm Springs where she found that he only wanted "to cuddle and kiss," and "the other just wasn't very important." Elvis went through his usual sweet and vulnerable routine with Ann—not necessarily a performance at all given the girls' motivation for their presence in the first place. Sex with Elvis was a score, not seduction.

One night while Ann was staying with Elvis in Las Vegas, they had smoked pot in bed. He went to sleep and wet the bed. Ann retreated to the high ground along the edge on her side. The next morning Elvis was laughing as he told the guys about how she had spent the night on this one narrow dry strip. "He didn't seem to be embarrassed," she marveled.

Ann knew that he had other women, and he knew she had other men. Elvis told her he did not like to think that she "had been with anybody else." But Ann was not bothered by the other women. For her, Elvis was too needy. She had her daughter to take care of, and she didn't need another child in Elvis. Before the end of the Las Vegas engagement, she happily passed the Elvis baton to Sheila Ryan.

Sheila was not an actress or a beauty queen. Her claim to fame was appearing on the cover and in the centerfold of *Playboy*. In February 1974, she found herself sitting all alone on a bar stool in Elvis's suite in the Hilton International waiting for her first meeting with the star. He was to come up and join her after his first show. "I looked like I was thirteen years old in those days," she later recalled. "I had an angelic little face, and really my personality went along with it." She was, she said, very young, naive, Midwestern, and "a blank canvas." Her early-adolescent but *Playboy*-worthy body got her to Elvis's suite; it was probably the "blank canvas" that kept her there.

Elvis came in "all sweaty" after his dinnertime performance below. He "half-hugged" her. Right away he commented on the way she was dressed—in slacks and not at all to his taste. He could fix that and would love doing so. They talked for a while, and then they went down for him to do the second show. When they returned, he acted "just like a little kid." He showed her a fire hat that a fan had given him and a baby bib. At some point he kissed her and then fell asleep. She thought it all very weird, got up, put on her clothes, and went home.

The next day Joe Esposito called her at home. "Goddammit, where are you?" he barked. "Boss is furious." Sheila half knew she was supposed to stay in Elvis's bed until he woke up, but she was "this little rebellious thing." She went back to the Hilton. Elvis was eating breakfast and was irritated. "I was quiet," Sheila said. "I was always very quiet, just kind of took it all in." After breakfast, Elvis had Las Vegas's most chic boutique send up racks of clothes. Sheila modeled while Elvis chose.

Afterward, Sheila spent a couple of nights with Elvis. Like so many other girls, she had misread his sexual preferences. "The sexual thing was never a big deal to him, you would think it was, but it wasn't... We had sex but what he liked best was the petting, the kissing." It was like "in high school and neck and neck and neck and grope and do whatever you're doing." She was shocked by the next transition. "It was adolescent," she said, "until all of a sudden you graduated into Mother." Very quickly, she found that she was supposed to take care of him, "to get him things in the middle of the night"—water, pills, Jell-O—and read to him. But also he would glide into romantic fits in which he would sing to her on the balcony high above Las Vegas or shower her with gifts that only embarrassed her.

Elvis took Sheila with him as he began his next tour with a performance in the auditorium at Oral Roberts University in Tulsa, Oklahoma. Three days later, in Monroe, Louisiana, however, he replaced her with Ann Pennington, the model. Lamar Fike picked Ann up at the airport while one of the other guys taxied Sheila to the airport for her flight out. "He had women in revolving doors," Lamar said. "They could run into each other at the airport and not know it."

Sheila Ryan lasted for well over a year. During his August–September 1974 run in Las Vegas, Elvis sent Linda away after four nights and brought Sheila in. In the Showroom on the last night, Monday, September 2, he put her in the special booth near the stage with Priscilla and Lisa Marie. He had Priscilla stand up and introduced her to the audience. "Boy, she's a beautiful chick," he exclaimed. "I'll tell you for sure. Boy, I knows 'em when I picks 'em, I think. Hot damn." Then he had six-year-old Lisa stand up. "Look at her jump up," he said to the crowd. "Pull your dress down, Lisa. You pull your dress down before you jump up like that again, young lady." Elvis was playing the responsible father, training his daughter to have ladylike modesty.

Finally, he had Sheila stand up and turn around. He introduced her as his "girlfriend." He had her show off the diamond ring he had given her. It took a while. "Sheila, hold it up," he ordered. "Hold it up. Hold the ring up. Hold the ring up. The ring. Your right hand. Look at that sonofabitch," he insisted. Everyone had to marvel at what a generous man he was.

After the introductions, Elvis launched into declarations about how he and Priscilla were the "best of friends." They divorced, he explained, "not because of another man or woman" but because he traveled so much. It was not fair to her, and he made the sacrifice. She got whatever "she wanted as a settlement...about two million dollars," he said. Elvis was a considerate man as well as a generous one.

He continued his discourse on his generosity by saying that he had given Priscilla a mink coat, but he added that Priscilla had also given him a Jaguar. Thus, she still cared about him. He began to talk about his own beloved Stutz Blackhawk, which he intended to give to her. "She liked this Stutz that I have," he said, before losing control of his thoughts and speech. "No it's called a stud...a Stutz. And she likes a stud (*laughs*) she likes the Stutz. Mike Stone ain't no stud, so forget it. She liked the Stutz, and so I'm gonna give her the Stutz...Stone better wish he was a stud. He's a..." Elvis paused, then concluded lamely, "nice guy." Some two thousand people sat and listened in silent embarrassment.

Elvis moved on to introduce his next song, one that he had been listening to on record over and over, testing the endurance of the guys with the repetition of the same dreary message. "Softly as I Leave You," Elvis said, was about a man dying in a hospital bed in the middle of the night with his sleeping wife lying beside him. As he passes he writes out his last message to his beloved, beginning with "Softly as I leave you..."

Earlier in the show, Elvis had complained that the microphone was too high. "I'm six-one-and-a-half and this sonofabitch is six-three-and-a-half," he said. Next he complained about a toothache. Then he complained to Charlie Hodge about the large bejeweled belt he wore. "Charlie, take this belt off, really. It's gonna cut me...castrate me...do somethin'...really." As Charlie took off the belt Elvis complained further that Charlie was choking him with the entangled microphone cord.

Years on a psychiatrist's couch might not have sufficed to untangle the painful emotional threads that made up Elvis's being at that point in his life, September 1974. One vital thread was his fear that he was not really the highly sexual man that he ought to be and that his failing was visible. He had sent Linda away during this run and publicly announced his possession of Sheila Ryan. He created a fantasy narrative that neither Mike Stone, nor any other man, had taken Priscilla away;

he had generously let her go. Mike Stone certainly was a "stud," and Elvis's flat denial could only acknowledge the fact that Stone was a virile, younger man, while Elvis was sliding into middle age.

Another thread running through Elvis's strange discourse was that love could only be expressed by garish and outlandishly expensive gifts publicly displayed. Rings, fur coats, cars, and, ironically, a $2 million divorce settlement bespoke true love. Lavish gifts made feelings for someone real. And the gifts had to be witnessed. Elvis's gifts were never secret.

Elvis relished the idea that Priscilla was giving him a Jaguar, but there is no record that Priscilla ever did so. Indeed, none of Elvis's intimates ever gave him any gift that amounted—by Elvis's materialistic values—to more than a trinket. Perhaps no one other than his fans altogether could ever have given him a gift high enough in dollar value to make him feel loved. His fans did that in the form of millions of dollars spent for his records and especially for the famously reasonably priced tickets for his always "sold out" performances. Elvis did relish the money that they gave him. "Charlie, you know how much money we made for working all of twelve hours onstage?" he once said to Charlie Hodge, full of warmth and good feelings. The answer was "a little over $800,000," and certainly he used that money to give himself garish, outlandishly expensive gifts that were conspicuously and publicly displayed.

Elvis was in trouble in the summer of 1974, and it was evident from the beginning of this September run in Vegas. He put a lot of new material into the opening night, and then took it out for the second night. He grew rebellious. After the midnight show several days later, with the aid of Red and Jerry, he climbed up a ladder in the Showroom to paint black the image of one of the Louis XIV ladies included in the room's Baroque decor. During later performances, he proudly pointed out his handiwork to his audiences. Two days later he canceled both performances for the night, pleading stomach flu.

A few days later Elvis put on a full-scale demonstration of his karate skills during the dinner show, using Red West as his fall guy. He had been boasting about his mastery of the art and showing off his moves more and more during the shows, but this was just too much. Finally, the Colonel said stop. Thereafter, Elvis confined himself to proudly passing out "certificates" of achievement onstage to singers and band members who had attended his karate classes in his suite.

SHEILA LEAVES

Elvis was compelled to feel that he was a generous man, but Sheila Ryan had difficulty expressing unbounded gratitude for Elvis's gifts. Joe tutored her. She had to understand that Elvis felt a great need to give things to people, he lectured, and people had to express great gratitude for the things he gave. Sheila was not materially minded. She was twenty-one and never owned anything in her life, she said. She did not know what to make of this man giving her a brand-new Corvette. She just said, "Thank you." Slowly Sheila learned to say, "Oh, God, it's beautiful, I love it." She felt so phony, but she did it.

Sheila found that her relationship with Elvis was not a matter of exchanging heavy sex for favors. "You gave and you got," she said, but not for sex. "I've read bits and pieces about his sexual behavior, and how perverse and bizarre it was, and it really wasn't. It was innocent...Adolescent innocence was what it was all about." Sheila concluded that Elvis "was just this guy who had this wonderful charisma and things got blown way out of shape. He was just this innocent little guy." It was really not as complicated as it seemed.

After the run in Las Vegas was over in early September, Elvis stayed on for a few days, going to shows with Sheila. Then he went to Los Angeles and flew back to Memphis with Linda.

Sheila was increasingly unwilling to go on tour with Elvis. She just wasn't much interested in Elvis, she concluded, and his interest in her was limited. "There wasn't much at stake. I was his friend, I was his little pal." She was relieved when he took Mindi Miller, a model and dancer, with him for the first part of his tour that began in Macon, Georgia, on April 4, 1975.

Elvis wanted Sheila to go with him for his third tour in 1975, seventeen days that began on July 8. Joe couldn't find her, so Elvis brought along the reigning Miss Georgia, Diana Goodman, whom he had previously picked out of a tour group at the gates of Graceland. When Joe did reach Sheila, she confessed that she was practically living with actor James Caan, so they agreed to tell Elvis that she had an ear infection and could not fly. Elvis responded with an offer to hire a low-flying plane to bring her to him. Sheila declined. Elvis seemed to understand and accept the end of their relationship. He said he would call after the tour.

The Kathy Blow-up

Within days of Sheila's rejection, Elvis began to disintegrate onstage. Traditionally, during every show at some point he would introduce the people who were onstage with him, usually with some adolescent attempts at humor. For instance, he was always introducing himself as someone else. "Hello, I'm Johnny Cash," he would say. Or Tom Jones, or Sammy Davis Jr., or Bill Cosby. Often, his humor was at the expense of someone else. He loved to pick on the diminutive Charlie Hodge. "Charlie does something," he would say, "I don't know what." Sometimes his insensitivity was outrageous, as when he introduced the Sweet Inspirations to a Las Vegas audience as "the young ladies that stood out in the sun too long." In March 1975, he had a camera do a close-up of Estelle Brown's new hairdo, comparing her to Stepin Fetchit, a weak-minded black character in white movies. Onstage, in front of two thousand people there to see Elvis, Estelle met the insult as best she could. "Oooh, I hate you!" she responded in a laughing tone. "I hate you!"

That July, Kathy Westmoreland became the prime target of Elvis's malicious stage humor. Kathy was no longer available as his bedmate, but unlike Priscilla and Sheila, she was right there with him during every performance on tour and in Vegas or Tahoe. Introducing Kathy during the performance in Richfield, Ohio, on July 18, 1975, Elvis said: "She will take affection from anybody, any place, anytime. In fact she gets it from the whole band." The next night in Uniondale, New York, he did it again. Kathy was livid. After the show, she grabbed Joe Esposito and said, "Get the word to him, tell Elvis to stop doing this to me. Tell him I've had it."

During the afternoon performance in Norfolk on the next day, he began the cruel attack again. Kathy pointed at him and said, "You had better stop this." Elvis stopped, went over, and kissed her on the cheek. Just before the evening show, Tom Diskin, the Colonel's man on the scene, cautioned him about such comments. Elvis, who never took criticism lightly, bridled. Reportedly, he attacked Kathy again onstage, but in a voice so low that only the people around him could hear. Allegedly he said, "She gives good head. Ask any man in the band."

Then he very audibly turned his guns on the Sweets. The press reported that Elvis declared that "he smelled green peppers and onions and that his backup singers, the Sweet Inspirations, had probably been eating catfish." No one knows exactly what he meant by that assertion, but white Southerners generally regarded catfish as one of the least desirable fish to eat and often associated it with black people of the lowest social order within black society.

Estelle Brown could only lower her head in response to such open cruelty. Elvis then attacked all the backup singers. "Estelle, Sweet Inspirations, Stamps, if you don't look up, I'm going to kick your ass," he raged. Estelle walked off the stage, and Kathy moved over to close the gap between her and the two remaining Sweets. As he began the introductions, he glared at the three women. "Sorry for any embarrassment I might have caused you, but if you can't take it, get off the pot," he said. It was not an apology. Sylvia Shemwell and Kathy responded by walking off the stage, leaving Myrna Smith the only female on the stage. During the performance, Elvis virtually forced her to accept a ring he took off of one of his fingers. It was as if he could think of nothing better to say or do.

Jerry Schilling, who would soon become Myrna's husband, tried to calm Elvis down, but he wouldn't have it. He would not apologize. He felt he didn't need those women. Tom Diskin persuaded the three singers to at least travel on with the troupe to the next venue, Greensboro, North Carolina. After some sort of exchange with Elvis, the Sweets did perform, but not Kathy. After the show, Kathy was invited into Elvis's bedroom, presumably for apologies and reconciliation. "I thought it was funny," Elvis said, regarding his comments. Kathy replied that he knew it was not funny. He shrugged.

Elvis was sitting on the bed in his karate pajamas outfit. He had a gun in one hand and a gift in the other—it was a wristwatch. He held both out toward Kathy and said, "Which do you want, this or this?" Kathy struggled to appear calm. She took the watch. She would stay on the tour, she said, then quit the show. Elvis grinned and shrugged. It was okay with him.

The next day they were to fly to Asheville, North Carolina, to perform. Elvis delayed his departure several times. When he was finally ready to go, not every member of the troupe slated to fly on his private plane was there. He took off without them. The plane had to fly Elvis to Asheville and return for those left behind.

In Asheville, Elvis needed to see a dentist, so Dr. Nick took him to a local practice. While the dentist was out of the treatment room, Elvis rummaged through his cabinets and stole some drugs. Nichopoulos was horrified but was unable to stop the pillaging. Back in Elvis's room at the Rodeway Inn, with Vernon present, he confiscated the pills. Elvis went wild, thrashing about and swearing. Then he went into the bathroom to put on his pajamas to take a nap before the show. He came out holding a Beretta at his side. For some reason, he threw his arm around his father's shoulder, and the gun went off. The bullet bounced off a chair and hit Dr. Nick on the chest. Fortunately, its force was largely spent. "All it did was give me a little burn on my chest," the doctor said. The guards rushed in and everyone was scared to death, but Elvis laughed it off. At some point during this stay, he shot out the television set in his room.

Elvis thought that the Asheville audiences should have been more responsive. During his last performance there on July 24, trying to rouse them up, he took requests for songs—as if to say he no longer knew what they wanted to hear. Finally, he gave a $6,500 ring to a fan and threw his guitar out to them—or at them.

At home again in Memphis, Elvis, as usual, gave out gifts instead of apologies. He had bought more than $85,000 worth of jewelry in flurries of gift-giving. He had also ordered a new airplane as a gift for the Colonel, which was delivered on the twenty-sixth and immediately returned by his unconsulted and astonished manager. On the twenty-seventh, he bought fourteen Cadillacs for $140,000 and gave them away, one going to Myrna, the Sweet who had not left the stage during the Norfolk show. On the twenty-ninth, he loaned Dr. Nick—who must still have carried "a little burn" on his chest from Elvis's bullet—$200,000 for the construction of his new house.

BLUE CHRISTMAS

Elvis barely made it to Las Vegas for rehearsals for his Monday, August 18, 1975, opening at the Hilton. He was overweight and tired. He sat down during much of the first performance. The second show became a sort of patchwork of requests from the audience. He tried to cancel both Wednesday performances at the last minute, but the Colonel would not let him. During these shows, he kept glancing at his watch. Before morning, all of the usual Elvis hype of photographs and broadsides had disappeared from the hotel lobby and elsewhere. There was only a small sign announcing that Elvis's engagement had been canceled because of illness. The Colonel was expert at damage control.

Dr. Nick put Elvis in Baptist Memorial Hospital in Memphis on August 21. Nothing to worry about, he announced to the world, just fatigue. In truth, Elvis was depressed. The manic highs he had manifested earlier in the summer, the gunplay, the boisterous "I don't need you, I'll do what I want," gave way to a feeling, as he said to his friend Jo Cathy Brownlee, that "the boy is just falling apart."

Jo Cathy, a schoolteacher and the press box hostess for the WFL team the Memphis Southmen, moved into Graceland and took care of him. She was going at it twenty-one hours a day. Elvis began to recover. Part of his therapy was zooming around Memphis with his gang on three-wheeled motorcycles he had bought that summer, smoking cigars, and wearing sunglasses. Spied by a UPI wire service reporter on September 15, he declared positively that he was feeling fine. Jo Cathy noted that the pills were coming into Graceland again, some from Las Vegas, some from local sources.

But Jo Cathy herself was now wearing thin for Elvis. One day near the end of October, when she arrived at Graceland, he told her to get what she needed and go home. He had a date. She gathered all her things in a laundry basket. She was hurt, and Elvis was not sympathetic. "Now you don't have to be a bitch about this whole thing," he said and stormed out of the room. Jo Cathy never came back.

On November 10, the *Lisa Marie* was delivered to the Memphis airport, where Elvis had based the Jetstar he had bought for himself in August and another plane he had bought as an investment. He now owned well over $2 million worth of airplanes. During the next couple of weeks, he flew everywhere, showing off the *Lisa Marie* with its lavish appointments. He was flying high, but he was almost out of cash. On November 25, he borrowed $350,000 from his bank, secured by a lien on Graceland.

Elvis earned only $180,000 for two weeks at the Hilton in December 1975. Even he began to realize, if only in his dreams, that he was in big trouble. Marian Cocke, his middle-aged and motherly nurse from Baptist Hospital, visited him in his bedroom at Graceland on Christmas Eve. He had awakened "in a rage," he told her. He dreamed that he had gone broke and found himself deserted by all those people who called themselves his friends. In fact, at that moment they were all waiting downstairs for him to deliver his Christmas gifts to them, and he did not want to go down. Finally, he took everybody up in the *Lisa Marie* for a ride around the city. His aunt Delta got drunk, used foul language, called Marty Lacker a "wall-eyed son of a bitch," and threatened to shoot him with the .38 pistol she carried in her purse. After they landed, Elvis gave out jewelry as usual, but later threatened to strip Aunt Delta, throw her over the wall, and exile her from Graceland, because she had so embarrassed him in front of his friends. Summoned to answer for her conduct afterward, she seemed not to remember what she had done and earnestly asked for forgiveness. Urged by Billy Smith, Elvis decided not to exile Aunt Delta.

PART IV

THE FALL

CHAPTER TEN

THE BODYGUARD BOOK

PHYSICAL ASSAULTS AND LEGAL SUITS

On September 7, 1973, Red West and two of the guys attacked and beat up a man named K. Peter Pajarinen outside of Elvis's suite at the Hilton Hotel. Pajarinen said that he had been invited as a "guest" to Elvis's quarters and insisted on his admission to what he surely thought would be a party with a lot of attractive girls. Two years later, he brought suit against Elvis. In May 1974, Red and the boys did it again. This time it was during an engagement at the Sahara Tahoe Hotel.

It was a bad time for Elvis. The *San Francisco Examiner* described an opening show as "listless, uninspired, and downright tired." Afterward, he missed two shows because, he complained, he had the "flu." Lamar Fike called such events "Vegas throat," meaning that Elvis just did not want to go on and offered illness as his excuse.

On this occasion Red and three other bodyguards beat up Edward L. Ashley, a real estate developer from Grass Valley, California. Ashley, up in Tahoe for a good time, thought that he had an invitation to an Elvis party. Indeed, he said that he had passed $60 to one of Elvis's retainers to obtain the invitation. He was denied entrance and in retaliation attempted to shut off the power in Elvis's suite. Two of the guys held Ashley down while two others beat him severely.

In October, Ashley brought suit against Elvis for more than $6 million. He claimed that Elvis watched the beating. Insiders knew that the guys always did what Elvis wanted them to do, whether he watched or not. Ashley said that he had suffered "severe lacerations of his lips, loosened teeth, possible fractured jaw, injury to the left ear, brain concussion," and more.

In Elvis's last years, the guys, like Elvis, began to really fear for their lives. "There were so many death threats," Billy Smith later said. Elvis's bodyguards became increasingly frustrated, uncertain, and quick to respond violently. On one occasion, Red rousted and roughly handled a guest in the Hilton Showroom because he was acting in a suspicious manner. The man turned out to be an FBI agent secretly planted to help protect Elvis. One of the guys indulged himself in extracurricular violence by getting into a barroom brawl with one of the "Tailhookers," US Navy carrier pilots who convened in Las Vegas every year. They tended to get very drunk, hire prostitutes, chase girls in ways unbecoming to officers and gentlemen, and behave generally very much like sailors on shore leave after months at sea with no alcohol and no women around.

On several occasions, in the alleged defense of Elvis, the guys caused bruises and drew blood. Only rarely did they crack bones or smash teeth, but the macho style seemed to feed upon itself and grow, the guards relishing their work too much. In their zeal to protect Elvis, they became a threat to the physical safety of others, his image, and his pocketbook.

Inevitably, all this mayhem generated lawsuits, and they were not frivolous. In 1976, six such suits against Elvis were pending. This was something new in Elvis's life. The courts might find that the assault by Elvis's guys against Ashley was not just an isolated incident but one event in a pattern of unwarranted and vicious assaults. The "Memphis Mafia," the appellation of which Elvis and the guys had been so proud, had become a liability. They were indeed, it seemed, a gang of sadistic bullies and thugs who thought themselves above the law. If the police and the criminal courts did not bring them to justice, the civil courts would.

Clearly, it was going to cost Elvis a lot of money just to hire lawyers to cope with the suits already filed, never mind the settlements that would probably ensue. Further, if Elvis lost even one case, it would establish a likelihood of guilt and put all the rest in jeopardy. And who knew how many other people who had been manhandled by the guys were out there waiting for revenge and a chance to get significant money out of what they saw to be Elvis's bottomless coffers? It was a crisis such as he had never faced before.

The suits were not going to go away, and Elvis's finances were already shaky. The Colonel was probably taking about half of the income produced by Elvis's work and fame, even though his contracts with Elvis would not show that. As much as a third of what Elvis got went to the federal government in income taxes. Fortunately for his fiscal survival, Tennessee had no income tax, and he steadfastly maintained his residence in that state. Even after sharing income with the Colonel and paying his taxes, Elvis was still making millions, but he was spending it all, sometimes faster than he made it. In November 1975, facing a cash flow problem, he was forced to mortgage Graceland to borrow $350,000 from his bank in Memphis, the National Bank of Commerce. Elvis had earned more than $100 million in the previous twenty years, but he was living from hand to mouth.

In January 1976, Elvis signed a new agreement with the Colonel splitting the proceeds from his performances on tour fifty-fifty instead of the two-thirds for Elvis and one-third for the Colonel previously agreed upon. Elvis readily agreed that the new arrangement was fairer than the old. In the tour business, Parker's labors seemed just as important as Elvis's in achieving high earnings. In March, however, Elvis was so short of cash that the Colonel gave him two-thirds of the proceeds from a tour with the understanding that Elvis would pay him back at the end of the year. But Parker continued the practice, even after the year ended. This meant that Elvis was running up a tremendous debt to the Colonel. If he fired the Colonel, he would be more than broke; if the Colonel sold his contract to another manager, Elvis would still owe someone a pile of money. The more he made, the more he owed. Someday would be pay-up day—1977, 1978, 1979, or later.

Meanwhile, he and Colonel Parker were milking the tours for all they were worth. Elvis was touring at a killing pace to maintain the revenue stream upon which everyone depended. Parker began to book Elvis into smaller towns with smaller auditoriums to exploit that market. This meant that Elvis had to perform more often to maintain his income level, and his diminishing energies were further taxed. There was a real question as to how long Elvis's increasingly sick and obese body and distressed psyche could continue at this pace.

THE FIRINGS

With the suits for assaults coming to a head, Elvis's career was in jeopardy. His image and his livelihood were in danger. One way to defend himself was to distance himself from his most conspicuously violent bodyguards. He yielded to advice and in July 1976 instructed Vernon to fire Red, Sonny, and Dave Hebler, a karate enthusiast they had brought into the group in 1973.

Vernon had long thought that the bodyguards were overpaid and underworked; nor was he fond of them personally. At last, he had a chance to manifest his dislike and keep money at the same time. Reputedly, Vernon later said that this was "one of the happiest moments in my life." Vernon gave Red West, Elvis's close friend for more than twenty years and head bodyguard, and Red's cousin Sonny West, who had served Elvis for almost as long as Red, no warning at all and only a week's severance pay.

The bodyguards heard no rumor of their coming dismissal and were taken totally by surprise. That morning, Vernon reached Sonny by phone at his dentist's office. Dave Hebler got the call while he was enjoying the swimming pool at his motel near the Memphis airport. Ironically, Red got his while he was at the office of a private detective talking about one of the several lawsuits pending against Elvis.

Vernon asked Sonny to come out to Graceland to see him. He and Sonny had just had a bitter fight after Vernon refused to pay for air travel for Sonny's wife and child to join him during Elvis's recent engagement in Shreveport, Louisiana. Sonny said that he was a grown man and could probably handle anything Vernon had to say over the phone.

"Well, things haven't been going too well," Vernon told him, warming up to his task, "and, well, we're going to have to cut back on expenses and we're going to have to let some people go."

"Oh, I see," Sonny replied, "and I guess I'm one of the ones that is going to be let go."

"Yes, I'm afraid so," Vernon said, then added with a shower of crocodile tears, "There will be others, too, unfortunately."

Sonny asked who else, but Vernon declined to say. Sonny returned to the motel where he and his family were staying. Morosely, he watched his wife and young son playing by the motel pool. He called Dave Hebler and found that Vernon had already summoned Dave to Graceland. Soon Red phoned Sonny.

"I've been fired, man," he said flatly.

The guys complained bitterly to each other and their friends about the cold and abrupt nature of their dismissal. Vernon was never skilled in personal relations, but Elvis would have been better served had Vernon honestly told them that they were being dismissed to improve Elvis's situation in the suits. Out of loyalty to Elvis, they should simply lie low for a time, and then they would be rehired.

The bodyguards knew full well that the real problem was not paying their salaries. They knew, too, that Elvis himself, not Vernon, ultimately had the power to decide who would come and who would go, and that he always found the money to do whatever he wanted to do. Fairly recently, Elvis had actually hired three new guys to join his security force, David Stanley and Ricky Stanley, Dee Stanley's sons, who claimed that they were Elvis's "brothers," and Dean Nichopoulos, Dr. Nick's son. They also knew that Elvis had specifically chosen to make the three of them, and not others, the scapegoats. Vernon's explanation was a bald-faced lie.

Red West felt especially betrayed. In his view he had given twenty years of his life and very nearly total and exclusive devotion to Elvis Presley, the one man in the world he most loved. He resented deeply—and justly—that his dismissal did not come from Elvis himself and was based on the flimsy and transparent excuse of financial necessity. Elvis had not only suddenly taken away Red's livelihood but had also insulted Red's manhood.

Elvis should not have expected Red to take this lying down. Red quickly saw a way to strike back with devastating effect and earn a lot of money at the same time. He would lead his two colleagues in writing a book that would tell all of Elvis's dirty secrets to the world. For years, the tabloids, such as the *National Enquirer*, had tried to penetrate Elvis's organization to get salaciously scandalous stories about him. But the discipline within the coterie was amazingly effective. Nobody inside ever said anything to journalists about any negative occurrences in

Elvis's private life. The rule of silence was often expressly and sometimes forcefully stated. Even those guys who left told no tales. Suddenly and unfairly expelled from the privileged circle, "the bodyguards" who knew all would tell all.

Very soon Red found a publisher to advance $125,000 to finance the process of writing and pay a royalty on the sales of the book. None of the bodyguards possessed great literary skills, but a professional tabloid writer, Steve Dunleavy, was added to the team.

ELVIS'S RESPONSE

Elvis's informers and friends picked up rumors of the book project almost as soon as it was conceived. In late August 1976, while on tour, Elvis summoned his staff to his hotel room in Mobile, Alabama. They found him sitting cross-legged on his bed, holding a sheaf of papers in his hand. Already he had a copy of the outline of the book.

"They're trying to kill me," he cried to the room at large.

"Who's trying to kill you?" someone asked.

In response, Elvis held up the papers. Friends in the publishing world had learned that a contract had been signed, and they had managed to obtain a copy of the proposal.

"I don't know how those guys could do this to me," Elvis wailed, verging on tears.

Over the next several weeks, rumors came in that the book would expose in detail Elvis's large, various, and perverted sexual appetites, especially for sex between girls and young women, his drug addiction, and his fits of violence. As with Priscilla's departure, Elvis could not imagine that he had done anything wrong to bring about this vicious betrayal. Also as with Priscilla's departure, he became obsessed with the matter. He "was completely absorbed by the book," a member of the inner circle, David Stanley, later recalled in his own tell-all book. "It was all he wanted to talk about."

During the fall of 1976, Elvis struggled desperately to get his ex-bodyguards to cancel the project. The book would destroy his image, he feared. His fans would turn away from him in revulsion, this monster

"Elvis" that the book depicted. He could not believe that he could not somehow persuade his ex-friends to abort the project.

There was some thought at first of threatening them physically, for instance, of somehow using Frank Sinatra's Mafia connections to pressure them into giving up on the venture. On occasion, Sinatra had announced his willingness to share his underworld contacts with Elvis. Wisely, Elvis retreated to try a more conventional approach—bribery. He sent his private detective, tough-talking John O'Grady, to offer each man $50,000 if they would give it up. No luck.

THIS IS ELVIS

Then, in October, about three months after the firings, Elvis telephoned Red himself. Unknown to Elvis, Red recorded the conversation on tape. He got the call at 7:00 a.m. in his motel room in Hollywood. Elvis was attempting to entice Red—and probably Sonny too—to come back into the fold and hence abandon the book project. He admitted that in the firing "maybe I did lose sight of…especially you, your family, and everything," but it was only "because of a lot of things that piled up on me." There followed a lengthy and rambling litany of the numerous ways in which he, Elvis, had been treated unfairly by both alleged friends and others. Whenever Red attempted to make the point that Elvis had treated him unfairly, Elvis rushed in with another example of the gross abuses he had suffered. Red's firing was not really his fault; it was all these other things. He seemed simply unable to say to Red that he was responsible for the callous manner of his firing and that he had done him wrong and was sorry.

Red had guessed correctly that Elvis would call him. Two days earlier, someone had phoned and asked the boys to put off writing the book. On the next day, Red called Graceland and talked to Charlie Hodge. Charlie then talked to Elvis. The following morning Elvis telephoned Red, who was ready and waiting with the tape recorder. He included a loosely transcribed and edited version of the exchange in his book. That transcript is a very fair representation of the conversation, and it is a rare opportunity to hear Elvis speaking directly for himself. This is the real Elvis at some length.

"Charlie [Hodge] told me about the talk you all had," Elvis began. "I guess I do owe you an explanation."

Elvis said that at the time of the firing he was "getting a lot of excess pressure," all because other people in his entourage, not Red, had done him wrong. Dr. Nick and Joe Esposito, along with a Memphis bond salesman named Mike McMahon, had looped him into a scheme to build two commercial racquetball courts costing $1.3 million dollars, he complained. McMahon was a crooked businessman who had altered the contract, he said, to make him responsible for any debts incurred by the company. "That son-of-a-bitch, he ain't no good," Elvis said. Elvis had signed the contract understanding that he was only putting in his name and no money. "I wouldn't have to put up a dime," he said. "Wouldn't be no money or nothin'."

Elvis said that Joe, Dr. Nick, and McMahon had all gone on a tour with him and pretended to have an interest in numerology, one of his passions, but they were really trying to get him to invest in their racquetball court venture. McMahon had cut himself into the deal for a management fee of $50,000 a year. He had gone to Nashville promoting the project and saying that he represented Elvis. "They had all these cards and shit printed up—chairman of the board," Elvis said, but nobody had consulted him. He had balked at putting in any cash, and they were going to court. It did not look good for Elvis, according to his lawyer. "The lawyer read to me the contract where it said that if anything happened I would stand good for the whole thing," Elvis said. "That was news to me."

Elvis was about to be sued for breach of contract by his physician, his road manager, and Mike McMahon. In addition, he was facing a raft of suits from people his bodyguards had beaten up.

"And those goddamn lawsuits," he complained. "You know how them lawyers are," he said. "There were six lawsuits in two years...They were trying to prove us insane." The problem was "them lawyers," and the defendant had become "us." The charge was interesting. He understood from his advisers that if they lost just one case, they might lose them all. He explained that the opposition lawyers were trying to "establish a pattern of insanity and violence. Like me shooting out that lamp up there." At first Red didn't know what he was talking about;

Elvis reminded him about the time he took a pistol to a chandelier in the Las Vegas Hilton. "Well, we was known as the wild bunch," Red replied.

Elvis's pitiful lament went on and on. "My daddy was sick," he said. "You know he was nearly dead. My family is strung all over the face of the United States." Elvis had an extra good reason to be upset by Vernon's illness. Vernon was not only sick; he had angrily blamed Elvis for his illness, even as Elvis himself was ill. Elvis, of course, was not blameless when it came to his father's health problems. His obsessive spending had stressed Vernon terribly, and Vernon never hid his distress from his son. Recurrently, Vernon saw himself broke and on the streets of Memphis again, pounding the pavement with holes in the soles of his shoes again, looking for a job. He was not a man to accept a return to poverty stoically. He loved the high life—including his share of the leftover girls—and he felt that he fully deserved it.

In truth, except for Lisa Marie, Elvis's "family" was not at all far away or scattered. An awful lot of it was right there in Graceland, on his payroll, and not about to leave. Furthermore, Lisa was gone because Priscilla was gone, and Red had told Elvis the truth when he said that Elvis had driven Priscilla away. Again, Elvis did not accept the consequences of his own actions. He was victimized and blameless...and clueless.

Elvis's litany of his miseries included the immediate and the physical. He and Charlie Hodge had had a songfest for some "little kids" the night before. One of the songs, he said, was "Love Is a Many Splendored Thing." They missed Red harmonizing with them. But Elvis's exertions for the pleasure of these small children had taken its toll. His fingers were blistered from playing the guitar, he complained, and his voice raspy from overuse.

"I'm not operating on but one cylinder either," Elvis whined.

Red was not rude to Elvis, and even expressed some sympathy for him in his terrible plight. But persistently and patiently, yet unsuccessfully, he attempted to bring him back to the injustice of his firing. Recurrently, Elvis slid back into recitations of his own problems.

"Yeah, it was cold," Red said, trying to focus Elvis on the nature of his dismissal. Elvis replied by declaring that he loved Red's wife, Pat, "and your family and everything."

"We gotta get back to my problem," Red said. "I just know about my problems." Again Elvis immediately began to talk about his own many problems.

Red tried once more. He said that the firing "was a shock to all of us." They had no warning. Suddenly, they had no income and they were all broke. "I sold my house. I hated to do that," Red said.

"You sold your house?" Elvis responded incredulously. Houses were important to him. At last, it seemed that Red had gotten his attention.

It was a "bad time," Red said.

"It was bad for me, too," Elvis responded, sliding away again. He complained that at the time he himself had just gotten out of the hospital and, "My daddy...I almost lost him."

Red declared that he wished Elvis himself had told him he was fired. "If I'd just heard from you, it would [have] been...it would have been easier to take," he said.

Elvis responded hesitantly. "I don't...I don't do that." Such things, he declared, were his daddy's business.

Red demurred. Certainly it was not his daddy's business in Red's case, and Elvis knew that Red was not just another employee. He had been one of Elvis's closest friends for over two decades and had served him loyally, literally body and soul. He did not deserve such treatment. Elvis excused himself on the grounds that he had to go off to Palm Springs to think about the racquetball court thing, and then he slid into a lengthy and bitter indictment of Dave Hebler.

He had been wrong about Hebler, he was really a bad guy, not one of the gang. "He hated all you guys," Elvis said, and for two years his comments on who he hated "just burned into my ear." Dave "was underhanded and sneaky."

If Elvis could split Red and Sonny, his old friends, away from Hebler, the newcomer, it might kill the bodyguard book. Further, if he could rehire Red and Sonny and leave Hebler out in the cold, they would abort the book, and they might make a scapegoat out of Hebler. Dave Hebler, a karate companion, was really the violent one, the story would run. It was he who was responsible for all the damage to those poor victims they had beaten up. With no money for a lawyer, Hebler would be vulnerable. Elvis was into his usually successful tactic of dividing and ruling.

In truth, Elvis was wrong about Hebler. He was not at all underhanded and sneaky in his response to being fired by Vernon. Of the three, he was the only one who pressed on relentlessly for a face-to-face confrontation with Elvis. After the dismissals, each had sought unsuccessfully to talk to Elvis in person. Each had attempted to contact him by phone, but he could not be reached. True to character, just before the firings Elvis had disappeared, flying to Palm Springs for a three-week rest.

Dave went after him. In Palm Springs, he discovered that Elvis had gone into even deeper seclusion by retreating to the special quarters that Dr. Elias Ghanem had built at his home in Las Vegas to accommodate his celebrity patients. At Dr. Ghanem's house, Dave knocked on the front door. When the doctor answered, Dave said, "I want to talk to Elvis."

Dr. Ghanem politely asked Dave to wait while he told Elvis he was there. After several minutes he came back.

"I'm sorry, but he doesn't want to see you," he said.

Elvis absolutely hated facing any criticism of his behavior. A confrontation with Dave was exactly the kind of thing that Red and Sonny had protected him against over the years. If karate champion Hebler lost control and got physical, Elvis would be in trouble. His refusal to confront Dave was probably prudent, if not courageous or honorable.

Elvis's indictment of Hebler to Red was lengthy. "I'd become a dollar sign to him," he said. "I'd become an object, not a person. But you know, I'm not that thing. I'm not that image that's built up. I'm myself."

Red rejected Elvis's thinly veiled invitation to turn against Hebler. Elvis had grossly misjudged the situation. Red was sorely wounded and still in pain.

Red wanted to know why they had picked him out for sacrifice. "All the other...a lot of other guys...," he said, "man, I thought I...that I was more important to the organization than they were. But I guess I wasn't. But I'm glad I found that out."

When Red became more assertive, Elvis became more aggressive. "I am not fucked up by any means," he declared. "On the contrary, I've never been in better condition in my life." He enjoyed his work, he insisted, and last winter he had "had a ball" on vacation in Vail, Colorado. He had shared everything with Red, but then Red had "turned around and tried to hurt me."

"Well that's after you hurt me," Red replied. "You hurt me...me and my family very bad, you know, left us out in the cold, so let's don't talk about me tryin' to hurt you."

Nobody was allowed to challenge Elvis like that, but instead of picking up his gun, Elvis slid to the defensive again. Red just didn't know all that was going on.

In fact, Red did know what was going on. "You hadn't been healthy in quite a while," he said. Red was probably referring specifically to Elvis's drug problem, but Elvis chose to consider it a reference to his physical health.

"Oh, yes, I am," he insisted. He had just "had an absolute physical, head to toe, in the last three weeks." It was required by his insurance company, Lloyd's of London. "That thing I had, that lower intestinal blockage, corrected itself," he insisted. Somehow people just did not understand that he was perfectly well. "I keep hearing this shit about [being] fat and middle aged," he railed.

"Suspicious minds" was the problem, he said. "Understanding solves all problems," he declared, relying as he so often did on the lyrics of his hit songs for words, wisdom, and authority. "Negative vibes" from others, especially Dave Hebler, not from himself or Red, had caused the firing. He had "just reached a boiling point." He hoped Red would understand. "It was just a temporary thing."

Red resisted the implied invitation to return to his job. He was not "really into the psychic thing," he said. Elvis replied that he wasn't either. It was just that he felt "terribly alone." "You know like that number eight." In numerology, Elvis was a number eight. He and all eights were "intensely lonely at heart," he indicated. "They feel they're lonely but in reality they have warm hearts toward the oppressed... But they hide their feelings in life and do just what they please."

Elvis said that he understood from Charlie Hodge that Red had said that he, Elvis, was "all fucked up." Elvis insisted, "I'm not. I got a daughter and a life, you know." What profits a man if he gains the world and loses his own soul? "I love to sing. That's been my thing, since two years old." These things proved that he was all right.

Finally, Elvis sensed that he would not be able to move Red during this conversation. He ended by declaring that he would help Red job-wise or otherwise, that his help "ain't got a goddamn thing to do with articles or no publications or none of that shit." He had heard "bits and pieces," but no one had laid out the whole thing for him. "I don't know nothing," he lied.

It was a long good-bye on the phone that ended as Elvis again slipped into his habit of quoting songs as if they were verses from the Bible. He indicated that you have to "listen to the dull and the ignorant because they too have their story to tell" (from "Desiderata") and "you never walked in that man's shoes and saw things through his eyes" (from Hank Williams's "Men with Broken Hearts"). The relevance of the quotes to Red's situation was not totally clear, but saying them seemed to help Elvis. He might be inviting Red to understand his position with the shoes metaphor, but it was not at all clear who was dull and ignorant.

At last, he closed with an expression of open-handed generosity, ultimately his way of begging. "That's why I [am] saying, anything I can do at all. Worried about the book? I don't...I don't think so. Not on my part. You do whatever you have to do. I just want you and Pat to know I'm still here."

It was a bizarre performance by Elvis, but bizarre was not unusual for him. He was trying hard to say something that Red wanted to hear. He hoped that an appeal to friendship and the expectation of some huge gift would kill the book project. "Anything I can do at all," he said, and reached out to embrace Red's wife with his generosity. Possibly the promise of a new house to replace the one they had lost might lead Pat to persuade her husband to return to the fold.

Elvis's insistence that he was not worried about the book was bravado, pure and simple. In fact, he was worried nearly to death about it.

THE BOOK

Elvis had good reason for his anxiety. Cast in the style of a tabloid exposé, the bodyguard book, published in August 1977, would depict

Elvis as Dr. Jekyll and Mr. Hyde. The back cover of the paperback edition would say it succinctly:

A devoted son. A generous friend. A model army recruit. A gifted entertainer. A beloved hero to millions. This is the Elvis Presley the world knows—and cherishes.

Brooding. Violent. Obsessed with death. Strung out. Sexually driven. This is the other side of Elvis.

In case the prospective reader found the bad Elvis unbelievable, the back cover ticked off real-life episodes described in the book:

Charms a beautiful young fan into joining him on a drug binge for two that nearly kills her...

Hurls a pool cue at a party guest who interrupts his game, injuring her breast...

Talks with his bodyguard about a "hit on the man who stole his wife..."

Has for years leaned heavily on uppers, downers.

The text lived up to the cover's promise. The book opened with Elvis ordering Sonny West to kill Mike Stone. It went on to describe how Elvis threw his pool cue at a girl who interrupted his game in his Hollywood house, severely injuring her breast, and seduced a seventeen-year-old fan during a Tahoe engagement and ended by allowing her to overdose almost lethally in his house in Palm Springs. The girl suffered permanent brain damage but refused to sue out of loyalty to Elvis. He talked to her briefly on only one occasion after the event. The book included a long sequence of episodes in which Elvis molested and debauched very young girls, engaging young girls to perform for him by mud wrestling in white panties, spying on couples having sex in one of his Hollywood houses by installing a two-way mirror in a bedroom, and using the same device to watch young women undressing in the pool house of another of his Hollywood homes. The disturbing scenes went on and on, and there was very substantial basis in fact for each. The trouble with the forthcoming book was that it was all too revealing of the chasm that lay between the good Elvis in the popular image and the bad Elvis that really was.

ELVIS WEPT

During the late summer and fall of 1976, Elvis's limited physical capacity was sorely taxed by three cycles of road tours. In late August and early September, he did thirteen shows in thirteen days in Deep South cities from San Antonio over to Jacksonville and back to Pine Bluff, Arkansas. In October, he did an exhausting run of fifteen shows in fourteen Midwestern cities. At the end of November he did a seven-day northwest coast tour, and then in December, after a one-week break, he rolled into fifteen shows in eleven days in Las Vegas.

His exhaustion manifested itself in his first performances in the Showroom of the Hilton. He forgot lyrics; he had to sit down during the show; he had to leave the stage and let the Stamps and the Sweets sing while he recuperated. That he was able to perform at all had a lot to do with the drug protocol that Dr. Nick established for him—and a six-step process that provided three packets of uppers to get him up for a performance and three packets of downers to bring him down afterward, plus painkillers all along to combat the effects of chronic constipation and other conditions.

During his run at the Hilton in December, the Reverend Rex Humbard, a leading evangelist, visited him in his dressing room. Recalling the meeting soon after Elvis's death, he said that Elvis was much concerned with the last days on earth for unredeemed mankind.

"Christ is gonna come real soon, isn't he?" queried Elvis. Then he spoke of the biblical prediction of the Second Coming following famine and pestilence. "We don't have long, do we?" he concluded.

Reverend Humbard asked permission to pray for Elvis. "Please do," Elvis replied, then "he started weeping." The minister was moved and pleased by the depth of Elvis's feeling. "He just emotionally shook and trembled," Humbard said. At that point, eight-year-old Lisa Marie walked into the room.

"Why is my daddy crying?" Lisa asked.

"It's all right, honey," Elvis said.

Soon after Elvis's death, Rex Humbard claimed that Elvis had found something spiritual in their meeting, that he had come back to Jesus Christ again. Some of Elvis's ardent fans have welcomed Reverend Humbard's account as convincing evidence that Elvis was indeed born again as a Christian before he died. His performance with Humbard, however, did not square well with the life he actually led. How did he come to the conclusion that the Second Coming was near? He certainly saw no evidence of famine or pestilence.

One might suspect that Elvis was doing to Reverend Humbard what he usually did to people he perceived as having some measure of power they could exercise over him in the world—politicians, journalists, Jaycees, and his fans. He told them what they wanted to hear. This is not to say that he thought he was deceiving them. For the moment, he not only played the part, he was the part.

The quality of Elvis's Christianity after his epiphany with the girls in the Overton Shell in July 1954 is murky. Thereafter, he was not at church every Sunday morning. He said that he did not go to church because his presence would be too disruptive. Clearly, he had a good knowledge of the Bible and sometimes preached to captive congregations of his friends and followers. His preaching, however, could not always be taken seriously by serious people. "Now listen all you sonsabitches," he might begin and launch into a homily drawn from his readings of life and the scriptures.

Elvis was not a model Christian, but he really did believe that he could lead others to true interpretations of the Bible. Priscilla had to attend his Bible study groups in his Hollywood mansion before they married. She would sit on the couch beside him, boiling with thinly hidden anger, while he offered guidance to flocks of young women sitting at his feet. She was particularly upset by the way they leaned forward to show their cleavage and squirmed eagerly in their tight skirts as they asked Elvis to share his saintly wisdom and satisfy their ardent desire to understand better the Holy Word. She was furious that he enjoyed his performance and theirs so much and seemed not to know what the girls were really doing. On one occasion, she was so outraged that she went into their bedroom and changed into the most sexually provocative attire she had, "a tight-fitting black sheath he had picked out himself." Dressed in her Bible study outfit, she came back to sit beside him again, but he ignored her and continued to shower his priestly attention on the girls.

LARRY GELLER AND EASTERN THOUGHT

Beginning in 1964, Elvis sought the ultimate answers not in Christian theology but in Eastern thinking. Moreover, his interest in final things became increasingly intense and was with him even on the morning he died. His tutor in these matters was a Hollywood hairdresser, Larry Geller. One day in April 1964, when he was summoned to Elvis's house in Bel Air to do his hair, he began to tell Elvis about his interest in Eastern religions. Elvis kept him for more than four hours.

Elvis's early biographer Albert Goldman described Larry as "a tall, slender, good-looking New York Jew." He was one of the first, Goldman said, in what became a common type: "the low-pressure, low-profile West Coast hippie spiritualist and health food faddist, who, as he labors every day at his manual craft, babbles endlessly about meditation, vitamin E, and the Third Eye."

For Elvis, it was as if a dam had broken and flooded his consciousness with a superior form of spirituality. Soon, Larry was prescribing books for Elvis to read, visiting him in Graceland, and having long philosophical discussions. Then he joined Elvis's paid coterie and became his most favored companion. He got to ride in the front seat alongside Elvis as he drove his bus back and forth between Los Angeles and Memphis. They talked endlessly about final things. After Larry came, the guys rode in the back of the bus and hated him. The guys hated Larry, but Elvis could not have cared less about their feelings. He was saved. He was born again.

Elvis was growing increasingly unhappy with his movie career as he contemplated the truly important things of life. Finally, in 1967, there came a time when he was scheduled to return to Hollywood from Memphis to make a particularly bad movie, *Clambake*. His weight had recently ballooned to two hundred pounds. He threw up flimsy excuses to delay his return, costing everyone money. On the morning he was supposed to go into the studio, March 9, 1967, he fell in his bathroom and hit his head, causing still further delay and expense. Officially it was announced that he had suffered a severe brain concussion, but a doctor X-rayed him and declared that nothing serious was wrong.

The Colonel had had enough. He called a meeting of Elvis and all the boys. He read the riot act to the guys and used the incident to blame Geller for the disruptions. Elvis cast his gaze down and would not even look at Larry as the Colonel hammered away at him. Colonel Parker summarily banned Larry from Elvis's presence, and Elvis did not say a word. Pressured by the Colonel and assisted by a very willing Priscilla, Elvis tossed Geller's books into an incinerator behind Graceland and burned them.

During the 1970s, Larry began coming over to Las Vegas from Los Angeles to visit Elvis, and gradually they became intimate again. He claimed to be the last person to talk to Elvis alive—by phone. Elvis again built up his library of books on spiritual matters. Vera Stanley Alder's *The Initiation of the World* was one of his favorites, and he insisted that Priscilla read it, a task she did not eagerly embrace and soon abandoned. "Are human beings potential gods, as they have been told, or are they merely the least of worms?" Alder posed this question in the introduction to *The Finding of the Third Eye* (1938) and devoted her writings to answering it. Modern science had devalued humanity, she insisted, but here and there among us is a seeker who, "while gathering his store of knowledge, may develop wisdom…and learn those few essential secrets through which he may attain the poise, power and creativeness which will ultimately develop him into a superman." These seekers "will be the builders of the new and promised Golden Age," she declared.

Lying in his bed upstairs in Graceland, Elvis read and read, underlined and made notes. Never before had he been such an assiduous student. Visitors would be amazed to see this cavelike bedroom strewn with books—and guns. When he traveled, he took a suitcase full of his books with him. Elvis was an earnest seeker after the higher truths that would give him definition and power over himself and everything around him. Who was he? What was his great mission in life? He clearly believed that the answers lay in Eastern rather than Western thinking, if the answers lay anywhere.

CHAPTER ELEVEN

SAVED

Elvis was ever mindful of the sudden and precipitous downfall of celebrities, and he dreaded the appearance of the bodyguard book. He had been exceedingly fearful that he would be forgotten while he was in the army in Germany. Afterward, he hated the Beatles, who had seized America's attention during his absence and gained wildly increasing popularity. With the Comeback Special in Vegas and the road shows, he had survived the Beatles and the movies, but now the sea of his troubles was rapidly rising. How would his fans respond to the book? How could he live without his fans? How could he survive without recurrently immersing himself in the warming waters of adulation? How could he go on without money?

Then rather suddenly the promise of salvation began to take shape in his mind. As usual with Elvis, what began as a thought quickly became a passion, and again as usual, after a time the passion faded. Salvation took the form of a young woman named Ginger Alden.

"I think I am in love" was the thought. Elvis made the declaration in the late fall of 1976. Ginger was twenty years old, a Memphian, and a beauty queen. Love, marriage, and a budding family with this beautiful young woman would create "a new Elvis," wash away the tales in the bodyguard book, and save him. His marriage to Priscilla had been a cover-up managed by the Colonel. Elvis would manage this one himself.

COURTSHIP

George Klein, always the eager procurer, provided the link. On November 19, 1976, he sent Elvis not one girl but two, the Alden sisters, both beauty queens. Terry, the older of the two, was the reigning Miss Tennessee–Miss America. She had won her crown as Miss Tennessee in the contest organized by the Jaycees in April 1976 and went on to compete in Atlantic City. She played classical piano. In February 1976, Ginger Alden had become the first runner-up in the Miss Tennessee–Miss Universe contest. Ginger had won other contests. She was the reigning Miss Mid-South Fair, and she had been Miss Traffic Safety. After high school she had worked as a saleswoman at Jeans, a clothing store. In December 1976, interviewed by the *Memphis Press-Scimitar* as Elvis's new girlfriend, she told the press that she had appeared in several commercials and was a student at the Memphis Academy of Arts.

By this time the procedure by which a new girl connected to Elvis in Memphis was well established. Arriving at Graceland at the designated time, she would be admitted by one of the staff and seated in the drawing room, just off the front entranceway. Sooner or later either Elvis or his agent would appear.

With the Alden girls it was Elvis himself who did the interview. On this first visit to Graceland, Ginger and Terry were accompanied by their older sister, Rosemary, already married, a mother, and not a rising professional in the beauty business. The three women sat in a row on the fifteen-foot long white couch. Elvis sat in a chair in front of them. It was as if Ginger and Terry were there to simply interview for a job. Rosemary was by nature a leader and a talker, and Terry was not far behind if at all. They volleyed the ball of conversation back and forth with Elvis. Ginger hardly said a word. Elvis liked what he saw and invited the Aldens to visit again.

Probably it was twenty-two-year-old Terry Alden, rather than Ginger, that George Klein had in mind for Elvis's attention. Tall, intelligent, self-confident, and engaging, she was compellingly attractive. If Terry ever had a chance with Elvis, however, she soon blew it. She was not one to bat her eyelashes and call men masterful. On a later occasion she challenged Elvis to an arm-wrestling match—elbows on table, opposing hands locked. Terry won, hands down and all too easily. Bad move. Nobody beats Elvis. Especially a girl.

Ginger was reticent and not easily readable. In her dark good looks, she was not unlike Priscilla or Elvis himself. But at five-eight and with appropriate fullness of figure, she was not a young girl. She was twenty. From the first, it seems, Elvis chose her—not as simply another in his usual game of revolving girls but as a possibly permanent bedmate. She had, as Billy Smith said, "that virginal look" that was so important to Elvis. In the order of Elvis's women, she ranked with Anita Wood, Priscilla Beaulieu, Kathy Westmoreland, Joyce Bova, and Linda Thompson— all convincing virgins with a chance of substantial tenure in Elvis's bed.

As he had with the Beaulieus and the Thompsons, Elvis engaged not just the girl but her whole family, and he did so with a rush and a magnitude that were unprecedented. It quickly became a more serious commitment than he had made to Linda and her family and much quicker and thicker even than his involvement with the Beaulieus. It left the Aldens reeling. They could hardly believe their good luck.

The Aldens, it developed, had encountered Elvis before, if only briefly. Mr. Alden had been a sergeant in the army induction center in Memphis when Elvis entered the service in 1958. Ginger had also met Elvis previously. In 1961, when she was a little girl, her mother, Jo Laverne Alden, took her to Libertyland, the Memphis amusement park. Elvis was there. Jo Alden, an ardent Elvis fan herself, took Ginger up to meet him. He patted the little girl on the head. He was twenty-six then, and Ginger was five.

In 1976 the Aldens still lived in Memphis. Mrs. Alden was working in the IRS processing center. In the late sixties and early seventies, after leaving the army, Mr. Alden worked as a department manager in Dixie Mart, a chain store. In the seventies he was a production worker at the Schlitz brewery. Their son, Michael, was a fireman in the Memphis Fire Department.

The transition to Ginger required one last highly charged encounter with Linda Thompson. In late November 1976, Elvis played in San Francisco. He wanted to bring Ginger in for that occasion, but Linda was already there and staying with Elvis in his suite in the Fairmont Hotel. Finally he arranged for Linda to leave, but Ginger arrived before Linda actually left Elvis's quarters. The guys had to stash Ginger in another room in the hotel for many anxious hours—without food, explanation, or communication of any sort. Finally, after Linda departed, one of the guys came and ushered Ginger into Elvis's presence. It was an insult for Ginger and a close call for Elvis.

In truth, Linda was ready to move on. Before she left, however, she ran up $30,000 on one of Elvis's credit cards. Everyone, including Elvis but excluding Vernon, said that Linda's action was totally appropriate. She had been lover, mother, nurse, companion, and confidant to an ailing Elvis for more than four years. She had earned her compensation and more. The only difficulty was that when she left she took the job description with her. Ginger Alden was no Linda Thompson.

In December 1976, Elvis brought Ginger, her mother, father, and her sisters out to Vegas on the *Lisa Marie* for the last two days of his engagement. He housed them at the Hilton Hotel and entertained them lavishly. "Don't let this one get away," Mr. Alden was heard to advise his daughter humorously.

Back in Memphis in January, the courtship with the Aldens continued apace. Mrs. Alden's father died in Harrison, Arkansas, her hometown. On January 3, Elvis, Ginger, and a dozen or so members of his staff flew up to Harrison, high in the Ozark Mountains near the Missouri line. One of the guys was already there to meet them at the airport with Elvis's Lincoln Continental.

After the funeral at 10:00 a.m. (which Elvis attended wearing his giant sunglasses), lunch at the Ramada Inn, and proper paying of respects to family and friends, the Lincoln Continental brought them back to the airport for the return flight to Memphis. Elvis generously paid for the funeral. He had paid for any number of weddings outside the family, but never a funeral. Elvis had involved himself with the families of his girlfriends before in order to achieve his ends, but never so much as he did with the Aldens.

By now Ginger was sleeping in Elvis's bed and spending time with him in his upstairs quarters at Graceland. If eyebrows might rise at the thought of such intimacy in an unmarried state, Mrs. Alden quickly lowered them with her even-tempered comment that she never worried about Ginger when she was with Elvis.

On January 5, Elvis and Ginger flew to Palm Springs for a week-long vacation at his house. Rosemary came along, and Lisa Marie came up from Los Angeles to help her father celebrate his forty-second birthday on the eighth. Elvis's Los Angeles dentist, Dr. Max Shapiro, and his fiancée also happened to come by for a visit. Dr. Shapiro made house calls and wrote prescriptions freely; he had built an extraordinary practice among celebrities in Bel Air and Las Vegas. Elvis persuaded them to marry on the spot at his expense. He bought the necessary rings and supplied flowers and music. Ginger served as the bridesmaid, and Larry Geller, Elvis's tutor in Eastern thought and religion, who had somehow acquired an official minister's license and ministerial clothing, came in to conduct the ceremony. Perhaps seduced by the sheer beauty of the proceedings, Elvis was heard to say that he might marry Ginger.

Back in Tennessee again, Ginger was supposed to go with Elvis to Nashville on Thursday, January 20, for a scheduled recording session for RCA. At the last minute, she backed out. Elvis postponed his departure for a day, and they had a prolonged and acrimonious argument. The next day he went to Nashville without her but would not go to the studio. He had a sore throat, he said. He spent much of his time in the hotel room calling Ginger. For three days the backup singers, the band, and the technicians waited in the studio for Elvis to appear. Finally, Elvis flew back to Memphis without recording anything at all. RCA paid everyone for the full week they were supposed to have worked.

Elvis was obsessed with having Ginger with him in Nashville, and he was in rebellion against RCA and the Colonel. Even before they went to Nashville he said to Billy Smith, "I'm not going to do it. If I have to, I'll say I'm losing my voice." He did that, Billy said, as a way of "getting back at Colonel *and* RCA."

ENGAGED

Elvis's intense involvement with Ginger and her family strongly suggested that he was into the traditional progression of love and courtship that would end in marriage. But Ginger was acting as if the relationship were not all that important to her. Elvis was not used to rejection. He was challenged, and he raised his bid substantially. He asked Ginger to marry him.

As Ginger later told the press, the marriage proposal came in the early morning hours of Wednesday, January 26. She and Elvis were together in Elvis's bathroom, which also often served as his sitting room. Elvis kneeled before her seated figure and asked her to be his wife. In the process he produced a green velvet box and drew forth a custom-made engagement ring valued at $50,000. Among Elvis intimates that figure would soon inflate to $70,000. Ginger agreed to become Mrs. Elvis Presley.

Elvis's jeweler, Lowell G. Hays, later told the story behind the ring. About 1:00 a.m. on the night of the engagement Elvis called him at home. He wanted an engagement ring with a giant diamond for Ginger, and he wanted it that night. Lowell said that he did not have such a diamond in his store but would get one the next day. Elvis, as usual, said now or never. The jeweler devised a creative solution. He reset the 11½-carat diamond that Elvis had in his own TCB ("Taking Care of Business") ring to produce the $50,000 piece. Nesting the ring in a green velvet box, he delivered it to Graceland before sunrise.

Elvis was so pleased with Lowell Hays's work that he gave him a new Mark V Lincoln Continental as a bonus. He also gave him an extraordinarily personal gift, his own highly treasured paperback book on the meaning of numbers. "It was as well read as any book I ever saw," the jeweler recalled. "It was obvious he had thumbed through it time and again for hours on end." Lowell found out something about himself that he never knew before. He was a four and Elvis was an eight. Hopefully he never looked up the Cantonese meaning of a four, or he would have discovered that he was thought to be "unlucky." Elvis's eight, on the other hand, indicates "sudden fortune" and "prosperity."

THE WEDDING PLAN

After Elvis's demise, Ginger told a detailed fantastic yet convincing story about how Elvis envisioned their marriage ceremony. It would be presided over by a justice of the United States Supreme Court rather than a minister of the Gospel. Honored guests would include FBI and federal narcotics agents and members of police departments from all across the nation. Unlike his wedding to Priscilla, which was not announced in advance at all, this one would be announced well beforehand to allow Elvis to milk the event fully for favorable publicity. One can almost see Elvis's mind working out the scenario, glorious in itself but also the solution to his problem with the bodyguard book. All those policemen in attendance at his wedding and a Supreme Court justice presiding would more than counterweigh slanderous tabloid stories about how he was a violent and drugged-out man who considered himself above the law. In consenting to preside over the marriage ceremony, a judge of the highest court in the nation would, in effect, declare him innocent of all charges.

Elvis's second marriage would be his own creation. He did not need the Colonel. Regardless of what he said publicly about their relationship, Elvis had long been bitter about the restraints that he felt Colonel Parker had placed upon his artistic creativity. He was not allowed to take a truly dramatic role for a movie comeback and enjoy a brilliant film career as had Frank Sinatra. Barbra Streisand had offered him a great role in *A Star Is Born*, and the Colonel had turned it down. Parker continued to keep him on a short leash. He would hardly even talk about a European tour, or one in Japan or Australia. Even as he passed into middle age, the Colonel continued to refer to him as his "boy," and he managed him accordingly.

Since the late 1960s, Elvis had wanted to fire the Colonel, but Parker had bound him hand and foot financially. Elvis made millions, but he had no millions to buy Tom Parker out. If he fired the Colonel he would essentially be broke. More recently, Parker had added insult to injury. There was a rumor, almost certainly true and probably deliberately leaked by the Colonel himself, that he was thinking of selling his management contract with Elvis. "Elvis was a lot of trouble," he was saying. In April or May 1977, he did tell Sam Thompson, Linda's brother and one of the bodyguards, that he intended to sell Elvis's contract. Now Elvis was going to take charge of his own life. To hell with the Colonel.

He would choose the woman he would marry, really marry, and his brilliant management of his image in these proceedings would put the

Colonel's management of his previous marriage in the shade. His marriage would save his image and career. Besides, he loved Ginger and wanted her by his side. He had courted her and her family assiduously, proposed to her on bended knee, and she had accepted. He was a romantic of the highest order, not a pervert or a womanizer. He would marry her and have children, especially, he hoped, a son.

Already his fans loved Ginger. He had her stand up in the Showroom of the Hilton and had the spotlight shine on her. He put on his usual show. "Turn around," he commanded. The audience had applauded with sincere warmth. Ginger began to speculate about her relationship to Elvis. "Maybe that's why I was put on Earth. If I could make Elvis happy, I would have served my purpose."

THE TROUBLE WITH GINGER

The real trouble with Elvis's plan for a new life with Ginger came from Ginger herself. It turned out that she was not as pliable as one might think on first impression. She had a mind and a will of her own, and she acted accordingly.

When Elvis set out on his first tour of 1977 on February 12, he insisted that Ginger come with him. He made the most of Ginger's presence on the tour. It was the usual routine that he relished so much. She would be publicly introduced as his girlfriend, the very image of love fulfilled. Affecting alarm, Elvis would command, "Sit down. You're hogging the spotlight." The fans loved this charming play. They melted into the romance; they were a part of it. The King had found his Princess. Elvis fans had come to yearn for Elvis's remarriage. Ginger later said that "they always would come up to me and say, 'You're what he's searched for a long time.' " They wanted him to find a girl to marry and have children with her.

Ginger was very young and bewildered by the bizarre world she had tumbled into. For starters, her fiancé was a generation older than she. He had experienced a life hardly imaginable for a girl who had grown up in post-Depression, postwar, prosperous Memphis. The heavy drugs all around, the guys, the tensions, and, most of all, the seclusion she had to endure to be with him taxed her severely.

Understandably, she began to yearn for the youthful sybaritic life she had before Elvis. She liked going to the bars and clubs frequented by people her own age, where racy guys like popular disc jockey George Klein hung out and handsome young men with trim, firm bodies flirted with her and asked her to dance. She must have been shocked by how quickly Elvis's charm could turn to anger and rage and his gifts into demands for her to perform as if she had no life and will of her own.

Elvis, of course, wanted her always with him or else waiting for him. She was supposed to go with him on tours and love it, love his fans, love the show business life as he loved it. She was supposed to be in his bed whenever he wanted her there, on the road or in Graceland, for as long as he wanted her there, and always when he was trying to go to sleep or waking up. But Ginger was not willing to follow Elvis every day for almost two grueling weeks of touring during each month of March, April, May, and June 1977. She did not want to lie in his bed in Graceland every morning when he was trying to go to sleep and be there every afternoon when he woke up no matter what else she wanted to do.

On one occasion Ginger simply balked at spending the night with him. They argued. She made ready to leave. Elvis insisted that she stay. As she got into her car and drove off, Elvis fired shots over her head, but she didn't stop. On another occasion, he ordered one of his minions to let the air out of her tires. Another time he threatened to lock the gates so she couldn't leave, but Billy Smith talked him out of the idea.

Elvis could not understand Ginger's desire to be apart from him sometimes. He suspected that she was seeing her old boyfriends. He put the guys on her trail. They came back with no evidence at all of infidelity. She would go to the clubs, but there was no other man out there to rival Elvis.

The truth was that Ginger liked the social life she had already been living, and she was deeply attached to her mother and two sisters and simply liked being with them. Eight days into the February tour, to keep Ginger happy, Elvis flew some of her family to Johnson City, Tennessee, and carried them on to Charlotte, North Carolina, for the last two days on the road. In Charlotte, he pulled a reluctant Terry Alden onto the stage and had her perform a classical piece on the piano. In early

March, he continued wooing the Aldens by taking Ginger and her sisters on vacation to Hawaii.

Ginger absolutely refused to go on the next tour, which began in Tempe, Arizona, on March 23. By then Elvis was in such bad shape that Dr. Nick had to put him on an IV, and Billy Smith had to load him onto the plane like some cumbersome bundle of cargo. His attire onstage during the tour was limited to the only two jumpsuits that he could squeeze into. His weight had swelled to well over two hundred pounds. He really was, as he had said to Red in October, "not operating on but one cylinder."

On the ninth day, in Baton Rouge, at the last minute he decided he could not go onstage at all. That show and the last three scheduled for the tour in Mobil, Macon, and Jacksonville had to be canceled. During the early morning hours of April 1, Elvis flew home. After stopping off at Graceland, he checked into Baptist Memorial Hospital. This certified his illness and allowed interested parties to collect insurance on the canceled performances. Even with the cancellations, the tour grossed almost a million dollars. Elvis and the Colonel got $375,000 of that. In spite of the new equal agreement, Parker allowed Elvis to keep two-thirds of their earnings, some $245,000.

On April 21, Elvis began his third tour of the year in Greensboro, North Carolina, and Ginger went with him. Elvis had only one jump-suit he could squeeze into. He was listless onstage, but Elvis fans were indefatigably loyal and were not much bothered by his weight. They filled the house to capacity again and again. If they were disappointed in a performance, they seldom showed it. Nine days into the tour he flew in Mrs. Alden and Rosemary to prevent Ginger's leaving. On May 3, they all flew home, and Elvis went into seclusion at Graceland for two and a half weeks. On May 6, he shot out a window in his bedroom.

During this tour, the *Nashville Banner* ran a story alleging that the Colonel was about to sell Elvis's contract. Parker immediately denied it, but everyone knew that something was up. The Colonel was a master at leaking information in ways that served his ends.

Elvis got home on May 4, and on the twentieth he began yet another tour in Knoxville, Tennessee. Ginger began with him, but on the seventh day, when he played in Binghamton, New York, she flew home to

Memphis. Elvis was exhausted, physically and emotionally. In Baltimore on the twenty-ninth he began "murmuring" and "swearing" onstage, and then walked off the stage entirely and remained off for about half an hour. The backup singers carried on as best they could. While he was in Baton Rouge on the thirty-first, making up for the performance he had canceled on the previous tour, newspapers abroad began to serialize the bodyguard book two months before its publishers released it in America.

Financially, this fourth tour of the year was a great success, grossing $2,309,000. Elvis got almost $800,000, two-thirds of the profit, but the Colonel stipulated that at the end of the year Elvis would give him back some $200,000 of that to conform to an agreement they had previously made whereby each would get half of the profits from tours. In effect, the Colonel had been loaning Elvis one-sixth of the profits they made from each tour since they signed that agreement in January 1976. Now Elvis agreed to pay back all those moneys at the end of 1977. It would be, of course, a staggering amount, and Elvis was barely surviving as it was. He was making fewer and fewer records, and none had hit No. 1 and sold a million copies since "Burning Love" in 1972. RCA was reduced to making records of tapes recorded on tour. Furthermore, the Hilton Hotel people were tired of his shenanigans and had not signed him up for another run. Touring still provided him with a large stream of income, but he spent it as fast as he made it. And the drugs he consumed as he kept up the break-neck pace were killing him.

Furthermore, the course of true love with Ginger was not running smoothly, despite Elvis involving himself thickly with the Alden family. In 1976, when Elvis first met the family, the Memphis City Directory indicated that the Aldens lived at 2999 South Perkins, which in the mid-1990s was the address of a small and very modest red-brick house on a wide and busy thoroughfare in a working-class neighborhood of eastern Memphis. The Aldens soon bought and moved into a larger, classically suburban, low ranch-style house at 4152 Royal Crest Place, a new house in an attractive new development on the southeastern edge of town.

After having been married for decades, Ginger's parents chose this particular time to divorce. Elvis stepped in to help Mrs. Alden. He not only made one of his lawyers available to help her secure her divorce; he also repaid Mr. Alden the $5,325 that he had invested in the new house. Further, he engaged a company to install a swimming pool and landscape the yard at a cost of $6,155. After Elvis's death, Mrs. Alden would sue the estate for the $35,000 she claimed Elvis had promised her to pay off the mortgage on her house. In the lower court she won; in the appeals court she lost.

Ginger did not respond to Elvis's generosity by making herself more available to him. She obviously did not like touring with him, and it became increasingly and painfully evident to Elvis that she did not like always hanging out in his bedroom in Graceland either. For days at a time she would not even come out to Graceland. "Where is she, man? Why don't she stay here?" Elvis would wail to Billy Smith. He desperately needed a girl he could count on, one who would be in his bed when he awoke and when he went to sleep.

ALICIA

Always on the job, George Klein found him one. She was Alicia Kerwin, another dark-haired Memphis beauty. Alicia was a twenty-year-old bank teller. She had no interest in beauty contests, and she was not even an Elvis fan. She seemed an unlikely candidate for his attention. At first, she declined George's invitation to visit Graceland, then on an impulse accepted.

Alicia drove out to Graceland on April 10. She arrived about 10:00 p.m. and was ushered into the drawing room. Jo Smith, Billy's wife, came down to interview her. Jo thought she was all right and brought her up to meet Elvis. Elvis and Alicia talked for about an hour. He explained his availability. He and Ginger had argued, he said. He was upset. He felt Ginger was too interested in his money. Elvis took a liking to Alicia right away.

Two days later, Elvis invited Alicia out to Graceland again. This time he received her in Lisa Marie's bedroom. He said that he was despondent over Lisa's return to California. Priscilla and Lisa Marie had flown in a week earlier. Priscilla's visit, apparently, was not purely social.

Before the month was out she would hold a $494,024.49 deed of trust on Graceland to secure money still owed her as part of the divorce settlement. In spite of his brag that he had given Priscilla what she wanted, obviously he had not put his money where his mouth was, and wisely Priscilla was taking no chances.

While Alicia was talking to Elvis, Ginger's sister Rosemary appeared. "She was real inquisitive and very rude and she wanted to know who I was and what I was doing there," Alicia recalled three years later. At that time, Alicia—it turns out—was talking to police officers pursuing a criminal investigation into the sources of Elvis's drugs. Rosemary, it seems, not only had access to Elvis's private precincts on the second floor of Graceland even when Ginger was not there, she also took a proprietary attitude toward her sister's fiancé and presumed to equate his engagement to Ginger with fidelity to Ginger. This had to be a shockingly new situation for Elvis. No one could challenge his freedom to invite a new young woman simply to visit his quarters. Neither Linda Thompson nor her relatives had ever dared such presumption. Then again, he had never proposed marriage to Linda.

On the next day, Elvis telephoned to invite Alicia to Graceland again. She said she had a date. "Break it," he urged. She said no. She was not overwhelmed by Elvis's fame. Like many other Memphians in those years, she barely knew who Elvis was—or cared. To them he was something like Beale Street, the famous black street in Memphis. They knew it was there, they knew it was famous all over America, but they didn't much care. Angrily, Elvis hung up on her. But "two seconds later" he called back and invited her to fly with him to Las Vegas on one of his jets. She accepted, she said, "because I'd never been there."

Billy and Jo Smith and some of the guys joined Elvis and Alicia on the trip. First they flew to Las Vegas, checking into the Hilton International Hotel, and then on to Palm Springs. The Smiths liked Alicia. Early on they had concluded that Ginger was not the right girl for Elvis. During one of Elvis's temper tantrums over Ginger's neglect, Billy declared that Elvis should look for a woman his own age. Elvis went wild. "What in the hell could a forty-two-year-old woman do for me?" he retorted angrily.

For three nights Alicia slept with Elvis in his bed in Las Vegas, and then spent two more in his bed in his Palm Springs house. One night in Palm Springs she thought he had stopped breathing. She rushed into Jo's room to sound the alarm. Jo said not to worry; it happened from time to time. Then the party returned to Memphis. In all of this there was no sex. Alicia was puzzled and amazed. Here she was sleeping with a man who was supposed to be one of the great sex idols of the world. Nevertheless, Elvis bought her a new car in Palm Springs, a Cadillac, and had it driven back to Memphis for her.

Three days after the party returned to Memphis, Elvis began his third tour of the year in Detroit. This time Ginger went with him, but on the eighth day Elvis had to fly her mother and Rosemary in to join them in Duluth, Minnesota. During the tour, Elvis called Alicia several times. He had to have a girl in his bed on tour regardless of how things might stand with his betrothed. Alicia, in his mind, was a good candidate in case Ginger defected.

It was June before Elvis called Alicia again. He needed to talk, he said. She drove down to Graceland. They talked for hours in his bedroom. It was like he wanted to go back in time to where she, at age twenty, then was. "He wished he could go out on Saturday night like everyone else," Alicia said. He wanted her to tell him all about the clubs she went to at night, crowded with young people. He wanted her to describe what it was like to walk into a club and not be singled out, to browse easily and gaze freely. He was more depressed than she had ever seen him, she said. He wanted her to stay with him until he went to sleep.

Alicia had already resolved to break off the relationship. The whole scene was just too weird. She was repulsed by the obsequious behavior of the young men who hung around Elvis. She thought David Stanley, Dee's son, was the worst at "bowing and scraping." David later told Geraldo Rivera in an interview for the television show 20/20 that he and other young members of Elvis's entourage sat around in the last months competing to see who would come closest to predicting the date of Elvis's death. He boasted that he was the winner of the contest, having "missed [by] about two days."

Alicia returned to Graceland one last time late that summer, arriving at 4:00 a.m. She read to Elvis for a long time before he went to sleep, then went to work at the bank. Once Ginger had appeared at Graceland while Alicia was there, and Elvis refused to see her. While she was at Graceland, Alicia recalled, Ginger phoned "a lot." Alicia said "she would ring the phone off the hook." The two girls who shared Elvis's bed that spring and summer would frequently see each other out in town—at a dress shop, from their cars at a stoplight, and "in clubs quite often"— but they never spoke to one another. Ginger had no rival in Alicia because Alicia had no great interest in Elvis. Soon she loaded her possessions into her new Cadillac he had given her, drove to Las Vegas, and became a blackjack dealer in the casinos.

BILLY SMITH

Back in Graceland, with almost two months of freedom before his next tour, Elvis retreated to his bedroom. He ordered George Klein to stay away. Also, he was tired of Lamar's smart-alecky comments and said he was thinking of firing him. The boys' club at Graceland was closing down. However, Charlie Hodge, who lived on the grounds, was allowed to come up to Elvis's room from time to time, and Dr. Nick was in attendance. He had installed a nurse, Tish Henley, in one of the mobile homes behind Graceland to manage Elvis's drug intake.

Increasingly, Elvis had come to rely on his cousin Billy Smith—and often also his wife, Jo—for emotional, physical, and managerial support. Indeed, in July 1976, when he fired Red, Sonny, and Dave, he ordered Billy to tell all the guys to stay away for a while. For years it had been their custom—and their job—to simply drop by in the late afternoons when Elvis got up, hang out with him, go with him to one of his late-night movies, or join in whatever fun thing he was into. When Elvis indicated his interest in paring down his social activities with the boys in the summer of 1976, Billy had come up with the idea of having only one of the guys "on duty" all the time, to do whatever chores might be necessary—such as setting up the midnight movies for Elvis in local theaters. The person would be on duty for a twelve-hour shift beginning at either noon or midnight. Billy was doing more and more of what the "foreman," Joe Esposito or Marty Lacker, had done previously.

It was clear that the list of those whom Elvis felt he could trust was shrinking and that he chose to have Billy and Jo Smith close to him because they were "family." They lived in a large mobile home just behind the big house at Graceland. They were dedicated to his well-being, and the services they performed for him had no bounds. From time to time, while on the road Elvis would come to their hotel room and crawl into bed with them. He would talk...and talk...and talk. Then he would fall asleep.

At Graceland they screened the endless stream of girls that George Klein sent from the bars and clubs of Memphis. Jo said that Elvis often sent her down to the drawing room to interview candidates. "If her fingernails are dirty, or if her toenails are dirty, she's a definite out," he would tell Jo. Jo would talk to the girl in the drawing room for a while, then go upstairs to report to Elvis. "I think she's real nice. I think you'd like her," she might say.

After some preliminaries the girl would be in her negligee propped up in the big bed next to Elvis, but he would not let Jo leave. (Sometimes it was Billy instead, but the routine would be the same.) Elvis would keep her with them, sitting in a chair by the bed or on the foot of the bed itself for an hour or more. He would not talk to the girl but rather to Jo. "Tell her about...," he would say to Jo, suggesting some story about himself, such as buying lamps for her double-wide mobile home. As Jo was finishing one story and about to leave, he would urge her to tell another. Sometimes the girl would say something, but mostly she just lay there and listened. Finally, before Jo was allowed to go she would have to explain to the girl that Elvis would not have sex with her because he needed to save "bodily fluids," either for an upcoming tour or to heal some tiny wound, such as a cut on his finger that he would hold up to show the girl as if to establish credibility. The girl needed to understand that he could have sex another time, but not just now.

As the older guys flaked away in the mid-1970s, as Linda Thompson spent more and more time in California pursuing her career, as the girls came and went, Billy came to spend twelve to eighteen hours a day with Elvis. While they were alone, he did whatever Elvis needed, but mostly they talked. In July and August 1977, with Billy always on call, it became virtually a twenty-four-hour-a-day job. They spent a lot of time doing take-offs on Monty Python films, dialogue and scenes that they knew by heart. It was silly teenage stuff, but they loved it.

Elvis talked about serious things too. He toyed with the idea of having plastic surgery to change his looks, disappearing, and living elsewhere. He would find a man with a terminal illness who looked like him and pay him to let the surgeon change his face to match his own. When the man died, he would be buried as Elvis Presley. Elvis could then live quietly elsewhere. "I'm giving up being Elvis Presley," he said. He soon dropped that thought.

Elvis went from erasing himself to perpetuating himself. He was obsessed with the idea of having a son. "He'll have my eyes and, of course, my face," he said. He would be an entertainer, and if Elvis chose the right woman, he would be "the best looking and the most perfect kid in the world." His name would be Elvis Presley Jr.

Lisa Marie's Last Visit

On the last day of July, Elvis's chief of security, Dick Grob, brought nine-year-old Lisa Marie from Los Angeles to Graceland for a two-week visit. For Elvis, this was supposed to be, at last, a long and satisfying time for closeness with his daughter. Recurrently in the past he had virtually begged Priscilla to send her for visits, but then failed to pay her a lot of attention after she arrived.

Billy Smith thought that Lisa idolized her father and was starved for his attention. Sometimes, when Elvis was available, she would crawl up onto his lap and put her arms around his neck. These were touching moments. But much of the time he was not available. He slept during the day while she was awake. Sometimes she would just go into his bedroom and wake him up. Elvis scolded her for interrupting his sleep. Occasionally persuaded to ride with her and a friend in her special golf cart around the Graceland grounds, he would take a turn and then leave them to ride by themselves.

Billy caught one scene perfectly. Elvis was sitting on the patio beside the house talking when Lisa ran up, eager to enlist her father's help.

"Daddy, my golf cart's got a flat on it, and I can't ride it anymore," she exclaimed.

"Okay, Lisa, Daddy's talking right now," Elvis said, brushing her aside and continuing his conversation.

"But, Daddy," she persisted, "won't you fix it for me so I can ride?"

After several such exchanges, Elvis exploded. "Goddammit, Lisa! Go get Earl." Earl Pritchard, Elvis's uncle by marriage, was the grounds manager and general repairman.

"But, Daddy," Lisa persisted, "I want you to fix it."

"Daddy don't fix flats, Lisa," Elvis responded. "Daddy's rich. He has people do that for him."

Lisa was a bright, spunky little girl, and, according to Billy Smith, she did find ways to get Elvis's attention, as well as that of other people. Sometimes she would ride her golf cart down to the gate and sign autographs for the fans. She was fully conscious of the power she had as Elvis Presley's daughter. Pert and sloe-eyed like her father, she could be a little rascal too. She developed one tactic that compelled notice. Reportedly, she would sometimes sign the autographs, "Fuck you, Lisa Marie Presley," and then hop on her cart and race up the hill. Billy called her "a pistol." Lamar Fike called her "the Little Fuhrer."

As a special treat for Lisa on this visit, Elvis rented out Libertyland for Lisa and their friends, including Ginger's little niece, Amber Alden. The reservation was for the early morning hours of Monday, August 8. Elvis had rented the park for the night many times before. He loved to crash his "bump 'em" electric car into other people's. Nobody except maybe Linda Thompson and Lisa Marie would ever bump Elvis's car seriously. As the time for the outing approached, Elvis called the event off on the excuse that the park staff had all gone home. Ginger finally cajoled him into doing it. Elvis rallied the staff and the games were on again. Lisa loved it.

Lisa Marie's room at Graceland was on the second floor just down the hall from Elvis's bedroom. Gladys and Vernon had first occupied the room, and later Minnie Mae. Now it contained Lisa's special bed—king-sized, with a canopy, and a headboard covered with simulated white fur. The mattress was raised so high that the child had to climb steps to get up to it. Some fifteen stuffed animals and dolls lounged around the room.

Because Elvis was so often asleep when Lisa was awake, she sometimes found company with her great-grandmother Minnie Mae and great-aunt Delta in their quarters downstairs just off the kitchen. She also had the fourteen-acre estate to explore, plus Billy and Jo's two little boys, a swing set, and her golf cart to play with.

Lisa might also visit with grandfather Vernon, but he was by nature not much fun. Moreover, he was not in good health that summer. He had suffered from ongoing mild heart issues in the spring of 1977. His heart condition, however, had not kept him from joining Elvis on his tours, where he, like the guys—including his two stepsons, David and Ricky Stanley—would cruise the crowds for girls and young women. Often enough there were keys on rings bearing hotel room numbers lying on the stage after a performance, thrown there as an invitation to Elvis but available to the guys and Vernon. Lamar Fike said Vernon had cheated on Dee "for years and with pretty much anything."

While on tour with Elvis in Denver, Colorado, in April, 1976, sixty-year-old Vernon found a thirty-six-year-old divorcee, a nurse named Sandy Miller. He brought Sandy and her two sons to Memphis and set them up in an apartment near Graceland. She was billed as his nurse, but no one was deceived.

Vernon's marriage to Dee was rapidly falling apart. Dee was getting out and socializing more, which Vernon did not like. Billy Stanley said that Vernon "told her he'd smash every bone in her face if she didn't keep her ass at home." With Sandy on the scene Dee was ready to accept divorce, but she wanted a quarter of a million dollars in return. Vernon was horrified. He got Elvis to try to persuade her to settle for less. Elvis told her that he would give her $10,000 right away to help her get started in life again. Dee wanted to become a songwriter, and presumably that lesser sum would enable her to begin that career, feel that she could earn her own living, and be less demanding of Vernon. She, however, stuck to her guns, went off to Santo Domingo, and secured her divorce with, Marty Lacker said, a settlement of $250,000.

On August 4, the publishers of *Elvis: What Happened?* released the bodyguard book that Elvis so feared and hated. He never read the book. Billy dissuaded him. But promotion geared up quickly and the air was full of it. In an interview for a Chicago radio station, Steve Dunleavy, the acid-tongued journalist who helped write the book, said that Elvis was nothing but "white trash." Elvis's death twelve days later made the book a smashing success. It sold more than three million copies. The authors were well paid, surely making much more than they would have received had they continued to work for Elvis.

THE LAST TOUR

As Elvis prepared to leave for Portland, Maine, and begin his tour in August 1977, he was banking on the double effect of the prospect of his new marriage and the usual magic that came with his live performances to drown the bodyguard book. He wanted this tour to be perfect. He called a meeting with some of his staff. The music would be changed to suit his mood, and he wanted everyone to be fully charged for the performances to come.

They would open in Portland on Wednesday evening, August 17, a thousand miles northeast of Memphis. New England, where Elvis had first played in Boston in 1971, was the region in America most alien to Elvis's native South. In his whole life, he had performed there only eleven times, and ten of these were in the last two years. On May 24, 1977, three months before his death, he went onstage in the Civic Center in Augusta, Maine, as far into the northeast of America as he would ever go.

The motivation for the depth of this regional invasion was almost surely financial. Elvis needed audiences. In his last years, he played in places he had never played in before and in towns and areas with relatively small populations. Two of the last six towns in which he performed were in South Dakota—Sioux Falls and Rapid City.

After Portland, the tour would work its way toward home—Utica, Syracuse, Hartford, Uniondale (New York), Lexington (Kentucky), Roanoke (Virginia), Fayetteville (Tennessee), Asheville, and finally Memphis, a triumphal procession. All the while, Ginger's lovely presence would be seen and eager anticipation aroused. On August 27, at home again in Memphis, during the first of two shows he would announce his engagement to Ginger. His fans, seeing their hopes and dreams for his happiness coming true through his marriage, would be filled with joy. The news would galvanize the world. "Elvis to marry!" the press would shout. The second show, in Memphis on August 28, would be sheer ecstasy.

Afterward, the media would celebrate the couple's every move. Later, the announcement of the wedding date would provide another grand opportunity for publicity and after that another period of eager anticipation. The wedding must not occur too soon or too late. It might be during the Christmas season, or perhaps on Elvis's birthday, January 8, 1978, to make that date a double celebration.

The details of the plans for the absolutely breathtaking wedding ceremony would be revealed to the public piece by piece, building toward the crescendo of the event itself. For months, the bodyguard book would have to do battle with images of Elvis and Ginger in love, devoted to one another and gliding happily toward marriage, children, and a resplendent family life at Graceland. The Colonel, too, would have to accept and follow Elvis's lead. He would not dare try to sell Elvis's contract or embarrass him financially in this time of rising admiration. Indeed, he would devote his considerable promotional talents to making the most of it.

In anticipating the tour and what was to follow, Elvis was coming alive again. Possibly his seclusion, several relatively restful weeks, and the unstinting tender love and care that he got from Billy and Jo Smith were therapeutic. He undertook to slim down for the tour and fit himself into a new jumpsuit. His special diet for losing weight was unnerving to the ordinary observer; he ate nothing but Jell-O. His diet on this occasion was not highly effective, nor were they usually. As Lamar said, Elvis would "go on a diet today and try to lose fifty pounds by one o'clock." Even his newly made suit proved too small. "Billy," he said to Billy Smith, "I'm just too damn fat."

DYING DAY

On Monday, August 15, Elvis woke up, as usual, in the afternoon. Billy found him keenly focused on the upcoming tour and increasingly enthusiastic about it. But also he talked on and on about the bodyguard book. What if someone in an upcoming audience yelled out, "Hey, drug addict!" or some such, what would he do? As Billy recalled, he ran through several possible responses he might make. He would say that writers said all sorts of things about him good and bad all the time; this was just more of the same. Or he would say that all his drugs were prescribed by his doctor for medical reasons and then introduce Dr. Nick, who would explain everything. But maybe there would be no challenge at all. He finally decided, as Billy remembered, that he would say that he was going to take some time off to get straight.

Ginger had agreed to come with him on this tour, and Mrs. Alden was fully supportive. In truth, it seemed that Mrs. Alden was very ambitious for Ginger to marry Elvis, perhaps even more so than the bride-to-be. On the previous Monday, Elvis and Charlie Hodge had gone over to the Aldens' house, where they had all stood around the piano singing gospel songs. The romance and, presumably, the matrimonial ship was again sailing smoothly.

About 10:30 on Monday evening, Elvis slid into his Stutz convertible along with Ginger, Charlie Hodge, and Billy Smith. Down the hill they raced, through the gates swung wide, and up Elvis Presley Boulevard toward Memphis. In his usual fashion of doing business after hours, he was off to see his dentist and friend, Dr. Lester Hofman.

Billy helped Elvis dress for the evening out. Elvis put on his black sweatsuit with the Drug Enforcement Administration patch on the back, black leather boots (which he could not zip up because his ankles were too fat), and aviator sunglasses. He stuck two .45 pistols in the waistband of his pants to complete his attire.

Dr. Hofman's office was just off Poplar Avenue, out east near White Station, about nine miles from downtown Memphis. During the 1950s and 1960s, White Station became the home of many Memphians who were rising high on the tide of postwar prosperity, including many who were born well-to-do and those whites who wanted to flee the increasingly black downtown. Kemmons Wilson, business tycoon, developer, and founder of Holiday Inn, had built his high-rise office building there, visible for miles around.

Elvis pulled his Stutz Blackhawk up to a side door of the building where it would not be seen and led his party into the dentist's office. Dr. Hofman refilled two of Elvis's teeth and cleaned them. It was a pleasant, chatty visit. Dr. Hofman volunteered to clean Ginger's teeth as the convivial evening continued.

Around midnight Elvis and his party drove back to Graceland. He had ordered one of his favorite movies, *MacArthur*, for that night at the Memphian Theater. Ricky Stanley, the guy on duty, had goofed. He could not get the film, so Elvis canceled the outing.

The Last Night

Elvis was in bad shape generally, but he was not always dysfunctional. His dentist, for example, saw nothing wrong with him less than twelve hours before he died. Later, Billy Smith would say that he was high about 60 percent of the time during his last years. Elvis was keyed up to a high pitch that last night. After the visit to his dentist, he took Ginger up to his quarters at Graceland, where Ginger said that he spent much of their time planning for the wedding. Interviewed by Geraldo Rivera for *20/20* in 1979, she recalled that Elvis sought her suggestions, and "he had gone into more detail about our wedding than he had gone into at any time ever before." Her wedding dress was already being made, he said. When Ginger indicated that the dressmakers didn't have her measurements yet, Elvis replied, "Well, they'll just have to come up here." This wedding would occur in Elvis's hometown, the Memphis he loved and would never leave. "This will blow them all aside," Ginger recalled Elvis saying as he finished projecting the image.

About 4:00 a.m., Elvis phoned Billy and suggested that he and Jo come out for a game of racquetball. The Smiths came over from their mobile home to the big house to join Elvis and Ginger. As the four of them walked along the cement walkway toward the two-story-high concrete blockhouse that contained the court, it was raining lightly. Jo complained about the rain. "Ain't no problem," Elvis said and raised his hands in a lazy, commanding gesture toward the sky.

Jo and Ginger went onto the court first, then Billy and Elvis. Jo was good at the game, and gave away no points to save either male or female egos. As he often did, however, Elvis fell into his own game of trying to hit his opponent, Billy, with the ball. He ended by overreaching himself in attempting a very hard serve and struck his leg with his racquet. Complaining, he raised his pants leg to examine and then rub the wound. Billy, who had been the object of his attack, made light of his injury. "Hell, if it ain't bleeding," he teased, "it ain't hurting." Elvis threw his racquet at him.

Elvis sat down at the piano in the lounge area in front of the court. He began to play gospel songs and sing. Elvis played the piano by ear. He had never had lessons. The piano, not the guitar, was his natural instrument. Billy remembered particularly that one song he played was not gospel. It was "Blue Eyes Crying in the Rain."

About six o'clock, Jo went home, Ginger went upstairs into the big bedroom, and Billy went with Elvis into his capacious upstairs bathroom. Billy washed and dried Elvis's hair, a usual ritual before Elvis went to bed. Elvis had a chair in his bathroom that was something like a barber's chair where he would sit to get his hair washed and sometimes to read.

Billy recalled that he talked about Alicia Kerwin, but most of all he talked about the bodyguard book. He was going to invite Red and Sonny up to Graceland and kill them himself. Billy dismissed the death threat as a way to let off steam.

Soon Ricky Stanley, the guy who was officially on duty from midnight until noon, brought in the first "hit" for Elvis to take. This was the first of three packets of pills in the protocol that Dr. Nick had established to put him to sleep. That night Elvis had also acquired some codeine pills from Dr. Hofman in case he had pain from the dental work. In addition, Elvis had called Dr. Nick about 2:15 a.m. saying that his teeth were hurting. In the past, he had suffered severe reactions to codeine, so it seemed logical that he should take a different kind of painkiller. Dr. Nick called in a prescription for six doses of Dilaudid, a very powerful drug often given to patients dying of cancer and other painful disorders. Elvis sent Ricky to the all-night pharmacy at Baptist Memorial Hospital to pick up the medicine. Later, when Ricky brought in the second of Dr. Nick's prescribed hits, Billy was still in the bathroom with Elvis and saw Elvis swallow the pills.

Billy left about 7:45 a.m. As he was leaving, Elvis said, "Billy... Son... this is going to be my best tour ever."

MORNING

When Ginger woke up in the big bed about 8:00 a.m., Elvis was in bed beside her, reading. He couldn't go to sleep.

"Precious, I'm gonna go in the bathroom and read for a while," he said.

"Don't fall asleep," Ginger said. They all knew that when Elvis was on downers he might fall asleep no matter where he was or what he was doing. Sometimes he would drop off in the middle of a sentence. He could fall out of a chair and hurt himself.

"I won't," he replied and shut the door to the bathroom.

Closed off in his bathroom, Elvis continued to read. He lay in that chair reading, the lamp bent to light the page.

About 8:30, Elvis called down to the kitchen for his third hit. They couldn't find Ricky, whose duty it was to deliver the packet to Elvis. Ricky had scored some drugs of his own and had, perhaps, either locked himself in a basement room or retreated to a motel room up the street to share his drugs with a girlfriend. Stories of where Ricky was when Elvis died evolved over the years. The kitchen staff had to telephone Dr. Nick's office downtown, where Tish Henley, Elvis's nurse, was working. She called her husband at the mobile home where they lived on Graceland's grounds, and he delivered the packet to the housekeepers downstairs.

Elvis's aunt Delta Mae Biggs was disgusted by Ricky's malfeasance. She thought that he was a "fat ass," and she took the bag containing the drugs up to Elvis's bathroom herself, along with a glass of water and the *Commercial Appeal*. Delta talked briefly with her nephew and departed. By then it was 9:00 a.m. She was the last person to see Elvis alive.

After Aunt Delta left, Elvis sat quietly in his bathroom and read. Probably a part of the time he was in the chair and part of the time he sat on the black leather padded seat of the low-slung, wall-hung, black ceramic commode. For several years, Elvis had suffered great pain from constipation, and he was used to spending time sitting on his toilet. He had two phones and an intercom within arm's reach.

THE BODY

Ginger woke up in Elvis's bed sometime before 2:00 p.m. Elvis was not in the room. She made a telephone call to her friend Cindy, who would join her on the tour. Cindy was just getting ready to leave work, go home, and pack for the trip. Ginger made another call to her mother at work at the Internal Revenue Service's Memphis center. Then she got dressed, applied her makeup, and did her hair. She needed to go out. She had things to do before they were to fly out that night.

Finally, Ginger began to wonder where Elvis was. Usually at this time of day he would be sleeping next to her in the big bed and she would slip quietly out of the bed and out of the house. If he was awake, she needed to tell him she would be gone for a while. He must be in the bathroom, she thought.

She went to the door and knocked. No response. Then she called softly, "Elvis." No answer. Again she called, "Elvis." Again no answer. Quietly, she entered the bathroom.

Elvis was kneeling on the floor like a Muslim in prayer. His face, turned slightly to one side, was almost buried in the three-inch-deep piles of the dark red rug. The book he had been reading had slipped from his hand and fallen open-faced to the floor. At first, Ginger was more concerned than alarmed. Elvis had passed out again.

Kneeling, she turned his head. She heard something like an expelling of breath that led her to think that he was all right. But she was startled by how dark blue his flesh was. His tongue was protruding, and he had bitten it. She raised his eyelid. His eyeball was blood red, no sign of any white at all, and it was staring lifelessly. For a few moments, she was in a state of shock. Then she reached for the intercom by the toilet and called the kitchen.

"Who's on duty?" she asked the maid.

"Al," came the answer. That was Al Strada, who first worked as a security guard at one of Elvis's Los Angeles houses and then became his valet and wardrobe person as well as a bodyguard.

"Would you tell Al to come up here really quick?" Ginger asked.

Al raced up the backstairs. Entering the bathroom, he saw Elvis on the floor.

Joe Esposito had arrived in town the night before and checked into the Holiday Inn up the street from Graceland. Shortly after 2:00 p.m., he drove over to Graceland, already beginning in his mind the countdown of the many things that had to be done before they took off in the *Lisa Marie* for Maine that night. Joe came in the back door just as Ginger's call came down to the kitchen. He rushed into Elvis's bathroom only seconds behind Al.

Together the two men turned Elvis over on his back. Grotesquely, the arms and legs remained frozen, so he seemed to be crouching, although upside down. With difficulty, they forced Elvis's limbs straight. He was wearing gold silk pajamas. The bottoms were down about his legs. The body was several feet away from the toilet, indicating that he either pitched forward and crawled the distance or struggled up, took a halting step or two, sank to his knees, and then fell forward. Later that afternoon, the investigator for the medical examiner detected a moist spot that smelled of vomit and bile where Elvis's face had rested against the carpet. He calculated from Elvis's height and the location of the spot that he had moved away from the toilet a few feet just before he died.

When Joe and Al turned Elvis over, they saw that he wasn't breathing. They feared that he had blocked his air passages with vomit. They had seen Elvis choking before. It was common practice to open his mouth and pull out the obstruction with their fingers. This time, however, they were not able to open his mouth. They attempted to pry open his jaws to no avail. With rising desperation, they knocked out his front teeth and made certain his air passages were open. Then they began mouth-to-mouth resuscitation and a rhythmic pumping of his chest.

The men ordered Ginger out of the room to spare her the awful sight. She left but immediately came back and began to press Elvis's chest also. She heard Lisa Marie calling as she came up the stairs. Running out, Ginger stopped the child in the hallway.

"What's wrong with Daddy?" Lisa asked.

"Nothing," Ginger responded, trying to hold the little girl.

"Something's wrong with my daddy," Lisa cried, struggling free. She turned and ran down the hall toward the dressing room, which had another door leading to the bathroom. Ginger called out to Al, who locked the other door just in time. Lisa then ran downstairs to tell her playmate that something was wrong with her father.

Amid the commotion, Joe began telephoning. First he tried to reach Dr. Nick at his office, only to find that he was out in East Memphis at Doctors' Hospital making his rounds. After leaving a message, he called the office of a nearby doctor that Graceland people sometimes used. The doctor asked him to bring Elvis to the office. Then Joe moved reluctantly to the last resort and dialed for the ambulance. This meant that the whole world would soon know that something was terribly wrong with Elvis Presley and his managers would have to come up with a good story. It was now 2:33 p.m. Joe told the dispatcher that someone was having trouble breathing at 3764 Elvis Presley Boulevard. He avoided giving Elvis's name as the person in distress, but he knew that the cat was already out of the bag.

At 2:37, Joe called the Colonel in Maine. Parker immediately began to take measures to control damage and prepared to fly to Memphis. Finally, Joe called Vernon, who was down in his office behind the house. Patsy Gambill and Vernon's girlfriend, Sandy Miller, were with him. Together the two women helped the wheezing, gray-haired old man up the stairs. Entering the bathroom, Vernon saw Elvis on the floor.

"Don't go, son!" he cried. "You're going to be all right!" Vernon was on the verge of collapse. They were afraid he would have another heart attack.

"My son is dead!" he wailed.

Charlie Hodge rushed in and tried to help Joe and Al revive Elvis. "Don't die!" he cried. "Please don't die!"

The order for the ambulance came to Fire Station No. 29 about three miles north of Graceland on Elvis Presley Boulevard, and Ulysses Jones and Charles Crosby responded immediately. But Elvis had stopped breathing about 9:30 that morning, five hours before the call came.

WHY ELVIS DIED

Pathologists doing the autopsy that evening would discover that about five feet of Elvis's lower colon was hugely distended and solidly blocked with chalky, whitish fecal matter. In places, it was stretched in diameter to about twice the normal two inches. Elvis had not effectively moved his bowels for some time.

That night, pathologists who were "running the gut," as they called the part of the autopsy that involved laying out the small and large intestines—about twenty-six feet—on a table and slicing them open lengthwise, had no difficulty at all deciding what caused this bizarre situation in Elvis's lower intestine. When someone takes downers over a long period of time, as Elvis had, the slowing down includes the digestive and elimination system. Elvis's bowels had simply lost much of their capacity for expelling waste.

If not medicated, Elvis would have suffered considerable pain. But he was medicated. The autopsy revealed that Elvis's body contained about ten times the amount of codeine a doctor would ordinarily have prescribed for pain. He might well have had his own supply of codeine in addition to that given to him by Dr. Hofman. No trace of the Dilaudid was found in his body, nor in Elvis's quarters.

In any event, Elvis had surely taken his three hits and other drugs as well. When the assistant medical examiner, Dan Warlick, came that afternoon to examine the scene, he found two empty syringes. One was in Elvis's office, next to his bedroom, on the desk in front of the placard that read ELVIS PRESLEY—THE BOSS. Warlick found the second syringe on top of the bookcase. He found no syringes in the bathroom, but a maid had thoroughly cleaned that space soon after the medics and the ambulance left. Dan Warlick also found the little black bag that Elvis called his "medicine chest." It was empty.

After considering carefully all of the substantial evidence available, the pathologists at Baptist Memorial Hospital concluded that Elvis had died of "polypharmacy." The codeine alone would have killed an ordinary person, but the doctors could not say that Elvis died of any one drug and exclude the others. Nor could they describe the exact effect on his body of the combination of several drugs found in lethal or large amounts. There was simply no way of knowing precisely how these drugs taken in various quantities at various times combined to affect this particular body.

Also, the doctors could not say exactly how the drugs acted in Elvis's body to kill him. Did he die of a heart attack? Did he suffocate? Certainly he did not simply doze off on the downers and die quietly in his sleep. He suffered horribly before he died. Tiny blood vessels hemorrhaged all over his upper body, as if exploded by high pressure. His eyes were blood red. His tongue protruded, and he bit it. He vomited.

Over time, experts offered several hypotheses as to what specific malfunction in Elvis's body did him in. For instance, Dan Warlick later suggested that his excessive straining at the stool might have caused his internal organs to move in such a way as to cut off the circulation of blood to his heart. Thus, it was a very painful death and one not caused directly by drugs. In this sense, Elvis had died of a heart attack after all.

The Will

Back in March, Elvis had been thinking pointedly about his children both present and prospective when he worked out the details of his last will and testament. In the wee hours of the morning of March 3, his lawyer Beecher Smith had come over with the finished document for him to sign. Vernon was there for the signing. Ginger, Charlie Hodge, and the lawyer's wife, Ann, witnessed Elvis's signature. Legally, only two witnesses were required, neither of whom could be a beneficiary of the will. Charlie, then, could not have been a beneficiary, and neither could

Elvis's prospective wife, Ginger. The lawyer perhaps brought his own wife to ensure that they had at least one qualified witness readily available. Elvis himself must have decided that Ginger and Charlie would both serve. He would like that—more "taking care of business," Elvis style. The signers did not need to read the will, only attest to the legitimacy of the signature. The will was not read aloud. Billy Smith was there. He said it was all done in "six or seven minutes—hardly any time."

Afterward, Elvis gave Billy a copy of the will and invited him to read it, but Billy put it away without reading it. A couple of nights later, Billy later recalled, Elvis got the will out and showed him one section on one page—a section on who got what. Billy did not remember the substance well. Two or three people would get $50,000; Grandma and five or six guys were mentioned; cars would go to some people like Aunt Delta.

Some people who were left out of Elvis's will as filed in the county courthouse claimed that he had handwritten another will in which everyone was taken care of, as he had repeatedly promised. Some speculated that Vernon persuaded Elvis to make a new will, then dictated the contents to the lawyer himself, and Elvis signed the document without reading it. The substance of the will filed in the Shelby County Probate Court in Memphis after Elvis's death could not have suited Vernon more perfectly, but no copy of the handwritten will has ever been discovered, and no clear and consistent memory of its contents has surfaced.

Elvis's will as duly filed provided that his entire estate, divided into equal parts, would go to his "lawful" children. Lisa Marie was a lawful child. Each child would receive his or her inheritance when he or she reached the age of twenty-five. Vernon would be the administrator and also one of three trustees, along with Elvis's accountant and a person named by his bank. Vernon himself would be supported out of the estate during his lifetime, and he was explicitly directed to take care of Minnie Mae for the rest of her life. Neither of them could be expected to tax the estate heavily. Vernon was in ill health (and would die in 1979); Minnie Mae was in her eighties (and would die in 1980). Vernon was to help other relatives only in the face of dire necessity. With Vernon in charge of the estate, that necessity would have to be dire indeed. Any of Elvis's relatives in need of funds would do better begging with tin cups on the sidewalks of downtown Memphis.

Elvis's will made no mention at all of any of the guys or the girls. Also, none of his relatives were named as specific and certain beneficiaries. Nor was his ex-wife, Priscilla. Nor was any mention made of a future spouse, one of whom might be the mother of Elvis Aaron Presley Jr.

How could this be? How could this man famously generous in life to friends, family, lovers, and even strangers cut out of his will all but his children, his sickly father, and his aging grandmother? How could he not give at least some token of recognition—at least a token $10,000—to his cousin Billy Smith and his wife, Jo? How could he pass over people who had truly loved him and served him faithfully for a goodly portion of their adult lives, people like Charlie Hodge and Linda Thompson? Probably, Elvis knew little of the contents of his will and Vernon was its primary author.

Elvis's will, in effect, was an insult to all those who had loved and served him faithfully. The paradox of his generosity in life and his lack of generosity in death seemed impossible to explain. But, taking the long view, perhaps there was no paradox. Perhaps, after all, he had not really been so generous in life. Of course, he did leave the music. And he left distinct shadows dancing to the beat of a jailhouse rock on our cultural walls and in our memories…dancing…dancing…

EPILOGUE

THE MEDITATION GARDEN

Elvis lies buried in the Meditation Garden at Graceland. He created the garden in 1966 as he moved ever more deeply into his contemplation of Eastern religion, thinking, and practice. He commissioned Marty Lacker's brother-in-law Bernie Grenadier, an interior decorator and landscaper, to design and oversee the project. It was located just beyond the swimming pool on the south side of the house. Originally the centerpiece of the garden was a shoulder-high fountain of water rising in the center of a low-walled circular pool twelve feet in diameter. The pool was circled by a walkway of tile and cement, bordered on the south side by eight white Ionic columns supporting a decorative white wooden trellis. Beyond the columns, a single step led up to a curved walkway. Just beyond the raised walkway, the southern border of the garden was marked by a high brick wall with four stained-glass windows, each depicting a vaguely religious scene. The bricks were from Mexico, and the stained-glass windows were brought by Bernie from Spain. The Meditation Garden was watched over from the east side by a classically perfect Jesus carved in marble by a Memphis artist, John McIntire. Jesus's arms are raised high and magnificently outstretched to welcome all humanity to salvation.

Vernon hated the garden, and he hated the Jewish landscape architect who had done the job. Elvis had been away in Hollywood throughout the construction. When he came home, Elvis listened to his father challenge Bernie's bills for labor, hesitated, but soon gave the production his approval. "Write the check," he said. No one could have imagined that a decade later Vernon would redesign the Meditation Garden to make it a monument dedicated to his own memory

325

almost as much as it was dedicated to prolonging the memory of his son.

In the fall of 1977, after thieves attempted to steal Elvis's body from Forest Hill Cemetery, Vernon decided to move both Elvis's and Gladys's remains to Graceland and bury them in the Meditation Garden just south of the pool containing the fountain. Vernon decided that the contractor he got for the project wanted too much money for the parts that required taking up the tile and cement walkway in that area, so he put the bodyguards still on the payroll to the task. Soon they were out there armed with jackhammers, hefting chunks of debris and cursing Vernon for this violation of their professional dignity. Vernon relished the sight. "They ain't working on Elvis's chain gang anymore," he declared proudly. "They're working on mine."

In the middle of the night on October 2, 1977, workers brought Gladys's and Elvis's remains back to Graceland. Vernon had pulled strings to get that part of the estate legally designated as a cemetery. The authorization stipulated that all cemeteries in Tennessee have to be reasonably available for visits by any interested persons. Therefore, early in the morning, before Graceland is open for paying visitors, anyone can visit Elvis's gravesite without charge.

Vernon chose to arrange the Presley family graves on the south side of the pool, heads together and facing away, bodies stretched out fanwise like fingers of an opened hand. Elvis is in the center. Vernon put Gladys two spaces to Elvis's left. Why he did so became apparent in 1979 when he died. Vernon had saved that space for himself. At last, Vernon was able to put himself in the center of his family, and separate his son from his wife.

Some visitors at the end of 1979 might have been shocked by the lopsided manner in which Vernon had arranged the three graves. There was no one permanently at rest on Elvis's right side, symbolically a highly significant space. One might have expected Vernon to put Elvis's mother in the place that would have honored the very special and powerfully close relationship that existed between them during her life.

Vernon understood his role in the memorials that appear on the bronze plaques that cover the graves of his wife and son. It is clear from the language that he had help. Vernon had such great difficulty with spelling and punctuation that one might question his claim as he entered prison in 1938 that he had attained a fifth-grade education. However, writing the epitaph for Gladys was easy because it was so short. She got only four lines in her inscription:

> *She was a great person, a great wife and mother.*
> *She was also loved by many.*
> *We love her dearly, and she is sadly missed.*
> *By Vernon Presley*

Vernon was proud of these random and rambling phrases.

Elvis's epitaph is much lengthier, almost overflowing the plate that covers his body. It gives his name and dates. Then he is described as the son of, first, Vernon Elvis Presley and, second, of Gladys Love Presley, and then as the father of Lisa Marie Presley. Next, Elvis gets eighteen rambling lines of high praise in trite phrases. He was a "gift from God," and he was "loved dearly." He had a "God-given talent" and "without a doubt he became most widely acclaimed." Also, he was a "great humanitarian" and "became a living legend in his own time."

Finally, Vernon declared, "We miss you son and daddy," thus slipping Lisa Marie into the scene again. He concluded using the first person singular, "I thank God that he gave us you as our son."

Vernon added the "taking care of business" sign at the bottom—*TCB* with a lightning bolt under the *C*. He again indicated in stone he was the composer of this memorial.

Just above Elvis's grave there sits a lantern on top of a low pedestal. It is the eternal flame, yet it always seems on the verge of dying. The flame flickers weakly and colorlessly in its six-sided clear glass container.

A close look at the right corner of the burial plot in the Meditation Garden reveals that there is one more family member represented. There Vernon placed a small bronze plaque on a low stone base to recall Elvis's stillborn twin:

In Memory of
Jessie Garon Presley
January 8, 1935

There is no body under the plaque and no overt indication of how Jessie fits into the family.

Asked why he did not bring Jessie's remains from the Priceville Cemetery in East Tupelo to lie with those of his mother and brother in the Meditation Garden, Vernon replied lamely that he did not know where the child was buried. Elvis himself as a young boy would climb the hill to the cemetery and visit the place where he understood that his brother lay. Elvis might have been guessing, but some relatives and friends surely knew where Jessie's body was buried, and little Jessie could have rejoined his family had his father cared enough to find him. Jessie Garon did not make that journey in Vernon's lifetime, but he might do so yet.

At the end of 1979 in the Meditation Garden there were two empty sites for graves on Elvis's right side. In 1980, Vernon's mother, Minnie Mae, died and took the spot next to Elvis. The second is still there, waiting.

———

In thinking about how the Presleys are arranged in the Meditation Garden, it is interesting to consider again how the family arrayed itself in the earliest photograph of Elvis, taken while Vernon was being held in the Lee County jail. In this picture, Elvis is standing on a bench while his mother sits on his right and his father sits on his left.

The futures of Elvis, his mother, and his father are eerily foreshadowed in that photograph. Gladys, a woman in a heavily male-dominated society, will labor ceaselessly to protect her husband and her son. Elvis is looking at the camera, about to do what he thinks the camera wants him to do. From age nineteen until the day he died, he strove to do what the living camera—his audience—wanted him to do. Gladys hates her son's drive; Vernon loves it, especially the reflected power he reaps as Elvis's father and his partial control over much of the river of money flowing out of his son's talent and ambition. As Elvis comes of age, Vernon—suffering from a "bad back"—becomes less and less able to earn money to support his family. Once Elvis begins to rake in the money, he jests that he has "retired" his father—at about age forty—and one does not hear about Vernon's bad back anymore.

While Gladys is alive, Elvis does not marry and have children as she so passionately wanted him to do. He is busy performing and partying. Gladys drinks more and more because Elvis will not allow her to protect him. Vernon is caught up immediately in Elvis's power and money. When Elvis is away, Vernon will play; he becomes the lord of the manor and increasingly abusive toward Gladys. Finally, powerlessness and alcohol kill her. She is barely in her grave before Vernon is conspicuously bedding down other women and strutting about so that others know that he is a manly man.

Then Elvis becomes Vernon's abuser. "Get out of the way, Daddy," he said as he was about to bulldoze the small house on the Graceland grounds that Vernon wanted to keep for storing things from his office. Before and after his mother's death, Elvis does not settle down as she begged him to do. He goes from one girl to many girls and with many girls to guns, badges, and drugs. As Elvis slips deeper into drugs, Vernon makes only a token effort to help him, to save his son's life. He relishes the attention he gets while on tour with Elvis; he is the father of the King. Vernon is always counting the money, and Elvis is not. Gladys did not count money either. She could never balance the household books even when Vernon was working. She was a compulsive consumer, as was her son. He used spending money like a whip to lash his father—repeatedly and almost viciously, as if to punish him for what he had done to his mother. Vernon at the end, at the very site of Elvis's death, in the very room in which he died, is with his new girlfriend, a woman about thirty years his junior, as he looks down at his son's body lying on the floor. After Elvis dies, Vernon can do as he likes. He does not marry the girlfriend. He chooses to bring the earthly remains of his wife and his son from a public cemetery to Graceland. He plants them exactly where he chooses—on either side of the space that he has reserved for himself. As in the early photograph, Elvis should have been in the middle with his mother on his right and his father on his left.

Vernon composes an epitaph that waves Gladys quickly away, and he appropriates as much of Elvis's glory for himself as he can. Graceland, even the Meditation Garden itself, for two years became his chain gang.

———

At Graceland the little boy wearing the man's hat is still looking at the camera. He is still giving his audience what it wants. Visitors to Graceland, including the Meditation Garden, do not dwell upon images of Vernon. They see Elvis. Each one feels the Elvis he or she wants and needs, the Elvis that they brought with them when they left their houses and headed down the highway for Memphis. Appropriately, the Meditation Garden is the last station on the tour of Graceland. It does encourage meditation. When visitors leave the garden, they talk earnestly with each other as they walk up the shady drive to meet the bus that will take them back to the reception center across the boulevard and into the world. They feel fulfilled, just as they felt fulfilled when they left his performances. That was Elvis's genius. It is as if the child is still there looking at the camera, ready to give whatever the camera asks.

OMAHA

Less than four months before Elvis's body came to rest in the Meditation Garden, CBS made a superbly revealing feature film of his last tour entitled *Elvis in Concert*. In images and interviews, it caught beautifully the truth that he had the love and loyalty of a host of middling Americans, male and female, young and old.

It begins on Sunday, June 19, 1977, on a highway near Omaha, Nebraska, leading to the Civic Auditorium Arena in which Elvis will perform that night. A highway sign marks it as one mile from the junction with Highway 680 and forty-eight miles from Lincoln, Nebraska. The auditorium building has a huge sign declaring that Elvis will perform that night at 8:30 in person. SOLD OUT, the sign blares, the usual Colonel Parker brag whether precisely true or not.

The parking lot has license plates from Colorado, Virginia, New York, South Dakota, Illinois, Ohio, Michigan, Wisconsin—no large cars, no small cars, just middle-sized cars, and one truck. The camera follows the crews putting together the stage, the lights, and the sound equipment for the performance. As the audience gathers in the late afternoon, numerous interviews capture beautifully the diversity of these people and why they were there:

A woman in her midthirties, long dark hair, dark eyes.

"He will always be the King no matter what," she says, shaking her head back and forth as if to prohibit any thought of dissent before it has even arisen.

An older woman in her fifties.

"I think he's a good clean fellow."

A woman in her midthirties, blond, sparkling blue eyes, shoulder-length hair.

"I've got a daughter about twelve years old, and I've talked about Elvis and about how great he was when I was growing up. She has no idea who the man is. And I think a kid can't grow up without knowing who Elvis Presley is."

A young woman about nineteen, deeply golden-blond hair, cool. Asked "Why Elvis?" she responds:

"I think it's a lot of the flashy clothes he wears and everything. And it seems like all women like that."

An older man.

"We're retired people, and...all ages come to see him, I think."

A young man, midtwenties, long dark hair, dark eyebrows, handsome.

"I like the stuff he buys, cars, all the rings, the clothes, it's quality, I mean. And I think he's a very religious person. I mean very. But he's human, I mean. I...he cusses onstage, but that's human, I mean. He's religious like...he's nice to people, I mean. He's...he's human."

A stout, strong-looking woman in her midtwenties, long straight jet black hair, no makeup, a wide friendly smile, wearing an Elvis button.

"He's so special and everything. And he's the best-looking guy in the world." She laughs, almost giggling.

A woman in her midthirties, short black hair, a wife and mom.

"This is about my twenty-eighth concert since 1972."

At this point the camera pans the gathering crowd: older women, kids, kids sleeping on their mothers' laps, popcorn, paper cups, one woman wearing a T-shirt that reads I'M NOT ELVIS. People are moving around while the crew is setting up the show.

A couple in their forties. They could be farmers. The man is talking.

"We lost our home Thursday in a tornado in Sioux City," he says. He and his wife went to the hospital. She got four stitches under her chin. He had twenty-three lacerations on his back—"like Jaws got ahold of me," he laughs. Their children's rooms were completely destroyed. Fortunately the kids were with their grandparents at the time. "I don't really feel like standing around too much," the man says, "but we still came down to see the King."

A young-looking woman, perhaps in her late thirties, with brown hair in a short, perky cut. She sports a flower over her ear and one on her collar.

"He's honest. That's the main thing. He's honest. And he...And he's got vibes, you know." She introduces her grown son, an Elvis fan since he was three; he's seen Elvis five times. "He's a really nice guy," the man says. "I really like the way he respects his mom."

A black man in his thirties.

"I give Elvis a lot of credit for bringing blues into rock and country. He's the first guy to ever do that, and I admire him for it. He has a lot of courage...I hope to name my kid after him some day...I just love the guy."

A man in his thirties, with a mustache, a receding hairline, and gold-rimmed glasses.

He still lives at home and is a post office worker. The pay is okay, but "just about all the money that I do make goes for seeing the Elvis shows...It's worth every penny of it." Elvis is religious, he says, even though he can't go to church every Sunday like regular people; you can tell by the way he sings spiritual songs. Onscreen Elvis ratchets up on "How Great Thou Art." Behind him in full voice are the Sweet Inspirations, Kathy Westmoreland, and J. D. Sumner and the Stamps Quartet.

A beautiful young woman, about twenty-five years old. Her long black hair falls just below her shoulders in front, parted in the middle to frame a smooth, oval face, dark eyes, and full lips. She is wearing a white top, open at the neck. She has a necklace bearing a cross. Why is Elvis important to her?

"It was when I was four years old, and he was on TV and he was kissing the polio poster child for that year. And I told my mother I'd give anything to be in her shoes. And I would to this day, still yet.

"And I bought my ticket through a girl that lives here in Omaha. And I was very lucky because she got twenty the day that the tickets went on sale. And she offered me two, my sister and I, and I was thrilled because I have been waiting to see him for so long." She shakes her head slowly back and forth, reflecting the exhaustion she had felt in that quest.

"And I was supposed to go see him in Wichita, Kansas, December the twenty-seventh of last year, and I had to go in the hospital for emergency surgery and was unable to go. And so this means the world to me [shaking her head and smiling bravely], because [pause, eyes raised to the sky] he's the greatest person that has ever walked and he sings beautiful and I would never pay to see anybody else, and I haven't and I won't. This is the only one, because I love Elvis with all my heart."

On the screen above, Elvis is singing while the Sweets and Kathy Westmoreland are singing and swaying:

> *Is your heart filled with pain,*
> *Shall I come back again,*
> *Tell me dear,*
> *Are you lonesome tonight?*

BIBLIOGRAPHIC ESSAY

I have spent my professional life working as an historian of American race relations. Themes involving race, class, and gender permeate Southern history, as they do this book. There are hundreds of books, a number of key ones used here, in English and other languages about Elvis. Of course there are thousands of newspaper and magazine articles. Everyone has a perspective on Elvis, often a personal one. Many of those around Elvis for a long time or for only a few days wrote books about him. Some of those who worked in his security detail or who knew him as a friend or as a romantic partner, however briefly, wrote books. His permanent home was Memphis, and local journalists knew him well, producing several excellent books from the Memphis perspective.

I set out to tell the story in a popular rather than scholarly fashion and removed the scholarly footnotes in one of my early drafts. This essay is meant to allow readers to follow the major primary and secondary sources I drew on during the years I was working on this study. I have not cited many informal sources that influenced me, people I met in Tupelo or in Memphis. My wife's mother, Mrs. Betty Carter Woodson, was a native of Memphis and had visited Graceland before Elvis acquired it. She and her friends shared with me many memories of Memphis in the 1940s and later. These conversations are not always cited, but they helped me gain insights into unique perspectives about Elvis. There are former neighbors, schoolteachers, church leaders, and school and family friends who still walk in the memory of those years when Elvis was finding his way as an artist. The *Memphis Press-Scimitar* is a repository of many items about Elvis from these years throughout the rest of his career, and afterward. The Memphis Public Library is a superb source for researching all aspects of the life of Elvis Presley, including the day of his death. The library has all the books, magazines, articles, and news-papers one might need in a special collection, along with an excellent staff. Of course the August 17, 1977, issue of the *Memphis Press-Scimitar* provides particularly detailed stories of that confused day. The New York Museum of Television and Radio is an invaluable source about Elvis, including a appearance of his on *The Today Show*, among other visual documents. Some special insights into Elvis's life with Priscilla can be seen in the following source: Museum of Television and Radio, New York City, Barbara Walters Special #32, "Priscilla Presley," ABC-TV, September 13, 1985.

INTRODUCTION

There are books and portions of books about his death, some by authors who knew Elvis. One excellent collection of stories comes from Charles C. Thompson II and James P. Cole's *The Death of Elvis: What Really Happened* (New York: Dell Publishing, 1991). Charles Thompson produced a striking "you are there" story for television, with Geraldo Rivera as the central reporter for the story. James Cole, a longtime writer for the Memphis newspapers, knew the story of Elvis's death well, and he also knew Memphis intimately. My "Introduction: The Death of Elvis" draws heavily upon this source. Thompson and Cole pages most used were 3, 22, 37–38, 42, 59–61, 70–71, 97–98, 104, 124, 126–27, 184–86, 240, 246, 260–64, 280–81, 295, 348, 350, 355–56, 374–77, 442–54, 469–74, 480. Richard H. Grob's *The Elvis Conspiracy* (Las Vegas, NV: Fox Reflections Publishing, 1979) provides more details, as does Albert Goldman's *Elvis* (New York: McGraw-Hill, 1981). Grob pages used were 244, 349–50, 355–58. Goldman pages used were 568–69. One of the most insightful of Elvis's biographers is Peter Guralnick, who wrote two seminal books about Elvis. Used here is his *Careless Love: The Unmaking of Elvis Presley* (Boston: Little, Brown, 1999), which touches on all aspects of Elvis's later life and is also rich on Elvis's career in Memphis. See especially page 625. This introduction benefited from material assembled by some members of Elvis's staff or security team in Steve Dunleavy's *Elvis Aaron Presley: Revelations from the Memphis Mafia* (New York: HarperCollins, 1995). See especially page 752.

PART I: THE BUBBLE

CHAPTER ONE: THE DREAM

Elvis made local tapes for his mother, and he had sessions with other players. One of his associates, Scotty Moore, contributed some of the early tapes to Memphis State University Library. There are people who contributed to a picture of Elvis in the early days, such as Gloria Roden, who with her husband, a physician, lived on Easter Egg Row in Memphis, and I talked to them as I was doing research in Memphis.

Peter Guralnick produced a very detailed view of the emergence of Elvis as an artist in his *Last Train to Memphis: The Rise of Elvis Presley* (Boston: Little, Brown, 1994), which provides quotes and details from Sam Phillips, a discoverer of Elvis, and some of Elvis's early associates. Pages used were 109, 159–60, 170–71, 188–210, 213–18, 224–33. Scotty Moore revealed many details of Elvis's early career in his *That's Alright, Elvis: The Untold Story of Elvis's First Guitarist and Manager, Scotty Moore, as Told to James Dickerson* (New York: Schirmer Books, 1997). Pages used were 54, 73, 75, 86, 91, 95, 96, 107–8. Another useful source about the early Elvis was Sam Wilder's interview with *TV Guide* in September 1956, page 110. Jerry Hopkins contributed a useful biography before Elvis's death, *Elvis* (New York: Simon and Schuster, 1971). Pages used were 54, 75, 79, 90–91, 107–8. Michael Gray and Roger Osborne compiled a very detailed chart of Elvis's life in their *The Elvis Atlas: A Journey Through Elvis Presley's America* (New York: Holt, 1996). The chronicle approach is very useful for checking details of his professional and personal lives. See pages 46, 52–54, 60, 63, 79, 91–93, 178–80. Peter Guralnick joined with Ernst Jorgensen to produce a very detailed record of Elvis's life with their *Elvis: Day by Day* (New York: Ballantine Books, 1999). See especially page 33. Former Elvis insiders also contributed some insights into the motivations of Elvis as an artist in Red West, Sonny West, and Dave Hebler, as told to Steve Dunleavy, *Elvis: What Happened?* (New York: Ballantine Books, 1977). See pages 20–21.

CHAPTER TWO: KILLERS OF THE DREAM

There was extensive coverage in newspapers and magazines as Elvis expanded his reach from the South to the nation and the world. Particularly useful in this chapter were the *New York Times*, October 28, 29, 1956;

the *Toronto Star*, October 29, 1956; and the *Memphis Press-Scimitar*, November 6, 1956. Elvis's films *Loving You, Jailhouse Rock,* and *King Creole* attempted to capture the youthful and handsome singer that Elvis was in his early career.

The Elvis Atlas: A Journey Through Elvis Presley's America (New York: Holt, 1996) by Michael Gray and Roger Osborne presents rich detail for these years when Elvis was evolving from poor Mississippi and Tennessee boy to stardom. Pages used were 74, 88, 93, 94–95, 99, 100–101, 126, 131, 178–81. Peter Guralnick's *Last Train to Memphis: The Rise of Elvis Presley* (Boston: Little, Brown, 1994) captures the development of Elvis in the early years. Pages used were 252, 254, 261–62, 284–85, 302–4, 338, 351–53, 356, 368–70, 379. With Ernst Jorgensen, Peter Guralnick put together the detailed daily summary of Elvis's activities in *Elvis: Day by Day* (New York: Ballantine Books, 1999). This book highlights the intense activities that characterized Elvis in some periods of his life, especially the early years when he was building his career. Pages used were 62–63, 73, 83, 89, 93, 99, 131. He attracted the attention of the Federal Bureau of Investigation, which created a file on Elvis worth reviewing.

PART II: WHY ELVIS?

CHAPTER THREE: VERNON AND GLADYS

Among the valuable primary sources was Works Progress Administration Records, Lee County, Mississippi Department of Archives and History, Jackson. Also useful was Lee County Courthouse, General State Docket 2, May 21, 1935–November 27, 1948, page 20. This document is in the spacious attic of the Lee County Courthouse. In the 1990s and the 2000s the attic was richly filled from knee-high to shoulder-high with original documents dealing with the official actions of the county government. I found useful the Warranty Deed Record, Book 4, D159–385, D159-568. Also, from the same source, I consulted Warranty Deed Record, Index Book B, D357–272. Also useful from Lee County Courthouse were the General State Dockets, 2, 5, 21, 35–11, 27, 43, various pages, indexed under *P*, State 2756. For some details about Vernon's imprisonment, see, Works Progress Administration Records, Lee County, Department of Corrections, subgroup 1: penitentiary, mf 17: convict register, pages 307–9. The Parchman Farm Records are in the Mississippi Department of Archives and History. Other primary sources useful for this chapter were Pontotoc County Courthouse, Court Records, Pontotoc, Mississippi; the Census of 1900, Lee County, Mississippi; and the Census of 1920, Itawamba County, Mississippi. Newspaper issues of interest were *Tupelo Daily Journal*, November 17, 1937, et seq.; *Tupelo Daily News*, April 16–18, May 27–28, 1938.

Elaine Dundy provides a rich tapestry of Elvis's family life in her *Elvis and Gladys* (New York: St. Martin's Press, 1985). This is certainly one of the most thorough studies of the relationships among family members, including the extended family. Pages used were 6–7, 10, 12, 57–64, 67, 70, 72–85, 93, 101–2. David M. Oshinsky has explored the prison system where Vernon was imprisoned in his *"Worse than Slavery": Parchman Farm and the Ordeal of Jim Crow Justice* (New York: Free Press, 1997). Pages used were 109, 110, 137, 143, 145, 147, 153–54, 162. Several other secondary sources proved useful. I used pages 14–16 from Alanna Nash, with Billy Smith, Marty Lacker, and Lamar Fike, *Elvis Aaron Presley: Revelations from the Memphis Mafia* (New York: HarperCollins, 1995); pages 267–80 from Frank E. Smith, *The Yazoo River* (New York: Rinehart, 1954); pages 3–21 and 25 from William F. Holmes, *The White Chief: James Kimble Vardaman* (Baton Rouge: Louisiana State University Press, 1970); and page 93 from Columbus B. Hopper, *Sex in Prison: The Mississippi Experiment with Conjugal Visiting* (Baton Rouge: Louisiana State University Press, 1970). Several of these sources explore the conditions of imprisonment in the South. As always, Peter Guralnick and Ernst Jorgensen, *Elvis: Day by Day* (New York: Ballantine Books, 1999) proves useful for details. See especially page 2. A useful source for examination of the culture of the era in the Deep South is the *Encyclopedia of Southern Culture*. This volume was edited by Charles Reagan Wilson and William Ferris, with Ann J. Abadie and Mary L. Hart as associate editors (Chapel Hill: University of North Carolina Press, 1989). The encyclopedia summarizes some pertinent findings by the scholar Steven Kasse, a 1973 UNC doctoral student. See page 1330. Kasse's dissertation was published by the UNC Press in 1989.

CHAPTER FOUR: EAST TUPELO AND TUPELO

Elaine Dundy's scholarly and perceptive study of the family provides rich details from this period. Her *Elvis and Gladys* (New York: St. Martin's Press, 1985) provides a look at family interactions in this transitional period of Elvis's life. Pages used were 86–87, 89–91, 93–95, 97, 102–7. Memphis journalist Bill E. Burk provides insights also into Elvis's personal life. I used pages 19–20 of Burk's *Early Elvis: The Humes Years* (Memphis: Propwash, 1990, 2003). Peter Guralnick's *Last Train to Memphis: The Rise of Elvis Presley* (Boston: Little, Brown, 1994) is very useful in this, as in other, chapters. Pages used were 16–17. Pages used from Guralnick and Ernst Jorgensen, *Elvis: Day by Day* (New York: Ballantine Books, 1999) were 3, 4, 6–7.

CHAPTER FIVE: MEMPHIS

Among the sources most useful in following various activities of the Presley family are the Memphis City Directory of the period and various telephone books over the years. The *Hume High School Herald*, a yearbook, also proved useful, especially for the year 1953. The Elvis Presley Collection in the Memphis Public Library is a rich resource for following early Elvis. One of the insiders, Bill E. Burk, has written a revealing picture of the high school student in his *Early Elvis: The Humes Years* (Memphis: Propwash, 1990, 2003). The 2003 edition includes a superb collection of photographs taken at Hume High School. I drew also on my research about William Faulkner, who grew up in Oxford, a culture with some similarities to Tupelo, East Tupelo, and Memphis. See Joel Williamson, *William Faulkner and Southern History* (New York: Oxford University Press, 1990).

Elaine Dundy's *Elvis and Gladys* (New York: St. Martin's Press, 1985) proved very useful. Pages used were 131–32, 134–35, 136, 139, 141–43, 145, 148–50, 151, 152–53. The detailed tracing of Elvis's total life by Peter Guralnick and Ernst Jorgensen, *Elvis: Day by Day* (New York: Ballantine Books, 1999), proved helpful in sorting out dates and events. Pages used were 1, 6, 8, 9, 10, 11, 15. Also useful was another book that details Elvis's life, Michael Gray and Roger Osborne, *The Elvis Atlas: A Journey Through Elvis Presley's America* (New York: Holt, 1996). Pages used were 28, 32, 33. Peter Guralnick's *Last Train to Memphis: The Rise of Elvis Presley* (Boston: Little, Brown, 1994) addressed the issue mentioned in chapter 5 about which song—there was a question—Elvis sang in one of his early public performances. Guralnick suggested Elvis sang "Till I Waltz Again with You," but there are other possibilities. Pages used were 32–33, 44, 49, 52, 53. Some of those who were to work with Elvis for all or a significant part of his career began to make personal observations in these years. See Alanna Nash, with Billy Smith, Marty Lacker, and Lamar Fike, *Elvis Aaron Presley: Revelations from the Memphis Mafia* (New York: HarperCollins, 1995), especially pages 22–23.

CHAPTER SIX: DIXIE LOCKE AND SAM PHILLIPS

In this chapter on women and Elvis, I drew background from my own *William Faulkner and Southern History* (New York: Oxford University Press, 1993). Pages used were 186–87, 193, 213–14. Other sources that provide insight into the role of gender in this South were Tammy Wynette and Joan Dew, *Stand by Your Man—An Autobiography* (New York: Simon and Schuster, 1979) and, for the part played by Elvis, Scotty Moore, *That's Alright, Elvis: The Untold Story of Elvis's First Guitarist and Manager, Scotty Moore, as told to James M. Dickerson* (New York: Schirmer Books, 1997). Pages used of Moore were 4–32, 35–48, 51, 53–57, 58–62, 63–65. For a look at other artists in the same general period, see Lyle Leverich, *Tom: The Unknown Tennessee Williams* (New York: Crown Publishers, 1995), pages 150–53. For a look at the evolution of Elvis's musical success, see *Elvis's 100 Greatest Hits* (Milwaukee: Leonard, 1978), page 55. Peter Guralnick and Ernst Jorgensen, *Elvis: Day by Day* (New York: Ballantine Books, 1997) provides photographs of Elvis's Memphis employment office record. See pages 7, 10, 12, 15.

As in other chapters, especially those that explore family and personal dynamics, Elaine Dundy provides many details in her *Elvis and Gladys* (New York: St. Martin's Press, 1985). Pages used were 108, 112, 160, 162–63, 171–73, 175–76, 178, 179, 180–81. The pages after page 112 provide photographs of key friends in these years. Useful here, as elsewhere, is Peter Guralnick, *Last Train to Memphis: The Rise of Elvis Presley* (Boston: Little, Brown, 1994). Pages used were 5–6, 42–43, 57, 60, 65, 67–74, 75, 83, 84, 85, 93–103, 106–7. Providing more insight into the high school influence was Bill E. Burk, *Early Elvis: The Humes Years* (Memphis: Propwash, 1990, 2003). See pages 109, 111–12.

CHAPTER SEVEN: A GIRL IN THE BED

I benefited from conversations with a number of people in understanding the Elvis of these years. This chapter reflects a conversation I had at dinner with Mrs. Robert Stoller, a source on Elvis, in her home just off Sunset Boulevard in Los Angeles and not far from UCLA, where I was giving talks in 1999. Parchman Farm records in the Mississippi Department of Archives and History, Jackson, and the *Memphis Press-Scimitar* provided background details on some aspects of Elvis's activities or activities of the larger family, including his parents, Vernon and Gladys. Priscilla herself provides details about her marriage, and the long periods before and after, in her *Elvis and Me* (New York: Berkley Books, 1986), written with Sandra Harmon. Her book contains a photographic record of their years together. Pages used were 48–54, 55–61, 62–64, 65–66, 184. Another look at Elvis and Priscilla's relationship is Suzanne Finstad, *Child Bride: The Untold Story of Priscilla Beaulieu Presley* (New York: Harmony, 1997). Pages used were 40, 45–66, 184. One of Elvis's intimates, Joe Esposito, with Elena Oumano, published *Good Rockin' Tonight: Twenty Years on the Road and on the Town with Elvis* (New York: Simon and Schuster, 1994). The useful pages are especially 181–82. Another acquaintance, Scotty Moore, provides some insights into this early transitional phase of Elvis's life in his *That's Alright, Elvis: The Untold Story of Elvis's First Guitarist and Manager, Scotty Moore, as told to James M. Dickerson* (New York: Schirmer Books, 1997). Pages used were 3, 92–93, 95. Charlie Hodge, another friend close to Elvis in this period, provides insights in his *Me 'n Elvis* (Memphis: Castle Books, 1988), written with Charles Goodman. The pertinent pages are 1–4, 10–13.

Several dependable sources provide details about Elvis's years in Memphis and in the army, and the transition, under the direction of Colonel Tom Parker, to a film career. See Peter Guralnick, *Last Train to Memphis: The Rise of Elvis Presley* (Boston: Little, Brown & Company, 1994), pages 38–39, 47–48, 66, 77, 78, 107–11, 114, 115, 150, 154–64, 184–85, 197–99, 200–201, 206, 220, 221, 348, 356–57, 422–23, 427, 447–80. Pertinent insights are revealed in Guralnick, *Careless Love: The Unmaking of Elvis Presley* (Boston: Little, Brown, 1999). Pages used were 10, 12–19, 22–24, 29–30, 37–44, 49, 56–59, 76–77, 107, 113–14, 116, 131–32, 206, 247, 261–65.

Also see Peter Guralnick and Ernst Jorgensen, *Elvis: Day by Day* (New York: Ballantine Books, 1999), pages 10, 49, 178, 182. Family dynamics and personal-life details are covered in a sensitive and scholarly fashion in Elaine Dundy, *Elvis and Gladys* (New York: St. Martin's Press, 1985), pages 148–49, 171, 174, 223, 227, 232, 233, 237, 242, 292–94, 305–6, 321–23, 326. We have seen sometimes a realistic view of Elvis from some of those who worked close to him, such as in Alanna Nash, with Billy Smith, Marty Lacker, and Lamar Fike, *Elvis Aaron Presley: Revelations from the Memphis Mafia* (New York: HarperCollins, 1995). See the preface, xv–xix, and pages 81–82, 89–92, 101–3, 108–20, 143, 157, 158, 160–66, 163, 174, 183, 185, 186, 195–96, 282, 358, 480–82, 564–65. Albert Goldman's study of Elvis was published only a few years after Elvis's death and provides a balanced look at Elvis's entire life. See Albert Goldman, *Elvis* (New York: McGraw-Hill, 1981), pages 207, 209–24, 252–54.

PART III: COMEBACK AND DIE

CHAPTER EIGHT: THE COMEBACK SPECIAL

The theatrical and television films are available, and this chapter draws on the CBS-TV film *Elvis*, known as "the Comeback Special," which highlighted Elvis's return to live performances, this time before mature nightclub audiences that included the girls, now women, who had squealed about two decades earlier. This is available from the New York Museum of Television and Radio. The lyrics of Elvis's music are likewise available via various sources. This chapter particularly draws from "If I Can Dream," with words and music by Walter Earl Brown. The Inventory of the Elvis Presley Estate, County Courthouse, Memphis, Tennessee, also provides some materials of the accomplishments of various aspects of Elvis's career. I drew from earlier research, Joel Williamson, *William Faulkner and Southern History* (New York: Oxford University Press, 1994), especially pages 322, 325–28, 340, including the photographs opposite page 249. Jerry Hopkins, as always, provides a more personal look at Elvis. See his *Elvis* (New York: Simon and Schuster, 1971), especially pages 335–51, 431. The same personal look is evident in Scotty Moore, *That's Alright, Elvis: The Untold Story of Elvis's First Guitarist and Manager, Scotty Moore, as told to James Dickerson* (New York: Schirmer Books, 1997). Pages used were 145–48. The more intimate look at Elvis's life here, as elsewhere, is provided by Alanna Nash, with Billy Smith, Marty Lacker, and Lamar Fike, *Elvis Aaron Presley: Revelations from the Memphis Mafia* (New York: HarperCollins, 1995). See pages 401–2, 449, 452–54, 459, 465, 468–70, 477, 479, 626–27.

Peter Guralnick's *Careless Love: The Unmaking of Elvis Presley* (Boston: Little, Brown, 1999) focuses especially on the disintegration of Elvis's career. See pages 185, 282–83, 294–304, 307–8, 311–15, 317, 343, 391, 443, 444. Another biographer, Albert Goldman, provides useful insights and facts into these transitional years in *Elvis* (New York: McGraw-Hill, 1981), especially pages 337, 403–39, 447, 531. You can follow the daily flow of Elvis's life in the period covered here in Peter Guralnick and Ernst Jorgensen, *Elvis: Day by Day* (New York: Ballantine Books, 1999), pages 174, 207–8, 236, 237, 240, 242, 245–57, 259, 261, 266, 275, 277, 370–71, 431–33, and in Michael Gray and Roger Osborne, *The Elvis Atlas: A Journey Through Elvis Presley's America* (New York: Holt, 1996), pages 138–39, 181–83. Insights into Elvis's fading relationship with his wife, Priscilla, emerge from Suzanne Finstad, *Child Bride: The Untold Story of Priscilla Beaulieu Presley* (New York: Harmony, 1997), page 213 and elsewhere. On Graceland see Karal Ann Marling, *Graceland: Going Home with Elvis* (Cambridge: Harvard University Press, 1996), page 184 and elsewhere.

CHAPTER NINE: GIRLS AND GUNS

Priscilla's book, with Sandra Harmon, *Elvis and Me* (New York: Berkley Books, 1986), provides many insights from her perspective. See especially pages 253–54, 259, 298, 299–300. Also revealing Priscilla's point of view is Suzanne Finstad, *Child Bride: The Untold Story of Priscilla Beaulieu Presley* (New York: Harmony, 1997), especially pages 184, 213–14, 216, 227, 231, 235–40. Many people who knew Elvis or Priscilla wrote books about him or her, such as members of the Memphis Mafia, the Graceland security team, or friends. Among those friends was Michael Edwards, *Priscilla, Elvis, and Me* (New York: St. Martin's Press, 1988). Edwards mostly knew Priscilla. See especially pages 210–13. Joyce Bova, who was supposed to become Elvis's wife after Priscilla, contributed a book of her own reflections. See Joyce Bova, as told to William Conrad Nowels, *Don't Ask Forever: My Love Affair with Elvis* (New York: Pinnacle Books, 1994), pages 69–89, 166–71, 173, 192, 235, 247, 284, 295–96, 332, 362, 393–94, 401–2. Another Memphis woman who knew Elvis intimately, and seemed deeply interested in his welfare, was Kathy Westmoreland, who with William G. Quinn wrote *Elvis and Kathy* (Glendale, CA: Glendale House Publishing, 1987). Westmoreland was a singer with Elvis for a period. See especially pages 57–58. Other insiders, here as elsewhere, provided perspectives of those around Elvis and his various female friends. See Alanna Nash, with Billy Smith, Marty Lacker, and Lamar Fike, *Elvis Aaron Presley: Revelations from the Memphis Mafia* (New York: HarperCollins, 1995), especially pages 204, 439, 486, 490–92, 500–502, 507, 508, 523–24, 526, 528, 532–33, 537–41, 571, 582, 583, 595, 632, 633, 638, 639, 658. Members of the Memphis Mafia contributed their version of Elvis with girls and guns. See Red West, Sonny West, and Dave Hebler, as told to Steve Dunleavy, *Elvis: What Happened?* (New York: Ballantine Books, 1997), especially pages 88 and 89. See Jerry Osborne's *Elvis: Word for Word* (New York: Harmony Books, 1999, 2000), especially pages 221, 230, 232–34, 237, 239, 242, 249, 252, 268, 288–89, 296. Another more personal view is provided by Charles Hodge with Charles Goodman, *Me 'n Elvis* (Memphis: Castle Books, 1988), page 3 and elsewhere. This chapter draws on the television films *Elvis* ("the Comeback Special") and *Elvis on Tour*.

Peter Guralnick's detailed look at Elvis's public and private life is *Careless Love: The Unmaking of Elvis Presley* (Boston: Little, Brown, 1994). See pages 389, 394–97, 401, 403, 408–12, 418–28, 433, 434, 438, 446, 451–56, 462, 471–73, 489–90, 526, 535–37, 540–41, 544, 551, 568–78, 581. Guralnick includes Kathy Westmoreland's words during an interview, pages 395–97. Guralnick and Ernst Jorgensen provide details about Elvis's activities in this period in their *Elvis: Day by Day* (New York: Ballantine Books, 1999), pages 215, 239–40, 280, 283, 285–87, 298, 300, 301, 316, 317, 350–51, 353. Also see Michael Gray and Roger Osborne's *The Elvis Atlas: A Journey Through Elvis Presley's America* (New York: Holt, 1996), especially page 151. Also see Albert Goldman, *Elvis* (New York: McGraw-Hill, 1981), especially pages 489–90.

PART IV: THE FALL

CHAPTER TEN: THE BODYGUARD BOOK

It is not surprising that Elvis tried to prevent the book the Memphis Mafia wrote from being published. Despite telephone calls and implicit bribes, the book appeared. See Red West, Sonny West, and Dave Hebler, as told to Steve Dunleavy, *Elvis: What Happened?* (New York: Ballantine Books, 1977), especially pages 1–6, 292, 322–32. The year of publication, 1977, was the year of Elvis's death. This book presents both a good and bad side of life behind the scenes. More looks at the darker side of Elvis can be found in Alanna Nash, with Billy Smith, Marty Lacker, and Lamar Fike, *Elvis Aaron Presley: Revelations from the Memphis Mafia* (New York: HarperCollins, 1995). This book came long after Elvis's death but provides details of this period. See pages 318–19, 355, 456, 478, 557–58, 587, 668–69, 675, 677–82, 686, 687. See David Stanley, *Life with Elvis* (Old Tappan, NJ: Fleming H. Revell, 1986), page 157, and Jerry Osborne, *Elvis: Word for Word* (New York: Harmony Books, 1999, 2000), pages 305–17, for more details of this period. On her former husband, see Priscilla Beaulieu Presley, with Sandra Harmon, *Elvis and Me* (New York: Berkley Books, 1986), pages 198–205, 231–34. Newspapers provided information and perspectives on all aspects of Elvis's public life. This chapter makes use of the August 30, 1977, issue of the *Memphis Commercial Appeal*.

The topic of this chapter was covered by Peter Guralnick in his *Careless Love: The Unmaking of Elvis Presley* (Boston: Little, Brown, 1999). See pages 173–74, 528–29, 598–99, 604. Biographer Albert Goldman, *Elvis* (New York: McGraw-Hill, 1981) provides some details on pages 363–65, 539–41. For tracking of details in Elvis's daily life, one can consult Peter Guralnick and Ernst Jorgensen, *Elvis: Day by Day* (New York: Ballantine Books, 1999), pages 328, 336, 354–55, and Michael Gray and Roger Osborne's *The Elvis Atlas: A Journey Through Elvis Presley's America* (New York: Holt, 1996), page 183 and various other pages.

CHAPTER ELEVEN: SAVED

Useful on the period of Elvis's death was the *Nashville Banner*, various issues following August 16, 1977. Also see the *Memphis Commercial Appeal*; this chapter drew especially on August 17, 1977, and, a year later, August 25, 1978. Also used was the *Memphis Press-Scimitar*, November 19, 1976, for a perspective on Elvis's career. The Memphis City Directory for 1976, among other city directories, was useful, as were pertinent records from the Clerk of Court of Shelby County. There is also a County Probate Inventory of the Elvis Presley Estate. One book is devoted entirely to Elvis's death, Charles C. Thompson II and James P. Cole, *The Death of Elvis: What Really Happened* (New York: Dell Publishing, 1991). See pages 142, 151, 153, 156–57, 196, 242–46, 255, 382, 396–97, 402, 430–35, 437, 484–86. The death was in his home at Graceland, still one of the most visited places. See Karal Ann Marling, *Graceland: Going Home with Elvis* (Cambridge: Harvard University Press, 1996), especially page 176. Useful for a personal perspective on Elvis is Charlie Hodge with Charles Goodman, *Me 'n Elvis* (Memphis: Castle Books, 1988), various pages.

Peter Guralnick provides details about the end of Elvis's life in his *Careless Love: The Unmaking of Elvis Presley* (Boston: Little, Brown, 1999), especially pages 261–65, 288, 608, 611, 613–16, 619, 622–24, 629, 631, 633, 637, 641. See also 341, 370–71, 372, 374, 375. More details about this period are in Michael Gray and Roger Osborne, *The Elvis Atlas: A Journey Through Elvis Presley's America* (New York: Holt, 1996), pages 182–83.

EPILOGUE

Less than four months before his death, CBS made a film of what turned out to be his last tour, *Elvis in Concert*. The theatrical films remain mostly unseen, although they are useful to watch. Graceland represents the way Elvis lived in private. See Karal Ann Marling, *Graceland: Going Home with Elvis* (Cambridge: Harvard University Press, 1996), pages 198, 203–8. Alanna Nash also provides perspectives. See Alanna Nash, with Billy Smith, Marty Lacker, and Lamar Fike, *Elvis Aaron Presley: Revelations from the Memphis Mafia* (New York: HarperCollins, 1995), pages 387–88, 731, 734, 735. Also see Elaine Dundy, *Elvis and Gladys* (New York: St. Martin's Press, 1985), page 128 and elsewhere.

OTHER SELECTED SOURCES

There are hundreds of books and thousands of scholarly and popular articles about Elvis Presley. This is a selective look at some of the major types of sources. Broadly speaking, there are both popular and scholarly sources that cover Elvis's short but diverse life as a singer, actor, and nightclub performer. Some concentrate on his personal life. There are sources that deal with special periods of his life, such as the film or nightclub years. There are more intimate sources produced by family, such as by his wife, Priscilla, or by friends and employees. There are a variety of different types of sources that deal with many special aspects of Elvis's life, such as a collection of poetry inspired by Elvis, or fiction in which Elvis is a major character.

347

Mary Hancock Hinds in 2001 published an annotated bibliography of Elvis materials. It covers all aspects of the literature dealing with Elvis. See Mary Hancock Hinds, *Infinite Elvis: An Annotated Bibliography* (Chicago: A Cappella Books, 2001). In addition to authors cited in the chapter-by-chapter bibliography, other authors have taken a scholarly approach to researching and telling the Elvis story embedded in the evolution of music or Southern history or culture. Among these studies are Michael T. Bertrand, *Race, Rock, and Elvis* (Chicago: University of Illinois Press, 2000), which argues that Elvis helped revise racial attitudes; Susan M. Doll, *Understanding Elvis: Southern Roots vs. Star Image* (New York and London: Garland Publishing, 1998); Erika Doss, *Elvis Culture: Fans, Faith, and Image* (Lawrence: University Press of Kansas, 1999); and Ted Harrison, *Elvis People: The Cult of the King* (London: Fount Paperbacks, 1992), which attempts to decipher how fans constructed a world view. One can find another assessment of Elvis in culture in George Plasketes, *Images of Elvis Presley in American Culture, 1977–1997: The Mystery Terrain* (New York: Harrington Park Press, 1997). Many details about Elvis's career are provided by Patsy Hammontree in *Elvis Presley* (Westport, CT: Greenwood Press, 1985). Also see Peter Harry Brown and Pat H. Broeske, *Down at the End of Lonely Street: The Life and Death of Elvis Presley* (New York: Dutton, 1997). This book contains many photographs. Albert Goldman, one of the major biographers of Presley, produced a detailed look at the last day of Elvis's life, *The Last 24 Hours* (New York: St. Martin's Paperbacks, 1991). There are many interpretative essays about Elvis's life, music and films. See Kevin Quain, ed., *The Elvis Reader: Text and Sources on the King of Rock'n' Roll* (New York: St. Martin's Press, 1992); and Kay Sloan and Constance Pierce, eds., *Elvis Rising: Stories on the King* (New York: Avon Books, 1993). Bill E. Burk was a Memphis journalist and friend of Elvis and his family. See his *Elvis Memories: Press Between the Pages* (Memphis: Propwash, 1985, 1993). The founder of *Elvis World* magazine, Burk assembled many stories about Presley from the *Memphis Press-Scimitar* in his column, "Good Evening." An insightful book about Southern history and culture of the period is by Jason Sokol, *There Goes My Everything: White Southerners in the Age of Civil Rights, 1945–1975* (New York: Alfred A. Knopf, 2006).

There are several chronologies of Presley's life and also photographic histories of major portions of his life. One source of pictures is *Life, Re-*

membering Elvis: The King at 75 (New York: Life Books, 2009). Another version by *Life* is *Life, Elvis Remembered: Twenty-Five Years Later* (New York: Warner Books, Inc., 1995). The book was assembled by Charles Hirshberg and the editors of *Life*. Photos of the touring Elvis are available in Robert Gordon, *Elvis: The King on the Road—Elvis Live on Tour 1954 to 1977* (New York: St. Martin's Griffin, 2001). Elvis's step-brother David E. Stanley, with Frank Coffey, put together a detailed chronology of Elvis's life in *Elvis Encyclopedia: The Complete and Definitive Reference Book on the King of Rock and Roll* (Santa Monica, CA: RR Donnelley & Sons, 1994, 1997). Lamar Fike contributed a foreword to this encyclopedia. Susan Doll's *The Films of Elvis Presley* (Lincolnwood, IL: Publications International, 1991) presents many special details, including photographs of Presley's film career days. Marie Clayton's *Elvis Presley: Unseen Archives* (New York: Barnes & Noble, 2003) also highlights the film career. Kim Adelman wrote *The Girls' Guide to Elvis* (New York: Broadway Books, 2002), and Frank Coffey provided *The Complete Idiot's Guide to Elvis* (New York: Alpha Books, 1997). Another guide for fans is Laura Levin and John O'Hara, *Elvis and You* (New York: Berkley Publishing Group, 2000). This book includes a bibliography of other Elvis sources.

A more inside look at Presley's family can be observed in Donna Presley Early and Edie Hand's *Precious Family Memories: A Personal Scrapbook* (Birmingham, AL: Edie Hand, 1997). This was written with Susie Pritchett. A detailed chronology of the musical career is available in Ernst Jorgensen, *Elvis Presley, a Life in Music: The Complete Recording Sessions* (New York: St. Martin's Press, 1998). This book has a foreword by Peter Guralnick. A more personal perspective on Presley's career can be seen in Cindy Hazen and Mike Freeman, *The Best of Elvis: Recollections of a Great Humanitarian* (Memphis: Explorations, 1992). These perspectives are combined with many photographs.

Some writers and scholars, friends, and family have written about special periods of Presley's career, sometimes from a very scholarly point of view, at others from a very personal perspective. Bill E. Burk has written about the early recording years in Memphis, a period rich in anecdotes about the young Elvis. See his *Elvis: The Sun Years* (Memphis: Propwash, 1997). Bobbie Ann Mason also wrote about this period in *Elvis Presley* (New York: Penguin, 2003) Lee Cotton wrote about the nightclub years of the 1970s in his *Did Elvis Sing in Your Hometown, Too?* (Sacramento, CA: High Sierra Books,

1977). Bill E. Burk also produced an insightful collection of pieces in his *Elvis Through My Eyes* (Memphis: Propwash, 1996). There are few studies specifically about Elvis as a soldier, but see Rex and Elisabeth Mansfield, with Marshall and Zoe Terrill, *Sergeant Presley: Our Untold Story of Elvis' Missing Years* (Chicago: ECW Press, 2002). This fills in this period of his life and presents many photographs of Presley as a soldier. Lucy de Barbin and Dary Matera's *Are You Lonesome Tonight? The Untold Story of Elvis Presley's One True Love and the Child He Never Knew* (New York: Villard Books, 1987) provides the perspective of a young woman who claimed to be Presley's daughter. Peter Whitmer explored the personal nature of Elvis, insofar as it could be studied, in his *The Inner Elvis: A Psychological Biography of Elvis Aaron Presley* (New York: Hyperion, 1996). Neal Gregory and Janice Gregory published a study about the reactions to Elvis's death by family and friends in Graceland, Memphis, the nation and world. See *When Elvis Died: Media Overload and the Origins of the Elvis Cult* (New York: Pharos Books, 1980). There are examples of journalistic treatment of Elvis's death from many places. Among many popular biographies of Presley are, for example, Richard Wootton, *Elvis!* (New York: Random House, 1985); and Tony Gentry, *Elvis Presley* (New York: Chelsea House, 1994). Wootton's book contains numerous photographs. Jim Curtin's *Elvis: Unknown Stories Behind the Legend* (Nashville: Celebrity Books, 1998), provides numerous stories about Elvis in a loose chronological order. Curtin did this book with Renata Ginter. After Presley's death, Graceland and the business confronted numerous challenges. But, like Elvis, it was an example of Elvis Presley Enterprises rising. See Sean O'Neal, *Elvis Inc.: The Fall and Rise of the Presley Empire* (Rocklin, CA: Prima Publishing, 1996). There are important audio productions, not to mention his millions of recordings. For example, see Earl Greenwood and Kathleen Tracy, *The Boy Who Would be King: An Intimate Portrait of Elvis Presley, by His Cousin* (Los Angeles: Publishing Mills, 1993).

One source rich in quotes from family members and friends, along with many photographs, is Rose Clayton and Dick Heard, eds., *Elvis Up Close: In the Words of Those Who Knew Him Best* (Atlanta: Turner Publishing, 1994). For the final years of his life, one can find many interviews with various people in Jerry Hopkins, *Elvis: The Final Years* (New York: Berkley Books, 1981). This book concentrates on the 1970s. Rick Stanley, with Paul Harold, produced *Caught in a Trap: Elvis Presley's Tragic Lifelong*

Search For Love (Dallas: Word Publishing, 1992). Alan Fortas spent more than a decade with Elvis and wrote *Elvis: From Memphis to Hollywood* (Ann Arbor, MI: Popular Culture, 1992). Some of these perspectives from those who worked or were close to Elvis are mentioned in our chapter-by-chapter summary of sources. Joyce Bova wrote, as told to William Conrad Nowels, *Don't Ask Forever: My Love Affair with Elvis* (New York: Pinnacle Books, 1994). For another female perspective see June Juanico, *Elvis: In the Twilight of Memory* (New York: Arcade Publishing, 1997). The introduction to this book is by Peter Guralnick. Few dispute the enormous power that Colonel Tom Parker had over Elvis's career; he was never in the historical spotlight like Elvis, but see James L. Dickerson, *Colonel Tom Parker: The Curious Life of Elvis Presley's Eccentric Manager* (New York: Cooper Square Press, 2001).

Elvis lives on in impersonations, in occasional sightings, and in poetry, fiction, and imagination, in addition to living on in his music, his film and television performances, and in spirit at Graceland, where his remains lie. Graceland is heavily visited, and Elvis Presley Enterprises is vigilant in protecting all interests of the ongoing career of Elvis, now dead for more than four decades. Will Clemens collected some of the poetry inspired by Presley's career in *All Shook Up: Collected Poems About Elvis* (Fayetteville: University of Arkansas Press, 2001). Some of the poems are sensitive and resonate with genuine feelings about Presley. Robert Mickey Maughon wrote a novel entitled *Elvis Is Alive: A Novel of Love, Sacrifice, and Redemption* (Nashville: Vaughan Printing/Cinnamon Moon, 1997). Greil Marcus continued, in a sense, conversations with Elvis after Elvis's death in his *Dead Elvis: A Chronicle of a Cultural Obsession* (New York: Doubleday, 1991). For a fantasy using Elvis's life see C. R. Sinclair, *Elvis A. Eagle: A Magical Adventure* (San Francisco: Scribe Press, 1996). Also see Samuel Charters, *Elvis Presley Calls His Mother after the Ed Sullivan Show* (Minneapolis: Coffee House Press, 1992). Another fictionalized look at Elvis supposedly talking to his mother is Gerald Duff's *That's All Right, Mama* (Dallas: Baskerville Publishers, 1995). Elvis had a deep interest in spirituality as he aged and inspired such books as David Rosen, *The Tao of Elvis* (San Diego: Harcourt, 2002). Rosen includes some sayings of, and about, Elvis. Among other special explorations, one can find Jonathan Goldstein and Max Wallace, *Schmelvis: In Search of Elvis Presley's Jewish Roots* (Toronto: ECW Press, 2002). For another special look at Presley, this time from a fan's perspective, see Frances Keenan, *Elvis, You're Unforgettable: Memoirs from a Fan* (Tampa Bay, FL: Axle Rod Publishing, 1997). Those imitating Elvis obviously have keen interest in Presley's life. For example, see William McCranor Henderson, *I, Elvis: Confessions of a Counterfeit King* (New York: Boulevard Books, 1997); or P. F. Kluge, *Biggest Elvis* (New York: Penguin, 1996).

Elvis remains a popular historical topic. Every year there are numerous studies about Elvis. If you type the words "Elvis Presley" into the search engine of the University of North Carolina Libraries website, you'll get a list of 468 books or other sources that touch on some aspect of Elvis's life. Of those, 19 have been produced or published in 2013 or so far (April) into 2014. In September 2014, Ginger Alden, to whom Elvis was engaged and who discovered his body, published *Elvis and Ginger: Elvis Presley's Fiancée and Last Love Finally Tells Her Story* (New York: Berkley Books), providing details of their intimate relationship and his death, 37 years ago. For historians at least (as for many faithful fans), one thing is clear: Elvis is alive.

INDEX